The Cytoskeleton: Cell Function and Organization

The Cytoskeleton: Cell Function and Organization

Proceedings of the
British Society for Cell Biology – The Company of Biologists Limited Symposium
Norwich, April 1986

Organized and edited by

Clive Lloyd
(Department of Cell Biology, John Innes Institute)

Jeremy Hyams
(Department of Botany and Microbiology, University College, London)

and

Richard Warn
(School of Biological Sciences, University of East Anglia)

SUPPLEMENT 5   1986
JOURNAL OF CELL SCIENCE
Published by THE COMPANY OF BIOLOGISTS LIMITED, Cambridge

Typeset, Printed and Published by
THE COMPANY OF BIOLOGISTS LIMITED
Department of Zoology, University of Cambridge, Downing Street,
Cambridge CB2 3EJ

© The Company of Biologists Limited 1986

ISBN: 0 948601 043

JOURNAL OF CELL SCIENCE SUPPLEMENTS

1 (1984) Higher Order Structure in the Nucleus
2 (1985) The Cell Surface in Plant Growth and Development
3 (1985) Growth Factors: Structure and Function
4 (1986) Prospects in Cell Biology
5 (1986) The Cytoskeleton: Cell Function and Organization

All supplements are available free to subscribers to *Journal of Cell Science* or may be purchased separately from The Biochemical Society Book Depot, P.O. Box 32, Commerce Way, Colchester CO2 8HP, UK

PREFACE

The 1986 Spring Meeting of the British Society for Cell Biology at the University of East Anglia, Norwich, marked a new departure for the Society. For the first time, a major BSCB meeting was organized in cooperation with the British Society for Developmental Biology as a step towards establishing closer ties. The meeting focused on three major themes, one of which, 'The Cytoskeleton: Cell Function and Organization', forms the basis of this volume. In thinking about our programme we were concerned not simply with catering for the specialist, but to put together a series of talks that would appeal to a broad cross-section of cell and developmental biologists. With this in mind, we chose to emphasize five main areas.

The first set of papers deals with microscopical techniques. Technical advances provide new insights into the organization of cytoskeletal proteins and in particular have allowed us to visualize cytoskeletal assemblies at work in living cells. Bob Allen was to have presented the inaugural lecture on new developments in video light microscopy but, sadly, died shortly before the symposium began. His co-worker, Dieter Weiss, presented their joint work at short notice and the first contribution is a tribute to Bob Allen's contribution to the visualization of living cytoplasm.

The second section deals with the roles of the three main classes of cytoskeletal filaments in organizing the cytoplasm. It includes two contributions on the relationship between the cytoskeleton and the nuclear matrix, underlining the point that fibrous proteins structure the whole cell and help organize its metabolic activity.

Section three is concerned with more dynamic aspects of the cytoskeleton. More is now being learned about the turnover of cytoskeletal proteins and how this contributes to the movement of arrays. This applies to the movement of cells, organelles and chromatids – all of which are represented.

So-called simple organisms have contributed greatly to our understanding of the cytoskeleton as is shown in the fourth section. Their cytoskeletons are not necessarily simpler but they have the advantage that their developmental cycles are often more accessible to experimentation and they are certainly more amenable to genetic analysis.

This leads on to the fifth section, which was organized jointly with the British Society for Developmental Biology. This final section shows the progress that is being made in understanding how the cytoskeleton contributes to the acquisition of polarity in multicellular tissues.

The aim, therefore, was to provide a list of speakers, spanning molecules and tissues. Generous support from The Company of Biologists Limited, and the sponsorship of Flow Laboratories, Unilever Research, Amersham International and CIBA Geigy ensured a strong list of international speakers. This (together with the fact that the weather provided no incentive to leave the lecture theatre) contributed to an enjoyable meeting and it is hoped that some of its flavour is conveyed in this volume.

Clive Lloyd
Jeremy Hyams
Richard Warn

THE CYTOSKELETON: CELL FUNCTION AND ORGANIZATION

CONTENTS

Continued overleaf

Contents

THE CYTOSKELETON IN DEVELOPMENT

J. Cell Sci. Suppl. 5, 1–15 (1986)
Printed in Great Britain © The Company of Biologists Limited 1986

VISUALIZATION OF THE LIVING CYTOSKELETON BY VIDEO-ENHANCED MICROSCOPY AND DIGITAL IMAGE PROCESSING

DIETER G. WEISS

Institut für Zoologie, Technische Universität München, 8046 Garching, Federal Republic of Germany* and Marine Biological Laboratory, Woods Hole, MA 02543, USA

SUMMARY

Two steps led to our present-day view of the cytoskeleton as a highly dynamic structure that is actively involved in force generation for various kinds of cell motility and, as a result, is itself often actively moving.

The first step was the introduction of video microscopy, especially of the Allen Video Enhanced Contrast-Differential Interference Contrast Microscopy (AVEC-DIC), which allows the visualization of cellular structures in the light microscope that are up to 10 times smaller than the limit of resolution. This enables one to see images of unfixed, unstained, native or purified microtubules and actin bundles, and their interaction with membrane-bound organelles.

The second step was the discovery of a system exceptionally well-suited to study microtubule and organelle movements, namely, the extruded axoplasm of the squid giant axon. From this axon the cytoplasm can be extruded free from surrounding plasma membrane, and individual microtubules and organelles can be separated from the bulk axoplasm.

The study of these native microtubules by AVEC-DIC microscopy yielded a great number of quite unexpected details of the dynamic behaviour of both the microtubules themselves and the motility associated with them.

INTRODUCTION: A TRIBUTE TO ROBERT D. ALLEN

The visualization of the 'living', i.e. unfixed, unstained, native, cytoskeleton is a topic whose progress has changed our image of the cytoskeleton from a more-or-less static and rigid framework to a dynamic matrix that is actively involved in the various kinds of intracellular and cellular motility. Furthermore, it has now been shown in several instances that some cytoskeletal filaments can themselves move actively (Travis *et al.* 1983; Allen *et al.* 1983, 1985*a*; Allen & Weiss, 1985; Vale *et al.* 1985*b*). This progress has been made possible by the rapid development of very powerful techniques in light microscopy, one of which (Allen Video Enhanced Contrast-Differential Interference Contrast (AVEC-DIC) microscopy) was developed by Robert D. Allen (Allen *et al.* 1981*a,b*; Allen & Allen, 1983; Allen, 1985). Our knowledge in the field of microtubule-based motility was dramatically advanced during the last four years when R. D. Allen and his collaborators applied this new

---

* Address for correspondence.

technique to especially well-suited cellular systems (Brady *et al.* 1982, 1985; Allen *et al.* 1982, 1983, 1985*a*; Allen & Weiss, 1985; Weiss & Allen, 1985; Travis *et al.* 1983; Hayden & Allen, 1984).

Robert D. Allen died in the Spring of 1986 at the age of 58 while actively developing his ideas for the advancement of light microscopy and the characterization of motility in living cells (see obituaries: Taylor, 1986; Rebhun, 1986). I consider it appropriate, therefore, to give a short review of the technique of AVEC-DIC microscopy, which made such progress possible, and then to summarize the recent findings of R. D. Allen, myself and our collaborators on microtubule-associated motility.

AVEC-DIC MICROSCOPY

The simple act of just adding a video camera and a monitor to a microscope may result in increased image contrast and brightness (Parpart, 1951), which may reveal more image detail than might be seen by just looking into the microscope. However, modern video microscopy uses specialized cameras and digital image processing systems to optimize image quality in three basic ways.

(1) Video-intensified microscopy (VIM) amplifies light-limited images so that very weak fluorescence and luminescence can be visualized (Reynolds *et al.* 1963; Willingham & Pastan, 1978; Reynolds & Taylor, 1980; Amato & Taylor, 1986). This technique has been used repeatedly to study cytoskeletal elements and their dynamic properties (Hayden *et al.* 1983; Yanagida *et al.* 1984; Amato & Taylor, 1986; Higashi-Fujime, 1986; Sanger *et al.* 1986, this volume; see also chapters in: Taylor *et al.* 1986).

(2) Video-enhanced microscopy allows one, by enhancing contrast, to resolve or at least to visualize objects both above and below the limit of resolution that, because of their limited contrast, could not otherwise be detected before. Video-enhanced contrast (VEC) microscopy was developed in the laboratories of S. Inoué (Inoué, 1981, 1986; Ellis *et al.* 1986) and of R. D. Allen (Allen *et al.* 1981*a,b*; Allen & Allen, 1983; Allen, 1985, 1986). Allen *et al.* (1981*a,b*) noted that analogue enhancement permitted the introduction of additional bias retardation, which, after offset adjustment, permitted much better visualization of minute objects by polarized light methods. This technique (AVEC microscopy) has been applied most successfully to the visualization of microtubules and microtubule-based cell motility *in vitro* (in motile cell extracts) and even in the intact living cell (Allen *et al.* 1982, 1983, 1985*a*; Allen & Weiss, 1985; Weiss, 1985; Vale *et al.* 1985*a,b*).

(3) Digital image processing is easily used once microscopic images have been picked up by a video camera and are converted to a digital signal. Image processors of all kinds can now be used to reduce noise in the image by filtering or averaging (for VIM and VEC microscopy), to further enhance contrast digitally (for VEC microscopy), or to perform measurements in the images (e.g. intensity, size, speed,

or form of objects). Only since procedures for noise reduction and contrast enhancement in real time, i.e. in video frequency, have become available has the microscopist
been able to generate optimized pictures while working with the microscope.

The typical steps required for obtaining optimal images with AVEC-DIC microscopy are summarized in Table 1. The first image processor designed especially
for microscopy and permitting all the steps mentioned was built by Hamamatsu
Photonics in 1983 in close collaboration with R. D. Allen. Subsequently, several
other systems have become available, few of which, however, enable all steps to be
performed in real time.

When the specimen is in focus, the microscope is adjusted for Köhler illumination,
but in contrast to visual observation, the condenser iris diaphragm should be
opened fully for video microscopy to maximize the practical resolution (Table 1). In
polarizing methods, the inherent loss of visual contrast that occurs at full aperture is
later regained electronically. The optimal compensator setting for visual inspection is
close to extinction, i.e. $1/50$ to $1/100\lambda$. For video-enhanced microscopy the contrast
is theoretically maximal at $1/4\lambda$. Owing to the enormous background brightness at
this setting, Allen recommended, as a good compromise, the compensator setting of
$1/9\lambda$ (Allen & Allen, 1981a,b; Allen & Allen, 1983). In order to achieve this
adjustment, Allen recommended the use of a de Sénarmont compensator (Allen *et al.*
1981a), while in its absence the retardation can only be estimated.

This analogue enhancement not only improves the contrast of the specimen but
also emphasizes dust particles, uneven illumination and optical imperfections. These
artifacts, called 'mottle', are superimposed on the image of the specimen. Therefore,
digital computers are used to filter these artifacts from the image. These steps,
mottle subtraction and digital enhancement (Table 1), can be seen in Fig. 1. The
final magnification on the video screen that should be achieved in order to make
optimal use of this technique is between $\times 5000$ and $\times 20\,000$. This requires optical

Table 1. *Image generation with the AVEC Photonic Microscope System**

	Step	Result
1 M	Open iris diaphragm fully	Optical image worsens
2 M	Set compensator to $1/9\lambda$	Optical image disappears, weak TV image appears
3 P	Analogue enhance (camera pedestal and gain control)	High-contrast TV image with disturbing background and uneven illumination (mottle)
4 M	Defocus	Specimen disappears, mottle remains
5 P	Store (freeze) mottle image and subtract it from incoming video images	Clear image appears; if contrast is weak, $\rightarrow 6$
6 P	Digital enhance (stretching the grey level histogram)	Optimal contrast and high-resolution image; if pixel noise is high, $\rightarrow 7$
7 P	Use rolling or jumping average	Noise reduction

M, microscope; P, processor or camera.
* Photonic Microscopy Inc., Oak Brooks, IL; Hamamatsu Photonics Europa, 8036 Herrsching,
FRG. Other equipment may require slight modifications of this procedure and may permit only
partial enhancement if all features are not provided.

D. G. Weiss

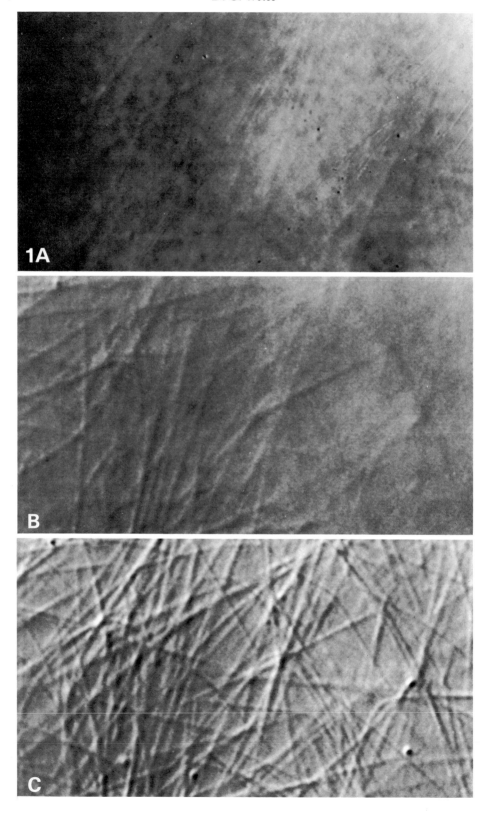

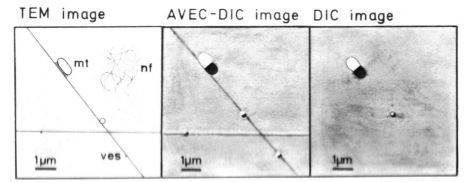

Fig. 2. Schematic representation of the visualization capabilities of different kinds of microscopy. Right: differential interference contrast microscopy (DIC) is one of the most powerful methods in light microscopy. DIC images are characterized by their typical shadow-cast appearance. The smallest objects visible are of an apparent size in the order of the theoretical limit of resolution (about 1/2 the wavelength of the light used). Left: in transmission electron microscopy (TEM) all membraneous and cytoskeletal elements of the cytoplasm can be resolved and imaged at their true size. TEM is, however, impossible on living or hydrated cells. Centre: AVEC-DIC microscopy permits visualization of biological, i.e. proteinaceous or membraneous, objects smaller than the limit of resolution if they are larger than 10–20 nm. These objects, however, would not appear at their real size, but inflated by diffraction to about the size of the resolution limit. Neurofilaments (10 nm) are visible in certain situations. See Allen (1985) for more detailed explanations. ves, axoplasmic or synaptic vesicles of about 60 nm diameter; mt, mitochondrion; nf, neurofilaments (10 nm filaments); the straight lines represent microtubules (25 nm diameter); the larger vesicular organelle is about 250 nm in diameter.

magnification of ×2000 to ×5000, which can usually be achieved only by the use of additional magnification changers and/or a zoom ocular. To reach satisfactory illumination at such high magnifications requires, according to our experience, a mercury arc lamp, usually the HBO 50W or a similar type. An excellent source for practical, technical and theoretical details related to most aspects of video microscopy is the recent book by Inoué (1986).

It should be emphasized that AVEC-DIC images contain some of the information in a coded way and, therefore, have to be interpreted similarly to electron-microscope (EM) images. Fig. 2 shows that, unlike EM images, which give true resolution of the objects depicted, the apparent sizes of objects seen in AVEC-DIC may not necessarily reflect their real size. In AVEC-DIC one has to note that objects smaller than the limit of resolution, which is in the range of 200–300 nm depending on the optics and the wavelength of light used, are inflated by diffraction to about this size (Fig. 2, centre). Also, the orientation of birefringent microtubules may affect their apparent thickness to some degree (Fig. 2, centre). While the size of the image does

Fig. 1. Video-enhanced differential interference contrast (AVEC-DIC) images of a preparation of three times cycled microtubules. A. Analogue enhancement not only enhances the specimen but also image imperfections (mottle). This image corresponds to step 3 in Table 1. B. Subtraction of the mottle by the image processor (step 5) yields an evenly illuminated, clean image free of shading. C. Digital enhancement is used to stretch the grey levels contained in image B over the whole range from white to black. Field width, 25 μm. Reproduced with permission from Allen (1985).

not enable one to decide whether one or several objects of a size smaller than the limit of resolution are present, the contrast does sometimes permit one to make this judgment. A pair of microtubules would, for example, have the same thickness as a single one, but the contrast would be about twice as high.

Which specimens are best suited for AVEC-DIC microscopy? Certainly not stained material or other objects, which already have high contrast. Specimens that are extremely weak in contrast or even invisible by conventional microscopy would be best suited. In this class fall micelles, liposomes and single or double-layer membraneous material, colloids (Kachar *et al.* 1984), cytoplasmic and other small vesicles (Allen *et al.* 1982), artificial latex particles of 70 nm and smaller (our unpublished observations), and cytoskeletal elements such as microtubules (Allen *et al.* 1983, 1985*a*) and actin bundles (Allen & Allen, 1982; Kachar, 1985). The AVEC-POL technique will also visualize very weakly birefringent objects such as individual microtubules (Allen *et al.* 1981*b*; Hard & Allen, 1985; Allen, 1985). When applied to bright-field microscopy, the VEC technique visualizes 5–20 nm diameter colloidal gold particles as are at present used in immunoelectron microscopy (De Brabander *et al.* 1986).

CELLULAR SYSTEMS STUDIED WITH AVEC-DIC MICROSCOPY

The new technique was rapidly applied by Allen, his collaborators and others to various cellular systems to study the role of microtubules in intracellular motility. It turned out that the lamellipodia of Foraminifera such as *Allogromia* were excellently suited for visualization of fine strands corresponding to microtubules or microtubule bundles along which particles were transported bidirectionally, and which themselves underwent very vigorous lateral and axial movements (Travis *et al.* 1983) (Fig. 3). These movements indicated for the first time a much more active role of microtubules in cytoplasmic transport and challenged the prevailing view that they were passive 'skeletal' elements.

A series of studies using cultured frog keratocytes conclusively demonstrated the role of microtubules in organelle transport within animal cells (Hayden *et al.* 1983; Hayden & Allen, 1984). Hayden & Allen showed that the filaments along which transport occurs were indeed microtubules, by applying VIM to visualize anti-tubulin antibody fluorescence and AVEC-DIC to show organelle movement on the same filament (Hayden *et al.* 1983). Furthermore, it was possible for the first time to prove that a single microtubule (later identified electron-microscopically) could transport organelles in both directions (Hayden & Allen, 1984). This bidirectionality (as it turned out later) seems to be a general feature of microtubule-based motility (Allen *et al.* 1983, 1985*a*; Koonce & Schliwa, 1985; Schnapp *et al.* 1985; Koonce *et al.* 1986).

More recently, the AVEC technique was applied to axons in which microtubules were thought to generate axonal transport of organelles. Although microtubules are too closely packed to be imaged individually (Allen *et al.* 1985*a*; Weiss & Gross, 1983), a fine analysis of particle movements yielded valuable information on the

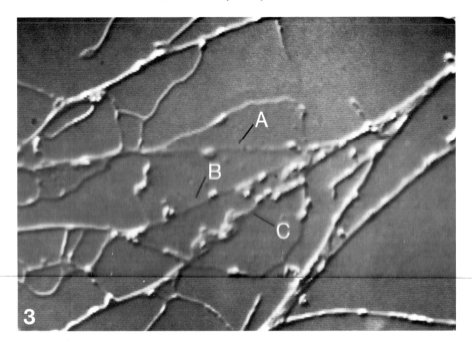

Fig. 3. Lamellipodium of *Allogromia* with three prominent filaments (A,B,C). Lamellipodia are flattened regions in the reticulopodial network that typically form where the organism has attached to positively charged substrata. These filaments consist of one or a few microtubules and can move both axially and laterally through the cytoplasm. ×2900; field width, 34 µm. Reproduced with permission from Travis *et al.* (1983).

arrangement of microtubules and their interaction with organelles (Weiss, 1985; Keller *et al.* 1985; Lynn *et al.* 1986). The true role of microtubules in axoplasmic transport was verified with the development of a cell-free transport system, namely, the axoplasm of the squid giant axon. A good review of what can be seen by his new method in the living cell is given by Allen (1985).

MICROTUBULE MOTILITY IN DISSOCIATED SQUID AXOPLASM

The transport of organelles in axons has for many years been regarded as a typical example of microtubule-based intracellular motility, although the exact mechanism of force generation was disputed (for review, see Grafstein & Forman, 1980; Weiss & Gross, 1982, 1983). Two types of concepts were suggested. One invokes direct action of force-generating enzymes on the organelles to be transported, linking them to microtubules (see Weiss & Allen, 1985; Weiss, 1986, for review). The other concept suggests that microtubule-associated force-generating enzymes act non-specifically upon their environment, thus producing microstreams along the surface of microtubules that could carry the materials to be transported (Gross, 1975; Weiss & Gross, 1982). One prediction of the latter hypothesis was the following: since microtubules have to absorb the recoil of the force-generation process that is supposed to be attached to them, a reactive force would be expected that would move the microtubules in the direction opposite to the main direction of organelle transport. This should occur only if microtubules were freed from the cytoskeleton (Weiss & Gross, 1982, 1983).

R. D. Allen and his collaborators were the first to study organelle movement in intact axons or in extruded axoplasm from squid. Together with Ray Lasek, Scott Brady and Susan Gilbert, Allen found that all organelles known from electron microscopy could be detected by video microscopy (Allen *et al.* 1982; Brady *et al.* 1982) and that individual filaments, probably single microtubules, did support transport in both directions (Allen *et al.* 1983). Biochemical studies by Ron Vale and Michael Sheetz, who were introduced by Allen to this preparation and, simultaneously, by Brady and Lasek (Brady *et al.* 1985), ruled out the possible involvement of actin/myosin in force generation (cf. Clapp, 1986).

These studies made it possible to test directly the hypothesis of whether microtubules would themselves move. In collaboration with R. D. Allen during the

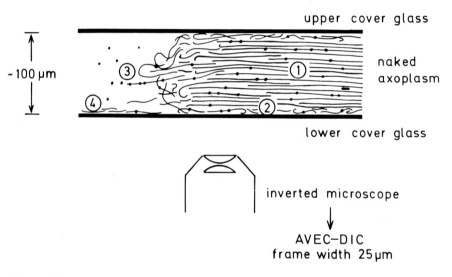

Fig. 4. Microscopy of the extruded axoplasm of the squid giant axon. The axoplasm cylinder is sandwiched between two cover glasses in a buffer developed by R. Lasek & S. Brady, which is composed of most of the soluble low molecular weight constituents of the axoplasm. Organelle movement in the interior (1) of the gel-like axoplasm is not different from the movement in intact axons. Here, the microtubules are usually not imaged individually because they are so densely packed that their diffraction images (Fig. 2) are overlapping. Good observation of individual microtubules is, however, possible at the surface of the axoplasm (2) where the parallel alignment is disturbed. Organelle transport is especially detectable where filaments protrude from the axon surface (3). Here the particles move along the microtubules, and after being released at the ends they disappear in Brownian motion. Some microtubules are found separate from the axoplasm and transport particles that settle onto them out of Brownian motion (4). These native microtubules are usually long and often form tangles or loose knots, whose loops undergo lateral movements and changes of diameter. Short microtubule segments originate in small numbers from the axoplasm surface and have been observed to glide away for up to several hundred μm. This can be observed more easily if the native microtubules are gently sheared into shorter pieces.

Fig. 5. Negative contrast electron micrograph of gently sheared squid axoplasm taken from an actively gliding preparation. Microtubules, characterized by their lengths, straightness and diameter, can be seen to settle to the surface randomly and individually. Typical neurofilaments are also abundant but are not visible by AVEC-DIC microscopy (cf. Figs 2 and 6). They are characterized by their irregular outline and bent shapes. Their deposition does not suggest a relationship to the microtubules or their possible direction of movement. The microtubules that are 25 nm in diameter appear here to have about twice this diameter, due to the negative staining procedure. ×9000; width, 12·5 μm. Electron micrograph by D. Seitz-Tutter.

summers of 1984 and 1985, we were able to produce routinely preparations of active axoplasm extruded from squid giant axons that contained single filaments capable of supporting ATP-dependent bidirectional transport for many hours (Fig. 4). Electron microscopy of these preparations verified that the filaments of the observed length and straightness were indeed microtubules (Fig. 5), which were never arranged in pairs or bundles but always singly (Allen *et al.* 1985*a*). The same finding was also made by Schnapp *et al.* (1985). These results made it clear that this was another microtubule-based motile system characterized by bidirectional movements along individual microtubules.

The properties of organelle movement on native microtubules are summarized in Table 2. A number of these findings have been reported similarly by Vale *et al.* (1985*a*), although there are several discrepancies, such as their finding that the transport of large organelles is size-independent (cf. Table 2, no. 8; and Allen *et al.* 1985*b*).

A remarkable and unexpected finding from these experiments was that careful homogenization of extruded axoplasm resulted in microtubule segments that could be observed to glide when near a surface (Fig. 6). The question of whether they would also move axially in the free medium remains unsolved, since the depth of focus in AVEC-DIC microscopy is less than $1\,\mu m$. The microtubules, which are many μm long, therefore cannot be kept in focus because they are subject to rapid

Table 2. *Properties of organelle movement on free microtubules*

1	Organelle transport is ATP-dependent. A reduction in ATP concentration causes a reversible reduction in transport velocity. V_{max} is $1-2\,\mu m\,s^{-1}$ depending on the preparation
2	Free particles that collide with nMTs* can attach to them anywhere along their length
3	Large organelles can detach anywhere, but small vesicles detach mainly at the end
4	The number of particles transported correlates with the number in suspension
5	In fresh preparations, transport is mainly unidirectional (anterograde)
6	In older preparations, an increasing number of large particles move also in the retrograde direction
7	Particles can overtake one another or pass in opposite directions, yet very seldom collide or interact
8	The velocity of retrograde organelles is inversely proportional to size, while the velocity of particles in the anterograde direction is independent of size
9	Latex beads (320 nm) are transported at similar velocities to that of organelles of comparable size
10	Taxol ($30\,\mu M$) has no detectable influence on particle transport
11	Particles can transfer from one of two intersecting nMTs to the other
12	One particle can be attached to and move along two nMTs, acting to deform or bend one or both nMTs
13	The force of attachment of particles to MTs is sufficient to deform a MT elastically. When the attachment breaks, the MT rebounds

*nMTs, native microtubules.

Table 3. *Repertoire of gliding behaviour displayed by native microtubules*

1	Long nMTs* can aggregate into tangles, knots, 'pretzels', or aster-like arrays showing vigorous particle transport
2	Curved microtubules change loop diameter resulting in lateral movement
3	Segments of nMTs $0.5-30\,\mu m$ long glide over glass in an ATP-dependent manner
4	Reducing the ATP concentration reduces the speed of gliding from $V_{max} = 0.7\,\mu m\,s^{-1}$ to a few $nm\,s^{-1}$, but does not affect the behaviour of gliding nMTs
5	The velocity of gliding is independent of the length of the nMT segment
6	nMT segments glide, usually, in a straight path, and do not noticeably roll either to the right or left while gliding
7	Gliding of nMT segments proceeds in the direction that would correspond to retrograde in the intact neurone, i.e. towards their $(-)$end
8	Gliding velocity of a MT is linearly correlated with but not equal to the speed at which it transports particles in the anterograde, but not in the retrograde, direction
9	Since taxol ($30\,\mu M$) has no effect, assembly and/or disassembly do not seem to be required for gliding
10	Gliding nMTs do not interact when they cross paths
11	When the forward progress of a gliding nMT is blocked by an obstacle, it 'fishtails' slowly from side to side through a series of serpentine shapes
12	Gliding nMTs occasionally follow a path determined by their own curved contour
13	nMTs bent into ring or C shapes rotate slowly near the glass surface
14	Small organelles sometimes fail to leave the frontal $(-)$end of gliding nMTs and remain there

*nMTs, native microtubules.

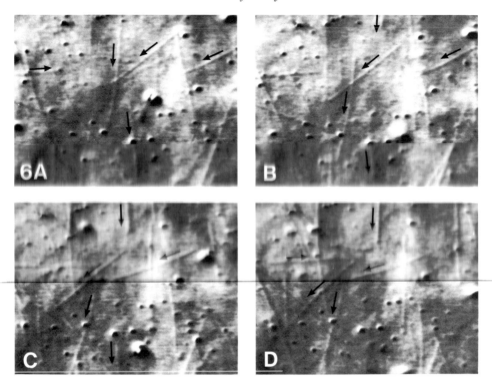

Fig. 6. A population of native microtubule fragments obtained by shearing is depicted at intervals of 5 s, to show the gliding behaviour. The direction of this movement depends upon the orientation in which the microtubules settled on the glass surface. Arrows show the directions of gliding. After video contrast enhancement following the steps given in Table 1 and using the Photonic Microscope System, the recorded images were subjected to further digital image processing. This included digital filtering, edge enhancement, contrast enhancement and shading correction steps, which were performed with the SIGNUM image processing system (SIGNUM GmbH, München, FRG). The image was photographed off-screen using a Ronchi ruling to reduce the video scan lines. Note that some of the particles depicted are firmly attached to the glass surface while others are in Brownian motion. This movement is therefore within the first μm above the glass surface. Some shading is caused by large particles undergoing Brownian motion in a slightly out-of-focus plane. $\times 3000$; width, $20\,\mu$m.

Brownian motion. Assuming that the asymmetry of velocity and direction in transport of large and small organelles that we observed was the same on free microtubules as in the intact axon, we were able to predict that the direction of gliding was towards the $(-)$end, i.e. retrograde (Allen *et al.* 1985*a*). This was shown simultaneously by Vale *et al.* (1985*c*). The whole repertoire of motility events associated with gliding microtubules is summarized in Table 3.

Meanwhile, several groups have used this preparation to purify proteins that are thought to be involved in force generation (Brady, 1985; Vale *et al.* 1985*d*; Hollenbeck & Bray, 1985). Similar microtubule-based movements and proteins have subsequently also been found in other systems, such as the sea-urchin egg (Scholey *et al.* 1985; Pryor *et al.* 1986).

The mechanism of force generation remains unsolved. Although the gliding of microtubules was predicted by the microstream hypothesis, there are other findings that indicate the involvement of a crossbridge-type mechanism (Lasek & Brady, 1985; Miller & Lasek, 1985; Langford *et al.* 1986). Allen *et al.* (1985*a*,*b*) concluded that the motive force for both anterograde and retrograde axonal transport resides with the native microtubule, which, when isolated, exhibits both bidirectional particle transport and gliding. Since gliding occurs in the complete absence of particle transport, the mechanism was suggested to be free-running. The bidirectionality was suggested to be caused by an elliptical stroke of the force-generating enzyme, an ATPase that imparts some force in both directions (Allen *et al.* 1985*a*,*b*). Yet another hypothesis has been put forward, which suggests that a soluble protein is the force-generating protein for anterograde movement when it is associated with vesicles, or for gliding when it is bound to the glass surface; in this hypothesis retrograde transport is attributed to another, as yet uncharacterized, protein (Vale *et al.* 1985*d*). It seems to be necessary to wait until the identification and characterization of these proteins is definitely established before serious models of the kind of mechanisms involved in these multi-faceted microtubule-associated movements can be produced.

CONCLUSION

It was my intention to show that AVEC-DIC microscopy is a most powerful tool in the field of cell motility and the cytoskeleton, which will find application in the near future to the study of cytoskeletal elements in a wide variety of cellular systems (Bray, 1985; Hollenbeck, 1985, 1986). It has fundamentally changed our views of the nature of the cytoskeleton. It is no longer possible to consider microtubules to be merely static 'structural' elements of the cytoskeleton. Rather, seen in the light of the new microscopy, native microtubules are now realized as being dynamic mechano-chemical units capable of generating the movement of organelles and of themselves.

The development of AVEC-DIC microscopy and its application to a most suitable system, the microtubules of squid giant axons, were just two contributions to cell biology for which we are greatly indebted to Robert D. Allen. He must have felt that these contributions marked a major breakthrough in cell motility when he presented, for the first time, our video tapes of gliding microtubules at the Cell Biology and Cell Motility Meetings at Tokyo and Nagoya in September 1984:

"In the meantime, we wonder whether we might have stumbled upon the long-sought force-generating system used in mitosis, meiosis, syngamy, and other MT-related motility and transport processes. It is too early to speculate in detail how such a force-generating system could be organized, but our present finding provides considerable leeway for testable hypotheses regarding mitotic mechanisms based on the particular form of MT gliding that we have discovered. Meanwhile, we already have a new concrete model system for exploring the basis for a previously unknown and unexpected motility process of possible widespread importance in cell biology." (Allen & Weiss, 1985).

I thank Jeff Travis for the critical discussions and helpful comments regarding many of the topics discussed here.

REFERENCES

ALLEN, N. S. & ALLEN, R. D. (1982). Video-enhanced microscopy – Better visibility of plant cell structures. *40th Ann. Proc. Electron Microsc. Soc. Am.*, pp. 182–185.

ALLEN, R. D. (1985). New observations on cell architecture and dynamics by video-enhanced contrast optical microscopy. *A. Rev. Biophys. Chem.* **14**, 265–290.

ALLEN, R. D. (1986). Video-enhanced microscopy. In *Optical Methods in Cell Physiology* (ed. P. De Weer & B. M. Salzberg), pp. 3–13. New York: Wiley.

ALLEN, R. D. & ALLEN, N. S. (1983). Video-enhanced microscopy with a computer frame memory. *J. Microsc.* **129**, 3–17.

ALLEN, R. D., ALLEN, N. S. & TRAVIS, J. L. (1981a). Video-enhanced contrast, differential interference contrast (AVEC-DIC) microscopy: A new method capable of analyzing microtubule-related motility in the reticulopodial network of *Allogromia laticollaris*. *Cell Motil.* **1**, 291–302.

ALLEN, R. D., BROWN, D. T., GILBERT, S. P. & FUJIWAKE, H. (1983). Transport of vesicles along filaments dissociated from squid axoplasm. *Biol. Bull. mar. biol. Lab., Woods Hole* **165**, 523.

ALLEN, R. D., METUZALS, J., TASAKI, I., BRADY, S. T. & GILBERT, S. P. (1982). Fast axonal transport in squid giant axon. *Science* **218**, 1127–1129.

ALLEN, R. D., TRAVIS, J. L., ALLEN, N. S. & YILMAZ, H. (1981b). Video-enhanced contrast polarization (AVEC-POL) microscopy: A new method applied to the detection of birefringence in the motile reticulopodial network of *Allogromia laticollaris*. *Cell Motil.* **1**, 275–289.

ALLEN, R. D. & WEISS, D. G. (1985). An experimental analysis of the mechanisms of fast axonal transport in the squid giant axon. In *Cell Motility: Mechanism and Regulation* (ed. H. Ishikawa, S. Hatano & H. Sato), pp. 327–333. Tokyo: University of Tokyo Press.

ALLEN, R. D., WEISS, D. G., HAYDEN, J. H., BROWN, D. T., FUJIWAKE, H. & SIMPSON, M. (1985a). Gliding movement of and bidirectional transport along native microtubules from squid axoplasm: Evidence for an active role of microtubules in cytoplasmic transport. *J. Cell Biol.* **100**, 1736–1752.

ALLEN, R. D., WEISS, D. G., SEITZ-TUTTER, D. & SIMPSON, M. (1985b). The dynamic microtubule theory of axonal and cytoplasmic transport, and a hypothesis regarding the mechanism. In *Microtubules and Microtubule Inhibitors 1985* (ed. M. De Brabander & J. De Mey), pp. 225–232. Amsterdam: Elsevier.

AMATO, P. A. & TAYLOR, D. L. (1986). Probing the mechanism of incorporation of fluorescently labeled actin into stress fibers. *J. Cell Biol.* **102**, 1074–1084.

BRADY, S. T. (1985). A novel brain ATPase with properties expected for the fast axonal transport motor. *Nature, Lond.* **317**, 73–75.

BRADY, S. T., LASEK, R. J. & ALLEN, R. D. (1982). Fast axonal transport in extruded axoplasm from squid giant axon. *Science* **218**, 1129–1131.

BRADY, S. T., LASEK, R. J. & ALLEN, R. D. (1985). Video microscopy of fast axonal transport in extruded axoplasm: A new model for study of molecular mechanisms. *Cell Motil.* **5**, 81–101.

BRAY, D. (1985). Cell motility – Fast axonal transport dissected. Editorial. *Nature, Lond.* **315**, 178–179.

CLAPP, P. (1986). Trucking down the axon. *MBL Science, Woods Hole* **2**, 9–16.

DE BRABANDER, M., NUYDENS, R., GEUENS, G., MOEREMANS, M. & DE MEY, J. (1986). The use of submicroscopic gold particles combined with video contrast enhancement as a simple molecular probe for the living cell. *Cell Motil. Cytoskel.* **6**, 105–113.

ELLIS, G. W., INOUE, S. & INOUE, T. (1986). Computer-aided light microscopy. In *Optical Methods in Cell Physiology* (ed. P. De Weer & B. M. Salzberg), pp. 15–30. New York: Wiley.

GRAFSTEIN, B. & FORMAN, D. S. (1980). Intracellular transport in neurons. *Physiol. Rev.* **60**, 1168–1283.

GROSS, G. W. (1975). The microstream concept of axoplasmic and dendritic transport. *Adv. Neurol.* **12**, 183–196.

HARD, R. & ALLEN, R. D. (1985). Flow birefringence of microtubules and its relation to birefringence measurements in cells. *Cell Motil.* **5**, 31–52.

HAYDEN, J. H. & ALLEN, R. D. (1984). Detection of single microtubules in living cells: Particle transport can occur in both directions along the same microtubule. *J. Cell Biol.* **99**, 1785–1793.

HAYDEN, J. H., ALLEN, R. D. & GOLDMAN, R. D. (1983). Cytoplasmic transport in keratocytes: Direct visualization of particle translocation along microtubules. *Cell Motil.* **3**, 1–19.

HIGASHI-FUJIME, S. (1986). Unidirectional sliding of myosin filaments along F-actin bundles *in vitro*. In *Cell Motility: Mechanism and Regulation* (ed. H. Ishikawa, S. Hatano & H. Sato), pp. 99–105. New York: Alan R. Liss.

HOLLENBECK, P. J. (1985). Organelle transport – A 3rd front for cell motility. Editorial. *Nature, Lond.* **317**, 17–18.

HOLLENBECK, P. J. (1986). Organelle transport – Moving in different directions. Editorial. *Nature, Lond.* **319**, 724–725.

HOLLENBECK, P. J. & BRAY, D. (1985). A novel 330 kD protein and its possible role in axonal transport. In *Microtubules and Microtubule Inhibitors 1985* (ed. M. De Brabander & J. De Mey), pp. 205–211. Amsterdam: Elsevier.

INOUE, S. (1981). Video image processing greatly enhances contrast, quality, and speed in polarization-based microscopy. *J. Cell Biol.* **89**, 346–356.

INOUE, S. (1986). *Video Microscopy.* New York: Plenum Press.

KACHAR, B. (1985). Direct visualization of organelle movement along actin filaments dissociated from Characean algae. *Science* **227**, 1355–1357.

KACHAR, B., EVANS, D. F. & NINHAM, B. W. (1984). Video-enhanced differential interference contrast microscopy: A new tool for the study of association colloids and prebiotic assemblies. *J. Colloid Interface Sci.* **100**, 287–301.

KELLER, F., GULDEN, J. & WEISS, D. G. (1985). Fine analysis of fast organelle transport in crayfish giant axons by AVEC-DIC microscopy: A study using digital filtering and FFT. *Eur. J. Cell Biol.* **36** (Suppl.) **7**, 33.

KOONCE, M. P., EUTENUER, U. & SCHLIWA, M. (1986). *Reticulomyxa*: a new model system of intracellular transport. *J. Cell Sci. Suppl.* 5, 125–129.

KOONCE, M. P. & SCHLIWA, M. (1985). Bidirectional organelle transport can occur in cell processes that contain single microtubules. *J. Cell Biol.* **100**, 322–326.

LANGFORD, G. M., ALLEN, R. D. & WEISS, D. G. (1986). Substructure of sidearms on squid axoplasmic vesicles and microtubules visualized by negative contrast electron microscopy. *Cell Motil. Cytoskel.* **6** (in press).

LASEK, R. J. & BRADY, S. T. (1985). Attachment of transported vesicles to microtubules in axoplasm is facilitated by AMP-PNP. *Nature, Lond.* **316**, 645–647.

LYNN, M. P., ATKINSON, M. B. & BREUER, A. C. (1986). Influence of translocation track on the motion of intra-axonally transported organelles in human nerve. *Cell Motil. Cytoskel.* **6**, 339–346.

MILLER, R. H. & LASEK, R. J. (1985). Crossbridges mediate anterograde and retrograde vesicle transport along microtubules in squid axoplasm. *J. Cell Biol.* **101**, 2181–2193.

PARPART, A. K. (1951). Televised microscopy in biological research. *Science* **113**, 483–484.

PRYOR, N. K., WADSWORTH, P. & SALMON, E. D. (1986). Polarized microtubule gliding and particle saltation produced by soluble factors from sea urchin eggs and embryos. *Cell Motil. Cytoskel.* **6** (in press).

REBHUN, L. (1986). Robert D. Allen (1927–1986): An appreciation. *Cell Motil. Cytoskel.* **6**, 249–255.

REYNOLDS, G. T., ALLEN, R. D. & INOUE, S. (1963). Evaluation of an image intensifier tube for microscopic observations. *Biol. Bull. mar. Biol. Lab., Woods Hole* **125**, 388–389.

REYNOLDS, G. T. & TAYLOR, D. L. (1980). Image intensification applied to light microscopy. *BioScience* **30**, 586–592.

SANGER, J. M., MITTAL, B., POCHAPIN, M. & SANGER, J. M. (1986). Observations of microfilament bundles in living cells microinjected with fluorescently labelled contractile proteins. *J. Cell Sci. Suppl.* 5, 17–44.

SCHNAPP, B. J., VALE, R. D., SHEETZ, M. P. & REESE, T. S. (1985). Single microtubules from squid axoplasm support bidirectional movements of organelles. *Cell* **40**, 455–462.

SCHOLEY, J. M., PORTER, M. E., GRISSOM, P. M. & MCINTOSH, J. R. (1985). Identification of kinesin in sea urchin eggs, and evidence for its localization in the mitotic spindle. *Nature, Lond.* **318**, 483–486.

TAYLOR, D. L. (1986). Robert D. Allen (1927–1986). *Nature, Lond.* **321**, 647.

TAYLOR, D. L., WAGGONER, A. S., MURPHY, R. F., LANNI, F. & BIRGE, R. R. (1986). *Applications of Fluorescence in the Biomedical Sciences*. New York: Alan R. Liss.

TRAVIS, J. L., KENEALY, J. F. X. & ALLEN, R. D. (1983). Studies on the motility of the Foraminifera. II. The dynamic microtubular cytoskeleton of the reticulopodial network of *Allogromia reticularis*. *J. Cell Biol.* **97**, 1668–1676.

VALE, R. D., REESE, T. S. & SHEETZ, M. P. (1985d). Identification of a novel, force-generating protein, kinesin, involved in microtubule-based motility. *Cell* **42**, 39–50.

VALE, R. D., SCHNAPP, B. J., MITCHISON, T., STEUER, E., REESE, T. S. & SHEETZ, M. P. (1985c). Different axoplasmic proteins generate movement in opposite directions along microtubules *in vitro*. *Cell* **43**, 623–632.

VALE, R. D., SCHNAPP, B. J., REESE, T. S. & SHEETZ, M. P. (1985a). Movement of organelles along filaments dissociated from the axoplasm of the squid giant axon. *Cell* **40**, 449–454.

VALE, R. D., SCHNAPP, B. J., REESE, T. S. & SHEETZ, M. P. (1985b). Organelle, bead, and microtubule translocations promoted by soluble factors from the squid giant axon. *Cell* **40**, 559–569.

WEISS, D. G. (1985). Dynamics and cooperativity in the organization of cytoplasmic structures and flows. In *Complex Systems – Operational Approaches in Neurobiology, Physics and Computers* (ed. H. Haken), pp. 179–191. Berlin: Springer.

WEISS, D. G. (1986). The mechanism of axoplasmic transport. In *Axoplasmic Transport* (ed. Z. Iqbal), chap. 20. Boca Raton, FL: CRC Press (in press).

WEISS, D. G. & ALLEN, R. D. (1985). The organization of force generation in microtubule-based motility. In *Microtubules and Microtubule Inhibitors 1985* (ed. M. De Brabander & J. De Mey), pp. 232–240. Amsterdam: Elsevier.

WEISS, D. G. & GROSS, G. W. (1982). The microstream hypothesis of axoplasmic transport: Characteristics, predictions and compatibility with data. In *Axoplasmic Transport* (ed. D. G. Weiss), pp. 362–383. Berlin: Springer-Verlag.

WEISS, D. G. & GROSS, G. W. (1983). Intracellular transport in axonal microtubular domains. I. Theoretical considerations on the essential properties of a force generating mechanism. *Protoplasma* **114**, 179–197.

WILLINGHAM, M. C. & PASTAN, I. (1978). The visualization of fluorescent proteins in living cells by video intensification microscopy (VIM). *Cell* **13**, 501–507.

YANAGIDA, T., NAKASE, M., NISHIYAMA, K. & OOSAWA, F. (1984). Direct observation of motion of single F-actin filaments in the presence of myosin. *Nature, Lond.* **307**, 58–60.

J. Cell Sci. Suppl. 5, 17–44 (1986)
Printed in Great Britain © The Company of Biologists Limited 1986

OBSERVATIONS OF MICROFILAMENT BUNDLES IN LIVING CELLS MICROINJECTED WITH FLUORESCENTLY LABELLED CONTRACTILE PROTEINS

JEAN M. SANGER*, BALRAJ MITTAL, MARK POCHAPIN AND JOSEPH W. SANGER

Laboratory for Cell Motility Studies in the Department of Anatomy, and the Pennsylvania Muscle Institute, University of Pennsylvania School of Medicine, Philadelphia, PA 19104, USA

SUMMARY

Fluorescently labelled contractile proteins (alpha-actinin and filamin) were used to study the dynamic nature of three types of microfilament bundles: myofibrils, stress fibres and polygonal networks. Cultured muscle and non-muscle cells that were microinjected with fluorescent alpha-actinin rapidly incorporated the labelled protein into Z-bands, stress fibre densities and the polygonal foci. Living, injected cells were then observed for varying periods of time, and changes in orientation and periodicity of the myofibrils, stress fibres and polygonal networks were recorded. Permeabilized cells were also reacted with fluorescently labelled proteins and with contractile protein antibodies in order to analyse further the changes taking place in the myofibrils and stress fibres. In both living cardiac myocytes and living skeletal muscle myotubes, contractile myofibrils were present in the same cell with non-contractile nascent myofibrils. The periodicities of small Z-bodies in the nascent non-contractile myofibrils were shorter than the Z-band spacings in the contractile myofibrils, yet both types of myofibrils contained muscle myosin. Over a period of 24 h, a nascent myofibril in a living, microinjected myotube was observed to grow from Z-body spacings of $0 \cdot 9$–$1 \cdot 3 \mu$m to full sarcomere spacings ($2 \cdot 3 \mu$m). During the same time, nascent myofibrils appeared *de novo* and Z-band alignment became more ordered in the fully formed myofibrils. Stress fibres were not observed to undergo the predictable type of growth seen in myofibrils, but stress fibre periodicities did change in some fibres; some shortened while others lengthened. The orientation of fibres shifted in cytoplasm of both mobile cells and stationary cells. Attachment plaques and foci also changed position and in some cases subdivided and/or disappeared. Models of stress fibres and polygonal networks are presented that suggest that the changes in the periodicities of the dense bodies in stress fibres and the distances between polygonal foci are related to the movement of the interdigitating actin and myosin filaments.

INTRODUCTION

Stress fibres, polygonal networks and myofibrils can be considered to be microfilament bundles, composed as they are of aligned arrays of actin microfilaments with associated proteins and interdigitating myosin proteins (Huxley, 1983; Weber & Groeschel-Stewart, 1974; Lazarides & Burridge, 1975; Lazarides, 1976). Observation of the periodic distribution of proteins along stress fibres has led to the suggestion that these fibres have a sarcomeric structure analogous to that of striated

* Author for correspondence.

muscle myofibrils (Gordon, 1978; Sanger & Sanger, 1980; Sanger *et al.* 1983*a*, 1985*a*). Stress fibres have been induced to contract (Isenberg *et al.* 1976; Kreis & Birchmeier, 1980) but it is not known if they have a contractile role in living cells. Stress fibres are more labile than myofibrils undergoing cycles of assembly and disassembly during the cell cycle (Sanger, 1975*a*,*b*) and in response to a variety of agents such as dimethyl sulphoxide (DMSO) (Sanger *et al.* 1980*a*,*b*, 1983*b*; Osborn & Weber, 1980), azide (Bershadsky *et al.* 1980) and cytochalasins (Weber *et al.* 1976) that do not alter myofibril structure (Sanger, 1974). The goal of our research is to observe the behaviour of microfilament bundles in living cells, to learn how they are assembled, whether their distribution changes as cells move, and whether, in the case of stress fibres, polygonal networks and nascent myofibrils, contraction can be observed.

MATERIALS AND METHODS

Cells

The cells used for these studies were three cell lines: PtK2, an epithelial line, and gerbil fibroma and 3T3, both fibroblastic lines (American Tissue Type Collection, Rockeville, MD); and primary embryonic chick cells from cardiac muscle (5-day embryos) and breast muscle (10-day embryos) (Sanger, 1974, 1977). The cell lines were cultured directly on glass coverslips (Sanger, 1975*a*,*b*) and the chick cells grown on collagen-coated coverslips (Sanger *et al.* 1986). Living cells were micro-injected in culture dishes as described (Pochapin *et al.* 1983; Sanger *et al.* 1985*b*) and returned to the incubator for a time ranging from half an hour to overnight. When living cells were to be observed over a time period greater than 1 h, they were mounted in a Dvorak-Stotler chamber (Nicholson Precision Instruments, Inc., Bethesda, MD) through which fresh culture medium was perfused and which was heated to 37°C with a hot-air heater. Cells that were to be observed for shorter periods of time were mounted with a Vaseline seal on a glass slide and kept at 37°C with a hot-air heater. Cells that were treated with antibodies or fluorescent alpha-actinin were permeabilized with either 0·02% Nonidet P-40 or chilled acetone (Sanger *et al.* 1983*a*, 1984*c*).

Proteins

Alpha-actinin was prepared from smooth and striated muscle (Feramisco & Burridge, 1980) or from calf brain (Duhaiman & Bamburg, 1984) and labelled with lissamine rhodamine sulphonyl chloride (LR) or fluorescein isothiocyanate (FITC) as previously described (Sanger *et al.* 1984*a*,*b*, 1986). A myofibril assay and gel electrophoresis of the fluorescent protein (Sanger *et al.* 1984*a*,*b*, 1986) were used to characterize the fluorescent alpha-actinin before its use in microinjected or permeabilized cells. Filamin from chicken gizzards was prepared according to the procedure of Feramisco & Burridge (1980) and labelled with iodoacetamido tetramethyl rhodamine (IAR). Antibodies to alpha-actinin, skeletal muscle and non-muscle myosins were prepared as described previously (Sanger *et al.* 1983*a*, 1986; Fallon & Nachmias, 1980).

Microscopy

Cells were viewed with a Zeiss 100× Planapochromat lens n.a. 1·3, and recorded on 35 mm film or videotape. To aid in observation of the low levels of fluorescence in the injected cells, the image from a SIT video camera (Dage-MTI, Inc., Michigan City, MI) was viewed directly on a video monitor or processed with an Interactive Video Systems (IVS) image processor (IVS, Concord, MA), or a Hughes 794 Image Processor (Hughes Aircraft, Inc., Carlsbad, CA) and subsequently photographed from the monitor with 35 mm film (Pochapin *et al.* 1983; Sanger *et al.* 1985*b*).

RESULTS AND DISCUSSION

Cardiac myocytes

When first isolated from embryonic hearts and placed in culture, cardiac myocytes are spherical. After attaching to the substrate the myocyte in Fig. 1 began to flatten by extending lamellipodia that actively ruffled, while at the same time the central rounded part of the myocyte contracted rhythymically. Over a period of 24–48 h, myocytes typically elongate and flatten as depicted by the cell in Fig. 2, which was transformed during 21 h in culture into the myocyte in Fig. 3. Although some myofibrils are visible in the flattened myocyte (Fig. 3), it is not possible to see myofibrils in rounder cells (Figs 1, 2), nor are myofibrils visible near the ruffling margins of the flattened myocyte (Fig. 3). In order to visualize all the myofibrils present in spreading cardiac myocytes, we have used fluorescently labelled alpha-actinin as a probe either injected into living cells or reacted with permeabilized cells. Alpha-actinin, a Z-band protein (Masaki *et al.* 1967), is an actin-binding protein (Goll *et al.* 1972; Podlubnaya *et al.* 1975), which can also bind to other alpha-actinin molecules (Masaki & Takaita, 1969). Previous studies have shown that fluorescent alpha-actinin binds to Z-bands and stress fibre densities in both injected and permeabilized cells (Sanger *et al.* 1984*a,b,c*; Geiger, 1981).

Fluorescently labelled alpha-actinin has been used to study the distribution of native alpha-actinin in a variety of systems (Sanger *et al.* 1984*a,b,c*; Lash *et al.* 1985). The fluorescent probe has the potential to reveal the smallest myofibril and enable us to observe the myofibrils in myocytes that are simultaneously contracting, extending lamellipodia and spreading on a substrate. Figs 4 and 5 show permeabilized myocytes comparable to the myocyte in Fig. 2. Myofibrils with full Z-band spacing ($2 \cdot 0$–$2 \cdot 3 \, \mu$m) are visible in the rounded central region of each cell, but not behind the lamellipodia. The cytoplasm between the ruffling margins of the cell and the region occupied by the fully formed myofibrils contains instead fibrils with punctate distributions of alpha-actinin spaced $0 \cdot 5$–$1 \cdot 5 \, \mu$m apart. Myofibrils running along the long axis of the cell have solid Z-bands in the centre (Figs 4, 5) and tail (Fig. 5) of the cell, beaded Z-bands (Figs 4, 5) distal to them and fine beaded fibrils that appear to splay out from the ends of the myofibrils. Similarly, periodic fibrils are also found at the periphery of fully spread myocytes such as are shown permeabilized and stained with alpha-actinin in Fig. 6.

Cardiac myocytes injected with fluorescent muscle or non-muscle alpha-actinin show comparable distributions of alpha-actinin in living cells (Figs 7, 8). Before injecting the cells, several technical problems had to be considered. It was of primary importance that fluorescently labelled proteins were prepared that retain their native ability to bind to other proteins, form filaments or retain their enzymic activity, as the case may be; while at the same time they need to emit a fluorescent signal that, when incorporated into cell structures, is bright enough to be detected with low light-level video cameras. When such proteins are injected into cells, observation of the fluorescence inside the living cells must be achieved with minimal levels of excitatory light to avoid damage to the cells and, secondarily, to limit bleaching of the

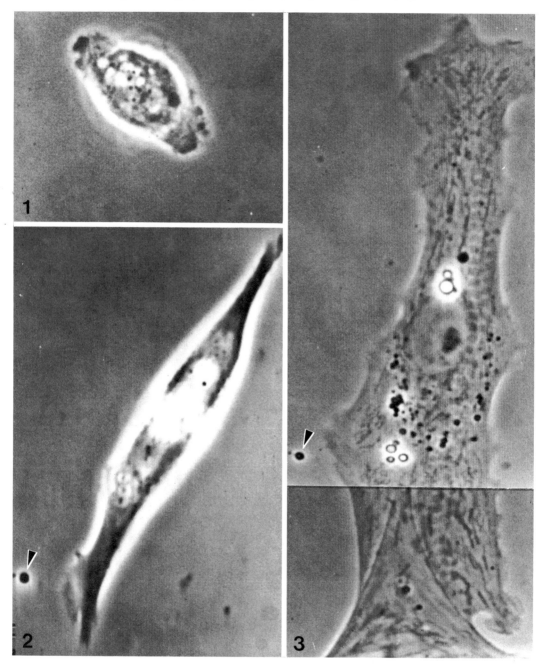

Figs 1–3. The cardiac myocytes were viewed with a Newvicon video camera on the second and third day in culture. The cell in Fig. 1, after 21 h in culture, contracted rhythmically and extended two lamellipodia from opposite sides of its rounded body. The myocyte in Fig. 2 was also contracting in the central region of the cell, and had flattened to a greater extent after the same time in culture. Fig. 3 shows the same myocyte as in Fig. 2, 21 h later. The cell has elongated and spread laterally, and myofibrils are visible in the cytoplasm. A stationary reference point on the substrate is indicated in Figs 2 and 3 (arrowheads). A fibroblast has moved onto the lower end of the myocyte in Fig. 3. Figs 1–3 same magnification. ×1250.

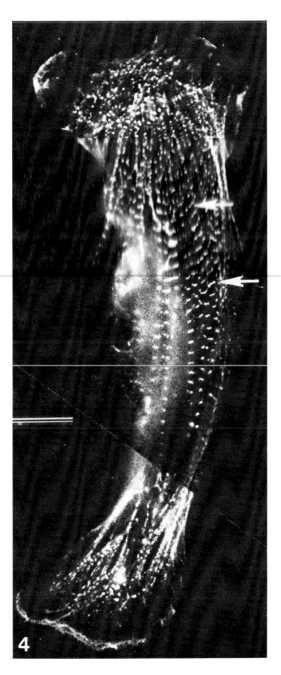

Fig. 4. Spreading cardiac myocyte with three lamellipodia permeabilized and re-acted with alpha-actinin–LR shows centrally positioned myofibrils merging with finer fibrils composed of closely spaced beads of alpha-actinin. In some cases, the Z-bands appear to be composed of laterally aligned beads of alpha-actinin (arrows). ×1700. Bar, 10 μm.

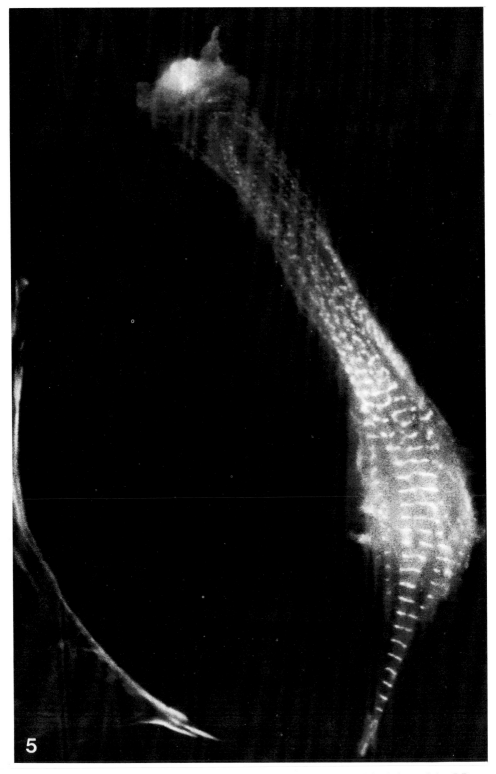

Fig. 5. A spreading cardiac myocyte permeabilized and reacted with alpha-actinin–LR has fully formed myofibrils that extend from a narrow tail to the bulbous cell body. Behind the ruffling end of the myocyte, fine beaded fibrils run parallel to the long axis of the cell. ×1900.

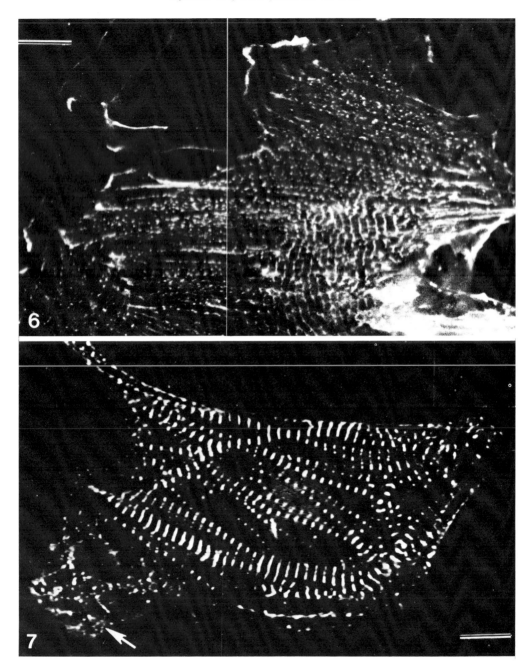

Fig. 6. A cardiac myocyte grown in culture for 7 days, permeabilized and reacted with alpha-actinin–LR contains parallel arrays of beaded fibrils in the peripheral cytoplasm adjacent to fully formed myofibrils. ×1400. Bar, 10 μm.

Fig. 7. Cardiac myocyte injected after 4 days in culture with smooth muscle alpha-actinin–LR. Most of the fluorescence is found in Z-bands of contracting myofibrils. A non-contracting region of the cell contains beaded aggregates of alpha-actinin (arrow). ×1450. Bar, 10 μm.

fluorescent dye. Before microinjection, we assay our labelled proteins using myo-fibrils and permeabilized cells (Sanger *et al.* 1984*a,b*). We minimize exposure of the living cells to light by using a SIT video camera coupled with an image processor that can enhance brightness levels and save consecutive frames of the image into memory where it can be displayed, recorded photographically or on video tape, and further analysed.

Although the resolution we have obtained so far with video recording of the myofibrils and finely periodic fibrils in the living cells is not as good as in the brightly stained permeabilized cells, the living injected cells beat in culture and enabled us to correlate structure with contractile activity. Rhythmic beating in living myocytes such as those illustrated in Figs 7 and 8 occurs only in areas populated with fully formed myofibrils (Z-band spacing $\simeq 2 \cdot 3 \, \mu$m). Areas of cytoplasm with beaded aggregates of alpha-actinin and fibrils with closely spaced beads of alpha-actinin (arrows in Figs 7 and 8) have not been observed beating. In some video sequences, a finely periodic fibril appeared to be ligated to a fully formed myofibril, and when the fully formed sarcomeres contracted, the nascent sarcomeres were pulled. Z-bands in the myofibril could be seen to move closer together during contraction but the spacing of the periodic beads of alpha-actinin along the fibril did not appear to change when the fibril was pulled.

In order to characterize further the non-contractile fibrils, cardiac myocytes were treated with both alpha-actinin and a monoclonal antibody to skeletal muscle myosin. We found that skeletal muscle myosin was present not only in the A-bands of fully formed myofibrils but also between the sites of alpha-actinin in the finely beaded fibrils (Sanger *et al.* 1986). We have suggested that these fibrils are nascent myo-fibrils and the beads of alpha-actinin nascent Z-bands (Sanger *et al.* 1984*c*, 1986). In a study of cultured chick cardiac cells using phase-contrast and polarized light microscopy, Rumery *et al.* (1961) reported that unbanded myofibrils that were non-contractile were present in varying numbers in heart muscle cells. The only contractions they observed were in striated myofibrils.

Myotubes

Myotubes cultured from embryonic chick breast muscle also incorporate micro-injected alpha-actinin into Z-bands regardless of the source of the alpha-actinin. If two types of alpha-actinin are coinjected into myotubes, they both become incorporated into Z-bands of contracting myofibrils (Fig. 9). The microinjected skeletal and cardiac muscle cells cannot distinguish between various forms of muscle and non-muscle alpha-actinins. McKenna *et al.* (1985) reported that microinjected cardiac fibroblasts and myocytes could not distinguish muscle actins from non-muscle actins. As is true in cardiac myocytes, both fully formed and finely periodic nascent myofibrils contain skeletal muscle myosin (Sanger *et al.* 1986) and can be found together in adjacent areas of cytoplasm. The nascent myofibrils are found most often at the ends of myotubes and in several such cells we have seen beating of fully formed myofibrils proximal to the myotube end with no contractile activity in the terminal nascent myofibrils. Periodic observations of a single area of an

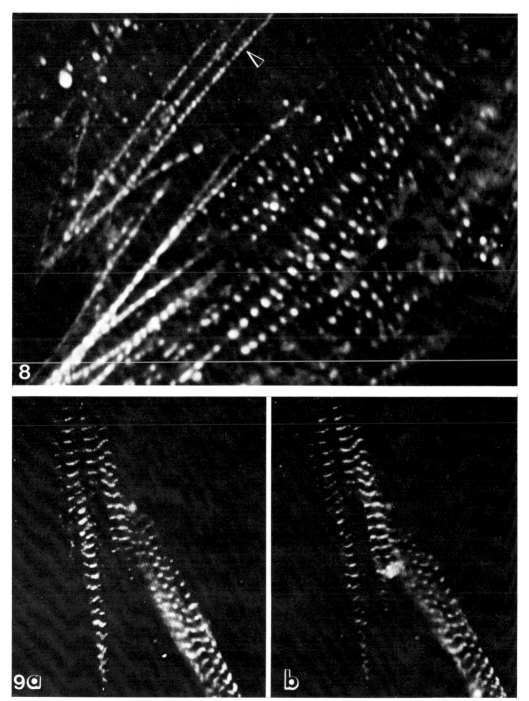

Fig. 8. A living cardiac myocyte injected after 3 days in culture with non-muscle alpha-actinin–LR. The myofibrils shown on the right side of the micrograph actively contracted whereas the fibrils on the left with a closely spread periodic arrangement of alpha-actinin (arrowhead) did not contract. ×2000.

Fig. 9. Two views of a myotube coinjected with smooth muscle alpha-actinin–FITC (a) and skeletal muscle alpha-actinin–LR (b). Both proteins are incorporated into the Z-bands with no preference evident in the fluorescence micrographs. ×1500.

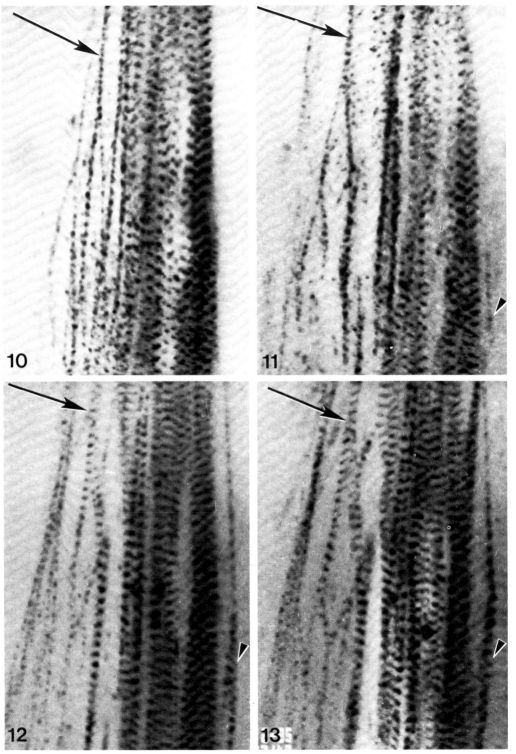

Figs 10–13. Area of a myotube injected with alpha-actinin–LR and viewed in reverse contrast to make the fluorescent periodicities easier to detect. Arrows point to regions of myofibrils where growth was detected. Arrowheads indicate fibrils that appeared to form *de novo* after first time point. ×1300.

    Fig. 10. First time point recorded.

    Fig. 11. Second time point 10 h later.

    Fig. 12. Third time point 25 h after the first point.

    Fig. 13. Fourth time point 30 h after the first point.

injected myotube over 30 h showed that Z-bodies in nascent myofibrils grew apart from periodicities of 0·9–1·3 μm to sarcomeric spacing of 1·6–2·3 μm (arrows in Figs 10–13). In addition to growth, *de novo* appearance of fibrils was also evident (arrowheads, Figs 12–13), as well as an increase in width of the myofibrils. Devlin & Emerson (1978) have reported the coordinate synthesis of actin, myosin, tropomyosin and alpha-actinin during vertebrate myogenesis. The increase in the width of the Z-band during myofibrillogenesis (Figs 10–13) may reflect the important role of alpha-actinin in binding the ends of new actin filaments to the Z-band (Goldstein *et al.* 1979). Sanger *et al.* (1984*a*) demonstrated that Z-bands in adult myofibrils are not capable of binding additional actin filaments. However, when exogenous alpha-actinin was added to these myofibrils, additional actin filaments bound to these Z-bands. These observations suggest that during myogenesis newly attached actin filaments could bind newly synthesized myosin filaments to the growing myofibril.

Observations of myofibril growth have been reported in insect systems by Aronson (1961) and Auber (1969), who showed that both filaments and sarcomeres grew during myogenesis. Aronson's (1961) study of living mite muscle also demonstrates that the onset of contractile activity occurred only after the thick filaments and sarcomere size grew to the adult length. We believe that a similar growth process occurs in the embryonic chick cardiac and skeletal muscle, but the relatively small sarcomere and A-band size characteristic of vertebrate muscle have made the growth until now difficult to detect.

Stress fibres

In non-muscle cells, microfilament bundles in the form of stress fibres are much more labile than the myofibrils in muscle cells (Sanger & Sanger, 1979; Sanger *et al.* 1983*b*). They have a banded appearance in the electron microscope (Fig. 14) and a periodic distribution of contractile proteins along their length (reviewed by Sanger *et al.* 1983*a*, 1985*a*). Stress fibres are found not only in tissue culture cells but in cells *in situ* (Rohlick & Olah, 1967; Byers & Fujiwara, 1982). Stress fibre periodicity is much shorter than the sarcomeric periodicity in vertebrate striated muscle. The shortest invertebrate muscle sarcomeres are 0·9 μm (Chapman *et al.* 1962), the longest 30 μm (Del Castillo *et al.* 1972), with all vertebrate sarcomeres measuring approximately 2·3 μm at rest length. Stress fibre periodicities as measured from alpha-actinin banding average approximately 0·8 μm in epithelial cells and 1·7 μm in fibroblast cells with variations within single cells and within a single fibre (Sanger *et al.* 1983*a*). Stress fibres show the same variation in periodicities with myosin antibody (Fig. 15) as is also seen in cells microinjected with alpha-actinin (Fig. 16). The myosin band itself is wider in the fibres that have the longer spacings as is also the case for tropomyosin localization (Sanger *et al.* 1983*a*).

Our current view of stress fibre structure is presented in Fig. 17, and is based on a variety of immunofluorescence (Weber & Groeschl-Stewart, 1974; Lazarides, 1976; Gordon, 1978; Sanger *et al.* 1983), electron-microscopic (Begg *et al.* 1978; Sanger & Sanger, 1980; Langanger *et al.* 1984, 1986) and microinjection studies (Kreis *et al.* 1979; Feramisco, 1979; Wehland & Weber, 1980; Sanger *et al.* 1984*b*). The model proposes that actin filaments are anchored in an interdigitating fashion in dense bodies that are composed in part of alpha-actinin. The actin filaments originating from one side of a dense body have uniform polarity (Begg *et al.* 1978; Sanger &

Fig. 14. Electron micrograph of PtK2 cell at low magnification showing periodic densities along the fibres. ×6300.

Fig. 15. Indirect immunofluorescence micrograph of a gerbil fibroma cell treated with an antibody to non-muscle myosin. Centre-to-centre spacings are longer in the fibres at the cell periphery than in the smaller fibres in the interior of the cell. Note that the length of the myosin bands is larger (arrowheads) in the longer centre-to-centre spacings and shorter in the smaller centre-to-centre spacings. ×1500.

Fig. 16. Fluorescence micrograph of a living gerbil fibroma cell microinjected with alpha-actinin–LR. The variation in periodicity between fibres is evident with the longer spacing in fibres at the margin of the cell (arrowhead). ×1500.

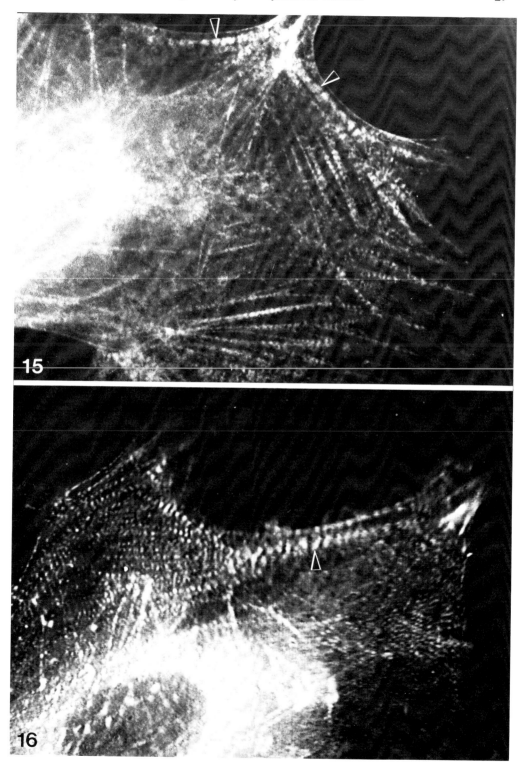

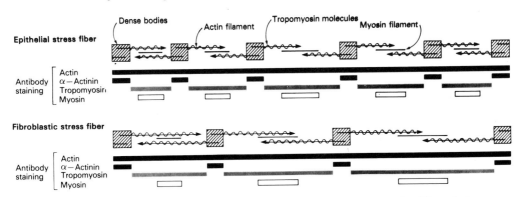

Fig. 17. Model of stress fibre structure in epithelial and fibroblastic cells. The relative positions of the proteins are the same for both types of cells, but the spacings between bands of protein are greater on the average in fibroblastic cells. The single myosin filaments in each band are depicted as varying in length to account for the variations observed in antibody staining. It is also possible that a staggered overlap of filaments of uniform length gives rise to immunofluorescence bands of varying length.

Sanger, 1980; Langanger *et al.* 1986) with the free ends of the actin filaments overlapping in the region midway between the dense bodies. Tropomyosin presumably binds to that region of the actin filament that is not bound to alpha-actinin. The absence of tropomyosin in the dense-body regions (Lazarides, 1976; Gordon, 1978; Sanger *et al.* 1983a) also gives us an indirect measurement of the maximum length of the tropomyosin-coated thin filaments in the sarcomere unit of the stress fibre. If the thin filaments extended any further than one dense body, the result would be solid tropomyosin staining as tropomyosin-coated microfilaments overlapped the dense body. Therefore, the banded pattern indicates the maximum lengths of the microfilaments, $0.9\,\mu m$ for epithelial cells and $1.7\,\mu m$ in fibroblasts. The variation in tropomyosin band length that we have previously reported (Sanger *et al.* 1983a) could be accounted for by a sliding together or apart of the overlapping tropomyosin-coated actin filaments. The actin would appear to be continuous along the length of the stress fibre unless the dense bodies moved apart until there was no overlapping of the actin filaments. This could account for the occasional observations of banded actin localization (Sanger, 1975c; Gordon, 1978).

Myosin filaments are shown interdigitating with the actin filaments in the central region between the dense bodies (Fig. 17). The variation in myosin bands implies that either myosin filaments are longer in some fibres than others or that there is a staggered arrangement of overlapping myosin filaments in the longer bands. Both variations in myosin filament length and overlapping of out-of-register groups of filaments have been reported in invertebrate muscle (Franzini-Armstrong, 1970). The immunoelectron-microscopic studies of Langanger *et al.* (1986) clearly show that the arrangement of myosin filaments in stress fibres is bipolar as it is in muscle (see review by Huxley, 1983). Thus stress fibre organization is compatible with an actin–myosin sliding analogous to that in muscle.

Although the actin filaments are illustrated as having a uniform length in the epithelial cells ($0.6\,\mu m$) and fibroblasts ($1.0\,\mu m$), the filaments could vary in length as has been reported in a few muscles (Robinson & Winegrad, 1979). As was stated above for tropomyosin staining it is unlikely that the pointed ends of the tropo-myosin-coated actin filaments extend beyond the dense bodies. In contrast to the capped ends of striated muscle actin filaments, the pointed end of the stress fibre actin filament may be uncapped (Sanger *et al.* 1984*a*,*b*). Ultimately we still have no idea why the sarcomeric units in epithelial and fibroblastic cells are different in their dimensions. The answer to this question should also yield insight into a similar phenomenon in invertebrate muscles where sarcomeric units have ranged from 0·9 μm to 30 μm, thin filaments from 0·5 μm to 15 μm and thick filaments from 0·6 μm to 25 μm (Chapman *et al.* 1962; Sanger & McCann, 1968; Del Castillo *et al.* 1972).

The ability to visualize stress fibre structure in living microinjected cells provides the potential for asking: do periodicities along a stress fibre change with time? Do stress fibres change their distribution inside cells? How are stress fibres assembled and disassembled during the cell cycle in response to agents that affect cell movement or shape? Figs 18–20 illustrate the changing distribution of alpha-actinin in a motile chick cardiac fibroblast that was photographed at 5-min intervals. During this time the cell formed lamellipodia in one direction and retracted a tail that extended in the opposite direction. The accompanying rearrangement of alpha-actinin occurs as an increase in attachment plaques at the base of the lamellipodia (Fig. 19, arrows) just before tail retraction, followed by the formation of a large aggregate of protein at the site where the tail retracted into the cell body (Fig. 20, arrow). In a study of tail retraction in chick embryo fibroblasts, Chen (1981) showed that there was an increased concentration of microfilaments at the retraction site. It will be of interest to see if other injected cells that undergo tail retraction also form additional attachment plaques shortly before retraction.

When stress fibres in the injected cells are observed at 5-min intervals, few changes in periodicities are evident in the fibres. Small changes occur, however, in at least a few fibres as shown in Figs 21 and 22, in which a cardiac fibroblast was photographed twice in 5 min. In this cell, these alpha-actinin bands moved apart in a stress fibre adjacent to the leading edge of the cell (top three arrowheads in Figs 21, 22). In another stress fibre, two bands moved closer together (two arrowheads, Figs 21, 22) as if contraction had occurred. The remainder of the resolvable stress fibre bands appeared unchanged.

Polygonal networks

Polygonal networks or nets have been observed on the dorsal surface in a wide variety of fibroblastic and epithelial cells in tissue culture (Lazarides, 1976; Rathke *et al.* 1979). Fig. 23 illustrates the dorsal edge of a chick cardiac epithelial cell with a small portion of a polygonal network. The circular dense foci of the network are connected to one another *via* bundles of microfilaments. Immunofluorescence work has demonstrated that the foci stain positively for alpha-actinin, actin and filamin, but negatively for tropomyosin and myosin (Lazarides, 1976; Rathke *et al.* 1979). Rathke *et al.* (1979) demonstrated that the microfilament bundles interconnecting

J. M. Sanger, B. Mittal, M. Pochapin and J. W. Sanger

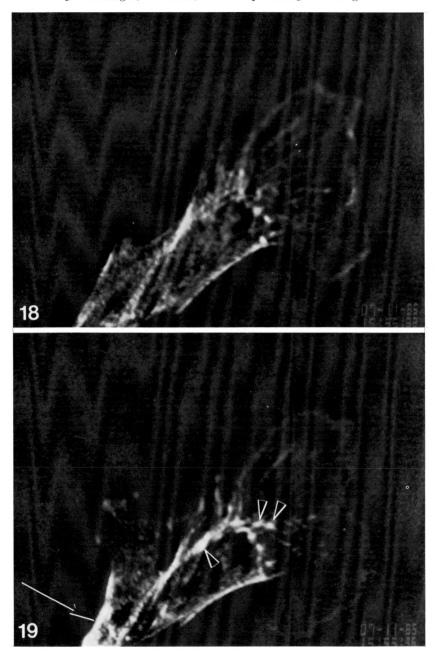

Figs 18–20. Cardiac fibroblast injected with alpha-actinin–LR and photographed at 5-min intervals. ×1100.

Fig. 18. Lamellipodia at one end of the cell with a tail extending out of the field at the opposite end of the cell.

Fig. 19. The changing shape of the lamellipodia 5 min later, an increased number of attachment plaques at the base of the lamellipodia (arrowheads), and an increased concentration of alpha-actinin in the region from which the tail extends (arrow).

Fig. 20. The fibroblast 5 min later with complete tail retraction and a large aggregate of alpha-actinin (arrow) at the point where the tail retracted into the cell body.

the foci are like stress fibres in their periodic antibody staining for myosin, alpha-actinin and tropomyosin. In fact, the fibres connecting foci of fibroblastic cells (Fig. 24) have the long periodicity characteristic of the stress fibres of those cells, whereas foci of epithelial cells (Fig. 25) are joined by fibres with short periodicity.

The activity of foci can be followed in cells injected with filamin-IAR, a protein that is co-localized with alpha-actinin in non-muscle cells (Rathke *et al.* 1979). 3T3 cells, a fibroblastic line, readily incorporate injected filamin into foci and stress fibres (Fig. 26). Twenty minutes later, the foci in the same cell (Fig. 27) have shifted in position with some adjacent foci moving closer to one another (Figs 26, 27, arrowheads) and others moving apart (Figs 26, 27, arrows).

Foci are also apparent in gerbil fibroma cells injected with alpha-actinin–LR (Figs 28–31). In this cell, also, rearrangements in foci occur within minutes. A cluster of foci (Fig. 28, arrow) transforms in 20 min into smaller bands of alpha-actinin, some of which are aligned into small stress fibres (Fig. 31, arrow). Two foci (Fig. 28, arrowheads) move apart after 5 min (Fig. 29, arrowheads) and after 20 min are no longer present (Fig. 31).

Fig. 32 is a diagram indicating the proposed relationship of the foci and the interconnecting bundles. Contraction of the fibres could cause the foci to move closer together or apart from neighbours. The position of filamin is not indicated in this diagram but is reported to be the dense bodies and on the thin filaments (Wang *et al.* 1975; Langanger *et al.* 1985, 1986). Langanger *et al.* (1986) have suggested that filamin may cross-link the actin filaments and prevent movement of the sarcomeric units in the stress fibres. Our results on living cells (Figs 10–22, 24–25) indicate that the filaments in the sarcomeric units can move by one another. If cross-linking by

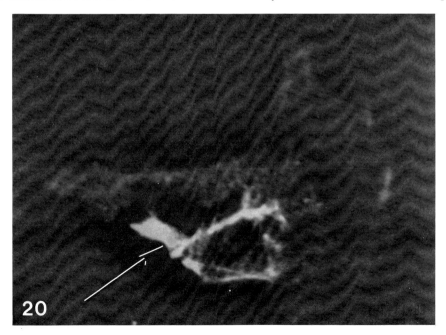

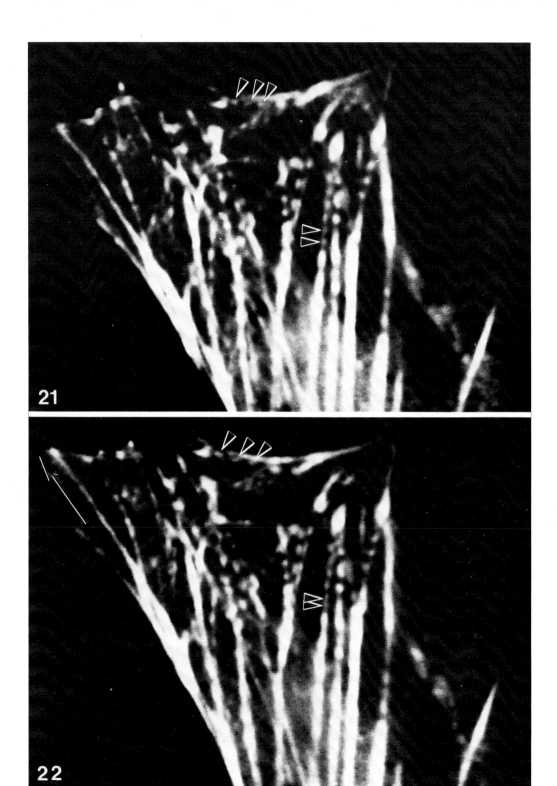

21

22

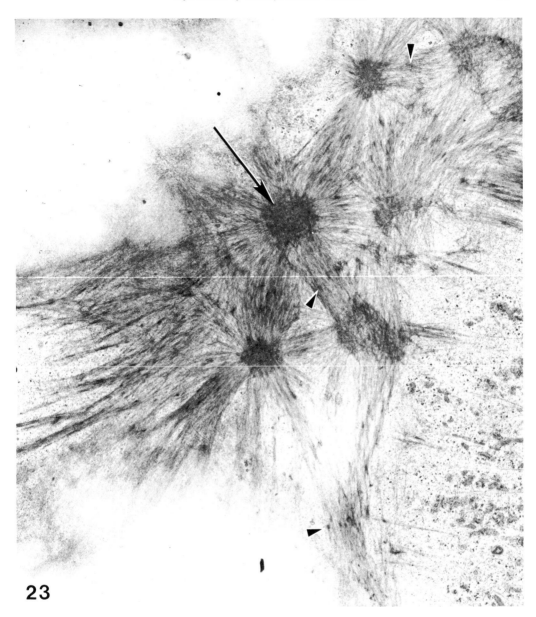

23

Fig. 23. An electron micrograph of a chick cardiac epithelial cell in culture. Note the large circular densities (foci) (arrow) in which actin filaments are embedded. Microfilament bundles interconnect the foci to form a polygonal network. Dense bodies (arrowheads) are observed among the microfilaments. ×26 000.

Figs 21, 22. Cardiac fibroblast injected with alpha-actinin–LR and photographed twice, 5 min apart. Three bands of alpha-actinin in a fibre running along the leading edge (top three arrowheads) move apart and two of the bands in a stress fibre running parallel to the axis of the cell move closer together (two arrowheads). The primary direction of movement of the cell was the direction of the arrow in Fig. 22. ×1800.

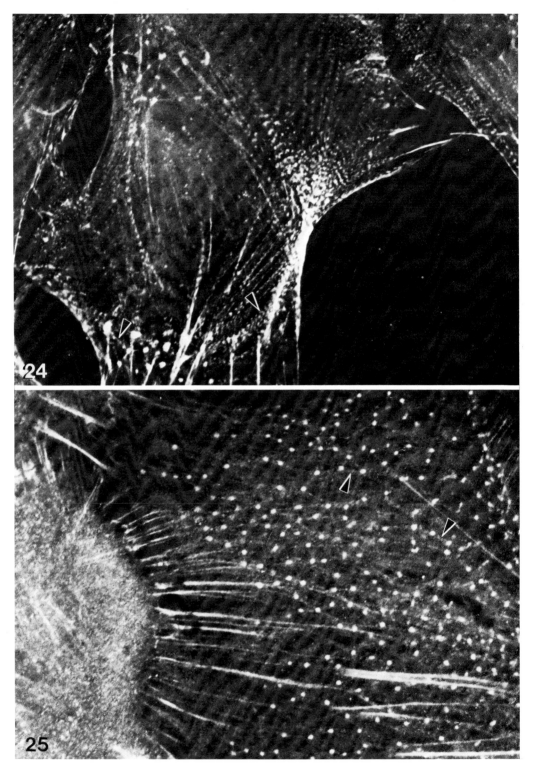

Figs 24–25. Immunofluorescent micrographs of two different cell types at the same magnification. ×1250.

Fig. 24. Gerbil fibroma cell stained with an alpha-actinin antibody. Note the long spacings in the interconnecting microfilament bundles (arrowheads).

Fig. 25. Bovine epithelial cell stained with the same alpha-actinin antibody. The periodicities of the bundles interconnecting the foci are short (arrowheads).

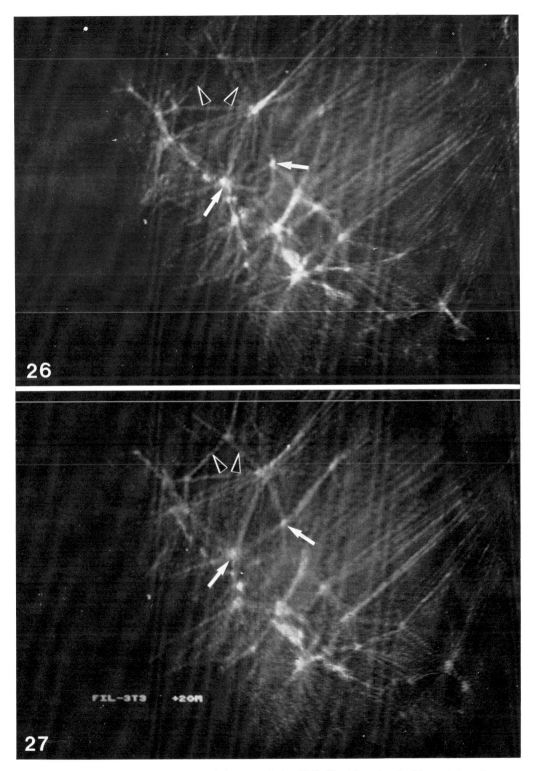

Figs 26–27. Two time points of the same living 3T3 fibroblast that had been injected with filamin–IAR. Fig. 26, 0 time; Fig. 27, 20 min later. Note the decreasing size of the triangle in the two figures. The sides (arrowheads) shorten while the base remains constant. Note the two foci moving further apart (arrows). A number of other changes in the polygonal networks and attached stress fibres can be detected by comparing the two figures. ×1600.

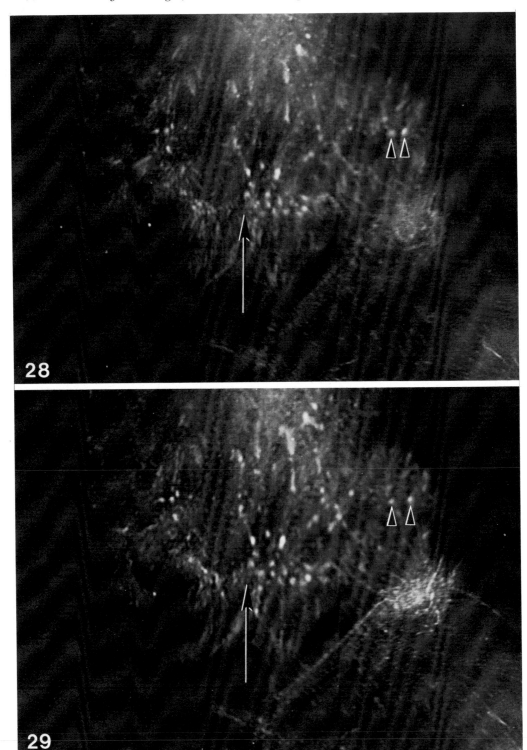

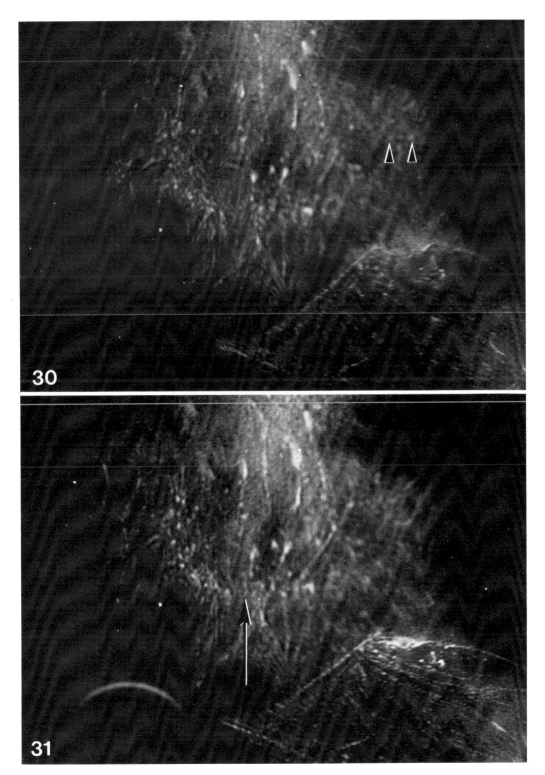

Figs 28–31. Four different time points from a gerbil fibroma cell microinjected with alpha-actinin–LR. A cluster of foci (arrow) in Fig. 28 after 20 min has been transformed into smaller bands of alpha-actinin some of which are aligned into small stress fibres (Fig. 31, arrow). Two foci (arrowheads) move apart after the first 5 min (Figs 28, 29, 30) and are no longer present after 20 min (Fig. 31). ×1600.

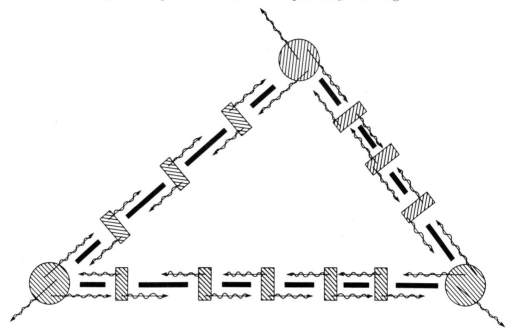

Fig. 32. A diagram illustrating the relationship of the foci and the sarcomeric inter-connecting microfilament bundles. The contraction of the sarcomeric units would result in the foci moving closer together. Contractions of adjacent sarcomeric units beyond the foci in this diagram would result in these foci being pulled further apart. Opposing contractile forces exerted on a single point from different directions could lead to a splitting of the foci into smaller foci.

filamin does occur in stress fibres inside living cells, a regulatory step would be needed before sliding movement could take place. The role of filamin has yet to be determined.

CONCLUSIONS

Immunofluorescence and related techniques developed over the past dozen years revolutionized our knowledge of the structure of the cytoskeleton. Following the lead of those who study motility in living cells (see, e.g., Trinkaus, 1984) these observations are being extended with studies in which antibodies and fluorescently labelled proteins are injected into living cells to probe the relationship between structure and function of cytoskeletal elements (see, e.g., Wang & Taylor, 1979; Wang, 1984, 1985; Feramisco, 1979; Kreis *et al.* 1979; Sanger *et al.* 1980; Burridge & Feramisco, 1980; Fuerchtbauer *et al.* 1983). Advances in video microscopy (Inoué, 1981; Allen *et al.* 1981) make possible improved resolution of the dynamic cytoskeletal network in living cells.

Almost exactly 23 years ago, a meeting organized by Professors R. D. Allen and N. Kamiya on 'Primitive Motile Systems in Cell Biology' was held at Princeton. The book edited by Allen & Kamiya (1964) was directed to scientists and students "interested in the movements in and of living cells". Allen & Kamiya wrote in their introduction to the published proceedings: "If it had not been for the invention of the microscope, the study of motility might well have remained restricted to the study of muscular contraction". We would like to paraphrase their statement. If it had not been for the development of low light-level TV cameras, image-processing equipment, and software (see reviews by Inoué, 1981; Allen *et al.* 1981; Walter & Berns, 1981), we and others would not be able to follow the dynamic behaviour of fluorescently labelled contractile proteins inside living cells.

This work was supported by grants from the National Institutes of Health (GM-25653 to J.W.S. and J.M.S.; HL-15835 to the Pennsylvania Muscle Institute) and the National Science Foundation (DMB 82–19920).

We are indebted to John M. Sanger, Neil R. Bigioni, Karen M. McSorley and Matthew K. Sanger for their capable photographic assistance during the course of this work.

REFERENCES

ALLEN, R. D., ALLEN, N. S. & TRAVIS, J. L. (1981). Video enhanced control, differential interference contrast (AVEC-DIC) microscopy: A new method capable of analyzing microtubule related movement in the reticulopodial network of *Allogromia laticollans. Cell Motil.* **1**, 291–302.

ALLEN, R. D. & KAMIYA, N. (1964). *Primative Motile Systems in Cell Biology.* New York: Academic Press.

ARONSON, J. (1961). Sarcomere size in developing muscles of a tarsonemed mite. *J. biophys. biochem. Cytol.* **11**, 147–156.

AUBER, J. (1969). La myofibrillogenèse du muscle strié. I. Insectes. *J. Microsc.* **8**, 197–232.

BEGG, D. A., RODEWALD, R. & REBHUN, L. I. (1978). The visualization of actin filament polarity in thin sections: evidence for the uniform polarity of membrane-associated filaments. *J. Cell Biol.* **79**, 844–852.

BERSHADSKY, A. D., GELFAND, V. I., SVITKINA, T. M. & TINTI, I. S. (1980). Destruction of microfilament bundles in mouse embryo fibroblasts treated with inhibitors of energy metabolism. *Expl Cell Res.* **127**, 421–429.

BYERS, H. R. & FUJIWARA, K. (1982). Stress fibers in cells *in situ*: immunofluorescence visualization with antiactin, antimyosin and anti-alpha-actinin. *J. Cell Biol.* **93**, 804–811.

BURRIDGE, K. & FERAMISCO, J. R. (1980). Microinjection and localization of a 130 K protein in living fibroblasts: a relationship to actin and fibronectin. *Cell* **19**, 587–595.

CHAPMAN, D. M., PANTIN, F. A. & ROBSON, E. A. (1962). Muscle in coelenterates. *Rev. Can. Biol.* **21**, 267–278.

CHEN, W.-T. (1981). Mechanism of retraction of the trailing edge during fibroblast movement. *J. Cell Biol.* **90**, 187–200.

DEL CASTILLO, J., ANDERSON, M. & SMITH, D. S. (1972). Proventriculus of a marine annelid: muscle preparation with the longest recorded sarcomere. *Proc. natn. Acad. Sci. U.S.A.* **69**, 1669–1672.

DEVLIN, R. B. & EMERSON, C. P. (1978). Coordinate regulation of contractile protein synthesis during myoblast differentiation. *Cell* **13**, 599–611.

DUHAIMAN, A. S. & BAMBERG, J. R. (1984). Isolation of brain alpha-actinin. Its characterization and a comparison of its properties with those of muscle alpha-actinins. *Biochemistry* **23**, 1600–1608.

FALLON, J. R. & NACHMIAS, V. T. (1980). Localization of cytoplasmic and skeletal myosins in developing muscle cells by double-label immunofluorescence. *J. Cell Biol.* **87**, 237–247.

FERAMISCO, J. R. (1979). Microinjection of fluorescently labeled alpha-actinin into living fibroblasts. *Proc. natn. Acad. Sci. U.S.A.* **76**, 3967–3971.

FERAMISCO, J. R. & BURRIDGE, K. (1980). A rapid purification of alpha-actinin, filamin and a 130,000 dalton protein from smooth muscle. *J. biol. Chem.* **255**, 1194–1199.

FRANZINI-ARMSTRONG, C. (1970). Natural variability in the length of thin and thick filaments on single fibres from a crab *Portunus depurator*. *J. Cell Sci.* **6**, 559–592.

FUERCHTBAUER, A., JOCKUSCH, B. M., MARUTA, H., KILIMANN, M. W. & ISENBERG, G. (1983). Disruption of microfilament organization after injection of F-actin copying proteins into living tissue culture cells. *Nature, Lond.* **304**, 361–364.

GEIGER, B. (1981). The association of rhodamine labeled alpha-actinin with actin bundles in demembranated cells. *Cell Biol. Int. Rep.* **5**, 627–634.

GOLDSTEIN, M. A., SCHROETER, J. P. & SASS, R. L. (1979). The Z lattice in canine cardiac muscle. *J. Cell Biol.* **83**, 187–204.

GOLL, D. E., SUZUKI, A., TEMPLE, J. & HOLMES, G. R. (1972). Studies on purified alpha-actinin. I. Effect of temperature and tropomyosin on the alpha-actinin/F-actin interaction. *J. molec. Biol.* **67**, 469–488.

GORDON, W. E. (1978). Immunofluorescent and ultrastructural studies of "sarcomeric" units in stress fibers of cultured non-muscle cells. *Expl Cell Res.* **117**, 253–260.

HUXLEY, H. E. (1983). Molecular basis of contraction in cross-striated muscles and relevance to motile mechanisms in other cells. In *Muscle and Nonmuscle Motility* (ed. A. Stracher), pp. 1–104. New York: Academic Press, Inc.

INOUÉ, S. (1981). Video image processing greatly enhances contrast, quality, and speed in polarization-based microscopy. *J. Cell Biol.* **89**, 346–356.

ISENBERG, G., RATHKE, P. C., HUELSMANN, N., FRANKE, W. W. & WOHLFARTH-BOTTERMANN, K. E. (1976). Cytoplasmic actomyosin fibrils in tissue culture cells: Direct proof of contractility by visualization of ATP-induced contraction in fibrils isolated by laser microbeam dissection. *Cell Tiss. Res.* **166**, 427–443.

KREIS, T. E. & BIRCHMEIER, W. (1980). Stress fiber sarcomeres of fibroblasts are contractile. *Cell* **22**, 555–561.

KREIS, T. E., WINTERHALTER, K. H. & BIRCHMEIER, W. (1979). *In vivo* distribution and turnover of fluorescently labeled actin microinjected into human fibroblasts. *Proc. natn. Acad. Sci. U.S.A.* **76**, 3814–3818.

LANGANGER, G., DE MEY, J., MOEREMANS, M., DANEELS, G., DEBRABANDER, M. & SMALL, J. V. (1984). Ultrastructural localization of alpha-actinin and filamin in cultured cells with the immunogold staining (IGS) method. *J. Cell Biol.* **99**, 1324–1344.

LANGANGER, G., MOEREMANS, M., DANEELS, G., SOBIESZEK, A., DEBRABANDER, M. & DE MEY, J. (1986). The molecular organization of myosin in stress fibers of cultured cells. *J. Cell Biol.* **102**, 200–209.

LASH, J. W., OSTROVSKY, D., MITTAL, B. & SANGER, J. W. (1985). Alpha-actinin distribution and extracellular matrix products during somitogenesis in the chick embryo. *Cell Motil.* **5**, 491–506.

LAZARIDES, E. (1976). Actin, alpha-actin, and tropomyosin interaction in the structural organization of actin filaments in nonmuscle cells. *J. Cell Biol.* **68**, 202–219.

LAZARIDES, E. & BURRIDGE, K. (1975). Alpha-actinin: immunofluorescent localization of a muscle structural protein in non-muscle cells. *Cell* **6**, 289–298.

MASAKI, T., ENDO, M. & EBASHI, S. (1967). Localization of alpha-actinin at Z-band. *J. Biochem., Tokyo* **62**, 630–632.

MASAKI, T. & TAKAITA, O. (1969). Some properties of chicken alpha-actinin. *J. Biochem., Tokyo* **66**, 637–643.

MCKENNA, N., MEIGS, J. B. & WANG, Y.-L. (1985). Identical distribution of fluorescently labeled brain and muscle actins in living cardiac fibroblasts and myocytes. *J. Cell Biol.* **100**, 292–296.

OSBORN, M. & WEBER, K. (1980). Dimethylsulfoxide and the Ionophore A23187 affect the arrangement of actin and induce nuclear actin paracrystals in PtK2 cells. *Expl Cell Res.* **129**, 83–91.

POCHAPIN, M., SANGER, J. M. & SANGER, J. W. (1983). Microinjection of lucifer yellow CH into sea urchin eggs and embryos. *Cell Tiss. Res.* **234**, 309–318.

PODLUBNAYA, Z. A., TSKHORVEBOVA, L. A., ZAALISHVILI, M. M. & STEFANENKO, G. A. (1975). Electron microscopic study of alpha-actinin. *J. molec. Biol.* **92**, 357–359.

RATHKE, P. C., OSBORN, M. & WEBER, K. (1979). Immunological and ultrastructural characterization of microfilament bundles: polygonal nets and stress fibers in an established cell line. *Eur. J. Cell Biol.* **19**, 40–48.

ROBINSON, T. F. & WINEGRAD, S. (1979). The measurement and dynamic implication of thin filament lengths in heart muscle. *J. Physiol., London* **286**, 607–619.

ROHLICK, P. & OLAH, I. (1967). Cross-striated fibrils in the endothelium of the rat myometral arterioles. *J. Ultrastruct. Res.* **18**, 667–676.

RUMERY, R. E., BLANDAU, R. J. & HAGEY, P. W. (1961). Observations on living myocardial cells from cultured 48-hour chick hearts. *Anat. Rec.* **141**, 253–262.

SANGER, J. M., MITTAL, B., POCHAPIN, M. B. & SANGER, J. W. (1986). Myofibrillogenesis in living cells microinjected with fluorescently labeled alpha-actinin. *J. Cell Biol.* **102**, 2053–2066.

SANGER, J. M., MITTAL, B. & SANGER, J. W. (1985a). Structure and assembly of microfilament bundles. In *Cell Motility: Mechanism and Regulation* (ed. H. Iskikawa, H. Sato & S. Hatano), pp. 461–476. Tokyo: University of Tokyo Press.

SANGER, J. M., POCHAPIN, M. B. & SANGER, J. W. (1985b). Midbody sealing after cytokinesis in embryos of the sea urchin *Arbacia punctulata. Cell Tiss. Res.* **240**, 287–292.

SANGER, J. M. & SANGER, J. W. (1980). Banding and polarity of actin filaments in interphase and cleaving cells. *J. Cell Biol.* **86**, 568–575.

SANGER, J. W. (1974). The use of cytochalasin-B to distinguish myoblasts from fibroblasts in cultures of developing chick striated muscle. *Proc. natn. Acad. Sci. U.S.A.* **71**, 3621–3625.

SANGER, J. W. (1975a). Changing patterns of actin localization during cell division. *Proc. natn. Acad. Sci. U.S.A.* **72**, 1913–1916.

SANGER, J. W. (1975b). The presence of actin during chromosomal movement. *Proc. natn. Acad. Sci. U.S.A.* **72**, 2451–2455.

SANGER, J. W. (1975c). Intracellular localization of actin with fluorescently labelled heavy meromyosin. *Cell Tiss. Res.* **161**, 432–444.

SANGER, J. W. (1977). Mitosis in beating cardiac myoblasts treated with cytochalasin-B. *J. exp. Zool.* **201**, 463–469.

SANGER, J. W., GWINN, J. & SANGER, J. M. (1980a). Dissolution of cytoplasmic actin bundles and the induction of nuclear actin bundles by dimethyl sulfoxide. *J. exp. Zool.* **213**, 227–230.

SANGER, J. W. & McCANN, F. V. (1968). Ultrastructure of moth alary muscles and their attachment to the heart wall. *J. Insect Physiol.* **14**, 1539–1544.

SANGER, J. W., MITTAL, B. M. & SANGER, J. M. (1984a). Analysis of myofibrillar structure and assembly using fluorescently labeled contractile proteins. *J. Cell Biol.* **98**, 825–833.

SANGER, J. W., MITTAL, B. & SANGER, J. M. (1984b). Interaction of fluorescently labeled contractile proteins with the cytoskeleton in cell models. *J. Cell Biol.* **99**, 918–928.

SANGER, J. W., MITTAL, B. & SANGER, J. M. (1984c). Formation of myofibrils in spreading chick cardiac myocytes. *Cell Motil.* **4**, 405–416.

SANGER, J. W. & SANGER, J. M. (1979). The cytoskeleton and cell division. *Meth. Achiev. exp. Path.* **8**, 110–142.

SANGER, J. W., SANGER, J. M. & JOCKUSCH, B. M. (1983a). Differences in the stress fibers between fibroblasts and epithelial cells. *J. Cell Biol.* **96**, 961–969.

SANGER, J. W., SANGER, J. M. & JOCKUSCH, B. M. (1983b). Differential response of three types of actin filament bundles to depletion of cellular ATP levels. *Eur. J. Cell Biol.* **31**, 197–204.

SANGER, J. W., SANGER, J. M., KREIS, T. E. & JOCKUSCH, B. M. (1980b). Reversible translocation of cytoplasmic actin into the nucleus caused by dimethyl sulfoxide. *Proc. natn. Acad. Sci. U.S.A.* **77**, 5268–5272.

TRINKAUS, J. P. (1984). *Cells into Organs. The Forces that Shape the Embryo*, 2nd edn. Englewood Cliffs: Prentice-Hall.

WALTER, R. J. & BERNS, M. W. (1981). Computer-enhanced video microscopy: Digitally processed microscopic images can be produced in real time. *Proc. natn. Acad. Sci. U.S.A.* **78**, 6927–6931.

WANG, K., ASH, J. F. & SINGER, S. J. (1975). Filamin, a new high-molecular-weight protein found in smooth muscle and non-muscle cells. *Proc. natn. Acad. Sci. U.S.A.* **72**, 4483–4486.

WANG, Y.-L. (1984). Reorganization of actin filament bundles in living fibroblasts. *J. Cell Biol.* **99**, 1478–1485.

WANG, Y.-L. (1985). Exchange of actin subunits at the leading edge of living fibroblasts: possible role of treadmilling. *J. Cell Biol.* **101**, 597–602.

WANG, Y.-L. & TAYLOR, D. L. (1979). Distribution of fluorescently labeled actin in living sea urchin eggs during early development. *J. Cell Biol.* **82**, 672–679.

WEBER, K. & GROESCHEL-STEWART, U. (1974). Antibody to myosin: the specific visualization of myosin-containing filaments in non-muscle cells. *Proc. natn. Acad. Sci. U.S.A.* **71**, 4561–4564.

WEBER, K., RATHKE, P. C., OSBORN, N. & FRANKE, W. W. (1976). Distribution of actin and tubulin in cells and glycerinated cell models after treatment with cytochalasin B. (CB). *Expl Cell Res.* **102**, 285–297.

WEHLAND, J. & WEBER, K. (1980). Distribution of fluorescently labeled actin and tropomyosin after microinjection in living culture cells observed with TV image intensification. *Expl Cell Res.* **127**, 397–408.

J. Cell Sci. Suppl. 5, 45–54 (1986)
Printed in Great Britain © The Company of Biologists Limited 1986

MYOSIN DISTRIBUTION AND ACTIN ORGANIZATION IN DIFFERENT AREAS OF ANTIBODY-LABELLED QUICK-FROZEN FIBROBLASTS

DURWARD LAWSON

Zoology Department, University College London, Gower Street, London WC1E 6BT, UK

SUMMARY

In cortical and subcortical areas of motile non-muscle cells myosin is found only on linear actin filament bundles that are aligned with the cell's long axis. Myosin is absent from actin filaments perpendicular to these bundles and from areas of cortical and subcortical actin, which has a complex geometrical array. These data suggest that in the non-muscle cell myosin exerts force in a unidirectional manner only, as it does in muscle. The presence of myosin up to the ends of cell processes suggests that, even in the cortex, this force transduction takes place over short-range distances. The absence of myosin rods *in vivo* but the presence of structures corresponding to single myosin molecules suggests that the force-generating unit for actomyosin-based movement in non-muscle cells is either a myosin dimer/small oligomer or single myosin molecule, attached to actin by their tail regions.

INTRODUCTION

Of the force-generating mechanisms available to eukaryotic non-muscle cells it is myosin, by its interaction with actin, that plays the major role (Kendrick-Jones & Scholey, 1981; Stossel *et al.* 1981). The basic mechanism used by the non-muscle cell to regulate myosin-based contraction is the same as that described for smooth muscle, namely control *via* phosphorylation/dephosphorylation of myosin regulatory light chains (Kendrick-Jones & Scholey, 1981; Kendrick-Jones *et al.* 1983; Scholey *et al.* 1980). However, it seems clear that the distribution (and very probably the organization) of non-muscle cell myosin will be different from that of smooth muscle cell myosin: a factor almost certainly dictated by the multiplicity of different movements undergone at different places at different times by the non-muscle cell (Stossel *et al.* 1981). Furthermore, the fact that the non-muscle cell requires force transduction on a much smaller scale than muscle tells us that we are looking for a much smaller myosin transduction unit than that found in smooth muscle. This has been shown by *in vitro* assembly of thymus (Scholey *et al.* 1980) and platelet (Niederman & Pollard, 1975) myosin into rods of only 20–30 myosin molecules compared with the several hundred myosins found in a muscle myosin rod (Pollard, 1981). However, *in vivo* in the non-muscle cell no one has yet clearly identified either (1) whether or not myosin rods/oligomer/dimers/or individual myosin molecules, are used as force-generating complexes or (2) precisely where these complexes are located.

The favoured techniques for visualizing myosin are (1) immunofluorescence (Pollard, 1981; Zigmond et al. 1979), where the limiting factor is the resolution of the light microscope; (2) thin-section electron microscopy, where the preparative protocols (such as OsO₄) are known to destroy myosin and the one-dimensional views/image superposition of this method are unsuitable for investigating the complex three-dimensional structure of the cytoskeleton (Herman & Pollard, 1981; Langanger et al. 1985; Niederman & Pollard, 1975; Small et al. 1978); and (3) whole-mount electron microscopy, where the critical-point drying involved induces distortions in the cytoskeleton (Schliwa & van Blerkom, 1981; Webster et al. 1978).

Helium-cooled rapid-freezing offers a way out of this impasse since the technique does not use OsO₄, freezes samples in less than 1 ms and, when coupled with deep etching, permits unique three-dimensional views inside cells (Hirokawa et al. 1982, 1983; Lawson, 1984). I have used this approach, in conjunction with colloidal gold and anti-myosin antibody, to localize myosin in different areas of non-muscle cells. The results show that myosin is: (1) distributed in either patches or myosin bands (both 275 nm long) only on linear actin filaments; (2) absent from actin filaments that are perpendicular to these actin bundles; and (3) present in some regions of the cortex but not others; a finding possibly related to the geometric organization of the actin filaments in these regions. Neither recognizable myosin rods nor individual molecules were ever seen *in vivo*, even in cell pre-treated with *N*-ethylmaleimide (Meeusen & Cande, 1979) or sodium azide. However, structures corresponding to individual myosin molecules were found when cells were detergent-permeabilized in the presence of free myosin. This suggests that the non-muscle cell uses either small oligomers/dimers or individual myosin molecules attached by their tails to actin as the means of generating actomyosin-based movement.

RESULTS

Subcortical myosin distribution

By deep etching antibody-labelled cells it is clear that there are two major types of myosin distribution present. These are either small, variably spaced patches 275 nm long and 10–20 nm wide (Figs 1, 2) or much larger myosin bands also 275 nm long but 0·5–1 μm wide with a periodicity of 200 nm (Fig. 2). Both are found on long actin filaments that appear aligned with the cell's long axis (Figs 1, 2, 3). In none of these areas was myosin found associated with actin filaments that are perpendicular to these actin filaments bundles (Fig. 4). Similarly, myosin was never found associated with the central 0·5–0·7 μm wide zone of actin geodomes (Fig. 5). Many small filaments 1–3 nm wide, 20–50 nm long and not labelled with anti-myosin are found in all of these areas (Fig. 4).

Cortical myosin distribution

At the sides of cells antimyosin was found up to the very edge of the cortex in 275 nm long patches (not shown). Large clearly delineated myosin bands like those found well inside the cell were not present in these regions (Fig. 6). At the ends of

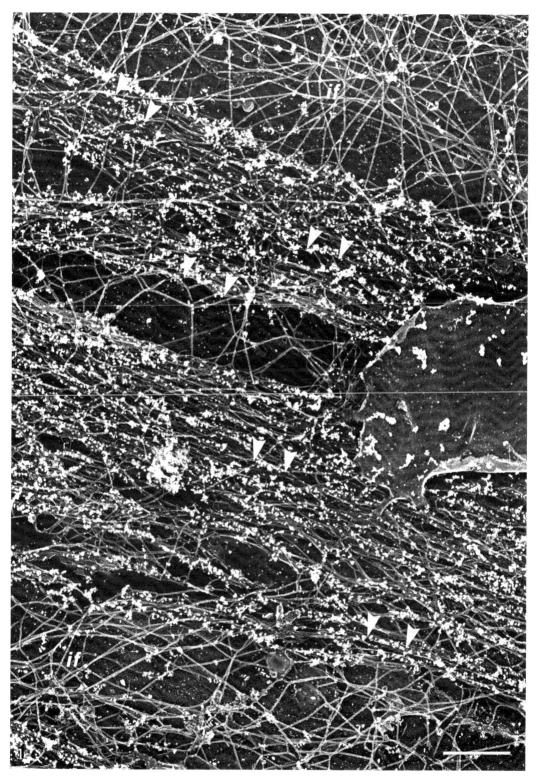

Fig. 1. Quick-frozen fibroblast labelled with anti-myosin, which is seen here distributed in variably spaced patches 275 nm long (double arrowheads) on actin bundles that are aligned with the cell's long axis. Intermediate filaments (*if*) course between these actin bundles. Bar, 0·5 μm.

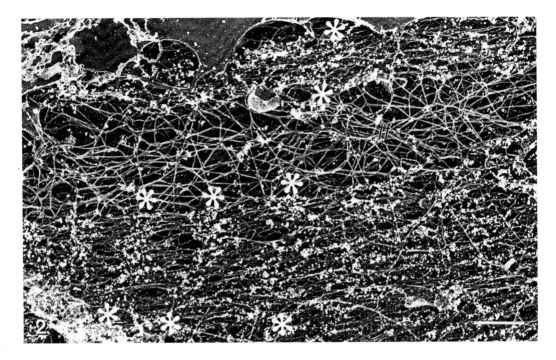

Fig. 2. Quick-frozen fibroblast labelled with anti-myosin, which is distributed in periodically spaced sarcomeres (asterisks), again 275 nm long but of varying widths. Note the unlabelled areas between the myosin bands. A large tangle of intermediate filaments (*if*) separate two stress-fibre bundles. Bar, 0·5 μm.

cells processes such as microspikes were heavily labelled, often nearly to their extremities, by patches and myosin bands (both 275 nm long) on linear-appearing actin filaments (Fig. 6). The most peripheral areas of the cortex were often unlabelled (Fig. 6).

Myosin rods/molecules in vivo *and* in vitro

Recognizable myosin rods were notable by their absence, even in cells preincubated in *N*-ethylmaleimide (Meeusen & Cande, 1979) or sodium azide. Furthermore, neither myosin rods nor molecules were apparent in cells extracted with detergent and then plunged, without rinsing, into glutaraldehyde (Fig. 7). Myosin rods were, however, preserved by the process of quick freezing when formed *in vivo* under ionic/detergent conditions identical to those used for permeabilizing cells (not shown). *In vivo* (with conditions identical to those used for the *in vitro* formation of rods), structures corresponding to the size and shape of individual myosin molecules (Heuser, 1983; Kendrick-Jones & Scholey, 1981), never rods, were seen only when cells were extracted with detergent in the presence of free myosin (Fig. 8).

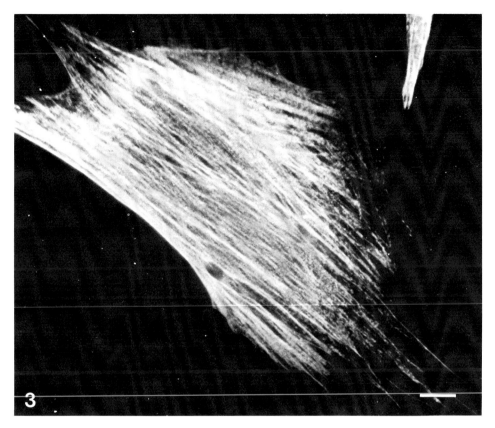

Fig. 3. Light micrograph of a fibroblast detergent-extracted and labelled with anti-myosin, which is periodically distributed on actin filaments aligned with the cell's long axis. Bar, 9 μm.

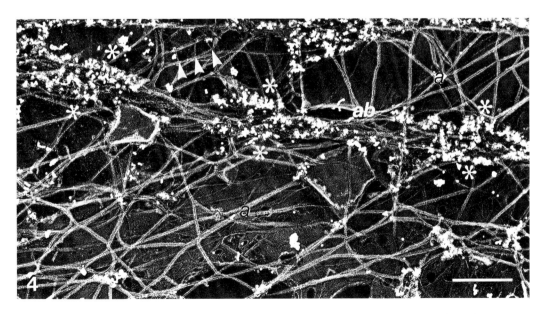

Fig. 4. Quick-frozen fibroblast labelled with anti-myosin. A small actin bundle (*ab*) is seen labelled, with several mini-myosin bands present (asterisks). Actin filaments (*a*) running perpendicular to this actin bundle are not labelled with anti-myosin. Small 1–3 nm filaments are clearly visible (arrowheads). Bar, 0·25 μm.

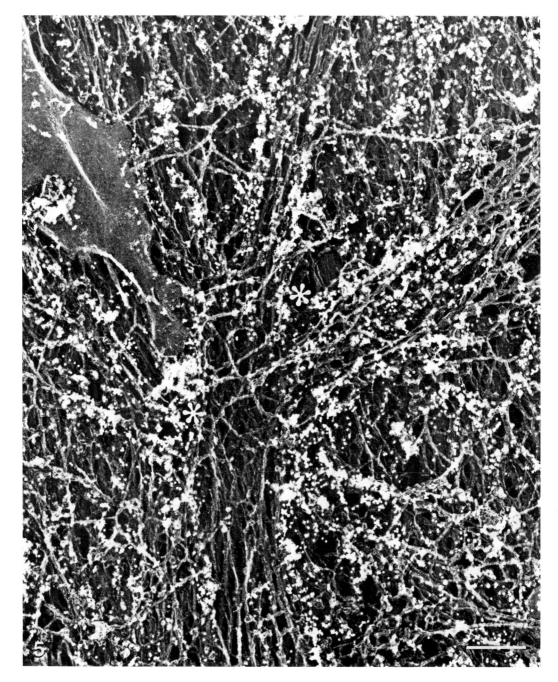

Fig. 5. Quick-frozen fibroblast labelled with anti-myosin. An actin-containing geo-dome (asterisks) not labelled with anti-myosin is seen at the top of the cell. Bar, 0·25 μm.

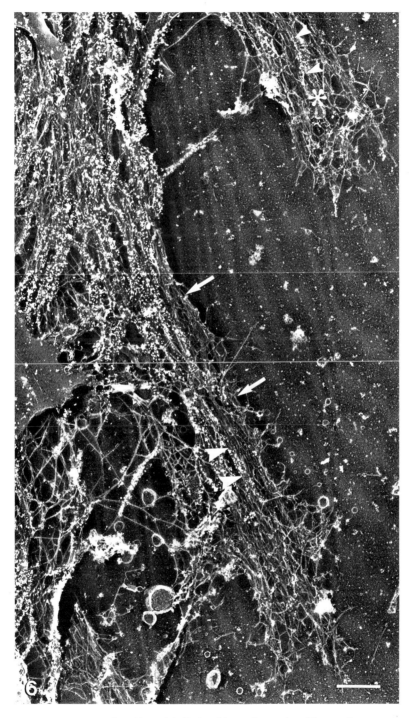

Fig. 6. Quick-frozen fibroblast labelled with anti-myosin. Two cell processes are seen, both labelled with anti-myosin, which extends well out towards the end of the process (asterisk). Anti-myosin is distributed in 275 nm long patches/mini-myosin bands (arrowheads). Note the unlabelled cortical edge of the lower microspike (large arrows). Bar, 0·5 μm.

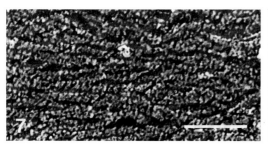

Fig. 7. Actin filaments in a fibroblast detergent-extracted, plunged without rinsing into glutaraldehyde and then quick frozen. Bar, $0.05\,\mu m$.

Fig. 8. Actin filaments in a fibroblast treated exactly as in Fig. 6 but detergent-extracted in the presence of $0.8\,mg\,ml^{-1}$ free myosin. Note the bilobed structure (arrowheads) corresponding to a single myosin molecule (see Kendrick-Jones & Scholey, 1981). Part of the tail is obscured by cell debris. Bar, $0.05\,\mu m$.

DISCUSSION

Myosin distribution and actin organization

In all these experiments, whether present in cortical or subcortical areas, myosin was restricted to those actin filaments that adopted a linear rather than a complex geometric configuration. Furthermore, these filaments were invariably aligned with the long axis of the cell. Combined time-lapse video/immunofluorescence experiments have shown that these filament bundles are parallel to the direction of cell movement (Lewis *et al.* 1982).

These observations, coupled with the finding, in these studies, that myosin was absent from actin filaments perpendicular to such bundles strongly suggest that in the non-muscle cell myosin acts as a unidirectional force transducer in a manner similar to its role in muscle (Huxley, 1969). A further similarity here is the organization of myosin (over large areas of the cell) into periodically spaced muscle-like myosin bands (Burridge, 1981; Langanger *et al.* 1985; Rathke *et al.* 1979; Webster *et al.* 1978; Zigmond *et al.* 1979). These data reinforce evidence that the cell can use stress fibres as an aid to transmitting force over considerable distances, possibly under conditions of isometric contraction, when it is in position on and has formed strong attachments to the substrate (Burridge, 1981). It is thus very likely that the characteristic multidirectional movement seen as non-muscle cells translocate (Lewis *et al.* 1982) is conferred by some of the large repertoire of actin-associated proteins (Pollard, 1984; Stossel *et al.* 1981; Weeds, 1982), which must, therefore, act as a fine control mechanism to modify the 'on/off/linear only' role played by myosin.

The fact that myosin was found up to the very edge of the cortex both at the sides and the ends of cells indicates that during non-muscle cell movement myosin exerts its effect on the delicate cortex over short rather than long-range distances. This indicates that the extension-movement of regions such as microspikes is myosin-mediated and is unlikely to be due to the rapid extension of actin filaments by the rapid polymerization of submembranous monomeric actin stores as has been suggested (Small *et al.* 1978).

The organization of specialized actin structures such as geodomes (Lazarides, 1976; Rathke *et al.* 1979) can be seen very easily in deep-etched replicas. Particularly clear is the interweaving of actin filaments as they approach the top of the geodome. What is still unknown is whether or not these actin filaments terminate at the plasma membrane or are simply linked laterally to it as they extend downwards again through the cell. The absence of myosin from these areas suggests that they are analogous to the Z line of skeletal muscle (Huxley, 1969). Many small 1–3 nm filaments were found in these experiments and have dimensions similar to α-actinin. While positive identification demands immunolabelling, their role here (seen for the first time *in vivo*) as actin cross-linkers closely parallels the *in vitro* role of α-actinin, which is known to cross-link and act as a spacer between actin filaments (Jockusch & Isenberg, 1981).

Myosin organization

No myosin rods have to date been unequivocally identified in any non-muscle cell. Conditions for their preservation should include: (1) correct ionic conditions (Kendrick-Jones *et al.* 1983); (2) stabilization with either *N*-ethylmaleimide (Karlsson & Lindberg, 1985; Meeusen & Cande, 1979) or sodium azide; and (3) neither OsO_4 nor dehydration protocols (Hirokawa *et al.* 1982; Niederman & Pollard, 1975). All of these parameters were met here, yet myosin rods could never be identified, but only structures corresponding to individual myosin molecules (Heuser, 1983; Kendrick-Jones & Scholey, 1981). The sizes of patches and sarcomeres in these experiments (275 nm) coupled with the length of a myosin molecule (170 nm) (Kendrick-Jones & Scholey, 1981) suggest that the structural form of non-muscle cell myosin could be either a bipolar dimer or a small oligomer (Langanger *et al.* 1985). It is equally likely, however, given the fact that only isolated myosin molecules were seen in cells permeabilized in the presence of free myosin (even although *in vitro* myosin forms rods in these conditions), that the non-muscle cell tranduces force using single myosin molecules. To do this demands that myosin must be attached to actin filaments either by its tail or by some other unidentified protein. Control of myosin assembly/interaction with actin would then involve the changes in local myosin concentration and actin organization found in these studies coupled with intracellular differences in ionic (Ca^{2+}) concentrations (Stossel *et al.* 1981).

This work was supported by a Wellcome Trust University Research Award to D. Lawson.

REFERENCES

BURRIDGE, K. (1981). Are stress fibres contractile? *Nature, Lond.* **294**, 691–692.
HERMAN, I. M. & POLLARD, T. D. (1981). Electron microscopic localization of cytoplasmic myosin with ferritin labelled antibodies. *J. Cell Biol.* **88**, 346–351.
HEUSER, J. E. (1983). Procedure for freeze drying molecules adsorbed to mica flakes. *J. molec. Biol.* **169**, 155–195.

HIROKAWA, N., KELLER, T. C. S. III, CHASAN, R. & MOOSEKER, M. S. (1983). Mechanism of brush border contractility studied by the quick freeze deep-etch method. *J. Cell Biol.* **96**, 1325–1336.

HIROKAWA, N., TILNEY, L. G., FUJIWARA, K. & HEUSER, J. E. (1982). Organization of actin, myosin and intermediate filaments in the brush border of intestinal epithelial cells. *J. Cell Biol.* **94**, 425–443.

HUXLEY, H. E. (1969). The mechanism of muscle contraction. *Science* **164**, 1356–1366.

JOCKUSCH, B. M. & ISENBERG, G. (1981). Interaction of α actinin and vinculin with actin: opposite effects on filament network formation. *Proc. natn. Acad. Sci. U.S.A.* **78**, 3005–3009.

KARLSSON, R. & LINDBERG, U. (1985). Changes in the organization of actin and myosin in non-muscle cells induced by *N*-ethyl maleimide. *Expl Cell Res.* **157**, 95–115.

KENDRICK-JONES, J., CANDE, W. Z., TOOTH, P. J., SMITH, R. C. & SCHOLEY, J. M. (1983). Studies on the effect of phosphorylation of the 20,000 M_r light chain of vertebrate smooth muscle myosin. *J. molec. Biol.* **165**, 139–162.

KENDRICK-JONES, J. & SCHOLEY, J. M. (1981). Myosin linked regulatory systems. *J. Muscle Res. Cell Motil.* **2**, 347–372.

LANGANGER, G., MOERMANS, M., DANEELS, G., SOBIESZEK, A., DE BRABANDER, M. & DE MAY, J. (1985). The molecular organization of myosin in stress fibres of cultured cells. *J. Cell Biol.* **102**, 200–209.

LAWSON, D. (1984). Distribution of epinemin in colloidal gold labelled quick-frozen, deep-etched cytoskeleton. *J. Cell Biol.* **99**, 1451–1460.

LAZARIDES, E. (1976). Actin, α actinin and tropomyosin in the structural organisation of actin filaments in non-muscle cells. *J. Cell Biol.* **68**, 202–219.

LEWIS, L., VERNA, J. M., LEVINSTONE, D., SHER, S., MAREK, L. & BELL, E. (1982). The relationship of fibroblast translocations to cell morphology and stress fibre density. *J. Cell Sci.* **53**, 21–36.

MEEUSEN, R. L. & CANDE, W. Z. (1979). N-ethylmaleimide modified heavy meromyosin: a probe for actomyosin interactions. *J. Cell Biol.* **82**, 57–65.

NIEDERMAN, R. & POLLARD, T. D. (1975). Human platelet myosin. II. *In vitro* assembly and structure of myosin filaments. *J. Cell Biol.* **67**, 72–92.

POLLARD, T. D. (1981). Cytoplasmic contractile proteins. *J. Cell Biol.* **91**, 156s–165s.

POLLARD, T. D. (1984). Actin binding protein evolution. *Nature, Lond.* **312**, 403.

RATHKE, P. C., OSBORN, M. & WEBER, K. (1979). Immunological and ultrastructural characterization of microfilament bundles, polygome nets and stress fibres in an established cell line. *Eur. J. Cell Biol.* **19**, 40–48.

SCHLIWA, M. & VAN BLERKOM, J. (1981). Structural interaction of cytoskeletal components. *J. Cell Biol.* **90**, 222–235.

SCHOLEY, J. M., TAYLOR, K. A. & KENDRICK-JONES, J. (1980). Regulation of non-muscle assembly by calmodulin-dependent light chain kinase. *Nature, Lond.* **287**, 233–235.

SMALL, J. V., ISENBERG, G. & CELIS, J. E. (1978). Polarity of actin at the leading edge of cultured cells. *Nature, Lond.* **272**, 638–639.

STOSSEL, T. P., HARTWIG, J. H. & YIN, H. L. (1981). Actin gelation and the structure and movement of cortical cytoplasm. In *Cytoskeletal Elements and Plasma Membrane Organisation* (ed. G. Poste & G. L. Nicolson), pp. 139–168. Amsterdam: Elsevier North-Holland Biomed. Press.

WEBSTER, R. E., HENDERSON, D., OSBORN, M. & WEBER, K. (1978). Three-dimensional electron microscopical visualization of the cytoskeleton of animal cells: immunoferritin identification of actin and tubulin containing structures. *Proc. natn. Acad. Sci. U.S.A.* **75**, 5511–5515.

WEEDS, A. (1982). Actin binding proteins: regulators of cell architecture and motility. *Nature, Lond.* **196**, 811–816.

ZIGMOND, S. H., OTTO, J. J. & BRYAN, J. (1979). Organization of myosin in a submembraneous sheath in well spread human fibroblasts. *Expl Cell Res.* **119**, 205–219.

J. Cell Sci. Suppl. 5, 55–68 (1986)
Printed in Great Britain © The Company of Biologists Limited 1986

STUDIES OF TEKTIN FILAMENTS FROM FLAGELLAR MICROTUBULES BY IMMUNOELECTRON MICROSCOPY

W. B. AMOS

Department of Zoology, Downing Street, Cambridge CB2 3EJ, UK

L. A. AMOS

MRC Laboratory of Molecular Biology, Hills Road, Cambridge CB2 2QH, UK

AND R. W. LINCK

Department of Anatomy, University of Minnesota, Minneapolis, Minn. 55455, USA

SUMMARY

Chemically resistant 2–3 nm filaments with a high α-helical content, isolated from sea-urchin sperm flagellar doublet microtubules, consist of proteins that have been named tektins. Polyclonal affinity-purified antibodies to tektins labelled sperm tails all along their lengths, as shown by indirect immunofluorescence microscopy, provided the specimens were not too well fixed. Results obtained for unfixed specimens studied by immunoelectron microscopy suggested the tektins are normally masked by tubulin. A monoclonal anti-tektin antibody labelled bare tektin filaments at longitudinal intervals of approximately 48 nm, which fits in well with the 96 nm longitudinal repeat of axonemes. We discuss a possible scheme for the regular interaction of tubulin monomers with an α-helical coiled coil.

INTRODUCTION

It has been shown by various workers that sea-urchin sperm flagellar doublet microtubules can be dissociated in a number of ways to produce chemically resistant ribbons of two to four protofilaments (Linck, 1976; Meza *et al.* 1972; Witman *et al.* 1972). These are thought to form one or more parts of the A-tubules of the outer doublets, in particular the region where the C-shaped B-tubule makes a junction with the A-tubule wall (Linck, 1982). The ribbons have been further fractionated with chemical agents to give highly insoluble 'tektin' filaments (Linck & Langevin, 1982).

In each species studied, the tektins consist of several distinct polypeptides varying somewhat in molecular weight (between 45 and $70 (\times 10^3) M_r$) and isoelectric properties. Their general properties suggest that they are much more closely related to the proteins of intermediate filaments (see, e.g., Fuchs & Hanukoglu, 1983) than to tubulin: they are highly insoluble in solutions containing Sarkosyl and urea; their sensitivities to limited proteolytic cleavage by *Staphylococcus aureus* protease are different from that of tubulin (Linck & Langevin, 1982); as a group they appear as fine fibrils with a high (71%) α-helical content, as shown by circular dichroism (Linck & Langevin, 1982); finally, X-ray fibre diffraction of the purified filaments gives patterns strongly characteristic of coiled-coil α-helical proteins (Beese, 1984).

Relatively stable components have been detected also in flagellar central singlet microtubules (Linck *et al.* 1981) and in microtubules from mitotic spindles (Jensen & Bajer, 1973). The latter may consist of the $55 \times 10^3 M_r$ non-tubulin protein, found by Hays & Salmon (1983) to be the major component of the calcium-resistant residue of isolated mitotic spindles from *Strongylocentrotus purpuratus* eggs. There is a possibility, therefore, that tektin-like polypeptides are a general feature of microtubules.

FRACTIONATION OF AXONEMES

The tektins of *S. purpuratus* flagellar microtubules consist of a group of three or more polypeptides that run on sodium dodecyl sulphate (SDS)–polyacrylamide gels in much the same region as α- and β-tubulin. Fig. 1, lanes a–c, shows the polypeptide compositions of the remaining polymers when axonemes are chemically disassembled. When A-tubules (Fig. 1, lane a) are treated with 0·5 % Sarkosyl, ribbons of two to four protofilaments (Fig. 1, lane b) remain (Linck, 1976) but only a fine filamentous fraction (Fig. 1, lane c) is insoluble in 0·5 % Sarkosyl plus 2 M-urea (Linck & Langevin, 1982). The tektin bands can be seen in each case. After a second extraction in Sarkosyl–urea, the 47, 51 and 55 ($\times 10^3 M_r$) bands together constitute more than 95 % of the Coomassie-stained protein. The ribbons of protofilaments contain other proteins in addition to tubulin and the three main tektin bands, in particular a pair of bands having apparent molecular weights of 77 and 83 ($\times 10^3$) (Linck & Langevin, 1982); their properties have not as yet been investigated.

Other species give rise to different sets of polypeptide bands on SDS–polyacrylamide gels but the filaments all look similar in the electron microscope (Linck & Langevin, 1982).

IMMUNOBLOTTING

Mouse antibodies that were raised against the Sarkosyl–urea-purified tektin filament complex were affinity purified using the antigen coupled to Sepharose 4B. On nitrocellulose blots of SDS–polyacrylamide gels, the purified anti-tektin antibodies reacted with all three main tektin bands from *S. purpuratus*, but disproportionately (Fig. 1, lanes e, h). They also cross-reacted with similar but not identical sets of proteins in SDS–polyacrylamide gel blots of axonemes from cilia and flagella of other sea-urchin species, but with reduced affinity (Linck *et al.* 1985).

Anti-tubulin antibodies did not bind to the tektin bands but did reveal a residual amount of tubulin in the original preparation (Fig. 1, lane i), below the level of detection with Coomassie Blue staining. Purified anti-tektins did not bind to tubulin on nitrocellulose blots (Fig. 1, lane k), but to be quite sure that the immunoglobulin G (IgG) fraction used for the structural work contained no trace of anti-tubulin activity, it was passed through a tubulin–Sepharose column.

To investigate the relationship between tektins and intermediate filaments, we also applied the 'universal' anti-intermediate filament (IF) monoclonal antibody (Pruss

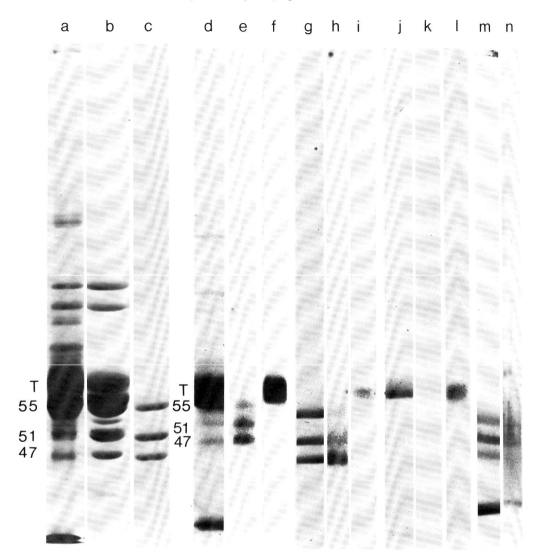

Fig. 1. Lanes a–c, polypeptide components of thermally fractionated A-tubules (see Linck & Langevin, 1981) from *S. purpuratus* sperm axonemes (a), Sarkosyl-insoluble protofilament ribbons (b) and Sarkosyl–urea-insoluble tektin filaments (c), separated by SDS–polyacrylamide gel electrophoresis and stained with Coomassie Blue. The apparent M_r values ($\times 10^{-3}$) are marked alongside the tektin bands. T indicates α-tubulin; β-tubulin has comigrated with the $55 \times 10^3 M_r$ band. Lanes d–n, antibody staining of nitrocellulose replicas from gels. Lanes d–f, whole axonemes; g–i and m–n, purified *S. purpuratus* tektins; j–l, purified bovine brain tubulin. Lanes d, g, j, m, Coomassie-stained gel strips; e, h, k, autoradiographs of strips of nitrocellulose incubated in affinity-purified mouse anti-tektin, followed by ^{125}I-labelled rabbit anti-mouse IgG; f, i, l, autoradiographs of nitrocellulose strips incubated in YL1/2 rat monoclonal anti-α-tubulin (Kilmartin *et al.* 1982), followed by ^{125}I-labelled rabbit anti-rat IgG. Lane n, an autoradiograph of a strip incubated in anti-intermediate filament monoclonal antibody (Pruss *et al.* 1981), followed by biotinylated rabbit anti-mouse IgG and finally by [35S]streptavidin.

et al. 1981) to gel blots. No reaction was detectable when the antibody was applied to blots from whole axonemes. However, on blots of purified filament protein, the 55 and 51 ($\times 10^3$) M_r tektin bands weakly but reproducibly bound the antibody, while the $47 \times 10^3 M_r$ band sometimes showed weak binding (Fig. 1, lane n). The antibody also revealed traces of some more slowly running material whose presence was not evident from Coomassie Blue staining. Though weak, the anti-IF antibody binding to both the tektin bands and the other material seems to be specific, since under the same conditions other antibodies such as anti-tubulins did not bind. This result suggests that tektins may contain a stretch of sequence similar but not identical to the common intermediate filament epitope.

Our purified anti-tektin antibodies did not appear to recognize mammalian intermediate filament proteins. This is not surprising in view of the species-specificity of the sera (see below). However, they do not even bind to nitrocellulose blots of mitotic spindles isolated from fertilized eggs of the same species (Amos *et al.* 1985), even though Hays & Salmon (1983) have shown that such spindle preparations include a $55 \times 10^3 M_r$ non-tubulin protein that may belong to the intermediate filament class. This lack of cross-reactivity is borne out by the results obtained by indirect immunofluorescence microscopy.

IMMUNOFLUORESCENCE STAINING

Sea-urchin sperm fixed with formaldehyde in sea water were stained all along their lengths after incubation with purified mouse anti-tektins, followed by FITC anti-mouse IgG (Linck *et al.* 1985; Amos *et al.* 1985). Similar results could be obtained for demembranated, purified axonemes (Fig. 2A) provided they were fixed in a suitable manner. Fixation simply in methanol cooled on solid CO_2 worked well. Fixation by formaldehyde in phosphate-buffered saline (PBS), followed by cold methanol, gave reasonable results. However, if the axonemes were kept during the early stages of aldehyde fixation in the axoneme-washing buffer of Linck & Langevin (1981), which includes 5 mM-$MgSO_4$ and 0·5 mM-EDTA, and is known to give good structural preservation at the electron microscope (EM) level, they did not stain with FITC. Anti-tubulin antibodies produced positive results for axonemes fixed in any of these ways, whereas staining did not occur under any conditions if pre-immune sera from the tektin-injected mice were used. These results suggested to us that a denaturation or unmasking of tektins is necessary for anti-tektin binding.

Staining could be obtained for axonemes from all species of sea urchin that were tried. However, the minimum concentration of anti-tektin required for a positive result was a hundred times higher for *Lytechinus pictus*, *Echinus esculentus* and *Psammechinus miliaris* than for *S. purpuratus*, the source of the original antigen.

The purified antibodies were also used to investigate a variety of structures containing microtubules. Since the antibodies showed reduced reactivity even when applied to axonemes of sea-urchin species other than *S. purpuratus*, we concentrated on material from echinoids, such as mitotic spindles and cytasters from eggs, and cilia and cytoplasmic microtubules of embryos (Amos *et al.* 1985).

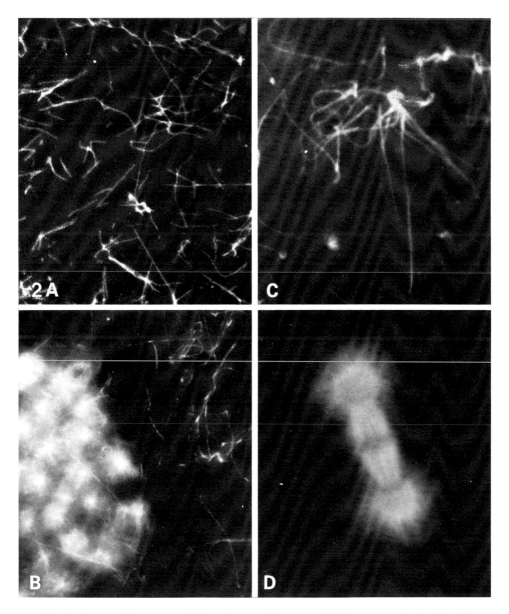

Fig. 2. Immunofluorescence light-microscopic images. A,C. Specimens incubated with polyclonal anti-tektin antibodies; B,D, specimens incubated with monoclonal anti-tubulin. FITC-labelled second antibody was applied in all cases. A. Purified axonemes from *E. esculentus* sperm; B, part of an *S. purpuratus* embryo with star-shaped intra-cellular microtubule arrays alongside cilia that have detached and become stuck to the slide; C comes from a similar specimen to B, except that the microtubule arrays were not labelled by anti-tektin; D shows an *S. purpuratus* egg mitotic spindle; anti-tektin gave no spindle staining under any of the conditions tried. ×200.

Ciliated embryos were obtained by fertilizing *L. pictus* eggs and leaving them to develop in artificial sea water. They were fixed in cold methanol, following the method that gave good anti-tektin staining for axonemes. After anti-tubulin treatment, the embryos were brightly fluorescent. Stained cilia were detected on all surfaces of the embryo and in its interior; each ectodermal cell contained a brightly stained star-shaped structure (Fig. 2B), presumably an array of cytoplasmic microtubules radiating out from a centrosome. Anti-tektin, on the other hand, stained only the cilia (Fig. 2C). This result shows that cilia, whose proteins differ from those of flagella in many cases (Linck, 1973), have components very like flagellar tektins. The cytoplasmic microtubules apparently do not.

This conclusion was supported by results of immunofluorescence experiments with spindles isolated from both *S. purpuratus* and *L. pictus* fertilized eggs or with multiple asters induced in unfertilized eggs (see Amos *et al.* 1985). No staining was observed with anti-tektin antibodies, no matter how the specimens were fixed, although anti-tubulin gave positive results in all cases (e.g. Fig. 2D).

IMMUNOELECTRON MICROSCOPY

Polyclonal antibodies

To study the molecular organization of tektin filaments in microtubules by electron microscopy, we used immunolabelling with 5 nm gold particles and uranyl acetate as negative stain (Linck *et al.* 1985). Gold-labelled anti-tubulin gave quite satisfactory results, though the gold appeared preferentially on singlet A-tubules and on protofilament ribbons (Fig. 3F,G); the tubulin in doublet microtubules may perhaps be masked by accessory proteins.

When preparations of *S. purpuratus* doublet or singlet microtubules, or protofilament ribbons, suspended in the axoneme buffer referred to above, were applied to carbon-coated grids and incubated with antibodies, first with the affinity-purified mouse anti-tektins and then with gold-labelled rabbit anti-mouse IgG, none of the specimens showed any sign of gold decoration. To 'unmask' the tektins, we briefly extracted microtubules on the grid with Sarkosyl–urea, before incubating with antibodies. The extraction *in situ* left behind filaments 2–3 nm in diameter, often twisted together into loose bundles (similar to the specimens shown in Fig. 4). It is not clear whether all the filaments in a bundle came from the same or different microtubules. After antibody treatment, the filaments were heavily decorated with gold. In control experiments, where no first antibody was used, the gold-labelled second antibody did not bind to the filaments.

In another series of experiments, *P. miliaris* axonemes were resuspended in a simple buffered saline instead of the axoneme buffer. Then the microtubules and protofilament ribbons all broke down into filaments and amorphous aggregates during the antibody incubations; the filaments became labelled with gold as in Sarkosyl–urea-extracted preparations. However, when 20 μM-taxol was included in the saline, the doublet microtubules disassembled only as far as protofilament ribbons during the incubations. Gold labelling was then mainly restricted to the

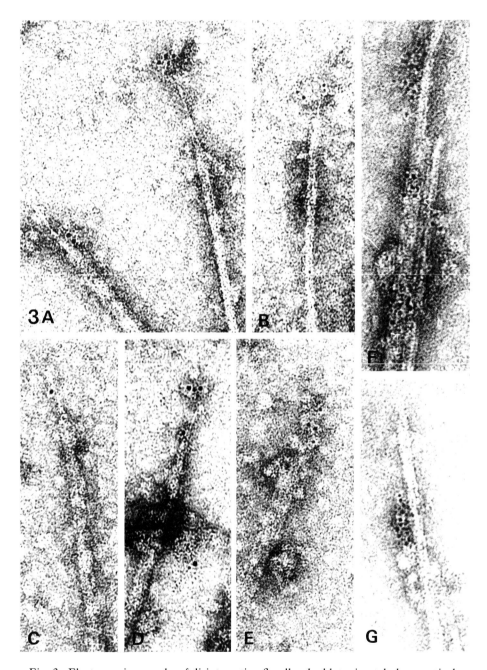

Fig. 3. Electron micrographs of disintegrating flagellar doublet microtubules negatively stained with uranyl acetate after incubation either (A–E) with polyclonal affinity-purified anti-tektin antibodies followed by gold-labelled second antibody; or (F,G) with gold-labelled monoclonal anti-tubulin (YL1/2; Kilmartin *et al.* 1982). In F,G, stable proto-filament ribbons protrude from the ends of fraying A-tubules. Gold particles show antibody binding along the lengths of both intact tubules and ribbons. In A–E, all the A-tubules have broken down completely and only ribbons are seen. The gold label is restricted to tektin filaments protruding from the ends of the ribbons. ×250 000.

broken ends of the ribbons, from which thin filaments 2–3 nm in diameter were often seen protruding (see Fig. 3A–E). These observations strongly support the theory that tektins are masked by tubulin in the intact microtubules.

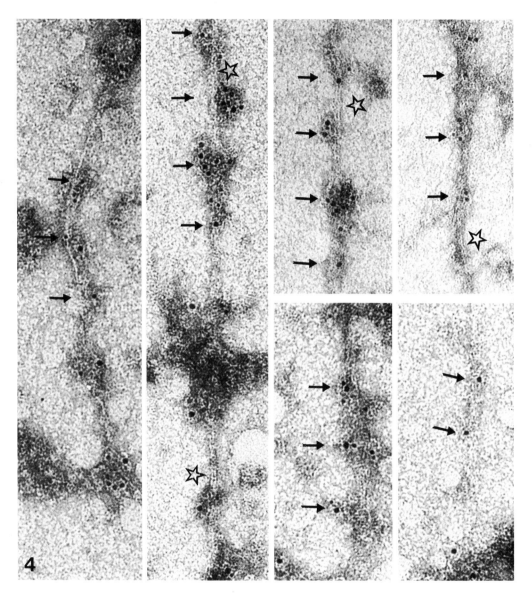

Fig. 4. Electron micrographs showing tektin filaments negatively stained with uranyl acetate after incubation with a monoclonal anti-tektin followed by gold-labelled anti-mouse antibodies. Arrows indicate the probable 48 nm axial spacing of equivalent antigenic sites, somewhat obscured by the clumping of the gold-labelled second antibody. In some regions one sees individual filaments 2–3 nm in diameter. Elsewhere, the filaments appear to be paired (☆) or even aggregated into sheets. Occasionally there are indications of an axial periodicity of the order of 3 nm, whose origin is not understood. ×330 000.

Studies with a monoclonal anti-tektin

A fusion of myeloma cells with spleen cells from one of the mice immunized with tektins produced several positive wells as assayed by immunofluorescence microscopy of sea-urchin axonemes. None of the supernatants stained mitotic spindles or cytoplasmic microtubules in HeLa cells. The supernatant from the cells in one well, which gave much brighter staining than the others, was used for immuno-electron microscopy of tektin filaments prepared by Sarkosyl–urea extraction of *P. miliaris* axonemes. The filaments became labelled with gold as before, except that now the labelling frequently appeared to be periodic (Fig. 4). Because the gold particles were attached to a secondary antibody, which amplifies any binding, the locations of the attachment sites of the primary antibody are less certain than if a gold-labelled primary antibody had been used. However, the small quantities of antibody available made the latter option impossible.

An estimate of the spacing of the binding sites was obtained by measuring the distances between the centres of adjacent clumps of gold particles. Fig. 5 shows the results for 54 intervals each defined by discrete clumps of gold. The uncertainty in each measurement is the sum of the diameters of the two clumps enclosing the gap. The distribution has a peak at around 48 nm. Since the highest values probably represent multiples of the basic repeat distance, they were not included in calculating the average. The actual distance between equivalent antigenic sites could be smaller than 48 nm; for example, one-half or one-third of this value. The clumps of label are

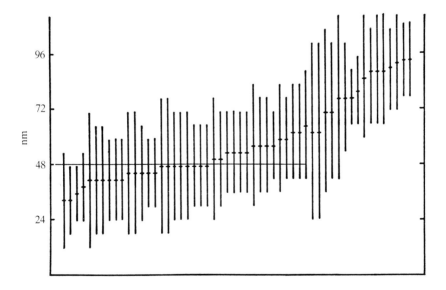

Fig. 5. Spacings of gold clumps on labelled tektin filaments such as those in Fig. 4. The measurements have been ordered according to the distance between the centres of each pair of clumps. The error bar shown for each measurement is the sum of the widths of the two clumps. The distribution peaks for a centre-to-centre spacing of around 48 nm and the average of the first 38 values is 47 ($\pm$8) nm. The remaining measurements show sufficient uncertainty to be accounted for as double spacings.

sufficiently large for spacings of this order to be obscured. However, a periodicity of around 48 nm seems to be the most likely.

DISCUSSION

The evidence suggests that most of the tektin polypeptides are assembled as continuous 2–3 nm filaments, though there may be fine projections not detected by electron microscopy. A length of about 48 nm per polypeptide in the form of a coiled α-helix would correspond to around 340 amino acid residues (roughly $37 \times 10^3 M_r$); this value agrees rather well with the estimated 71 % α-helix for tektins. There is sometimes some indication in electron-microscopic images (e.g. Fig. 4A) of globular domains along the filaments, with a periodicity of around 3 nm, significantly less than the 4 nm tubulin monomer repeat. It is not clear whether these are due to components other than the main tektin polypeptides, to the non-α-helical regions of the latter or simply to variations in charge distribution along a coiled coil, being shown up by the binding of the uranyl acetate stain.

We have not yet determined where exactly the tektin filaments are located in the A-tubule wall. It is clear that the antigenic sites are blocked in the intact structure, either by tubulin or some of the other associated proteins, such as the 77 and 83 $(\times 10^3) M_r$ polypeptides of *S. purpuratus*. It seems unlikely that the antigenic sites were exposed in our experiments by a drastic conformational change of the tektin filament itself, as the conditions used to produce staining were mostly quite mild. Thus, the most probable arrangement is a tektin filament running along a groove between two protofilaments, as in the model drawn in Fig. 6. Alternatively, tektins might themselves form certain protofilaments, in association with other non-tubulin polypeptides. Either way, they (and any side projections) probably have a stabilizing effect on the region of the wall into which they are incorporated. We do not know whether there is more than one stable protofilament ribbon per A-tubule or whether the different tektin polypeptides form homo- or heteropolymers. Answers to such questions should come from more detailed structural studies with a wider range of specific antibodies.

For a filament running straight alongside a tubulin protofilament, a periodicity of approximately 48 nm would correspond fairly closely with the axial extent of 12 tubulin monomers. This would be half of the overall axial repeat of doublet microtubules as defined by the groups of radial spokes and other accessory structures (see Fig. 6). Indeed, the tektins, being longitudinal elements, are quite likely to be involved in ordering the axial spacing of such components, as suggested by Linck (1982). The 29 % 'random chain' portions of the polypeptides may perhaps extend sideways to organize laterally distant accessory structures.

A further aspect of the possible role of tektins as longitudinal rulers along microtubules is that they may also define the ultimate length of the axonemes (Amos *et al.* 1985). Stephens (1977) made an extensive study of protein synthesis during ciliogenesis in sea-urchin embryos and found that a small number of minor components are synthesized in a short burst, either after fertilization or after experimental deciliation, whereas tubulins and dyneins are not newly synthesized for the purpose. The newly synthesized polypeptides were incorporated almost totally into the growing cilia. It is interesting that the major species was component 20, which is found in the Sarkosyl-resistant residue of the A-tubule and therefore is probably a

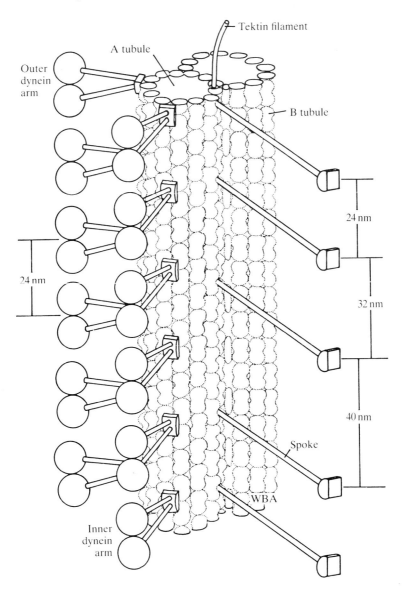

Fig. 6. Model of a short piece of doublet microtubule from a sea-urchin sperm axoneme, with many of its accessory structures. The drawing shows where a 2–3 nm tektin filament may be located in the A-tubule wall, close to the inner junction with the B-tubule. There may actually be more than one such filament, here or elsewhere in the A-tubule. Other accessory proteins are thought to be located in this region, including some material at the junction with a 16 nm periodicity (see Amos *et al.* 1976). The row of radial spokes is also attached fairly close to this region.

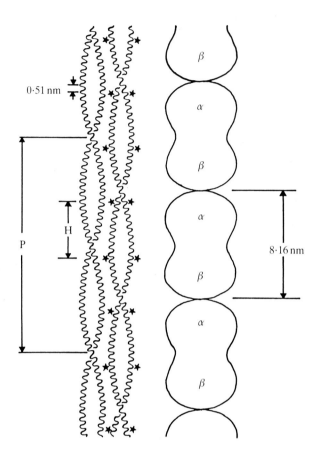

Fig. 7. Possible model for a 2–3 nm α-helical filament (left) compared with a tubulin protofilament composed of dimers (right). All lateral spacings in the 2–3 nm filament are exaggerated for clarity. In a coiled coil, each α-helix is thought to be supercoiled in a way that shortens the axial repeat distance from 0·55 nm (as in a straight α-helix) to 0·51 nm and reduces the number of residues per turn from 3·6 to 3·5; all coiled-coil α-helical proteins that have been sequenced, including myosin, tropomyosin and various types of intermediate filament, show a strong 3·5 residue period of hydrophobic groups, which form the interactions between the two chains (McLachlan & Stewart, 1982). The super-helix of such a coiled coil is thought to have a pitch (P in diagram) of 13·7–22 nm (see Phillips et al. 1980; McLachlan & Stewart, 1976; Crewther et al. 1983). Intermediate filaments are thought to differ from myosin and tropomyosin in that the basic unit is not just a simple coiled-coil dimer but a tetramer, arranged as a pair of coiled coils (Crewther et al. 1983). In addition to the 3·5 residue repeat, McLachlan & Stewart (1982) detected in sections of the sequences of vimentin and desmin a pattern of positively and negatively charged groups (symbolized by ★ in the diagram) with a period of 28 residues, which would correspond to eight turns of a coiled coil or an axial distance (H) of 4·08 nm. These groups may be involved in forming the tetramers and higher orders of assembly in 10 nm filaments. If, as we suspect, tektin filaments are similar to the basic tetrameric subfibrils of intermediate filaments, a 28-residue period would exactly match the tubulin monomer axial spacing. Furthermore, we predict that the pitch (P) of the supercoil may match the 16 nm periodicity detected in flagellar doublet microtubules near the junction between A- and B-tubules (see Fig. 6). A 48 nm distance along a tektin filament would then correspond to three complete superhelical turns.

component of the ciliary tektins. As suggested by Stephens, the apparently limited supply of this component might be the controlling factor in limiting the growth of the cilia.

It seems likely that microtubules in other cellular structures also possess some means of controlling their lengths in the presence of pools of tubulin required for different purposes. Although the negative results for spindles and cytasters could mean that tektins are absent from the constituent microtubules, there may be tektin-like proteins present but with no strong antigenic determinants in common with flagellar tektins. Again, a wider range of antibodies may answer this question. Since other microtubules are required to be much less stable than flagellar microtubules, it would not be surprising if they had associated proteins similar to tektins in some respects but different in others. The calcium-insoluble filaments described by Hays & Salmon (1983) may represent such components.

Finally, the question arises as to how closely related tektins are to *bona fide* intermediate filament proteins. Work in progress on the amino acid sequences of tektins should finally resolve this question. As emphasized before, many of their properties are similar and the weak reaction with the anti-intermediate-filament antibody suggests some homology in the sequence. We have discussed the necessity for tektin filaments to match up with the axial periodicities of the tubulin proto-filaments. The nominal 4 nm monomer periodicity in microtubules has actually been measured as 4·05–4·10 nm (Mandelkow *et al.* 1977; Baker & Amos, 1978), probably the most accurate estimate, 4·09 nm, being that of Wais-Steider *et al.* (1986). McLachlan & Stewart (1982) detected a regular pattern of charged residues in the primary sequences of the intermediate filament proteins desmin and vimentin with a period of 28 residues and pointed out that the axial extent of this repeat is similar to the tubulin monomer repeat in a microtubule. The match is actually even better than they thought. In a coiled coil, a 28-residue periodicity would correspond to an axial distance of 4·08 nm, a value remarkably close to the tubulin monomer repeat (see Fig. 7). Also, the total length of an individual intermediate filament protein monomer is thought to be around 44 nm (Crewther *et al.* 1983), only slightly shorter than our estimate of 48 nm for the length of a tektin monomer. Desmin and vimentin may not themselves interact directly with tubulin, but they may possibly be derived from an ancestral protein that evolved within a microtubule wall!

We are grateful to Dr B. H. Anderton for a generous supply of anti-intermediate-filament antibody; also to Dr J. V. Kilmartin for advice and gold-labelled anti-tubulin.

REFERENCES

Amos, L. A., Linck, R. W. & Klug, A. (1976). Molecular structure of flagellar microtubules. In *Cell Motility* (ed. R. Goldman, T. Pollard & J. Rosenbaum), pp. 847–867. New York: Cold Spring Harbor Laboratory Press.

Amos, W. B., Amos, L. A. & Linck, R. W. (1985). Proteins similar to flagellar tektins are detected in cilia but not in cytoplasmic microtubules. *Cell Motil.* **5**, 239–250.

Baker, T. S. & Amos, L. A. (1978). Structure of the tubulin dimer in zinc-induced sheets. *J. molec. Biol.* **123**, 89–106.

BEESE, L. (1984). Ph.D. thesis, Brandeis University, Waltham, Mass., USA.

CREWTHER, W. G., DOWLING, L. M., STEINERT, P. M. & PARRY, D. A. D. (1983). Structure of intermediate filaments. *Int. J. biol. Macromol.* **5**, 267–274.

FUCHS, E. & HANUKOGLU, I. (1983). Unraveling the structure of the intermediate filaments. *Cell* **34**, 332–334.

HAYS, T. S. & SALMON, E. D. (1983). A non-microtubular component of sea urchin isolated spindles. *J. Cell Biol.* **97**, 44a.

JENSEN, C. & BAJER, A. (1973). Spindle dynamics and arrangement of microtubules. *Chromosoma* **44**, 73–89.

KILMARTIN, J. V., WRIGHT, B. & MILSTEIN, C. (1982). Rat monoclonal anti-tubulin antibodies derived by using a new nonsecreting rat cell line. *J. Cell Biol.* **93**, 576–582.

LINCK, R. W. (1973). Chemical and structural differences between cilia and flagella from the lamellibranch mollusc *Aequipectens irradians. J. Cell Sci.* **12**, 951–981.

LINCK, R. W. (1976). Flagellar doublet microtubules: fractionation of minor components and α-tubulin from specific regions of the A-tubule. *J. Cell Sci.* **20**, 405–439.

LINCK, R. W. (1982). The structure of microtubules. *Ann. N.Y. Acad. Sci.* **383**, 98–121.

LINCK, R. W., AMOS, L. A. & AMOS, W. B. (1985). Localization of tektin filaments in microtubules of sea urchin sperm flagella by immunoelectron microscopy. *J. Cell Biol.* **100**, 126–135.

LINCK, R. W. & LANGEVIN, G. L. (1981). Reassembly of flagellar B($\alpha\beta$)-tubulin into singlet microtubules: consequences for cytoplasmic microtubule structure and assembly. *J. Cell Biol.* **89**, 323–337.

LINCK, R. W. & LANGEVIN, G. L. (1982). Structure and chemical composition of insoluble filamentous components of sperm flagellar microtubules. *J. Cell Sci.* **58**, 1–22.

LINCK, R. W., OLSEN, G. E. & LANGEVIN, G. L. (1981). Arrangement of tubulin subunits and microtubule-associated proteins in the central-pair microtubule apparatus of squid (*Loligo pealei*) sperm flagella. *J. Cell Biol.* **89**, 309–322.

MANDELKOW, E., THOMAS, J. & COHEN, C. (1977). Microtubule structure at low resolution by X-ray diffraction. *Proc. natn. Acad. Sci. U.S.A.* **74**, 3370–3374.

MCLACHLAN, A. D. & STEWART, M. J. (1976). The 14-fold periodicity in α-tropomyosin and the interaction with actin. *J. molec. Biol.* **103**, 271–298.

MCLACHLAN, A. D. & STEWART, M. J. (1982). Periodic charge distribution in the intermediate filament proteins desmin and vimentin. *J. molec. Biol.* **162**, 693–698.

MEZA, I., HUANG, B. & BRYAN, J. (1972). Chemical heterogeneity of protofilaments forming the outer doublets from sea urchin flagella. *Expl Cell Res.* **74**, 535–540.

PHILLIPS, G. N., FILLERS, J. P. & COHEN, C. (1980). Motions of tropomyosin. *Biophys. J.* **32**, 485–502.

PRUSS, R. M., MIRSKY, R., RAFF, M. C., THORPE, R., DOWDING, A. J. & ANDERTON, B. H. (1981). All classes of intermediate filaments share a common antigenic determinant defined by a monoclonal antibody. *Cell* **27**, 419–428.

STEPHENS, R. E. (1977). Differential protein synthesis and utilisation during cilia formation in sea urchin embryos. *Devl Biol.* **61**, 311–329.

WAIS-STEIDER, C., WHITE, N. S., GILBERT, D. S. & EAGLES, P. A. M. (1986). X-ray diffraction from neurofilaments and microtubules in axoplasm. *J. molec. Biol.* (in press).

WITMAN, G. B., CARLSON, K. & ROSENBAUM, J. L. (1972). *Chlamydomonas* flagella. II. The distribution of tubulins 1 and 2 in the outer doublet microtubules. *J. Cell Biol.* **54**, 540–555.

J. Cell Sci. Suppl. 5, 69–97 (1986)
Printed in Great Britain © The Company of Biologists Limited 1986

INTERMEDIATE FILAMENT NETWORKS: ORGANIZATION AND POSSIBLE FUNCTIONS OF A DIVERSE GROUP OF CYTOSKELETAL ELEMENTS

ROBERT D. GOLDMAN*, ANNE E. GOLDMAN, KATHLEEN J. GREEN, JONATHAN C. R. JONES, STEPHANIE M. JONES AND HSI-YUAN YANG

Department of Cell Biology and Anatomy, Northwestern University Medical School, Ward Building, 303 East Chicago Avenue, Chicago, Illinois 60611, USA

SUMMARY

Immunofluorescence and electron microscopic observations demonstrate that intermediate filaments (IF) form cytoplasmic networks between the nucleus and cell surface in several types of cultured cells. Intermediate filaments interact with the nuclear surface, where they appear to terminate at the level of the nuclear envelope. From this region, they radiate towards the cell surface where they are closely associated with the plasma membrane. On the basis of these patterns of IF organization, we suggest that IF represent a cytoskeletal system interconnecting the cell surface with the nucleus. Furthermore, IF also appear to interact with other cytoskeletal components including microtubules and microfilaments. In the former case microtubule–IF interactions are seen in cytoplasmic regions between the nucleus and the cell membrane, whereas microfilament–IF interactions occur in the cortical cytoplasm. IF also appear to be cross-linked to each other; especially in the case of the IF bundles that occur in epithelial cells. In order to determine the molecular and biochemical bases of the organizational state of IF we have developed procedures for obtaining IF-enriched 'cytoskeletons' of cultured cells. In these preparations IF–nuclear and IF–cell surface associations are retained. Thus, these preparations have enabled us to begin to study various IF-associated structures (e.g. desmosomes) and associated proteins (IFAPs) using biochemical and immunological methodologies. To date, the results support the idea that IF and their associated proteins may comprise the cell type specific molecular infrastructure that is involved in transmitting and distributing information amongst the major cellular domains; the cell surface/extracellular matrix, the cytoplasm and the nuclear surface/nuclear matrix.

INTRODUCTION

Intermediate filaments (IF) are cytoskeletal components found in many types of cells. They are usually ≈10 nm in diameter, and contain alpha-type proteins in a coiled-coil configuration. Despite their morphological, physical and chemical similarities, they in fact represent a very large and diverse family of cytoskeletal elements (Zackroff *et al.* 1981; Steinert *et al.* 1984; Wang *et al.* 1985). The diversity of IF is especially evident when their polypeptide composition is compared between different cells from different tissues of the same organism. This has led numerous investigators to attempt to categorize cells on the basis of differences in the immunological, molecular and biochemical properties of the structural subunits of their IF. To date, the largest subgroup of IF proteins to be described are the

---

*Author for correspondence.

keratins. In mammalian cell systems, there may be 30 or even more keratins (Moll *et al.* 1982; Steinert *et al.* 1984; Sun *et al.* 1986). This large group of IF proteins is distinguished by their relative insolubility, their diversity and their abundance in epithelial cells. The type or types of keratin family members expressed in any individual epithelial cell type varies with the state of cellular differentiation and the location of the cell (Zackroff *et al.* 1981; Steinert *et al.* 1984; Wang *et al.* 1986; Sun *et al.* 1985).

In contrast to these differences within the keratin sub-group, there are also obvious similarities amongst the keratin subunits. For example, there are antibodies that react with a variety of keratins, indicating that they possess antigenic similarities. On comparative biochemical grounds the keratins are known to be serine- and glycine-rich and more recent sequencing data have suggested that these serine + glycine-rich residues are located in terminal domains (Steinert *et al.* 1984; Wang *et al.* 1986).

There are also other types of IF proteins, the most extensively studied being vimentin, which is the major structural protein found in mesenchymal cells such as fibroblasts (Zackroff *et al.* 1981; Steinert *et al.* 1984; Wang *et al.* 1986). In addition, the major building blocks of neuronal IF (the neurofilament triplet proteins), the glial IF proteins, and the major protein of muscle IF, which has been called either desmin or skeletin, have also been studied intensively in recent years (Zackroff *et al.* 1981; Steinert *et al.* 1984; Wang *et al.* 1985).

Besides the major structural subunits comprising IF in different cell types, there is also some evidence for the existence of IF-associated proteins (IFAPs). These are diverse and appear to be cell-and-tissue type specific. For example, filaggrin is a specific IF–IF cross-bridging protein found in skin and related tissues (Steinert *et al.* 1981). Filaggrin is a very basic protein, which may act to cross-link individual keratin-containing IF into bundles (tonofilaments) *via* their serine + glycine-rich terminal domains. Another very different IFAP has been described in BHK cells, which appears to form cross-bridges between neighbouring BHK IF. *In situ*, these bridges appear to be intermittent and may be involved in the formation of cytoplasmic IF networks (Yang *et al.* 1985; Lieska *et al.* 1985). In epidermal cells, there is some evidence that a protein called desmoplakin, a major component of desmosomes, may also be an IFAP (Jones & Goldman, 1985).

Recently, we have demonstrated that there are keratin-like proteins in mesenchymal cells, such as cultured BHK and 3T3 cells, which do not form IF under normal conditions. These proteins appear to be localized at the nuclear surface where they form an insoluble polymer system known as the nuclear lamina (Aaronson & Blobel, 1975; Gerace *et al.* 1978, 1984; Zackroff *et al.* 1984; Goldman *et al.* 1984, 1985, 1986). Furthermore, Linck *et al.* (1985) have suggested that the tektins, components of the outer doublet microtubules of cilia, are also intermediate filament-like proteins. These findings are intriguing, as they demonstrate that not all members of the IF protein family form 10 nm diameter filaments. In the case of the nuclear lamina proteins, they appear to possess several keratin-IF-like properties including their high content of glycine and serine, their alpha-helical content, their cross-reactivity with antibodies directed against IF-forming epidermal keratins and their primary sequence derived from cDNA clones (Zackroff *et al.* 1984; Goldman *et al.* 1984, 1985, 1986; McKeon *et al.* 1986).

The fact that there is remarkable diversity amongst IF structural and associated proteins, and the fact that there are additional IF protein family members that can form polymeric systems other than IF, must presumably reflect functional significance. In this report, we review some of our work that has been aimed at determining the functions of the IF system.

RESULTS AND DISCUSSION

The cytoplasmic distribution of IF in cultured animal cells

Immunofluorescence observations of various types of cultured cells indicate that IF are generally distributed between the nuclear and cell surfaces in cultured fibroblastic cells, such as mouse 3T3 and baby hamster kidney (BHK). When BHK cells are observed by indirect immunofluorescence, using an antibody preparation directed against the major BHK IF structural protein of 55000 molecular weight (55 K, termed vimentin), a complex network of fibrils is seen to radiate from a juxtanuclear mass towards the cell surface (Fig. 1) and individual IF frequently appear to approach the cell surface very closely (Green & Goldman, 1986). A more dramatic way in which to show the association between IF and the nuclear and cell surfaces is to observe cells during attachment, spreading and shape formation. Following trypsinization and replating, rounded up BHK cells contain a large juxtanuclear cap enriched in IF structural protein (Fig. 2; and Goldman & Follett, 1970; Goldman & Knipe, 1973). As cell spreading progresses, this cap gives rise to fibres that radiate away from the nucleus towards the cell surface (Fig. 3; and Goldman & Follett, 1970; Goldman & Knipe, 1973). Similar observations have been made on all fibroblasts studied to date, on cultured nerve cells such as neuroblastoma (Fig. 4; and Goldman *et al.* 1981), and on several types of epithelial cells (Goldman *et al.* 1973; Jones *et al.* 1982).

The most extensive and dramatic IF networks that can be resolved in the fluorescence microscope are seen in many types of epithelial cells with polyclonal antibodies directed against epidermal keratin. For example, in cultured mouse keratinocytes, these networks are comprised of tonofibrils (IF bundles). These form a complex cage surrounding the nucleus, from which they radiate towards the cell surface (Fig. 5; and Jones *et al.* 1982). During the early stages of attachment and spreading of such cells, the network of tonofibrils can be seen to surround the nucleus. As cells begin to spread upon a substrate, individual tonofibrils are seen to extend into the expanding regions of cytoplasm from the concentrated juxtanuclear mass and move towards the cell surface (Fig. 6).

We have observed another example of nuclear–cell surface reorganization of tonofibrils in cultures of primary newborn mouse keratinocytes (PME) (Jones *et al.* 1982; Jones & Goldman, 1985). These cells are capable of attaching, spreading and dividing in low Ca^{2+} conditions (Hennings *et al.* 1980; Jones *et al.* 1982; Hennings

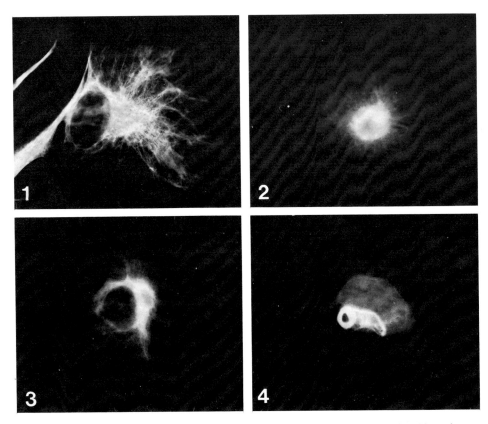

Fig. 1. A BHK cell observed ≈6 h following attachment to a glass coverslip. Note that the IF network is concentrated in a perinuclear region and radiates from this region towards the cell surface. Cells were fixed and processed for indirect immunofluorescence using an antibody directed against the BHK 55 K IF protein (Green & Goldman, 1983). ×750.

Fig. 2. A BHK cell observed ≈30 min following attachment to a glass coverslip. Note the juxtanuclear accumulation of IF as seen by immunofluorescence with the same antibody and preparative procedure described for Fig. 1. ×600.

Fig. 3. A BHK cell observed ≈2 h following attachment to a glass coverslip. Indirect immunofluorescence was carried out as described in Fig. 1. Note that IF are beginning to become redistributed into the spreading regions of cytoplasm. ×690.

Fig. 4. A mouse neuroblastoma (Nb2a) cell observed ≈2 h after attachment and processed for indirect immunofluorescence as described in Fig. 1. Note the juxtanuclear ring apparently connected to some IF-containing fibrils. ×625.

& Holbrook, 1983; Jones & Goldman, 1985). However, even though the cells are extensively spread under these culture conditions, tonofibrils are seen primarily in large perinuclear accumulations (Fig. 7; and Jones *et al.* 1982; Jones & Goldman, 1985). When the Ca^{2+} concentration is increased to normal levels, the tonofibrils move rapidly towards regions of the cell surface in contact with other cells (Fig. 8; and Jones *et al.* 1982; Jones & Goldman, 1985). When IF associate with the cell surface, desmosome assembly takes place. Desmosomes can be distinguished in this culture system by using immunofluorescence methods with antibodies directed against desmosomal components, such as desmoplakin (Figs 9, 10; and Mueller & Franke, 1982; Jones *et al.* 1985).

The IF patterns seen in the different cell types described above have some general features in common, including the fact that they appear to have radiating networks between the nuclear and cell surfaces. These observations with the light microscope are readily confirmed at higher resolution with the electron microscope. In the case of fibroblasts such as BHK or 3T3 cells, arrays of 10 nm diameter IF can be seen in the region immediately adjacent to the nuclear surface. These frequently appear to terminate at the nuclear surface (Fig. 11; Goldman *et al.* 1984, 1985, 1986). In mouse epidermal cells an elaborate cage composed of IF bundles can be seen to surround the nucleus, which readily accounts for the images resolved by light microscopy described above (Fig. 12; and Jones *et al.* 1985). Frequently, IF can be seen apparently terminating in close proximity to the nuclear pore complexes (Jones *et al.* 1982, 1985; Goldman *et al.* 1985).

At the level of the cell surface there are numerous types of IF–plasma membrane interactions as revealed by electron-microscopic observations. IF can be found in close association with the cell surface in cultured BHK and chicken embryo (CEF) fibroblasts (Fig. 13; and Green & Goldman, 1986). In the case of CEF, plasma membrane-associated IF are frequently seen in regions in which the outer cell surface contains an accumulation of extracellular matrix material, which by immunofluorescence and immunogold-labelling criteria contains fibronectin (Green & Goldman, 1986). IF are also seen in close proximity to the microfilament bundles that accumulate subjacent to the plasma membrane in the specialized regions known as the 'fibronexus' (Fig. 14; and Green & Goldman, 1986). These latter regions are

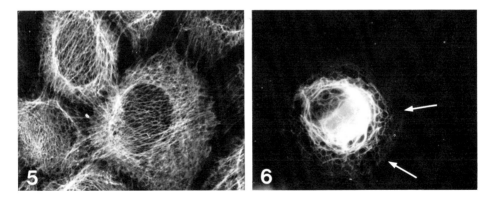

Fig. 5. The overall pattern of tonofibrils in well-spread cells obtained from a mouse skin epidermis cell line (PAM) is most readily observed by indirect immunofluorescence using, in this instance, a monoclonal antibody preparation directed against mouse keratin (Jones *et al.* 1985). Note the network of tonofibrils surrounding the nucleus and extending to the cell surface. ×1000.

Fig. 6. An early stage in the spreading process (≈2h after attachment to a glass coverslip) of a PAM cell prepared as described for Fig. 5. Note that most tonofibrils surround the nucleus and some are beginning to move into the spreading cytoplasm. Arrows mark the position of the edge of the cell. ×960.

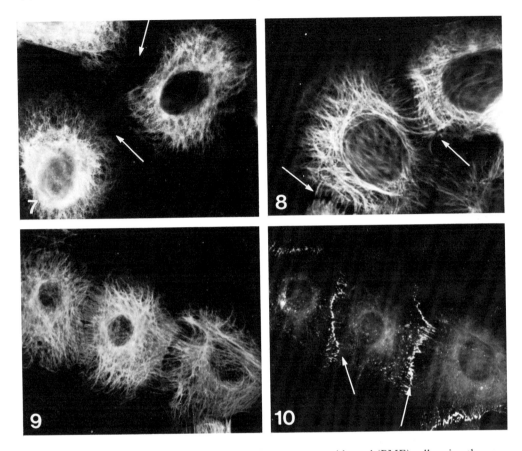

Fig. 7. Indirect immunofluorescence of primary mouse epidermal (PME) cells using the keratin antibody preparation as described for Fig. 5. These cells have been maintained in low Ca^{2+}-containing medium for 48 h and have established cell–cell contacts (arrows). Note that tonofibrils are concentrated around the nucleus and have not extended to the cell surface. ×700.

Fig. 8. A similar preparation of PME cells as described for Fig. 7, except that they have been exposed to normal Ca^{2+} levels for ≈3 h. Note that tonofibrils have moved to the cell surface, especially in areas of cell–cell contact (arrows). ×850.

Figs 9,10. Double indirect immunofluorescence micrographs of PME cells maintained in normal levels of Ca^{2+} for ≈4 h to show keratin-containing tonofibrils (Fig. 9) and desmosomes (arrows) (Fig. 10) (see Jones *et al.* 1984). ×675.

specialized membrane domains that are thought to represent sites of interactions between submembranous microfilament bundles and extracellular matrix components, especially fibronectin (Singer, 1979).

In addition to these ultrastructural observations, double-label immunofluorescence studies have been carried out in CEF, which indicate that, although there is not an extensive degree of overlap between the patterns generated by antibodies directed against CEF IF structural protein and fibronectin, there are regions in every cell in which a close association is seen between the two patterns (Figs 15, 16; and

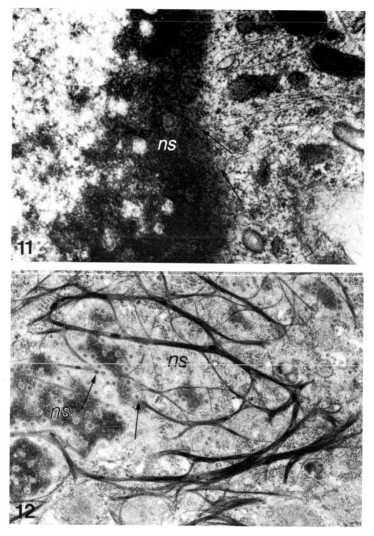

Figs 11, 12. Electron micrographs of thin sections of a BHK cell (Fig. 11) and a PME cell (Fig. 12) fixed and prepared as described (Starger *et al.* 1978). Note the close association between individual IF (arrows in Fig. 11) or IF bundles (arrows in Fig. 12) with the nuclear surface (*ns*). Fig. 11, ×28 000; Fig. 12, ×10 500.

Green & Goldman, 1986). Similar observations have been made using fibronectin antibody in conjunction with the immunogold-labelling procedure (Fig. 17; and Green & Goldman, 1986). Additional evidence to support the possibility that IF associate with a 'cell membrane complex', which acts in some unknown fashion to link IF with the outer cell surface, stems from the observation that trypsinization of cells, which removes surface-bound fibronectin, induces the retraction of IF away from the plasma membrane. However, when CEF are removed from their growth substrates in the absence of trypsin, IF–cell surface associations are retained (Green & Goldman, 1986).

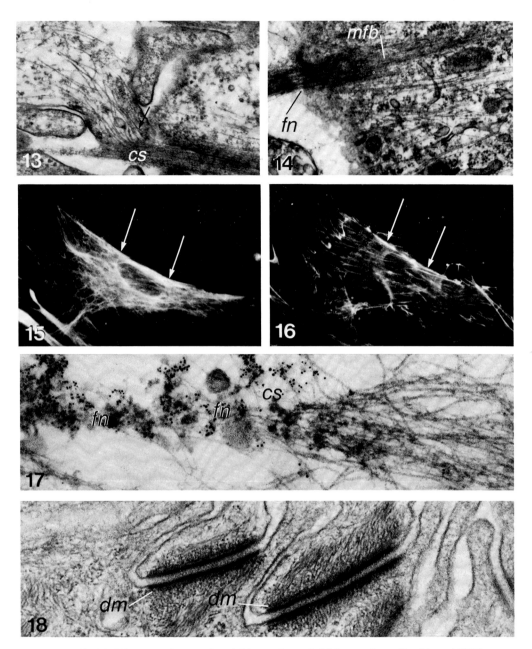

Figs 13, 14. Electron micrographs of thin sections of chicken embryo fibroblasts (CEF) cells to show IF associations (arrows) with the cell surface (*cs*; Fig. 13) and cell surface-associated microfilament bundles (*mfb*) in the region of the fibronexus (*fn*; Fig. 14). Fig. 13, ×55 000; Fig. 14, ×35 750.

Figs 15, 16. Double-label immunofluorescence micrographs of the same CEF cell showing IF organization (Fig. 15) and fibronectin distribution (Fig. 16), prepared as described by Green & Goldman (1986). Regions of close association between the two patterns are indicated by arrows. ×450.

Fig. 17. An electron micrograph of a region at the surface of a CEF cell prepared for indirect immunogold localization using fibronectin antibody as described by Green & Goldman (1986). Note the IF that approach the cell surface zone (*cs*) and the gold labelling in the extracellular fibres containing fibronectin (*fn*). ×87 500.

Fig. 18. An electron micrograph showing two desmosomes separating epithelial cells comprising the oral mucosa of bovine tongue (Jones *et al.* 1987). Note the close proximity of IF and desmosomal plaque material (*dm*). ×60 000.

Epithelial cells also exhibit obvious IF–cell surface interactions at the level of the desmosome – a double-membrane-containing structure, each half of which is associated with a cell–cell adhesion site (Arnn & Staehelin, 1981). Desmosomes are especially abundant in epidermal cells, where they are associated with keratin-containing IF. Indeed, IF appear to be attached to the innermost region of the submembranous plaque, which is associated with the cytoplasmic face of desmosomes (Fig. 18; and Arnn & Staehelin, 1981; Jones *et al.* 1987). As the bundles of IF approach the desmosomal plaque they appear to loop in and out of the fine fibrillar material associated with the plaque (Kelly, 1966). Recently, we have provided evidence that suggests that at least one of the desmosomal plaque proteins, desmoplakin 1, is associated with IF prior to the formation of desmosomes (Jones & Goldman, 1985).

The results of these morphological studies support the hypothesis that the IF system forms a cytoskeletal network that links the nuclear surface with the cell surface in cultured fibroblasts and epithelial cells (Goldman *et al.* 1985). We have also been able to show that IF interact with the two other major cytoskeletal elements, microtubules and microfilaments.

IF interactions with other cytoskeletal components: microtubules and microfilaments

One of the most obvious cases of IF interaction with microtubules (MT) can be seen in the cytoplasmic region between the nucleus and the cell surface of cultured fibroblasts that have been permitted to flatten on a solid substrate, such as a plastic Petri dish or a glass coverslip. Numerous IF can be seen in this region by electron-microscopic examination of thin-sectioned cells. In these areas, parallel arrays of IF and MT can be found (Fig. 19). Possible cross-bridging elements between these two cytoskeletal components have been reported elsewhere (Goldman & Knipe, 1973). Further support for this interaction also stems from the finding that in the presence of microtubule disrupting agents such as vinblastine or colchicine, the majority but not all of the IF visualized by immunofluorescence collapse around the nuclear surface (Fig. 20; and Starger *et al.* 1978; Green & Goldman, 1983, 1986). These latter arrays of IF are similar to those seen in cells observed during the early stages of attachment and spreading (see Figs 2, 3, above). Similar MT–IF configurations have been reported in nerve cells (Goldman *et al.* 1981).

IF also appear to be closely associated with submembranous microfilaments. In fibroblasts, we have been able to demonstrate, utilizing both immunofluorescence and electron microscopy, two types of MF–IF associations. One of these is apparent in the early stages of spreading in cultured CEF. In about 50 % of these cells, one or more phase-dense nodules are apparent within the cytoplasm in close association with stress fibres (microfilament bundles). These structures stain intensely with rhodamine-labelled phalloidin, indicating the presence of F-actin. When double stained with an antibody preparation directed against the CEF IF structural protein, these actin-rich nodules appear as focal centres from which IF-containing fibres radiate (Figs 21, 22; and Green & Goldman, 1986). In addition, numerous IF can be

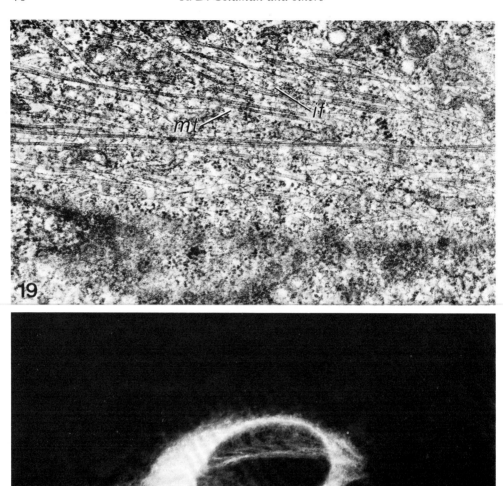

Fig. 19. Parallel arrays of IF (*if*) and MT (*mt*) seen in the cytoplasmic region between the nuclear and cell surfaces in BHK cells prepared for thin-section electron microscopy. ×40 000.

Fig. 20. A colchicine-treated (10 µg ml⁻¹ in culture medium) BHK cell prepared for indirect immunofluorescence using an antibody directed against the BHK 55 K (vimentin) subunit. Note the large juxtanuclear fluorescent cap. ×1100.

seen coursing parallel to stress fibres in fully spread CEF by immunofluorescence (Green & Goldman, 1986). Electron-microscopic examination of the nodules supports the light-microscopic findings; they appear as an outpocketing of a microfilament bundle that contains electron-dense fine fibrillar material closely associated

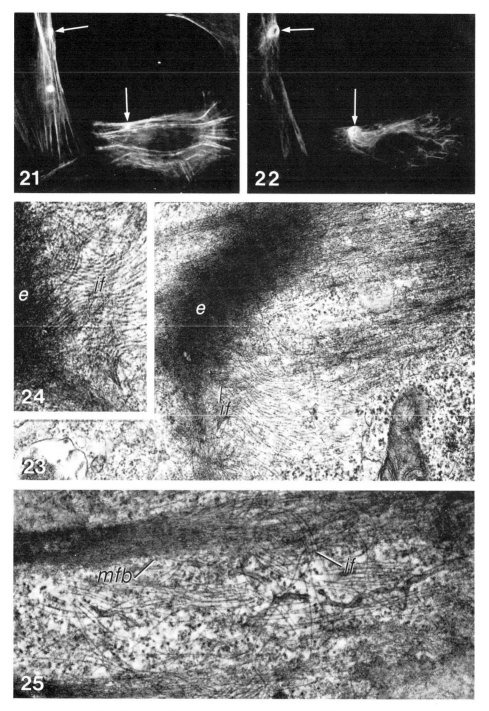

Figs 21, 22. Double-label fluorescence observations of CEF cells showing the distribution of F-actin, visualized using rhodamine-labelled phalloidin (Fig. 21), and IF (Fig. 22) (Green *et al.* 1986). Note the presence of actin-rich nodules or focal centres that are closely associated with IF (arrows). ×1200.

Figs 23, 24. Electron micrographs of a thin section through a 'nodule' of a spreading CEF cell. Note the electron-dense fibrillar material (*e*) and associated IF (*if*). Fig. 24 is a region taken from Fig. 23, but at higher magnification. Fig. 23, ×36 000; Fig. 24, ×51 500.

Fig. 25. An electron micrograph of a thin section through a submembranous region of a spread CEF cell showing a microfilament bundle (*mfb*) and associated IF (*if*). ×50 000.

with IF (Figs 23, 24; and Green & Goldman, 1986). The fine fibrillar material probably represents the F-actin-enriched region of the nodule as seen by fluorescence microscopy. In addition, as mentioned above for fluorescence, we have seen close associations between MF bundles and IF by electron microscopy in spread CEF (Fig. 25; and Green & Goldman, 1986).

IF also interact with IF as determined ultrastructurally. For example, parallel arrays of IF are seen both in the juxtanuclear caps in the early stages of spreading in BHK cells and, during spreading, in the cytoplasm between the nucleus and cell surface (Figs 26, 27; and Goldman & Follett, 1970; Goldman & Knipe, 1973; Goldman et al. 1973). In epithelial cells, IF bundles can be found that form the tonofibrils resolved by light optical methods (Jones et al. 1982). These consist of tightly packed parallel arrays of IF (Fig. 28). In the case of epidermal cells, these latter arrays are cross-linked by a protein called filaggrin (Steinert et al. 1981).

The preparation of IF-enriched cytoskeletons: their morphological, biochemical and immunological properties

When cultured cells are extracted with high ionic strength detergent-containing solutions (0·6 M-KCl, 1 % Triton X-100 in phosphate-buffered saline) and subsequently treated with DNase I (Starger & Goldman, 1977; Zackroff & Goldman, 1979), a so-called cytoskeletal preparation is formed that is greatly enriched in IF. Despite these rather drastic lysis conditions, the IF-enriched cytoskeletons appear to retain their overall shape in both fibroblasts and epithelial cells, as determined by whole-mount electron-microscopic observations (Figs 29, 30; Jones et al. 1982; Green & Goldman, 1986). In addition, these cytoskeletons are virtually devoid of other major cytoplasmic structural proteins such as tubulin and actin. In the case of fibroblast cytoskeletons, elements of the extracellular matrix can also be seen in their normal location (Fig. 30; and Green & Goldman, 1986). In the cell centre lies a nuclear remnant and between this latter structure and the cell surface there are large numbers of fibrous components that represent IF networks (Figs 29, 30; and Jones et al. 1982; Green & Goldman, 1986).

When such preparations are fixed and embedded for conventional electron-microscopic observations, more detailed views of the morphological properties of these cytoskeletons can be obtained. Beginning at the level of the nuclear surface, an obvious 'nuclear ghost' is present that is decorated on its cytoplasmic face with large numbers of IF (Figs 31–34; and Jones et al. 1982; Goldman et al. 1985). The nuclear ghost contains fine fibrillar material that represents the nuclear lamina region (Figs 31, 32, 34; Jones et al. 1982; Goldman et al. 1985). Nuclear pore complexes are frequently seen embedded in this latter region (Figs 31, 32, 34; and Jones et al. 1982; Goldman et al. 1985). In the case of fibroblast-derived cytoskeletons, IF at the cytoplasmic surface of the nuclear ghost appear to be anchored to a network of finely fibrous material (Figs 31, 32). In epidermal cell preparations, IFB are frequently seen to splay apart as they approximate the nuclear ghost and individual IF appear to terminate at the level of the nuclear pore complexes (Fig. 34; and Jones et al. 1982). The cytoplasmic networks of IF appear to be in their usual organizational states.

Very few other cytoplasmic constituents can be detected (Figs 35, 36; and Jones *et al.* 1982; Jones & Goldman, 1985; Green & Goldman, 1986). At the level of the cell surface, close associations between IF and the extracellular matrix are retained (Fig. 35; and Green & Goldman, 1986). Frequently, in these regions, there appear

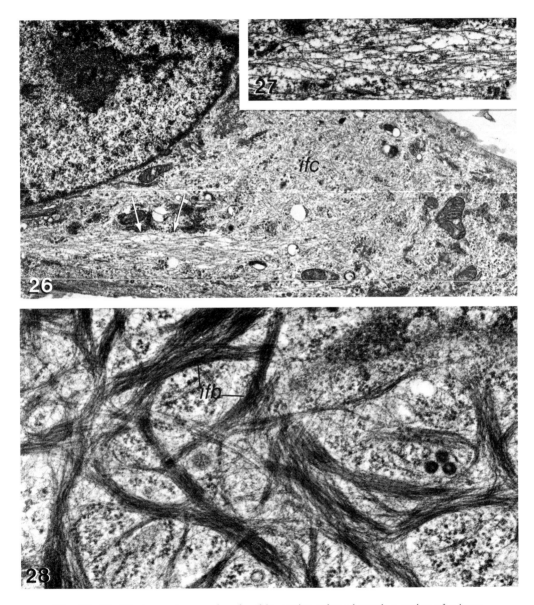

Figs 26, 27. Electron micrographs of a thin section taken through a region of a juxta-nuclear accumulation of IF (*ifc*) with an associated loosely packed parallel array of IF (arrows). Fig. 27 is a higher-magnification view of the parallel array seen in Fig. 26. Fig. 26, ×11 650; Fig. 27, ×20 000.

Fig. 28. An electron micrograph of a thin section cut through the cytoplasm of a spread PME cell to show IF bundles (*ifb*). ×42 600.

to be residual elements of the plasma membrane (membrane ghost material) (Fig. 30; and Green & Goldman, 1986). In the case of cultured keratinocytes, desmosomes as well as their connections with IF are retained (Fig. 36; and Jones *et al.* 1982; Jones & Goldman, 1985).

The biochemical properties of these IF-enriched cytoskeletal preparations have been analysed in some detail (e.g. see Starger & Goldman, 1977; Zackroff & Goldman, 1979; Steinert *et al.* 1982; Jones *et al.* 1982). SDS–PAGE (sodium dodecyl sulphate–polyacrylamide gel electrophoresis) analyses indicate the presence of relatively few polypeptides; the major components being the IF structural proteins. Since these vary from cell type to cell type, this is reflected in differences in the major proteins comprising their cytoskeletons. For example, in BHK preparations, two major polypeptides are apparent, of molecular weights 54 K and 55 K (the 54 K component is frequently termed desmin and the 55 K, vimentin) (Fig. 37; and Starger & Goldman, 1977), whereas in the case of PME cells, several bands of the keratin-type of IF structural protein are resolved (Fig. 38; and Jones *et al.* 1982; Jones & Goldman, 1985).

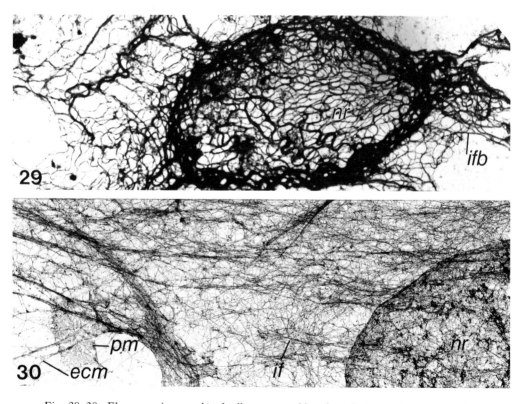

Figs 29, 30. Electron micrographs of cells grown and lysed on electron-microscope grids. Fig. 29 shows the IF bundle (*ifb*) network including the juxtanuclear IF cage, which remains when mouse epidermal cells are prepared according to Jones *et al.* (1982). Fig. 30 shows a region of a CEF prepared as described by Green & Goldman (1986). Note the nuclear remnant (*nr*), IF (*if*), elements of the extracellular matrix (*ecm*), and remnants of the plasma membrane (*pm*). Fig. 29, ×3500; Fig. 30, ×9100.

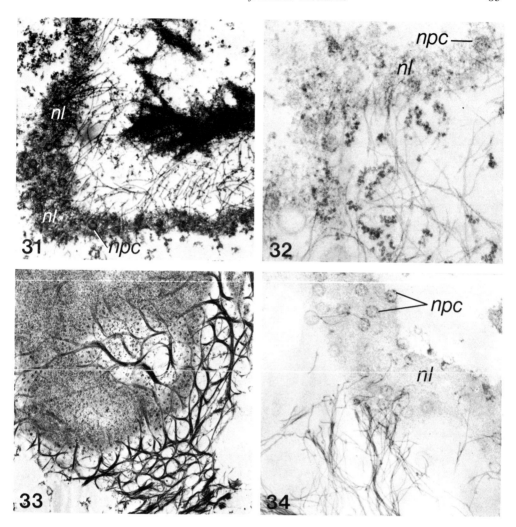

Figs 31–34. Electron micrographs of thin sections of the nuclear regions of IF-enriched cytoskeletons of CEF (Fig. 31), BHK (Fig. 32) and PME (Figs 33, 34) cells. Note the close associations between IF and the nuclear surface and in some cases nuclear pore complexes (*npc*). The nuclear lamin region is also evident (*nl*). Fig. 31, ×23 800; Fig. 32, ×48 000; Fig. 33, ×3700; Fig. 34, ×37 000.

Besides the major building-block proteins that make up the walls of IF, there are numerous other proteins that are consistently found in these IF-enriched cytoskeletons. In the majority of such preparations studied to date, which include several types of fibroblasts, epithelial cells and nerve cells, we have identified several proteins in the 60–70 K range (Fig. 37). In the case of BHK cytoskeletal preparations, there are four polypeptides of 60 K, 65 K, 67 K and 70 K (Fig. 37; and Zackroff *et al.* 1984). We have been able to purify these proteins as paracrystalline arrays (Figs 39, 40) and to demonstrate their keratin-like nature on the basis of their amino acid composition, their alpha-helix content and their cross-reactivity with antibodies directed against keratin (Zackroff *et al.* 1984; Goldman *et al.* 1986). Antibodies directed against these proteins have been prepared and when used in indirect immunofluorescence they generate a bright ring around the edge of the

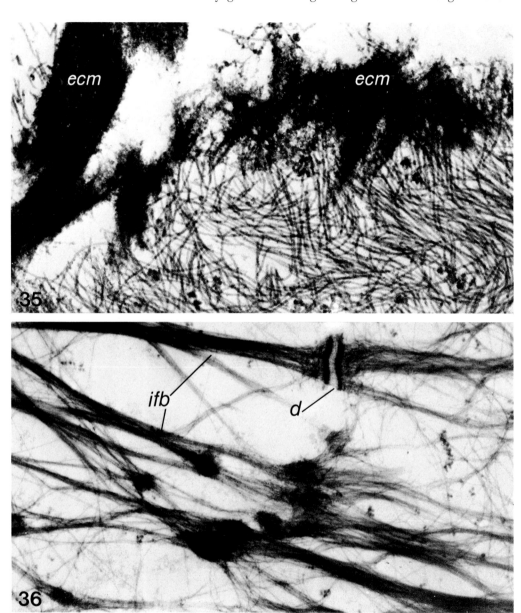

Fig. 35. An electron micrograph of a thin section through a region of the surface of a CEF IF-enriched cytoskeleton showing IF and fibronectin-enriched structures in the ECM (*ecm*). ×43 000.

Fig. 36. An electron micrograph of a thin section through a region of the surface of contacting PME cell cytoskeletons showing IF bundles (*ifb*, arrows) and a desmosome (*d*). ×45 000.

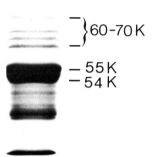

−300 K

}60-70 K

− 55 K
− 54 K

Fig. 37. SDS–PAGE analysis of a BHK cytoskeletal preparation containing the major 54 K (desmin) and 55 K (vimentin) IF structural proteins as well as the 60–70 K and 300 K components.

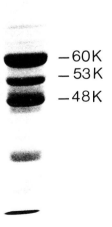

−60K
− 53K
−48K

Fig. 38. SDS–PAGE analysis of a cytoskeletal preparation of PME cells. Note the major keratin IF structural proteins of 48, 53 and 60 K.

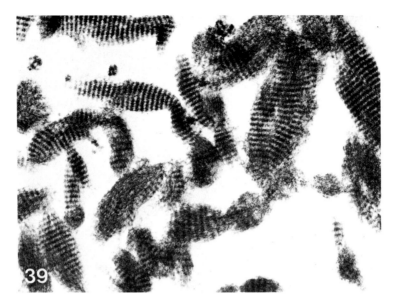

Fig. 39. An electron micrograph of a thin section through a pellet of paracrystals prepared from BHK IF-enriched cytoskeletons as described by Goldman *et al.* (1986). ×40 500.

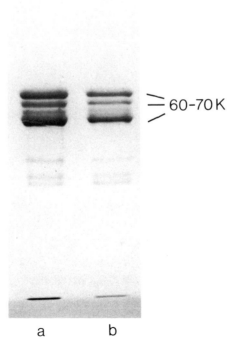

a   b

Fig. 40. SDS–PAGE analysis of paracrystals as prepared from BHK cytoskeletons (lane a) and a fraction of morphologically identical paracrystals prepared from *bona fide* nuclear lamins isolated from BHK nuclei (lane b) (Goldman *et al.* 1986). Note the enrichment of the four 60–70 K proteins seen in Fig. 37.

nucleus and diffuse fluorescence throughout the nuclear matrix (Fig. 41; and Goldman *et al.* 1985, 1986), indicating that this set of IF-like proteins is concentrated at the nuclear surface. From their size and cellular location, these proteins appear to be very similar to a set of nuclear matrix-derived proteins, which have been termed the nuclear lamins (Gerace *et al.* 1984), and which are thought to comprise the nuclear lamina. Indeed, we have been able to demonstrate that *bona fide* nuclear lamins derived from isolated BHK nuclei (Fig. 40) form identical paracrystalline arrays as described for the 60–70 K proteins that co-isolate in the IF-enriched cytoskeletal preparations (Goldman *et al.* 1986). Furthermore, antibodies directed against the nuclear lamins recognize the 60–70 K cytoskeletal polypeptides and *vice versa* (Goldman *et al.* 1986). Moreover, it has recently been shown that nuclear lamin sequences derived from cDNA clones are homologous to keratin sequences (McKeon *et al.* 1986).

   Therefore it appears that the peripheral region of the nucleus contains a set of IF-like proteins. This latter term is used to describe these proteins, which have numerous biochemical and immunological properties indicating their similarities to the IF protein family, yet they appear to be incapable of forming IF either *in situ* or *in vitro*. These 60–70 K keratin-like proteins are probably major structural constituents of the fine fibrillar material associated with the ends of the IF as seen in Fig. 32. We find these results intriguing as they suggest, but by no means prove, that the 60–70 K proteins may comprise a binding domain to which the cytoskeletal IF may be anchored, albeit indirectly (see below; Goldman *et al.* 1985, 1986). These results are even more provocative if one considers the possibility that the nuclear lamina and its constituent proteins are thought to be involved in the attachment of chromatin to the nuclear surface, and in this fashion may be involved in regulating gene activity (Gerace *et al.* 1984). It is conceivable, therefore, that an insoluble, relatively amorphous IF-like protein system localized at the nuclear surface may interact with the cytoplasmic IF system, providing a skeletal continuum involved in nuclear–cytoplasmic communication. However, it should be emphasized that this is speculative as there are no known molecular connecting links between cytoplasmic IF and the nuclear IF-like system. If such connecting links exist, they would probably be in the form of complex transmembranous elements or transnuclear pore-complex components (Goldman *et al.* 1986).

   There are also higher molecular weight components in the IF-enriched cytoskeletal preparations, some of which have been investigated using biochemical and immunochemical approaches. For example, in fibroblasts such as BHK and CEF there is a doublet or triplet of polypeptides at approximately 220 K, which by immunoblotting analyses are recognized by fibronectin antibody preparations (Fig. 42; and Green & Goldman, 1986). Furthermore, fibronectin is absent in the cytoskeletal preparations if they are prepared from freshly trypsinized cells, lending support to the idea that IF are part of a 'cell membrane complex', as mentioned above (Green & Goldman, 1986).

   In the case of BHK cytoskeletal preparations we have initiated studies on a 300 K protein, which we have termed the 300 K IFAP (IF-associated protein) (Yang *et al.*

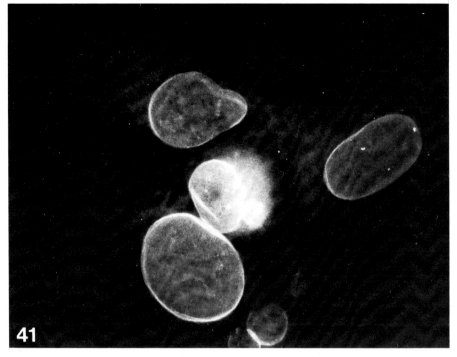

Fig. 41. An indirect immunofluorescence micrograph of BHK cells fixed and reacted with a monoclonal antibody that reacts with the 60–70 K proteins present in the IF-enriched cytoskeletons. Note the ring of fluorescence at the edge of the nucleus. ×1100.

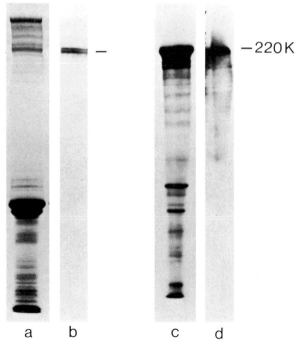

Fig. 42. Western immunoblotting analyses to demonstrate the presence of fibronectin in the IF-enriched preparations obtained from BHK (lanes a, b) and CEF (lanes c, d) cells. Lanes a, c, Amido Black-stained preparations of the polypeptides transferred to nitrocellulose. Lanes b, d, immunoblots using an antibody preparation directed against fibronectin. Note that in both preparations polypeptides of ≈220 K are recognized by the antibody preparation.

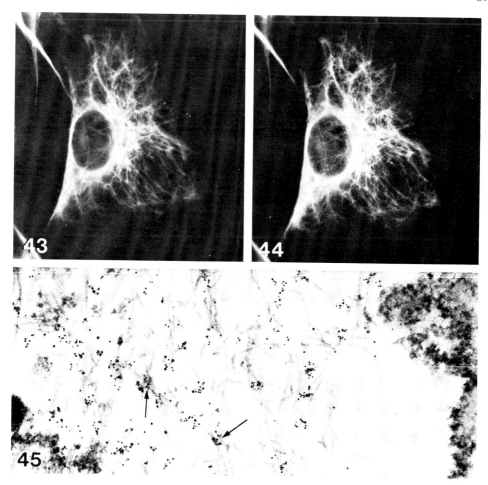

Figs 43, 44. Double-label immunofluorescence of BHK cells using an antibody preparation directed against the 55 K (vimentin) IF subunit (Fig. 37) and a monoclonal antibody preparation directed against the 300 K IFAP (Fig. 43). Note the coincidence of the patterns generated by these antibody preparations. ×750.

Fig. 45. An electron micrograph of a thin section of a BHK cell prepared for indirect immunogold localization using a monoclonal antibody preparation directed against the 300 K IFAP as described by Yang *et al.* (1985). Note that gold particles are present mainly in areas where IF appear to associate with each other (arrows). ×71 500.

1985). A monoclonal antibody has been prepared that reacts specifically with this protein and in double-label immunofluorescence assays, it appears to co-localize with IF (Figs 43, 44; and Yang *et al.* 1985). Observations made using the immunogold method at the ultrastructural level, indicate that this protein is localized in areas of close association between IF, indicating an involvement in cross-linking IF to IF (Fig. 45). More recently, we have been able to purify this protein and to demonstrate that it forms complexes with *in vitro*-reconstituted IF (Lieska *et al.* 1985).

We have also spent considerable time studying some of the high molecular weight proteins associated with IF in cultured epidermal cells (Jones & Goldman, 1985).

One of these turns out to be desmoplakin (Franke *et al.* 1983), a proposed component of the desmosomal plaque (see above). Indeed, the possibility that desmoplakin might represent another species of IFAP is suggested by its association with bundles of IF found in juxtanuclear complexes long before desmosome assembly occurs in PME cells grown in medium containing low levels of calcium (Figs 46, 47; and Jones & Goldman, 1985). This association has also been shown by immunogold localization (Jones & Goldman, 1985) and by immunoblotting analyses of IF-enriched cytoskeletal preparations made before and at various times after the initiation of desmosome assembly, following the switch to higher levels of calcium in the growth medium (Fig. 48; and Jones & Goldman, 1985). Moreover, once desmosome assembly has occurred and normal IF–desmosome complexes have formed along the borders of contiguous epidermal cells, cytoskeletons can be prepared using the method described above. We have found that the cytoskeletal preparations of these cells retain their intercellular desmosomal contacts by morphological criteria (see Fig. 36; and Jones *et al.* 1982; Jones & Goldman, 1985), and that desmoplakins 1 and 2 are both major constituents of the IF-enriched cytoskeletons (Fig. 48; and Jones & Goldman, 1985).

At this juncture it is worth reviewing briefly some of our work on the desmosomal system, specifically with regard to its subfractionation into constituent cytoplasmic and cell surface domains. With regard to the cell surface domains, we have been able

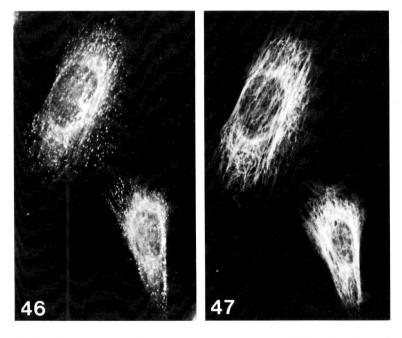

Figs 46, 47. Double-label indirect immunofluorescence of PME cells using a desmoplakin antibody preparation (Fig. 46) and a keratin antibody preparation (Fig. 47). The cells were maintained in medium containing low levels of Ca^{2+} for 48 h prior to fixation. Note that under these conditions desmoplakin-staining bodies (Fig. 46) appear concentrated in a juxtanuclear region where IF bundles (Fig. 47) are also found. ×900.

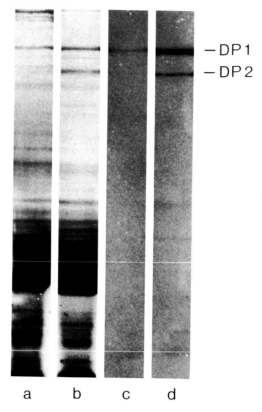

Fig. 48. Western immunoblotting analyses of PME cytoskeletal preparations isolated from cells maintained in low levels of Ca^{2+} (lanes a, c) or from PME cells 24 h following the initiation of desmosome assembly by increasing the extracellular Ca^{2+} concentration (lanes b, d). Lanes a, c, Amido Black-staining of polypeptides in these preparations. Lanes c, d, immunoblots using an antibody preparation directed against desmoplakin. Both cytoskeletal preparations possess high molecular weight polypeptides that are recognized by desmoplakin antibodies. In the case of the cytoskeletons isolated from PME cells maintained in low Ca^{2+} medium, a 250 K polypeptide (desmoplakin, DP1) appears present. However, both desmoplakins 1 and 2 (DP1 and DP2) are present in the cytoskeletal preparations isolated from PME cells 24 h following the initiation of desmosome assembly.

to determine that there are glycoproteins present that represent cell-type-specific adhesion molecules. The first clues that suggested that desmosomes might contain specific cell–cell adhesion (CAM) molecules came from studies of human auto-antibodies found in patients with pemphigus, a blistering disease of the skin (Beutner *et al.* 1970; Lever & Schaumberg-Lever, 1983). In this disease, blister formation is coincident with a loss of cell–cell adhesion in the epidermis, followed by cell death (Beutner *et al.* 1970; Lever & Schaumberg-Lever, 1983). This process is known as acantholysis. The acantholytic process takes place either in the suprabasal cell layer or in the upper cell layers of the epidermis. In the former case, the disease subclass is termed pemphigus vulgaris, while in the latter case it is called pemphigus foliaceus (Beutner *et al.* 1970; Lever & Schaumberg-Lever, 1983).

Immunofluorescence analyses have indicated that at least some of the antibodies found in the serum of patients with this autoimmune disease are directed against desmosomal components (Figs 49, 50; Jones *et al.* 1984, 1986*a*), and that these sera induce the separation of adherent keratinocytes in culture (Jones *et al.* 1984). Furthermore, immunoblotting analyses using cell-free preparations of bovine desmosomes (Fig. 51; and Jones *et al.* 1986*a*) indicate that there are several major antigens with which pemphigus serum samples react. In the case of pemphigus vulgaris, the majority of patients exhibit a reaction with a 140 K glycoprotein found primarily in bovine tongue mucosa desmosomes (Jones *et al.* 1986*a*), while in some pemphigus foliaceus patients, the most obvious consistent reaction is with a doublet of proteins in the 160–165 K range (Fig. 51; and Koulu *et al.* 1984; Jones *et al.* 1986*a*). The pemphigus vulgaris reaction is not detectable in desmosomes derived from a closely related stratified squamous epithelial tissue obtained from the epidermis of cow snouts (Jones *et al.* 1986*a*). Since these initial observations, we have prepared rabbit antibodies directed against this 140 K protein. We have been able to determine that this antibody preparation induces cell separation in living cultured mouse keratinocytes possessing desmosomal junctions, and furthermore recognizes a cell surface component (Jones *et al.* 1986*b*). More recently we have been able to demonstrate that this glycoprotein is present in membrane fractions obtained from bovine tongue desmosomes following extraction with urea (Fig. 52; and Jones *et al.* unpublished). Indeed, the 140 K protein possesses the characteristics of a cell adhesion molecule, i.e. it is a glycoprotein located on the cell surface, and an antibody directed against it disrupts cell–cell interactions (Edelman, 1982).

We have also been attempting to determine the nature of the cytoplasmic domains of isolated desmosomes (Fig. 53). In the urea-soluble fraction of desmosome preparations there is enrichment for desmoplakin and several polypeptides in the 50–65 K range that react with keratin antibodies. However, we have been unable to assemble IF from this urea-soluble fraction when it is placed into keratin assembly buffers. Indeed, under these conditions, a precipitate is formed that contains fibrillar material with no obvious IF (Fig. 54; and Jones *et al.* unpublished). This material appears to be morphologically similar to the fine fibrillar region that comprises the innermost (cytoplasmic) portion of the desmosome to which IF appear to attach *in situ* (Jones *et al.* 1986*b*). We are tempted to speculate that the interaction of desmoplakin with these keratins may reflect a mechanism by which IF associate with the desmosomal plaque. On the basis of these observations we hope to be in a position to study the 'chain' of molecules that is involved in interactions between the IF bundles of neighbouring cells *via* their desmosomal junctions.

SUMMARY AND CONCLUSIONS

The data reviewed in this paper provide support for the hypothesis that the IF system and its associated proteins may represent a chain of molecular connecting links between the nucleus and the cell surface. To date, we believe that we have characterized a number of links in this chain that has suggested to us that the IF

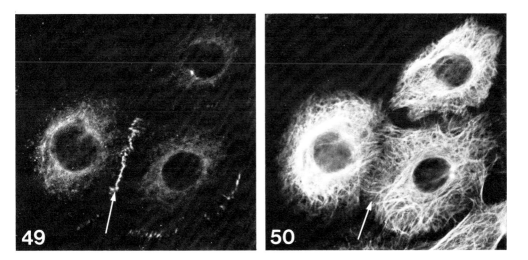

Figs 49, 50. Desmosome possessing PME cells prepared for double-label indirect immunofluorescence using a pemphigus vulgaris serum sample (Fig. 48) and a keratin antibody preparation (Fig. 49). Note that the pemphigus autoantibodies generate a staining pattern along areas of cell–cell contact where IF bundles of neighbouring cells associate and where desmosomes are located (arrows). ×800.

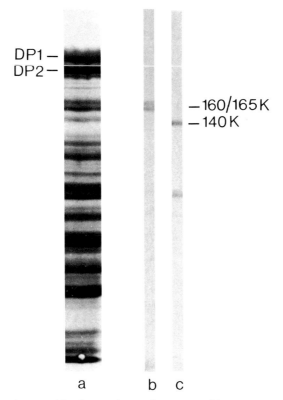

Fig. 51. Western immunoblotting analyses of two pemphigus serum samples using a bovine tongue mucosa desmosome-enriched fraction as a substrate (Jones *et al.* 1986*a*). Lane a, Amido Black staining of the polypeptides present in the desmosome-enriched fraction. Autoantibodies present in the serum of the pemphigus foliaceus patient recognize 160/165 K polypeptides in the desmosome fraction (lane b), while autoantibodies in the serum from a pemphigus patient with pemphigus vulgaris recognize a 140 K polypeptide in the same preparation. The desmoplakins are also indicated (DP1 and DP2 in lane a).

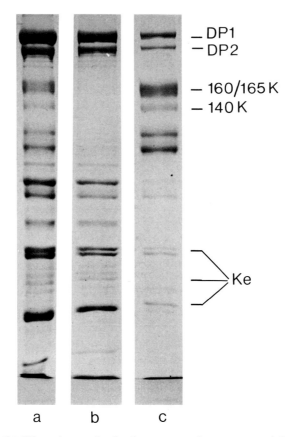

DP1
DP2

160/165 K
140 K

Ke

a   b   c

Fig. 52. SDS–PAGE analyses of a bovine mucosa desmosome-enriched preparation (lane a) and the 9·5 M-urea-soluble (lane b) and -insoluble (lane c) fractions of the same desmosome preparation (Jones *et al.* 1986). Note the enrichment of the 160/165 K and 140 K polypeptides in the urea-insoluble fraction (lane c). The soluble fraction (lane b) is enriched in desmoplakin 1 and 2 (DP1 and DP2) and certain keratin-like polypeptides (ke).

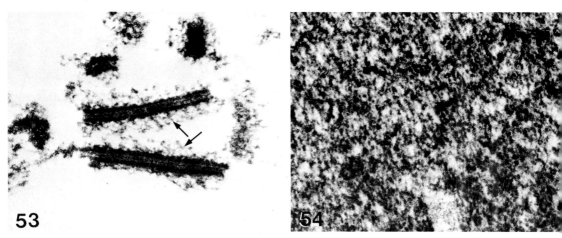

53   54

Figs 53, 54. Electron micrographs of an enriched preparation of bovine mucosa desmosomes (Fig. 53) and fibrillar material reconstituted from the 9·5 M-urea-soluble component of such a preparation (Fig. 54) (Jones *et al.* 1986). Note the similarity between the fibrillar material associated with the desmosome plaque (Fig. 53) (arrows) and the 9·5 M-urea-soluble reconstituted fibrillar material (Fig. 54). ×61 500.

networks in cells may represent a type of variable cytoplasmic infrastructure upon which other reactions or interactions take place. These may include interactions with the plasma membrane–extracellular matrix, interactions with other cytoskeletal components such as microtubules and microfilaments and the nuclear surface–nuclear matrix. Such a system may function in many aspects of cell surface–nuclear interactions, cell–cell adhesion and intercellular cytoskeletal interactions that are important in tissue structure and homeostasis.

We thank Drs James Arnn and Andrew Staehelin for the gift of the desmoplakin antiserum. Dr Ken Yamada kindly provided an antibody directed against fibronectin. We also thank Ms Laura Davis, Manette McReynolds and Jack Gibbons for their assistance in the preparation of the manuscript.

Research support has been provided by grants to Dr Robert D. Goldman from the National Cancer Institute and the National Institutes of General Medical Sciences.

REFERENCES

AARONSON, R. & BLOBEL, G. (1975). On the attachment of the nuclear pore complex. *Proc. natn. Acad. Sci. U.S.A.* **72**, 1007–1011.

ARNN, J. & STAEHELIN, L. A. (1981). The structure and function of spot desmosomes. *Dermatology* **20**, 330–339.

BEUTNER, E., CHORZELSKI, T. & JORDAN, R. (editors) (1970). Autosensitization. In *Pemphigus and Bullous Pemphigoid*, pp. 5–116. Springfield, IL: Charles C. Thomas.

EDELMAN, G. M. (1983). Cell adhesion molecules. *Science* **219**, 450–457.

FRANKE, W., MOLL, R., MULLER, H., SCHMID, E., KUHN, C., KREPLER, R., ARTLIEB, U. & DENK, H. (1983). Immunocytochemical identification of epithelium derived human tumors using antibodies to desmosomal plaque proteins. *Proc. natn. Acad. Sci. U.S.A.* **80**, 543–547.

GERACE, L., BLUM, A. & BLOBEL, G. (1978). Immunocytochemical localization of the major polypeptides of the nuclear pore-lamina fraction. Interphases and mitotic distribution. *J. Cell Biol.* **79**, 546–566.

GERACE, L., COMEAU, C. & BENSON, N. (1984). Organization and modulation of nuclear lamina structure. *J. Cell Sci. Suppl.* **1**, 137–160.

GOLDMAN, A. E., MAUL, A. E., STEINERT, P. M., YANG, H.-Y. & GOLDMAN, R. D. (1986). Keratin-like proteins that coisolate with intermediate filaments of BHK-21 cells are nuclear lamins. *Proc. natn. Acad. Sci. U.S.A.* **83**, 3839–3843.

GOLDMAN, R. D., BERG, C., BUSHNELL, A., CHANG, C., DICKERMAN, N., MILLER, M., POLLACK, R. & WANG, E. (1973). *Fibrillar Systems in Cell Motility. Ciba Symp.*, no. 14, *Locomotion of Tissue Cells*, New York, pp. 83–107. New York: Elsevier-North Holland.

GOLDMAN, R. D., CHOJNACKI, B., GOLDMAN, A., STARGER, J., STEINERT, P., TALIAN, J., WHITMAN, M. & ZACKROFF, R. V. (1981). Aspects of the cytoskeleton and the cytomusculature of non-muscle cells. In *The Cytoskeleton and Nervous System. Neurosci. Res. Prog. Bull.* vol. 19 (ed. F. D. Schmitt), pp. 59–82. Mass: MIT Press.

GOLDMAN, R. & FOLLETT, E. (1970). Birefringent filamentous organelle in BHK-21 cells and its possible role in cell spreading and motility. *Science* **169**, 286–288.

GOLDMAN, R. D., GOLDMAN, A. E., GREEN, K., JONES, J., LIESKA, N., TALIAN, J., YANG, H. & ZACKROFF, R. (1984). Intermediate filaments: Their interactions with various cell organelles and their associated proteins. *J. submicrosc. Cytol.* **16**, 73–74.

GOLDMAN, R., GOLDMAN, A. E., GREEN, K., JONES, J., LIESKA, N. & YANG, H. (1985). Intermediate filaments: Possible functions as cytoskeletal connecting links between the nucleus and the cell surface. *Ann. N.Y. Acad. Sci.* **455**, 1–17.

GOLDMAN, R. D. & KNIPE, D. (1973). Functions of cytoplasmic fibers in non-muscle cell motility. *Cold Spring Harbor Symp. Quant. Biol.* **37**, 523–534.

GREEN, K. J. & GOLDMAN, R. D. (1983). The effects of taxol on cytoskeletal components in cultured fibroblasts and epithelial cells. *Cell Motil.* **3**, 283–305.

GREEN, K. J. & GOLDMAN, R. D. (1986). Evidence for an interaction between the cell surface and intermediate filaments in cultured fibroblasts. *Cell Motil. Cytoskel.* (in press).

GREEN, K. J., TALIAN, J. & GOLDMAN, R. D. (1986). Relationship between intermediate filament and microfilaments in cultured fibroblasts: Evidence for common foci during cell spreading. *Cell Motil. Cytoskel.* (in press).

HENNINGS, H., MICHAEL, D., CHENG, C., STEINERT, P. & HOLBROOK, K. (1980). Calcium regulation of growth and differentiation of mouse epidermal cells in culture. *Cell* **19**, 245–254.

HENNINGS, H. & HOLBROOK, K. (1983). Calcium regulation of cell–cell contact and differentiation of epidermal cells in culture. *Expl Cell Res.* **143**, 127–142.

JONES, J. C. R., ARNN, J., STAEHELIN, L. A. & GOLDMAN, R. D. (1984). Human autoantibodies against desmosomes: Possible causative factors in pemphigus. *Proc. natn. Acad. Sci. U.S.A.* **81**, 2781–2785.

JONES, J. C. R. & GOLDMAN, R. D. (1985). Intermediate filaments and the initiation of desmosome assembly. *J. Cell Biol.* **101**, 509–517.

JONES, J. C. R., GOLDMAN, A., YANG, H.-Y. & GOLDMAN, R. D. (1985). The organizational fate of intermediate filament networks in two epithelial cell type during mitosis. *J. Cell Biol.* **100**, 93–102.

JONES, J. C. R., GOLDMAN, A., YUSPA, S., STEINERT, P. & GOLDMAN, R. D. (1982). Dynamic aspects of the intermediate filament network in keratinocytes. *Cell Motil.* **2**, 197–213.

JONES, J. C. R., YOKOO, K. M. & GOLDMAN, R. D. (1987). Is the hemidesmosome a half desmosome? An immunological comparison of the mammalian desmosome and hemidesmosome. *Cell Motil. Cytoskel.* (in press).

JONES, J. C. R., YOKOO, K. & GOLDMAN, R. (1986*a*). Further analysis of pemphigus autoantibodies and their use in studies on the heterogeneity, structure and function of desmosomes. *J. Cell Biol.* **102**, 1109–1117.

JONES, J. C. R., YOKOO, K. & GOLDMAN, R. D. (1986*b*). A cell surface-desmosome associated component: Identification of a tissue specific cell adhesion molecule. *Proc. natn. Acad. Sci. U.S.A.* (in press).

KELLY, D. E. (1966). Fine structure of desmosomes, hemidesmosomes, and an adepidermal globular layer in developing newt epidermis. *J. Cell Biol.* **28**, 51–72.

KOULU, L., KUSIMI, A., STEINBERG, M., KLAUS-KOVTUN & STANLEY, J. (1984). Human autoantibodies against a desmosomal core protein in pemphigus foliaceus. *J. exp. Med.* **160**, 1509–1518.

LEVER, W. & SCHAUMBERG-LEVER, G. (1983). *Histopathology of the Skin.* 6th edn, pp. 106–114. Scranton, PA: J. B. Lippincott Co.

LIESKA, N., YANG, H. Y. & GOLDMAN, R. D. (1985). Purification of the 33K intermediate filament (IF) associated protein and its *in vitro* recombination with IF. *J. Cell Biol.* **101**, 802–812.

LINCK, R. W., AMOS, L. & AMOS, W. (1985). Localization of tektin filaments in microtubules of sea urchin flagella by immunoelectron microscopy. *J. Cell Biol.* **100**, 126–135.

McKEON, F. D., KIRSCHNER, M. W. & CAPUT, D. (1986). Homologies in both primary and secondary structure between nuclear envelope and intermediate filament proteins. *Nature, Lond.* **319**, 463–468.

MOLL, R., FRANKE, W., SCHILLER, D., GEIGER, B. & KREPLER, R. (1982). The catalog of human cytokeratins: Patterns of expression in normal epithelial tumors and cultured cells. *Cell* **31**, 11–24.

MUELLER, M. & FRANKE, W. (1982). Biochemical and immunological characterization of desmoplakins I and II, the major polypeptides of the desmosomal plaque. *Differentiation* **23**, 189–205.

SINGER, I. (1979). The fibronexus: A transmembrane association of fibronectin-containing fibers and bundles of 5 nm microfilaments in hamster and human fibroblasts. *Cell* **16**, 675–685.

STARGER, J. M., BROWN, W., GOLDMAN, A. & GOLDMAN, R. (1978). Biochemical and immunological analysis of rapidly purified 10 nm filaments from baby hamster kidney (BHK-21) cells. *J. Cell Biol.* **78**, 93–109.

STARGER, J. M. & GOLDMAN, R. D. (1977). Isolation and preliminary characterization of 10 nm filaments from baby hamster kidney (BHK-21) cells. *Proc. natn. Acad. Sci. U.S.A.* **74**, 2422–2426.

STEINERT, P. M., CANTIERI, J. S., TELLER, D. C., LONSDALE-ECCLES, J. D. & DALE, B. A. (1981). Characterization of a class of cationic proteins that specifically interact with intermediate filaments. *Proc. natn. Acad. Sci. U.S.A.* **78**, 4097–4101.

STEINERT, P. M., IDLER, W., AYNARDI-WHITMAN, M., ZACKROFF, R. & GOLDMAN, R. (1982). Heterogeneity of intermediate filaments assembled *in vitro*. *Cold Spring Harbor Symp. quant. Biol.* **46**, 465–474.

STEINERT, P. M., JONES, J. C. R. & JONES, R. D. (1984). Intermediate filaments. *J. Cell Biol.* **99**, 22s–27s.

SUN, T., TSENG, S., HUANG, A., COOPER, D., SCHERMER, A., LYNCH, M., WEISS, R. & EICHNER, R. (1986). Monoclonal antibody studies of mammalian epithelial keratins: A review. *Ann. N.Y. Acad. Sci.* **455**, 307–329.

WANG, E., FISCHMAN, D., LIEM, R. & SUN, T. (1986). Intermediate filaments. *Ann. N.Y. Acad. Sci.* **455**, 832.

YANG, H.-Y., LIESKA, N., GOLDMAN, A. E. & GOLDMAN, R. D. (1985). A 300,000 mol. wt. intermediate filament-associated protein in baby hamster kidney (BHK-21) cells. *J. Cell Biol.* **100**, 620–631.

ZACKROFF, R. V. & GOLDMAN, R. (1979). *In vitro* assembly of intermediate filaments from baby hamster kidney (BHK-21) cells. *Proc. natn. Acad. Sci. U.S.A.* **76**, 6226–6230.

ZACKROFF, R. V., GOLDMAN, A. E., JONES, J., STEINERT, P. & GOLDMAN, R. D. (1984). The isolation and characterization of keratin-like proteins from cultured cells with fibroblastic morphology. *J. Cell Biol.* **98**, 1231–1237.

ZACKROFF, R. V., STEINERT, P. M., AYNARDI-WHITMAN, M. & GOLDMAN, R. D. (1981). *Intermediate Filament in Cytoskeletal Elements and Membrane Organization* (ed. G. Post & G. L. Nicholson), pp. 55–97. New York: Elsevier/North Holland.

J. Cell Sci. Suppl. 5, 99–119 (1986)
Printed in Great Britain © The Company of Biologists Limited 1986

ASSOCIATION OF RNA WITH THE CYTOSKELETON AND THE NUCLEAR MATRIX

EDWARD G. FEY, DAVID A. ORNELLES AND SHELDON PENMAN

Department of Biology, Massachusetts Institute of Technology, 77 Massachusetts Avenue, Cambridge, MA 02139, USA

SUMMARY

Heteronuclear RNA (hnRNA) is preferentially associated (76%) with the nuclear matrix in mammalian cells. Active mRNA, in the form of polyribosomes, is associated (>97%) with the cytoskeletal framework. In this report, we present evidence that the association of both hnRNA and mRNA with structural networks of the cell may be essential features of gene expression.

To study the association of polyribosomes with the cytoskeletal framework, cytochalasin D was used to release mRNA from the cytoskeletal framework. Protein synthesis was inhibited by cytochalasin D in direct proportion to the release of mRNA. The released mRNA is unaltered in its translatability as measured *in vitro* but is no longer translated in the cytochalasin-treated HeLa cells. The residual protein synthesis occurs on polyribosomes that are reduced in amount but display a normal sedimentation distribution. The results support the hypothesis that mRNA binding to the cytoskeletal framework is necessary, though not sufficient, for translation.

Further fractionation of the cytoskeletal framework separates nuclear constituents into three distinct protein fractions. Chromatin proteins and 94% of the DNA are released by 0·25 M-ammonium sulphate after inter-nucleosomal DNA is cut with DNase I. The resulting structure retains 76% of the hnRNA in the form of ribonucleoprotein and is designated the RNP-containing nuclear matrix. The proteins of hnRNP complex are those associated with the nucleus only if RNA is intact. These proteins and 97% of the hnRNA are released after brief digestion with RNase A.

Visualizing the nuclear matrix using resinless sections shows that nuclear RNA plays an important role in the organization of the nuclear matrix. Electron micrographs of resinless sections show the interior of the matrix to be a three-dimensional network of thick filaments bounded by the nuclear lamina. The filaments are densely covered with 20–30 nm electron-dense particles, which may contain the hnRNA. The RNP-depleted matrix is disordered and the interior fibres aggregated. These results suggest that hnRNA is involved in the spatial organization of the interior of the nuclear matrix.

INTRODUCTION

We have developed an *in situ* fractionation protocol for mammalian cells that involves extraction with detergents and salt, and digestion with nuclease. This procedure is optimized to preserve cell morphology as retained by the structural elements of the cell. In the initial step, virtually all phospholipid and approximately 70% of the protein is removed from the cell by extraction in a buffer containing 0·5% Triton X-100 (Fey *et al.* 1984). The resulting cytoskeletal framework is a complex structure that retains > 97% of the polyribosomes. Considerable evidence indicates that eukaryotic polyribosomes are bound to the structural networks of the cell. Biochemical evidence for this association is largely based on detergent extraction, which removes the soluble phase from cell structure. In these studies, polyribosomes remain bound to the detergent-isolated cell structures (Ben-Ze'ev *et al.* 1981; Cervera *et al.* 1981; Fulton *et al.* 1980; Howe & Hershey, 1984; Lenk & Penman, 1979; Lenk *et al.* 1977; van Venrooij *et al.* 1981). There are mRNA molecules free in the cytoplasm but these are not translated (Cervera *et al.* 1981).

Morphological studies show that the spatial distributions of polyribosomes and mRNA are not random. Polyribosomes in 3T3 cells are preferentially localized in perinuclear regions (Fulton *et al.* 1980). A discrete distribution of actin, tubulin and vimentin mRNA in fibroblasts and myoblasts has been described (Singer & Ward, 1982; Lawrence & Singer, 1986) as well as a differential localization for histone and actin mRNA in the *Xenopus* oocyte (Jeffery, 1984). Such topographical concentrations are difficult to envisage without an underlying, organizing structure to which the polyribosomes and mRNA can bind. Those studies using both detergent extraction and morphological criteria found that the amount and the spatial distribution of polyribosomes were similar before and after the extraction (Fulton *et al.* 1980). It is, therefore, unlikely that the observed polyribosome binding to skeletal structures is due to extraction artifacts. Other components of the protein-synthetic apparatus, including initiation factors (Howe & Hershey, 1984) and an aminoacyl-tRNA synthetase complex (Mirande *et al.* 1985), also appear structure-bound. Furthermore, immunofluorescence experiments have indicated the co-localization of a protein homologous to the cap binding protein with elements of the cytoskeleton (Zumbe *et al.* 1982; reviewed by Nielsen *et al.* 1983).

This report examines the association of polyribosomes with the cytoskeletal framework using cytochalasin D (CD) to disaggregate polyribosomes and release mRNA. These data show that when mRNA is released from the cytoskeletal framework it ceases translation. Most important, the mRNA remaining on the cytoskeletal framework functions at a normal rate. In contrast, the reticulocyte, with its presumably soluble protein-synthetic system, shows no sensitivity to the drug.

When the cytoskeletal framework is further fractionated using ionic detergents, DNase I and ammonium sulphate, the resulting structure is called the ribonucleo-protein (RNP)-containing nuclear matrix (Fey *et al.* 1986). When prepared in the presence of inhibitors of ribonuclease, the nuclear matrix, a structure composed of <5 % of the total cellular protein, is obtained in association with 76 % of the hnRNA.

The distribution of hnRNA in the nucleus was first examined by Bernhard using EDTA regressive staining. These studies suggested that non-nucleolar fibrillo-granular RNP domains existed throughout the interchromatinic regions of the nucleus (Bernhard, 1969; Bernhard & Granboulan, 1963; Moneron & Bernhard, 1969; Puvion & Bernhard, 1975; Swift, 1963). High-resolution autoradiography showed labelled nuclear RNA in these fibrillogranular domains (Fakan & Bernhard, 1971; Fakan *et al.* 1976; Nash *et al.* 1975). The data showed that perichromatinic granules and fibrils near the borders of condensed chromatin contain both nascent and steady-state RNA.

More recent studies of the nuclear matrix have largely been done on isolated nuclei. Chromatin is removed by exposure to high salt (2 M-NaCl) followed by nuclease digestion (Berezney & Bucholtz, 1981; Berezney & Coffey, 1977; Brasch, 1982; Comings & Okada, 1976; Fisher *et al.* 1982). These procedures produce a nuclear matrix with much of the hnRNA still bound (Jackson *et al.* 1981; Long *et al.* 1979; Miller *et al.* 1978; Ross *et al.* 1982; van Eekelen & van Venrooij, 1981). Histones are removed in these procedures causing the chromatin to extend as DNA loops that remain firmly attached to the matrix at sites corresponding to DNA replication points (Berezney & Coffey, 1975; Jackson *et al.* 1984; McCready *et al.* 1980; Mirkovitch *et al.* 1984; Pardoll *et al.* 1980; Vogelstein *et al.* 1980). Steroid receptor binding sites are found on the matrix (Barrack & Coffey, 1980; Diamond & Barrack, 1984) and some actively transcribed genes are preferentially associated with this matrix (Ciejek *et al.* 1983; Dyson *et al.* 1985; Hentzen *et al.* 1984; Maundrell *et al.* 1981; Mirkovitch *et al.* 1984; Nelkin *et al.* 1980; Robinson *et al.* 1982; Ross *et al.* 1982; Small *et al.* 1985).

The procedure described here preserves several important nuclear constituents in the final preparation. In particular, the procedure retains the proteins of the hnRNP complex that are removed by extraction with 2 M-salt (Beyer *et al.* 1977). Several reports of an RNA constituent of non-chromatin nuclear structure have appeared (Berezney, 1980; Brasch, 1982; Comings & Okada, 1976; Gallinaro *et al.* 1983; Herman *et al.* 1978; Kish & Pederson, 1975; Narayan *et al.* 1967; Miller *et al.* 1978; Puvion & Bernhard, 1975). This report shows that chromatin removal is possible without disrupting the RNP-filament domains and suggests that intact hnRNP filaments are essential to the organization of the nuclear matrix.

RESULTS

Purifying the cytoskeletal framework and the RNP-containing nuclear matrix

The fractionation protocol used to obtain both the cytoskeletal framework (CSKF) and the RNP-containing nuclear matrix is described schematically in Fig. 1. The procedure is generally applicable to both suspension and monolayer cells and has been described in detail (Fey *et al.* 1986). Briefly, the cell is fractionated using a sequence of buffers with varied salt and detergent compositions. The CSKF is obtained after removal of Triton-soluble components, and then the nuclear matrix is obtained after further fractionation of the CSKF. Subfractions of the cell are obtained with distinct RNA and protein compositions (Fig. 1). The fractionation also preserves aspects of cellular morphology that are displayed by structural elements of the cell (Fig. 2). The intact cells (Fig. 1A, Fig. 2A) are first extracted with Triton X-100. This extraction removes 70% of cell proteins and almost all of the phospholipids in the 'soluble' (SOL) fraction. The polyribosomes (>97%) remain associated with the CSKF (Fig. 3A). Extraction with Triton X-100 removes much of the 'microtabecular lattice' (Fig. 2A; and Wolosewick & Porter, 1979) leaving the cytoskeletal framework (Fig. 2B). Fig. 2B shows a resinless section micrograph of a HeLa cell after phospholipids and soluble proteins have been removed. The dense trabecular lattice, seen in the intact cell (Fig. 2A), is no longer present. The micrograph of the CSKF (Fig. 2B) reveals the fine structure of filament networks in the cytoplasm. In the nucleus, filaments are visible in the diffuse regions of euchromatin and are continuous with the perichromatin filaments. Some of these

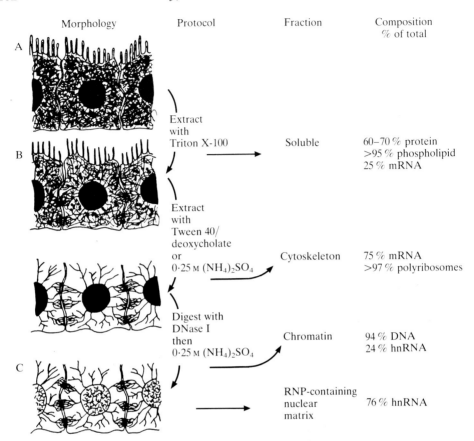

Morphology	Protocol	Fraction	Composition % of total

Fig. 1. Fractionation protocol depicting the morphological structures obtained after successive fractionation steps. Intact monolayer (or suspended) cells (A) are first extracted with a buffer containing 0·5 % Triton X-100 for 10 min at 4°C (for all buffer compositions see Fey *et al.* (1984)). The Triton-soluble proteins, which represent 60–70% of the total cellular protein, are removed leaving the cytoskeletal framework (B). Polyribosomes are quantitatively (>97%) associated with the cytoskeletal framework (CSKF). The polyribosomes and approximately 25% of the cell protein are released from the CSKF by extraction with either 0·25 M-ammonium sulphate or a Tween 40/ deoxycholate-containing buffer. The RNP-containing nuclear matrix (C) is obtained after digestion in 100 μg ml^{-1} DNase I followed by extraction with 0·25 M-ammonium sulphate. hnRNA (76%) is associated with this nuclear matrix structure that is composed of only 5% of the total protein.

Fig. 2. Transmission electron micrographs comparing an intact HeLa nucleus and a HeLa nucleus after extraction with Triton X-100. Intact cells (A) and cells extracted with Triton X-100 (B) were prepared as unembedded sections as described by Fey *et al.* (1986). The intact cell (A), seen in a 0·2 μm section, appears as a 'microtrabecular' structure as described by Wolosewick & Porter (1979). The extracted cell (B) shows the cytoskeletal framework (*cy*), the structure that remains after phospholipid and 70% of the cellular protein is removed. The extracted cell is less dense than the intact cell, yet virtually all the polyribosomes are retained in the cytoplasmic networks and aspects of differentiated chromatin organization are clearly retained in the extracted nucleus (*n*). A fibrillogranular network (*f*) is observed throughout the extracted nucleus. *l*, lamina boundary. Bar, 0·2 μm.

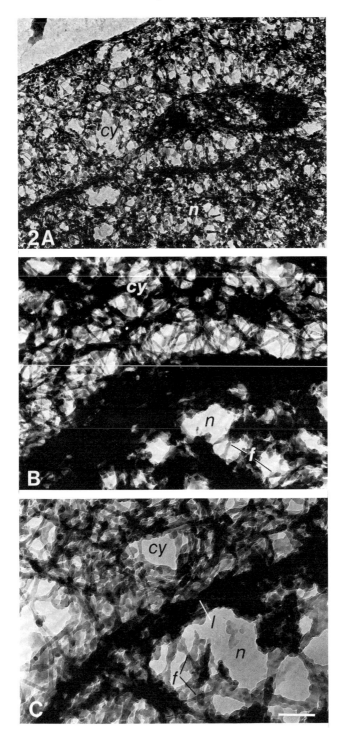

nuclear components are shown below to correspond to RNP structures previously suggested by differential nuclear staining (Fakan & Bernhard, 1971; Fakan *et al.* 1976; Puvion & Bernhard, 1975).

In the second step of the fractionation, the cytoskeletal proteins are extracted with a buffer containing Tween 40/deoxycholate or 0·25 M-ammonium sulphate. The polyribosomes and approximately 25 % of the total protein are removed from the cell scaffold after this extraction. This fraction has been designated the 'cytoskeleton' (CSK) fraction. The remaining structure is incubated in a digestion buffer containing DNase I, and after digestion the DNA and associated histones are released from the nucleus by extraction in 0·25 M-ammonium sulphate. The DNA (94 %), histones and approximately 10 % of the total protein are released by this digestion/extraction in the 'chromatin' (CHROM) fraction. The RNP-containing nuclear

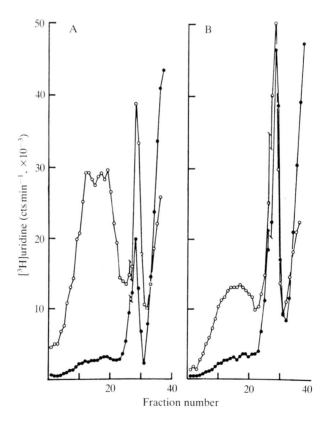

Fig. 3. Distribution of polyribosomes between the SOL and CSK fractions of control and CD-treated HeLa cells. Monolayer cultures of HeLa cells were labelled with [³H]uridine overnight, exposed to dimethylsulphoxide (DMSO) (A) or 8 μg ml⁻¹ CD for 20 min (B) and fractionated as described in Materials and Methods. Material from equivalent numbers of cells was loaded onto each sucrose gradients. (●——●) SOL fraction; (○——○) CSK fraction. Total gradient radioactivity recovered from control cells was 1·29×10⁶ cts min⁻¹; from CD-treated cells, 1·23×10⁶ cts min⁻¹. Values plotted for fractions above number 26 are scaled down by a factor of 0·6. In both cases, the polyribosomes are quantitatively (>97 %) associated with the cytoskeletal framework.

matrix (Fig. 1C, Fig. 2C), consisting of $< 5\%$ of the total protein and 76% of the hnRNA is obtained after the chromatin.

Release of polyribosomes from the CSKF by cytochalasin D

The drug cytochalasin D (CD) was used to study the association of polyribosomes with the CSKF. Treatment of cells with CD has almost no effect on the measured protein content and composition of the CSKF. Suspension-grown HeLa cells were prelabelled with [^{35}S]methionine, treated with CD and fractionated as described above. The soluble components are released by non-ionic detergent extraction. The resulting nuclei-containing CSKFs are further extracted with the mixed detergent, Tween-40 and deoxycholate, in low ionic strength buffer. This second extraction removes most of the CSKF proteins from the nucleus. The fraction solubilized by the mixed detergent is termed the cytoskeleton and it includes many cytoplasmic components of the CSKF, including the filamentous actin and essentially all of the cell polyribosomes (Lenk *et al.* 1977). The separated nuclear fraction includes the chromatin and associated proteins, hnRNP, and the nuclear matrix (Capco *et al.* 1982; Fey *et al.* 1986). In accord with other reports, the intermediate filaments are retained with the isolated nucleus (Bravo *et al.* 1982; Capco *et al.* 1982; Fey *et al.* 1984; Fey *et al.* 1986; Staufenbiel & Deppert, 1982; Woodcock, 1980).

Cytochalasin D does not alter the composition of protein fractions

The data in Table 1 show that there is no loss of total [^{35}S]methionine-labelled protein after treatment with cytochalasin D. Therefore, processes leading to significant reduction in cell mass, such as cytoplasmic extrusion and enucleation, were not significant during the course of these experiments. The data in Table 1 further show that exposure to CD has no gross effect on the composition of the CSK fraction. Electrophoretograms of the [^{35}S]methionine-labelled proteins in the SOL and CSK fractions were examined by Ornelles *et al.* (1986). The pattern of labelled CSK proteins obtained from cells exposed to 2 μg ml^{-1} CD was indistinguishable from the control. The CSK proteins obtained from cells treated with 64 μg ml^{-1} CD were also similar to the control though two differences were apparent at the high drug

Table 1. *Distribution of [^{35}S]methionine-labelled proteins following a 30-min exposure to cytochalasin D*

Subcellular fraction	Cytochalasin D (μg ml^{-1})		
	0	2	64
SOL	1325	1343	1302
CSK	314	320	296
NUC	146	149	152
Total	**1785**	**1812**	**1750**

NUC, nuclear fraction.
Expressed as the acid-precipitable radioactivity per 1000 cells.

concentration. There was an apparent increase in the amount of CSK proteins migrating in the region of actin at 42–44 ($\times 10^3$) M_r and a small reduction in proteins migrating in the lower molecular weight range, between 18 and 27 ($\times 10^3$) M_r. Proteins in this lower molecular weight range include the ribosomal proteins (Lastick & McConkey, 1976). Their decrease may reflect the loss of polyribosomes from the CSKF at the higher concentration of CD (described below).

CD releases polyribosomes from the CSKF and inhibits protein synthesis

Although CD does not change the protein composition of the CSK fraction, high levels of the drug do dissociate polyribosomes from the cytoskeletal framework. To show this, HeLa cell RNA was labelled for 12 h with [^{3}H]uridine. The cells were then exposed to CD for 30 min and the polyribosomes prepared. Fig. 3 shows the resulting polyribosome profiles and their partition between the SOL and CSK fractions. Fig. 3A shows that greater than 97 % of the polyribosomes are bound to the cytoskeleton framework. This value is in agreement with previous results (Cervera *et al.* 1981; Lenk *et al.* 1977). Polyribosomes from cells exposed to 8 μg ml^{-1} CD are shown in Fig. 3B. This concentration of CD inhibits protein synthesis by approximately 50 %. The amount of polyribosomes is also reduced by 50 % at this drug concentration. Although reduced in amount, the size (or sedimentation distribution) of the polyribosomes that remain associated with the CSKF is unchanged by CD. Few, if any, other inhibitors of protein synthesis produce this type of polyribosome sedimentation distribution (Vazquez, 1979).

Previous results suggested that polyribosomes are linked to the cytoskeletal framework by their mRNA (Cervera *et al.* 1981; Lenk *et al.* 1977). Other experiments showed that mRNA not bound to the CSKF is also not translated. Taken together, these observations suggested that the binding of mRNA to the CSKF may be obligatory for its translation. The experiments presented here show that CD releases portion of the polyribosomes from the CSKF and removes a fraction of the mRNA from translation. The remaining polyribosomes are associated with the CSKF evidently function normally. This phenomenon could be explained if CD released a portion of mRNA from the CSKF and this ceased functioning while the mRNA remaining bound continued to be translated. This hypothesis is supported by the findings described below in which the release of mRNA from the cytoskeletal framework is shown to parallel closely the inhibition of protein synthesis.

Distribution of mRNA

When the distribution of poly(A)$^+$ mRNA was measured using incorporation of [^{3}H]uridine or selection by poly(U) hybridization (Ornelles *et al.* 1986), approximately 75 % of the mRNA was found associated with the cytoskeletal framework in control cells. The remaining 25 % of poly(A) RNA was in the SOL fraction and was not associated with polyribosomes. Cytochalasin D displaces mRNA from the cytoskeletal framework in a dose-dependent manner (Ornelles *et al.* 1986). The amount of mRNA released closely parallels the inhibition of protein synthesis. The data from several experiments are summarized in the bar graph in Fig. 4. At each dose, the proportion of poly(A) retained on the CSKF corresponds to the level of protein synthesis remaining. These data, together with the normal sedimentation profile of the polyribosomes that remain associated with the CSKF, imply that the inhibition of protein synthesis induced by cytochalasin D may be the direct result of the release of mRNA from the cytoskeletal framework.

The experiments described here support the hypothesis that CD inhibits protein synthesis by disrupting the association between mRNA and the cytoskeletal framework. It was of interest to examine what effect the drug would have on protein synthesis in a cell that has no apparent cytoskeletal framework (Rifkind *et al.* 1969). The effect of CD on protein synthesis in intact rabbit reticulocytes was determined. Reticulocytes were prepared from anaemic rabbits and used within 16 h of isolation at which time more than 99% of the cells excluded Trypan Blue. The reticulocytes were washed in PBS and diluted in serum-free MEM with 1/10 the normal amount of methionine and the cells were pulse-labelled with [^{35}S]methionine after a 30-min exposure to the drug. Suspension-cultured HeLa cells were treated in a similar manner. Fig. 5 shows the acid-precipitable radioactivity expressed as a percentage of the untreated culture in the two cell types. HeLa cells show the expected inhibition of protein synthesis. In contrast, the rabbit reticulocytes show no detectable inhibition of protein synthesis over the range of concentrations of CD tested.

Heteronuclear RNA is associated with the nuclear matrix

The skeletal framework, obtained by detergent extraction in physiological buffer, is extracted with double detergent or with buffered 0·25 M-ammonium sulphate as

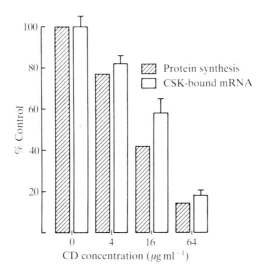

Fig. 4. Concomitant inhibition of protein synthesis and release of mRNA from the cytoskeletal framework. The inhibition of protein synthesis represented at each concentration indicated is obtained from the best fit of a dose–response curve (Ornelles *et al.* 1986). The % poly(A)$^+$ RNA retained is expressed as % of the cytoplasmic poly(A)$^+$ retained on the cytoskeletal framework in untreated cells. The S.E.M. for each group is indicated (0 μg ml^{-1}, $n = 7$; 4 μg ml^{-1}, $n = 4$; 16 μg ml^{-1}, $n = 3$; 64 μg ml^{-1}, $n = 5$).

described above. The solubilized proteins are largely from the cytoplasm and constitute a unique subset of cellular proteins (Fey *et al.* 1986). Few proteins in this fraction are shared with the remaining nuclear fractions described below. The intermediate filaments remain associated with both intact nuclei and extracted matrix preparations.

Removal of chromatin from the nucleus

DNA and the associated chromatin proteins are separated from the nuclear matrix using conditions that preserve the stability of RNP complexes (Beyer *et al.* 1977). Our experiments show that high ionic strength (2 M-NaCl), often used to remove histones prior to digestion of chromatin, significantly alters the interior nuclear morphology (Fey *et al.* 1986). In the experiments described here, chromatin is first digested with purified DNase I in physiological buffer (100 mM-NaCl, 10 mM-PIPES, pH 6·8, 3 mM-MgCl$_2$). The nuclease cuts the DNA between the nucleosomes and chromatin is eluted as DNA–nucleosome complexes after the addition of 0·25 M-ammonium sulphate. Vanadyl adenosine is present to inhibit ribonuclease activity and prevent hnRNA degradation. This chromatin fraction contains 94 % of the DNA, greater than 95 % of the histones and 70 % of the non-histone nuclear proteins (Table 2).

To follow the partition of histones during fractionation, HeLa cells were labelled for 2 h with [^{3}H]lysine and fractionated. The lysine-labelled nuclear proteins were analysed on a 15 % polyacrylamide gel. The electrophoretogram in Fig. 6 shows that

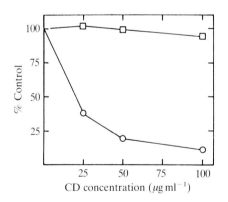

Fig. 5. Failure of CD to affect protein synthesis in intact reticulocytes. Cells were washed with PBS and resuspended at 5×10^7 reticulocytes or 10^6 HeLa cells per ml in medium containing 1/10 normal methionine. CD in DMSO carrier was added to the concentrations indicated, adjusting the amount of DMSO to 2 % of culture volume in all cases. The cultures were incubated for 30 min with the addition of 150 μCi ml^{-1} [^{35}S]methionine during the final 10 min of the treatment. The cells were extensively washed in PBS then lysed in buffer containing sodium dodecyl sulphate (SDS). Samples were decolorized by H$_2$O$_2$ and NaOH and the acid-precipitable radiolabelled proteins were determined. The results are expressed as % of the untreated sample where the control level of incorporation represented 2·08 cts min^{-1} per HeLa cell, 0·23 cts min^{-1} per reticulocyte. HeLa protein synthesis (O——O); reticulocyte protein synthesis (□——□).

the first exposure to ammonium sulphate, prior to digestion with DNase, releases histone H1 but the core histones remain with the nucleus. Subsequent elution with 0·25 M-ammonium sulphate after the DNase I digestion releases >95% of the core histones in the chromatin fraction.

Table 2. *Distribution (%) of nuclear components after fractionation*

Fraction	Protein*	hnRNA†	DNA‡
CHROM	70	24	94
N·RNP	4	73	4
NM·IF	26	3	2

CHROM, chromatin fraction; N·RNP, nuclear RNP; NM·IF, RNP-depleted nuclear matrix.
* Protein was determined on the basis of labelling with [^{35}S]methionine (see Fey *et al.* 1986).
† hnRNA was measured by pulse-labelling with [^{3}H]uridine in the presence of 0·05 μg ml^{-1} actinomycin D (see Fey *et al.* 1986).
‡ DNA was measured after labelling cells with [^{3}H]thymidine for 12 h (see Fey *et al.* 1986).

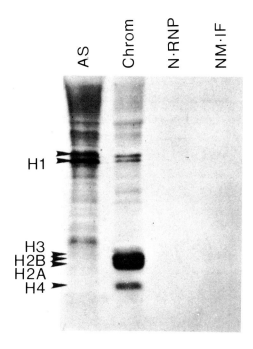

Fig. 6. Localization of histones in the nuclear fractions. HeLa cells were labelled for 2 h with [^{3}H]lysine and fractionated as described in Materials and Methods. Protein fractions from 2×10^{7} cells were separated by gel electrophoresis on a 15% polyacrylamide gel (Laemmli, 1970). Histones were identified on the basis of molecular weight and preferential labelling with lysine. The majority of the core histones (>95%) were localized in the chromatin fraction (Chrom). Fewer than 5% of the core histones were released in the initial elution with ammonium sulphate (AS). The initial salt elution released a significant proportion of histone H1. Trace amounts of histones were observed in the nuclear RNP (N·RNP) and the RNP-depleted nuclear matrix (NM·IF) fractions.

E. G. Fey, D. A. Ornelles and S. Penman

Proteins of the nuclear RNP complex

The RNP filaments of the matrix are an important component of matrix architecture. A brief digestion of the RNP-containing matrix with RNase A removes 97 % of the hnRNA (Table 2). Consequently, proteins associated with the matrix by RNA are released quantitatively. These proteins, referred to here as nuclear RNP, comprise about 4 % of the total nuclear protein (Table 2).

Fig. 7A shows a two-dimensional gel electrophoretogram of proteins from the nuclear RNP fraction. The gel has about 30 major protein spots that are predominantly greater than $30 \times 10^3 M_r$ and have a wide range of isoelectric points.

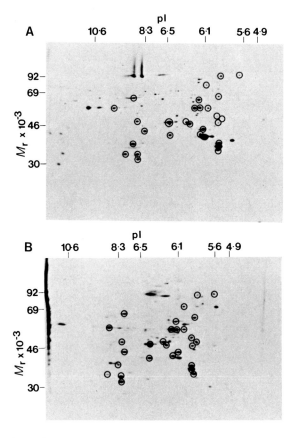

Fig. 7. Comparison of proteins released by treatment with RNase with hnRNP proteins obtained from a standard preparation. HeLa nuclear proteins released by treatment with RNase (A) were obtained as described for Fig. 2. hnRNP complexes (B) were isolated according to the method of Pederson (1974). Proteins (200 cts min^{-1}, $\times 10^{-3}$/fraction) were separated by two-dimensional gel electrophoresis (O'Farrell, 1975). The nuclear RNPs (A) were compared with proteins obtained from a preparation of hnRNP obtained after sucrose gradient separation of a nuclear sonicate (B). Proteins in the nuclear RNP fractions (A) that are common to the hnRNP fraction (B) are indicated by circles. A majority of proteins observed in the hnRNP fraction are also components of the RNA-containing nuclear matrix.

These ribonucleoproteins were compared with those in the nuclear RNP preparation described by Pederson (1974). Ribonucleoprotein particles were prepared from labelled nuclei by sonication. The particles were purified by sedimentation in a sucrose density gradient and proteins were analysed by two-dimensional gel electrophoresis (Fig. 7B). The proteins of the Pederson RNP particle mostly have M_r values greater than 30×10^3. More than 90 % of the Pederson proteins are the same as the RNP proteins obtained here (Fig. 7A).

Electron microscopy of the nuclear matrix preparations

The morphology of the nucleus at different steps in the fractionation was examined using transmission electron microscopy (TEM) of unembedded sections (Capco *et al.* 1984). Fig. 8 shows the resinless-section images of the three nuclear preparations described here. Fig. 8A shows the nucleus of the cytoskeletal framework, Fig. 8B the structure of the RNP-containing nuclear matrix and Fig. 8C the nuclear matrix after the removal of nuclear RNP.

The embeddment-free image of cytoskeletal framework (Fig. 8A) clearly shows the protein filament networks of the cytoplasm and nucleus. Networks of fine filaments extend throughout the nucleus and terminate at the nuclear lamina (arrows; Fig. 8A). Filamentous structures are visible in the diffuse regions of euchromatin and are continuous with the perichromatin filaments. These nuclear components probably correspond to the RNP structures previously suggested by differential nuclear staining (Fakan & Bernhard, 1971; Fakan *et al.* 1976; Puvion & Bernhard, 1975).

Morphology of the RNP-containing nuclear matrix

After digestion with DNase I and elution with 0·25 M-ammonium sulphate, the nuclear matrix is obtained almost free of chromatin. Most of the hnRNA (76 %) remains tightly associated with the nuclear matrix (Table 1). Fig. 8B shows the morphology of the RNP-containing nuclear matrix in a resinless section. This image offers a clear view of the structures inside the nucleus after the chromatin has been removed. The section is thin (0·2 μM) compared to the HeLa cell nucleus (10 μM), so that few sections include the dense nuclear lamina. Fig. 8B shows the interior of the RNP-containing nuclear matrix to be rich in filament networks. A set of 10 nm filaments exterior to the nuclear lamina boundary (*l*) are probably intermediate filaments of vimentin and cytokeratin (Franke *et al.* 1979). The stereoscopic view in Fig. 9 shows that these filaments terminate directly on the surface of the nuclear lamina.

The interior region of the RNP-containing nuclear matrix is filled with an anastomosing network of filaments. Dense clusters of electron-opaque 25–30 nm granules, associated with the fibres, are now visible (*p*, Fig. 8B). These 25–30 nm granules correspond in size to the RNP particles described by Beyer *et al.* (1977), Pederson & Davis (1980), Pullman & Martin (1983) and Samarina *et al.* (1968). The nucleoli (*nu*, Fig. 8B) are large, dense bodies enmeshed in the nuclear matrix filaments. Some empty regions appear in the matrix fibre network, which may result from tearing during sectioning.

Altered morphology of the RNP-depleted nuclear matrix (NM–IF)

Digestion of the RNP-containing nuclear matrix with RNase A removes the RNP components of the nucleus and leaves the nuclear matrix with the associated intermediate filaments. We have previously designated this structure the nuclear matrix–intermediate filament (NM–IF) scaffold (Fey & Penman, 1984, 1986; Fey *et al.* 1984) to denote the apparent role of the intermediate filaments in tissue architecture. Removing the nuclear RNA greatly alters interior matrix morphology. Fig. 8C shows the RNP-depleted matrix (or NM–IF scaffold). Intermediate filaments remain associated with the cytoplasmic face of the nuclear lamina (arrows). Fig. 8C shows the resinless-section image of the RNP-depleted nuclear matrix. The morphology is greatly altered from the RNP-containing nuclear matrix in Fig. 8B. Removal of hnRNP results in marked distortion of overall nuclear shape. Few dense aggregates replace the interior network of 20–30 nm filaments. Many of the 20–30 nm granules of the interior fibres of the RNP–matrix have been removed by the digestion, suggesting that they contain RNA. The marked reorganization effected by RNase indicates a role of nuclear RNP in organizing the nuclear interior.

A powerful feature of embeddment-free electron microscopy stems from its imaging the entire contents of a sample and not just the stained surface of a section. Consequently, the resinless sections offer striking stereoscopic views of three-dimensional organization that can be obtained in no other way. Fig. 9 shows a stereoscopic micrograph of a $0.2 \mu m$ section of the RNP-containing matrix taken at $5° (\pm)$ tilt angles. The stereoscopy shows the lamina (l) to be a spherical shell with cytoplasmic filaments fibres terminating throughout its exterior surface. The nuclear

---

Fig. 8. TEM comparing fractionated HeLa nuclei in unembedded resin-free sections. Nuclei obtained after extraction with Triton X-100 (A), RNA-containing nuclear matrices (B), and RNA-depleted nuclear matrices (C) were prepared as described by Fey *et al.* (1986). Nuclear preparations were fixed in glutaraldehyde, postfixed in OsO_4 and embedded in the removable embedding compound diethylene glycol distearate (DGD). A. The organization of chromatin is seen after extraction with Triton X-100. The retention of differentiated regions of heterochromatin (h), euchromatin (e) and nucleoli (nu) is observed in this section. Detail of filaments in the perichromatinic space (p) and the association of cytoplasmic filaments with the nuclear lamina (arrows) are also observed. B. Chromatin and associated proteins were removed as described, and the resulting RNP-containing nuclear matrix revealed a dense interior matrix of fibres (f) that extends throughout the nucleus, forming continuous associations between nucleoli and the nuclear lamina (l). Cytoplasmic filaments were again observed in association with the nuclear lamina (arrows). C. Nuclear RNA was removed with RNase A and the RNA-depleted nuclear matrices were examined as above. The RNP-depleted nuclear matrices display a distortion of nuclear shape. The interior of the nuclear matrix, after digestion with ribonuclease, is composed of large filament aggregates (fa). These structures are larger than the filaments (f) seen in (B). These aggregates appear condensed and fragmented. Both the loss of gross nuclear shape and the distortion of the interior by digestion with RNase suggest that RNA is an important structural component of the nucleus. Unembedded sections are $0.2 \mu m$ thick. Bars, $1.0 \mu m$.

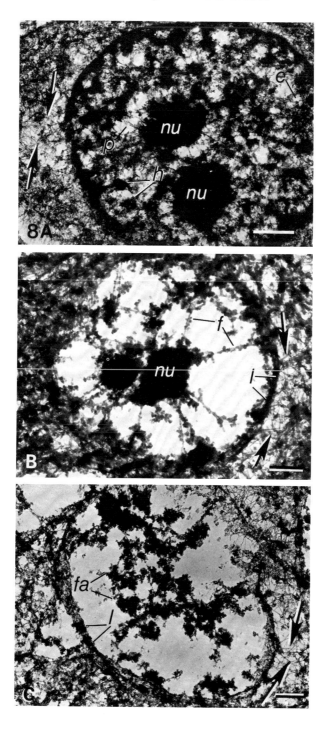

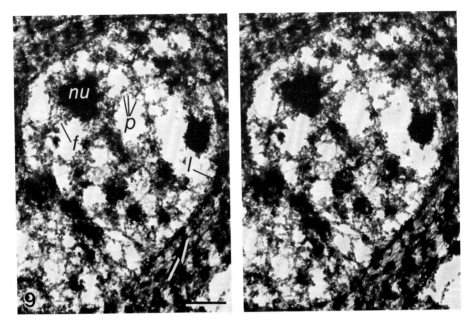

Fig. 9. Stereo transmission electron micrograph of the RNA-depleted nuclear matrix. Sections (0·2 μm thick) of RNA-depleted nuclear matrix were examined in stereo (total tilt 10°, ±5°). Although there is distortion of the structure of the nuclear in the NM–IF preparation, many aspects of three-dimensional cellular organization are retained. The lamina (*l*) retains an interaction with the system of cytoplasmic filaments (arrow) that has a regularity in three dimensions observed in the RNP–matrix structure (Fig. 6). The filament aggregates inside the nucleus (*f*) show little structural regularity and have lost the continuity characteristic of the filaments in the RNP-containing nuclear matrix. See Fig. 8 legend for abbreviations. Bar, 1·0 μm.

interior contains a dense nucleolus (*nu*) held apparently suspended in position by a dense network of matrix filaments.

DISCUSSION

In this report, we examine the association of RNA with the non-membranous structural elements of the cell. In the cytoplasmic space mRNA molecules, in the form of polyribosomes, are quantitatively (>97 %) associated with the cytoskeletal framework. Inside the nucleus greater than 75 % of the hnRNA is associated with the nuclear matrix after removal of 94 % of the chromatin. Both of these interactions may be of considerable biological significance. The association of polyribosomes with the CSKF may be necessary for translation (Cervera *et al.* 1981). The association of hnRNA with the nuclear matrix may be necessary for transcription (Jackson *et al.* 1981). A population of hnRNA molecules may also play a structural role in the organization of chromatin domains in differentiated nuclei.

Cytochalasin D was used to probe the interaction of polyribosomes with the CSKF. The release of mRNA from the CSKF by CD is used to probe this interaction. At sufficiently high concentrations, CD inhibits protein synthesis in an unusual manner. CD reduces the amount of polyribosomes in proportion to the degree of inhibition. The remaining polyribosomes, which retain an association with the CSKF, are unaltered in their sedimentation distribution. This pattern of inhibition could not result from simple lesions in initiation or elongation that lead to altered polyribosome distributions (Vazquez, 1979). The results are consistent with a model where, in the presence of CD, a portion of the mRNA molecules is withdrawn from active translation. In parallel with this withdrawal from translation, the mRNA molecules are released from the CSKF to the soluble phase. The mRNAs released from the CSKF cease translation while the mRNA remaining bound to the CSKF translates normally. Since a number of investigators have shown that removing the ribosomes from the mRNA by a variety of means does not release mRNA from the CSKF (Bonneau *et al.* 1985; Cervera *et al.* 1981; Howe & Hershey, 1984; van Venrooij *et al.* 1981), the release of these molecules is probably prior to and not a consequence of the cessation of translation. A likely interpretation of the results is that freeing mRNA from the CSKF removes it from translation.

CD is an effective but unusual inhibitor of protein synthesis. The inhibition becomes noticeable at concentrations just above those commonly used to alter cell morphology. The polyribosome profiles in Fig. 3 show the unusual mode of protein synthesis inhibition. The polyribosomes in cytochalasin-D-treated cells are reduced in amount but exhibit a normal sedimentation distribution. The reduction of polyribosome mass closely parallels the reduction in protein synthesis (Fig. 3, Fig. 4). This implies that the remnant polyribosomes, which remain associated with the CSKF, are functioning at near normal rates. Few, if any, inhibitors have this effect on the protein-synthetic machinery. Inhibitors of initiation decrease the average polyribosome size while inhibitors of elongation reduce the rate of protein synthesis without a concomitant reduction in polyribosome mass (Vazquez, 1979). In both cases the number of active mRNA molecules does not change. The cessation of mRNA function accompanies, and may be the result of, release from the CSKF.

CD does not appear to affect directly the components of protein-synthetic system. It has no effect when added to an initiating reticulocyte *in vitro* system. This suggests that the drug does not act at the level of initiation and elongation, and is in agreement with the normal polyribosome sedimentation distribution obtained in the presence of the drug (Fig. 3). The reticulocyte seems to have little cytostructure and its polyribosomes are distributed uniformly throughout the cytoplasm (Rifkind *et al.* 1969). It seems likely that there is no cytoskeletal role *in vivo* for the highly specialized protein synthesis of the reticulocyte. The data in Fig. 5 are consistent with this hypothesis. Levels of cytochalasin D that strongly inhibit HeLa cells have no effect on protein synthesis in the intact reticulocyte. The results are consistent with the proposal that in cells with a cytoskeletal-associated protein-synthetic system, mRNA binding to the CSKF is necessary, though clearly not sufficient, for translation.

The nature and purpose of the association of protein synthesis with structural elements of the cell remain unknown. There may be several reasons for the association of mRNA with the CSKF. The seemingly obligatory binding of mRNA for translation may reflect a need for positioning the molecule near appropriate initiation (Howe & Hershey, 1984) or other regulatory factors, including the cap-binding protein (Zumbe *et al.* 1982) and high molecular weight aminoacyl-tRNA synthetase complexes (Mirande *et al.* 1985). The binding of mRNA may also have a topographical significance. Such localization may be important for the placement of protein products at the cellular level (Capco & Jackle, 1982; Fulton & Wan, 1983).

The interaction of hnRNA with the nuclear matrix is not well characterized at the molecular level. The experiments described in Fig. 7 suggest that the proteins associated with the hnRNA are a distinct subset of nuclear non-histone proteins. These proteins correspond closely to the proteins in the hnRNP complex described by Pederson (1974). Removal of the hnRNA and associated proteins from the nuclear matrix after digestion with RNase A results in a dramatic loss of the fibrillogranular organization of the nuclear interior (Fig. 7). We propose that some of hnRNA transcripts may function solely as components of the nuclear matrix and have no function as mRNA precursors. This hypothesis is supported by the observations of Darnell and coworkers (Salditt-Georgieff *et al.* 1981; Salditt-Georgieff & Darnell, 1982). In these studies, 50–75 % of the primary nuclear RNA transcripts were shown not to appear as mRNA molecules. The sequence composition of the non-message hnRNA transcripts is under investigation.

We gratefully acknowledge the expertise and patience of Gabriella Krochmalnic with the electron microscopy.

This work was supported by grants from the National Institutes of Health, CA 08416 and CA 37330, and from the National Science Foundation, DCB 8309334. During part of this work, D.A.O. was the recipient of a National Science Foundation fellowship.

REFERENCES

BARRACK, E. R. & COFFEY, D. S. (1980). The specific binding of estrogens and androgens to the nuclear matrix of sex hormone responsive tissues. *J. biol. Chem.* **255**, 7265–7275.

BEN-ZE'EV, A., HOROWITZ, M., SKOLNIK, H., ABULAFIA, R., LAUB, O. & ALONI, Y. (1981). The metabolism of SV40 RNA is associated with the cytoskeletal framework. *Virology* **111**, 475–487.

BEREZNEY, R. (1980). Fractionation of the nuclear matrix. I. Partial separation into matrix protein fibrils and a residual ribonucleoprotein fraction. *J. Cell Biol.* **85**, 641–650.

BEREZNEY, R. & BUCHHOLTZ, L. A. (1981). Dynamic association of replicating DNA fragments with the nuclear matrix of regenerating liver. *Expl Cell Res.* **132**, 1–13.

BEREZNEY, R. & COFFEY, D. S. (1975). Nuclear protein matrix: association with newly synthesized DNA. *Science* **189**, 291–292.

BEREZNEY, R. & COFFEY, D. S. (1977). Nuclear matrix isolation and characterization of a framework structure from rat liver nuclei. *J. Cell Biol.* **73**, 616–637.

BERNHARD, W. (1969). A new staining procedure for electron microscopical cytology. *J. Ultrastruct. Res.* **27**, 250–262.

BERNHARD, W. & GRANBOULAN, N. (1963). The fine structure of the cancer cell nucleus. *Expl Cell Res. Suppl.* **9**, 19–53.

BEYER, A. L., CHRISTENSEN, M. E., WALKER, B. W. & LESTOURGEON, W. M. (1977). Identification and characterization of the packaging proteins of core 40S hnRNP particles. *Cell* **11**, 127–138.

BONNEAU, A. M., DARVEAU, A. & SONENBERG, N. (1985). Effect of viral-infection on host protein-synthesis and messenger-RNA association with the cytoplasmic cytoskeletal structure. *J. Cell Biol.* **100**, 1209–1218.

BRASCH, K. (1982). Fine structure and localization of the nuclear matrix in situ. *Expl Cell Res.* **140**, 161–171.

BRAVO, R., SMALL, J. V., FEY, S. J., LARSEN, P. M. & CELIS, J. E. (1982). Architecture and polypeptide composition of HeLa cytoskeletons. Modification of cytoarchitectural polypeptides during mitosis. *J. molec. Biol.* **154**, 121–143.

CAPCO, D. G. & JACKLE, H. (1982). Localized protein synthesis during oogenesis of *Xenopus laevis*: analysis by in situ translation. *Devl Biol.* **94**, 41–50.

CAPCO, D. G., KROCHMALNIC, G. & PENMAN, S. (1984). A new method of preparing embeddment-free sections for transmission electron microscopy: applications to the cytoskeletal framework and other three-dimensional networks. *J. Cell. Biol.* **98**, 1878–1885.

CAPCO, D. G., WAN, K. M. & PENMAN, S. (1982). The nuclear matrix: three-dimensional architecture and protein composition. *Cell* **29**, 847–858.

CERVERA, M., DREYFUSS, G. & PENMAN, S. (1981). Messenger RNA is translated when associated with the cytoskeletal framework in normal and VSV infected HeLa cells. *Cell* **23**, 113–120.

CIEJEK, E. M., TSAI, M.-J. & O'MALLEY, B. W. (1983). Actively transcribed genes are associated with the nuclear matrix. *Nature, Lond.* **306**, 607–609.

COMINGS, D. E. & OKADA, T. A. (1976). Nuclear proteins. III. The fibrillar nature of the nuclear matrix. *Expl Cell Res.* **103**, 341–360.

DIAMOND, D. A. & BARRACK, E. R. (1984). The relationship of androgen receptor levels to androgen responsiveness in the Dunning R3327 rat prostate tumor sublines. *J. Urol.* **132**, 821–827.

DYSON, P. J., COOK, P. R., SEARLE, S. & WYKE, J. A. (1985). The chromatin structure of Rous Sarcoma provirus is changed by factors that act in trans in cell hybrids. *EMBO J.* **14**, 413–420.

FAKAN, S. & BERNHARD, W. (1971). Localization of rapidly and slowly labeled nuclear RNA as visualized by high resolution autoradiography. *Expl Cell Res.* **67**, 129–141.

FAKAN, S., PUVION, E. & SPOHR, G. (1976). Localization and characterization of newly synthesized nuclear RNA in isolated rat hepatocytes. *Expl Cell Res.* **99**, 155–164.

FEY, E. G., KROCHMALNIC, G. & PENMAN, S. (1986). The nonchromatin substructures of the nucleus: The ribonucleoprotein(RNP)-containing and RNP-depleted matrices analyzed by sequential fractionation and resinless section electron microscopy. *J. Cell Biol.* **102**, 1654–1665.

FEY, E. G. & PENMAN, S. (1984). Tumor promoters induce a specific morphological signature in the nuclear matrix–intermediate filament scaffold of Madin-Darby canine kidney (MDCK) cell colonies. *Proc. natn. Acad. Sci. U.S.A.* **81**, 4409–4413.

FEY, E. G. & PENMAN, S. (1986). The morphological oncogenic signature: Reorganization of epithelial cytoarchitecture and metabolic regulation by tumor promoters and by transformation. *Devl Biol.*, vol. 3. *The Cell Surface in Development and Cancer* (ed. M. Steinberg). New York: Plenum.

FEY, E. G., WAN, K. M. & PENMAN, S. (1984). Epithelial cytoskeletal framework and nuclear matrix–intermediate filament scaffold: Three-dimensional organization and protein composition. *J. Cell Biol.* **98**, 1973–1984.

FISHER, P. A., BERRIOS, M. & BLOBEL, G. (1982). Isolation and characterization of a proteinaceous subnuclear fraction composed of nuclear matrix, peripheral lamina and nuclear pore complexes from embryos of *Drosophila melanogaster*. *J. Cell Biol.* **92**, 674–686.

FRANKE, W. W., SCHMID, E., WEBER, K. & OSBORNE, M. (1979). HeLa cells contain intermediate filaments of the pre-keratin type. *Expl Cell Res.* **118**, 95–109.

FULTON, A. B., WAN, K. M. & PENMAN, S. (1980). The spatial distribution of polyribosomes in 3T3 cells and the associated assembly of proteins into the skeletal framework. *Cell* **20**, 849–857.

FULTON, A. B. & WAN, K. M. (1983). Many cytoskeletal proteins associate with the HeLa cytoskeleton during translation *in vitro*. *Cell* **32**, 619–625.

GALLINARO, H., PUVION, E., KISTER, L. & JACOB, M. (1983). Nuclear matrix and hnRNP share a common structural constituent with premessenger RNA. *EMBO J.* **2**, 953–960.

HENTZEN, P. C., RHO, J. H. & BEKHOR, I. (1984). Nuclear matrix DNA from chicken erythrocytes contains β-globin gene sequences. *Proc. natn. Acad. Sci. U.S.A.* **81**, 304–307.

HERMAN, R., WEYMOUTH, L. & PENMAN, S. (1978). Heterogeneous nuclear RNA–protein fibers in chromatin-depleted nuclei. *J. Cell Biol.* **78**, 663–674.

HOWE, J. G. & HERSHEY, J. W. (1984). Translational initiation factor and ribosome association with the cytoskeletal framework fraction from HeLa cells. *Cell* **37**, 85–93.

JACKSON, D. A., COOK, P. R. & PATEL, S. B. (1984). Attachment of repeated sequences to the nuclear cage. *Nucl Acids Res.* **12**, 6709–6726.

JACKSON, D. A., MCCREADY, S. J. & COOK, P. R. (1981). RNA is synthesized at the nuclear cage. *Nature, Lond.* **292**, 552–555.

JEFFERY, W. R. (1984). Spatial-distribution of messenger-RNA in the cytoskeletal framework of *Ascidian* eggs. *Devl Biol.* **103**, 482–492.

KISH, V. M. & PEDERSON, T. (1975). Ribonucleoprotein organization of polyadenylate sequences in HeLa cell heterogeneous nuclear RNA. *J. molec. Biol.* **95**, 227–238.

LAEMMLI, U. K. (1970). Cleavage of structural proteins during the assembly of the head of bacteriophage T4. *Nature, Lond.* **277**, 680–685.

LASTICK, S. M. & MCCONKEY, E. H. (1976). Exchange and stability of HeLa ribosomal proteins *in vivo*. *J. biol. Chem.* **251**, 2867–2875.

LAWRENCE, J. B. & SINGER, R. H. (1986). Intracellular localization of messenger RNAs for cytoskeletal proteins. *Cell* **45**, 407–415.

LENK, R. & PENMAN, S. (1979). The cytoskeletal framework and poliovirus metabolism. *Cell* **16**, 289–301.

LENK, R., RANSOM, L., KAUFMANN, Y. & PENMAN, S. (1977). A cytoskeletal structure with associated polyribosomes obtained from HeLa cells. *Cell* **10**, 67–78.

LONG, B. H., HUANG, C.-Y. & POGO, A. O. (1979). Isolation and characterization of the nuclear matrix in Friend erythroleukemia cells: chromatin and hnRNA interactions with the nuclear matrix. *Cell* **18**, 1079–1090.

MAUNDRELL, K., MAXWELL, E. S., PUVION, E. & SCHERRER, K. (1981). The nuclear matrix of duck erythroblasts is associated with globin mRNA coding sequences but not with the major 40S nuclear RNP. *Expl Cell Res.* **136**, 435–445.

MCCREADY, S. J., GODWIN, J., MASON, D. W., BRAZELL, I. A. & COOK, P. R. (1980). DNA is replicated at the nuclear cage. *J. Cell Sci.* **46**, 365–386.

MILLER, T. E., HUANG, C.-Y. & POGO, A. O. (1978). Rat liver nuclearskeleton and ribonucleoprotein complexes containing hnRNA. *J. Cell Biol.* **76**, 675–691.

MIRANDE, M., LECORRE, D., LOUVARD, D., REGGIO, H., PAILLIEZ, J. P. & WALLER, J. P. (1985). Association of an aminoacyl-transfer RNA–synthetase complex and of phenylalanyl-transfer RNA–synthetase with the cytoskeletal framework fraction from mammalian cells. *Expl Cell Res.* **156**, 91–102.

MIRKOVITCH, J., MIRAULT, M.-E. & LAEMMLI, U. K. (1984). Organization of the higher-order chromatin loop: specific DNA attachment sites on nuclear scaffold. *Cell* **39**, 223–232.

MONNERON, A. & BERNHARD, W. (1969). Fine structural organization of the interphase nucleus in some mammalian cells. *J. Ultrastruct. Res.* **27**, 266–288.

NARAYAN, K. S., STEELE, W. J., SMETANA, K. & BUSCH, H. (1967). Ultrastructural aspects of the ribonucleoprotein network in the nuclei of Walker tumor and rat liver. *Expl Cell Res.* **46**, 65–77.

NASH, R. E., PUVION, E. & BERNHARD, W. (1975). Perichromatin fibrils as components of rapidly labeled extranucleolar RNA. *J. Ultrastruct. Res.* **53**, 395–405.

NELKIN, B. D., PARDOLL, D. & VOGELSTEIN, B. (1980). Localization of SV40 genes within supercoiled loop domains. *Nucl. Acids Res.* **8**, 5623–5633.

NIELSEN, P., GOELZ, S. & TRACHSEL, H. (1983). The role of the cytoskeleton in eukaryotic protein synthesis. *Cell Biol. Int. Rep.* **7**, 245–254.

O'FARRELL, P. H. (1975). High-resolution two-dimensional electrophoresis of proteins. *J. biol. Chem.* **250**, 4007–4021.

ORNELLES, D. A., FEY, E. G. & PENMAN, S. (1986). Cytochalasin releases mRNA from the cytoskeletal framework and inhibits protein synthesis. *Molec. cell. Biol.* **6**, 1650–1662.

PARDOLL, D. M., VOGELSTEIN, B. & COFFEY, D. S. (1980). A fixed site of DNA replication in eukaryotic cells. *Cell* **19**, 527–536.

PEDERSON, T. (1974). Proteins associated with heterogeneous nuclear RNA in eukaryotic cells. *J. molec. Biol.* **83**, 163–184.

PEDERSON, T. & DAVIS, N. G. (1980). Messenger RNA processing and nuclear structure: Isolation of nuclear ribonucleoprotein particles containing β-globin messenger RNA precursors. *J. Cell Biol.* **87**, 47–54.

PENMAN, S. (1966). RNA metabolism in the HeLa cell nucleus. *J. molec. Biol.* **17**, 117–130.

PULLMAN, J. M. & MARTIN, T. E. (1983). Reconstitution of nucleoprotein complexes with mammalian heterogeneous nuclear ribonucleoprotein (hnRNP) core proteins. *J. Cell Biol.* **97**, 99–111.

PUVION, E. & BERNHARD, W. (1975). Ribonucleoprotein components in liver cell nuclei as visualized by cryo-ultramicrotomy. *J. Cell Biol.* **67**, 200–214.

RIFKIND, R. A., CHUI, D. & EPLER, H. (1969). An ultrastructural study of early morphogenetic events during the establishment of fetal hepatic erythropoiesis. *J. Cell Biol.* **40**, 343–365.

ROBINSON, S. I., NELKIN, B. D. & VOGELSTEIN, B. (1982). The ovalbumin gene is associated with the nuclear matrix of chicken oviduct cells. *Cell* **28**, 99–106.

ROSS, D. A., YEN, R. W. & CHAE, C. B. (1982). Association of globin ribonucleic acid and its precursors with the chicken erythroblast nuclear matrix. *Biochemistry* **21**, 764–771.

SALDITT-GEORGIEFF, M. & DARNELL, J. E. (1982). Further evidence that the majority of nuclear RNA transcripts in mammalian cells do not contribute to mRNA. *Molec. cell. Biol.* **2**, 701–707.

SALDITT-GEORGIEFF, M., HARPOLD, M., WILSON, M. & DARNELL, J. E. (1981). Large heterogeneous nuclear ribonucleic acid has three times as many 5' caps as polyadenylic acid segments, and most caps do not enter polyribosomes. *Molec. cell. Biol.* **1**, 177–185.

SAMARINA, O. P., LUKANIDIN, E. M., MOLNAR, J. & GEORGIEV, G. P. (1968). Structural organization of nuclear complexes containing DNA-like RNA. *J. molec. Biol.* **33**, 251–263.

SINGER, R. H. & WARD, D. C. (1982). Actin gene expression visualized in chicken muscle tissue culture by using in situ hybridization with a biotinylated nucleotide analog. *Proc. natn. Acad. Sci. U.S.A.* **79**, 7331–7335.

SMALL, D., NELKIN, B. & VOGELSTEIN, B. (1985). The association of transcribed genes with the nuclear matrix of *Drosophila* cells during heat shock. *Nucl. Acids Res.* **13**, 2413–2431.

STAUFENBIEL, M. & DEPPERT, W. (1982). Intermediate filament systems are collapsed onto the nuclear surface after isolation of nuclei from tissue culture cells. *Expl Cell Res.* **138**, 207–214.

SWIFT, H. (1963). Cytochemical studies on nuclear fine structure. *Expl Cell Res. Suppl.* **9**, 54–67.

VAN EEKELEN, C. A. G. & VAN VENROOIJ, W. J. (1981). HnRNA and its attachment to a nuclear protein matrix. *J. Cell Biol.* **88**, 554–563.

VAN VENROOIJ, W. J., SILLEKENS, P. T. G., VAN EEKELEN, A. G. & REINDERS, R. J. (1981). On the association of mRNA with the cytoskeleton in uninfected and adenovirus infected human KB cells. *Expl Cell Res.* **135**, 79–91.

VAZQUEZ, D. (1979). *Inhibitors of Protein Biosynthesis*. Berlin: Springer-Verlag KG.

VOGELSTEIN, B., PARDOLL, D. M. & COFFEY, D. S. (1980). Supercoiled loops and eukaryotic DNA replication. *Cell* **22**, 79–85.

WOLOSEWICK, J. J. & PORTER, K. R. (1979). Microtrabecular lattice of the cytoplasmic ground substance. Artifact or reality? *J. Cell Biol.* **82**, 114–139.

WOODCOCK, C. L. F. (1980). Nucleus-associated intermediate filaments from chicken erythrocytes. *J. Cell Biol.* **81**, 67–82.

ZUMBE, A., STAHLI, C. & TRACHSEL, H. (1982). Association of a M_r 50,000 cap-binding protein with the cytoskeleton in baby hamster kidney cells. *Proc. natn. Acad. Sci. U.S.A.* **79**, 2917–2931.

J. Cell Sci. Suppl. 5, 121–128 (1986)
Printed in Great Britain © The Company of Biologists Limited 1986

THE ROLE OF MICROTUBULE POLARITY IN THE MOVEMENT OF KINESIN AND KINETOCHORES

T. J. MITCHISON

National Institute for Medical Research, London NW7 1AA, UK

SUMMARY

Microtubules are important for organizing and directing many types of intracellular motility. Recently progress has been made in the analysis of two types of motility at the molecular level: the movement of axonal vesicles driven by kinesin, and the movement of chromosomes driven by the kinetochore. Both require ATP for movement *in vitro*. Kinesin-driven movement is unidirectional, towards the microtubule plus end, while movement of the kinetochore is bidirectional. These similarities and differences are discussed and incorporated into a new model for the kinetochore–microtubule interface.

INTRODUCTION

The internal contents of cells are in a state of constant motion, but their overall predictable morphology and asymmetry implies that this movement must be subject to spatial organization over large distances. Microtubules are linear elements that follow rather straight courses over long distances through cytoplasm, and are thus suited to coordinating intracellular transport. Since their discovery, it has been appreciated that microtubules play an important role in directing the movement of chromosomes during mitosis, and of other organelles throughout the cell cycle (Porter, 1966). Until recently the only system in which microtubule-dependent motility could be analysed at the molecular level was the ciliary axoneme where the favourable spatial organization and high local concentration permitted the identification of dynein as an ATPase that produces force against microtubules (Gibbons, 1981). More recently, the combined application of video-enhanced differential interference contrast microscopy (Allen *et al.* 1981) and biochemistry to squid axoplasm has permitted the isolation of a novel force-producing ATPase, kinesin (Vale *et al.* 1985a,c). The classic problem of chromosome movement has also come under renewed attack, and although we are still far from a molecular analysis, it is now possible to discuss the movement of the kinetochore along the microtubule at a mechanistic level. In this article I will review recent progress on the ways in which kinesin and kinetochores move along microtubules, and in particular the influence of the polarity of the microtubule lattice. The comparison may suggest some new approaches to these mechanistically related but biologically very different problems.

MICROTUBULE POLARITY

Microtubules are formed by helical polymerization of their subunit protein, tubulin (reviewed by Kirschner, 1978). Such a helical polymer is necessarily polar, because the asymmetric subunits are all aligned in the same direction along the lattice. In fact tubulin is a dimer of similar α and β subunits, so the micro-tubule could be pseudo-bipolar if α and β were arranged head-to-head in the dimer. However, the strong 4 nm repeats in the microtubule lattice, evident from X-ray diffraction (Cohen *et al.* 1971) and electron microscopy (Amos *et al.* 1976; Mandelkow *et al.* 1986) suggest that α and β are arranged in the same direction in the lattice, and head-to-tail in the dimer. Thus if one thinks of the amino acids exposed by each subunit on the microtubule surface as forming a molecular arrow, then all the arrows are pointing in the same direction. As well as being expressed on the surface lattice, this polarity means that the two ends of the microtubule are different, probably with all α subunits exposed on one end, and all β on the other; though which is the plus end is not yet known.

Assays for the polarity of microtubules have utilized both differences at the ends of the lattice, manifest as different growth rates (Bergen & Borisy, 1980), and visual-ization of polarity in the surface lattice by the asymmetric binding of further tubulin oligomers (hook decoration; Heidemann & McIntosh, 1979), or dynein (Haimo *et al.* 1979). The hook decoration assay has been widely applied to microtubules in cells, showing that under most circumstances the plus, or fast-growing end, is distal to the cell centre (Euteneuer & McIntosh, 1981*a*). The uniform polarity of cytoskeletal microtubules means that they can determine not just the tracks that organelles follow, but also the direction of movement (McNiven *et al.* 1984). The importance of direction is well illustrated by the axon, where completely different classes of organelles are transported towards and away from the cell body (Grafstein & Forman, 1980). Microtubules running parallel to the axon, with uniform polarity (plus ends distal to the cell; Heidemann *et al.* 1981), probably direct this traffic (see below).

The mechanism that controls the polarity of microtubules within cells is not known, but specific nucleating structures probably play an important role. The centrosome nucleates microtubules with their plus end distal *in vitro* (Bergen *et al.* 1980). The reason for this is unknown, but it seems likely that a component of the centrosome must recognize and effectively cap the minus end. The kinetochore can also nucleate *in vitro* (Telzer *et al.* 1975), but apparently lacks a specific end inter-action since microtubules grow out with both polarities (Mitchison & Kirschner, 1985*a*). Mechanisms for determining polarity other than nucleation at centrosomes must exist, however, to account for its specification in microtubules not attached to the centrosome, such as those in some axons (Chalfie & Thomson, 1979). In addition, the reorganization of microtubule polarity in severed melanophore arms (McNiven *et al.* 1984) suggests that the microtubule cytoskeleton may be most stable with plus ends distal to the cell centre even in the absence of conventional nucleating sites.

KINESIN: DIRECTIONALITY OF A PURIFIED TRANSLOCATOR

Kinesin is a protein that was purified from squid axoplasm on the basis of its ability to promote latex bead movements along taxol-stabilized microtubules and movement of the microtubules relative to the glass substrate (Vale *et al.* 1985*a*). The properties of kinesin are most easily explained by a model in which the molecule can bind non-specifically to negatively charged surfaces, and specifically to the surface of the microtubule through an active site. In the presence of ATP the molecule can then walk along the microtubule lattice, presumably hydrolysing the nucleotide, although this has not yet been demonstrated.

Kinesin-promoted movement appeared to be unidirectional, since all beads moved in the same direction along a single microtubule, which itself moved in the opposite direction along the substrate (Vale *et al.* 1985*c*). In order to determine the direction of movement relative to the polarity of the lattice, it was necessary to observe it on a microtubule substrate of known polarity. This was provided by astral arrays nucleated *in vitro* by centrosomes. Conditions for forming arrays of known polarity had been previously established (Mitchison & Kirschner, 1984*a*), but some modification was required to make unfixed, taxol-stabilized arrays. At achievable centrosome concentrations ($10^7 \, ml^{-1}$) only a tiny fraction (<0·2%) of input tubulin can be converted into nucleated microtubules. Thus asters must be separated from free tubulin before taxol addition to avoid production of large numbers of free microtubules. This was accomplished by sedimenting asters through glycerol-containing cushions, which also served to stabilize the unfixed microtubules against depolymerization prior to taxol addition. This technique was a modification of the one previously used in preparing asters for electron microscopy (Evans *et al.* 1985).

Kinesin, ATP and latex beads were added to the immobilized astral arrays, which were observed by video-enhanced differential interference microscopy. Bead movement was observed to be uniformly centrifugal, i.e. towards plus ends. At the same time distal microtubule segments moved centripetally, driven by kinesin on the substrate (Vale *et al.* 1985*b*). Thus kinesin is a plus-end-directed translocator. This specificity reinforces the idea that a kinesin active site makes a stereospecific protein–protein interaction with repeated sites on the microtubule lattice. Since directionality comes from the kinesin–microtubule interface it is not influenced by factors such as the orientation of kinesin on the bead surface. Presumably active movement requires more than one binding site, so the molecule remains attached to the microtubule while reaching out for a new attachment. Whether a single kinesin molecule (which contains more than one copy of the predominant $120 \times 10^3 \, M_r$ polypeptide; Vale *et al.* 1985*a*) can move on its own is not known.

The introduction of the directionality assay led to the discovery in axoplasm of a second motile activity, acting towards minus ends (Vale *et al.* 1985*b*). This differed from kinesin by both pharmacological and immunological criteria. The potent inhibition of minus-end-directed motility by vanadate and *N*-ethylmaleimide suggests a relationship to axonemal dynein, which is also thought to exert force towards minus ends (Sale & Satir, 1977).

IMPLICATIONS FOR THE PHYSIOLOGICAL ROLE OF KINESIN

The polarity results suggest that if kinesin is indeed a motor for fast axonal transport, then it is responsible for anterograde movement. At present the relationship between the bulk of kinesin, which is present in the soluble cytoplasmic pool (Vale *et al.* 1985*c*), and vesicle-bound forms is unknown, though preliminary work suggests a receptor protein on vesicles (Vale *et al.* 1985*c*). This is a very interesting direction for future research since it may hold the key to the specification of the direction of vesicle transport. At present the simplest model to account for the directionality of axonal transport invokes two different receptors, one for kinesin and one for the retrograde factor. One class of organelles would bind kinesin and move anterograde along the unipolar axonal microtubules, while another would bind the retrograde transporter and move back towards the cell body.

Kinesin was purified initially from axons, but is also present in other cell types such as sea urchin eggs (Scholey *et al.* 1985) and fibroblasts (R. D. Vale, personal communication). It seems likely to play a general role in organelle transport towards the cell periphery, and a balance between kinesin and minus-end-directed translocation could be important for positioning organelles within cells. The apparent lack of specificity for transport substrates *in vitro* suggests that kinesin could also generate tension between microtubules and other cytoskeletal elements. The polarity results suggest, for example, a role in pulling kinetochore microtubules polewards (J. R. McIntosh, personal communication), and perhaps stretching intermediate filaments towards the periphery of the cell.

CHROMOSOME MOVEMENT *IN VIVO*

The movement of chromosomes on the spindle can be considered a special case of an organelle moving with the help of a microtubule, in which movement is intimately coupled to microtubule dynamics. Chromosomes are attached to the spindle by microtubules with their plus ends terminating at the kinetochore (Euteneuer & McIntosh, 1981*b*). When chromosomes move towards or away from the pole, kinetochore microtubules must add or lose subunits, while remaining attached (for reviews, see Nicklas, 1971; Pickett-Heaps *et al.* 1982). We probed these dynamics by microinjecting biotin-labelled tubulin subunits into living cells at metaphase, and following their incorporation into microtubules by immunoelectron microscopy (Mitchison *et al.* 1986). Subunits incorporated at the kinetochore, giving rise to kinetochore microtubules with labelled segments proximal to the kinetochore, and unlabelled segments distal. The labelled segments elongated with time while spindle length remained constant, suggesting a continuous polewards flux of subunits during metaphase. This treadmilling (Margolis & Wilson, 1981) of the kinetochore microtubules corresponds to plus-end-directed motility of the stationary kinetochores. When cells injected in metaphase went into anaphase, labelled segments proximal to the kinetochore were lost, suggesting that kinetochore microtubules shorten by disassembly at the kinetochore. Thus anaphase movement corresponds to minus-end-directed motility of the kinetochore, and this structure is capable of bidirectional movement with respect to the microtubule lattice, in apparent distinction to kinesin and dynein. However, these data do not permit us to draw direct conclusions about force generation by the kinetochore, because of the complexity of the spindle, and the possibility of multiple force-generating mechanisms. Movement of the kinetochore relative to the microtubule lattice is likely to be at least in part a response to external forces acting on the microtubules, and in order to clarify the situation the kinetochore–microtubule interaction must be studied in isolation.

CHROMOSOME MOVEMENT *IN VITRO*

During an analysis of the interaction of microtubules with isolated chromosomes *in vitro*, we observed that proximal microtubule assembly could occur at the kinetochore in the presence of ATP (Mitchison & Kirschner, 1985*b*). Furthermore, in the presence of ATP the kinetochore could move along the surface lattice of taxol-stabilized microtubules, apparently towards the plus end, at a maximal rate of $2–3\,\mu\mathrm{m\,min^{-1}}$ (about $1/10$ the rate of kinesin-induced bead movement *in vitro*). These observations were made by following the position of a biotin-labelled microtubule segment relative to the kinetochore by fixing at time intervals and analysing populations. This method is less satisfactory than real-time observation for analysing movement; for example, rapid, intermittent motion could not be distinguished from slow, continuous motion. Thus there is an urgent need for reanalysis of *in vitro* chromosome movement by video-enhanced microscopy, pending which the conclusions, particularly concerning the polarity of movement, must be treated with caution. Nevertheless, the results strongly suggest that the kinetochore–microtubule connection is mediated by an ATPase that binds to the surface lattice.

STRUCTURE OF THE KINETOCHORE–MICROTUBULE INTERFACE

The ability of the kinetchore to hold on to the microtubule end while subunits are added or lost necessitates multiple contacts to the lattice. It seems unlikely that 13 contacts to the protofilaments at the end of the lattice would be sufficient, and the most plausible structure seems to be a sliding collar, making multiple contacts with the surface lattice, a structure first graphically suggested by Margolis & Wilson (1981). This structure helps explain both the *in vivo* and *in vitro* data, but the exact nature of the individual binding sites in the collar remains to be addressed. Do they mediate specific protein–protein interactions with the lattice, respecting its polarity as with kinesin, or is the interaction less specific? Is their attachment and detachment from the lattice a simple reversible binding reaction, or part of a unidirectional enzymic cycle?

The bidirectional movement of the kinetochore *in vivo* argues against its being an active directional translocator like kinesin or dynein, and the translocation observed *in vitro* was if anything in the wrong direction to explain anaphase movement. I think it is most likely that the flux at the kinetochore *in vivo* is imposed by external forces on the microtubule. Assembly (plus-end-directed movement) could be driven by polewards pulling on kinetochore microtubules (perhaps by kinesin, see above). Such forces would achieve congression if they acted along the length of micro-tubules, so that total force was dependent on kinetochore-to-pole distance. Dis-assembly (minus-end-directed movement) could perhaps be driven by an elastic element pulling on the chromosome (Pickett-Heaps *et al.* 1982), but I prefer the idea that the thermodynamic drive to disassembly alone is sufficient to move chromosomes polewards (Inoue & Sato, 1967). GDP-liganded microtubules have a strong thermodynamic drive towards disassembly, even while other, possibly GTP-capped microtubules, continue to assemble (Mitchison & Kirschner, 1984*b*).

Hill (1985) has described a model kinetochore with multiple binding sites to the lattice, and a simple activation energy per site for slipping from one position on the lattice to a neighbouring one. Using a small amount of binding energy per site ($1.5 \, \text{kcal mol}^{-1}$) and proportionally reasonable activation energies for slipping, the model kinetochore will stay firmly attached as it follows a shrinking microtubule. In such an equilibrium binding model the binding energy per site is limited by the need for the kinetochore not to slow down the rate of microtubule disassembly too much: anaphase movement ($1-3 \, \mu\text{m min}^{-1}$; Nicklas, 1971) is not very much slower than free plus-end disassembly *in vitro* ($12 \, \mu\text{m min}^{-1}$; Mitchison & Kirschner, 1984*b*). If the equilibrium model is correct, then the kinetochore–microtubule connection is likely to be mediated by multiple weak bonds that have low activation energies for sliding, such as electrostatic interactions. Conceivably, the microtubule–kinetochore

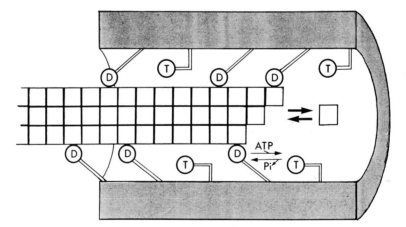

Fig. 1. Model for the kinetochore–microtubule interaction. The kinetochore acts as a sliding collar on the microtubule, with many individual sites that interact with the lattice. Individual binding sites are ATPase molecules that have a high affinity for the lattice in the ADP (D) conformation, and dissociate on ATP binding (T). The plus end of the microtubule is free to add and lose subunits (squares). In the absence of external force, GDP-liganded subunits will tend to dissociate, and the kinetochore will slip down the disassembling microtubule in order to maximize the number of sites still bound to the lattice. If an external force pulls the microtubule polewards (left in figure) while the kinetochore is fixed, subunits will add to the end, since assembly within the kinetochore collar is favoured by formation of bonds with the ATPase sites. Thus the collar acts as a reversible transducer between assembly dynamics and force, even though the ATPase cycle is unidirectional.

interaction could be that of a negatively charged rod in a positively charged hole. In this case individual binding sites would be very different from kinesin, and might not notice the polarity of the lattice. The *in vitro* movement data, however, suggest a different model, in which the individual sites are in fact more like kinesin, that is ATPase molecules that bind tightly to the lattice when liganded with ADP, and dissociate on ATP binding (Fig. 1). Unlike kinesin the kinetochore ATPase would not be strongly directional, that is it would tend to rebind to the lattice at the same position from which it dissociated. Thus the kinetochore on its own would not be an active translocator in the presence of ATP (though it might display a weak plus-end-directed bias as detected *in vitro*). In the absence of ATP, a rigor complex would be formed that caps the microtubule against disassembly (Mitchison & Kirschner, 1985*b*). This model kinetochore should act as a transducer between assembly dynamics and force in the same way as Hill's equilibrium model does, except that the constraints on the rate constants are removed. Binding is strong in the ADP-liganded state, mediated by specific protein–protein interactions, and weak in the ATP-liganded state, as is probably the case for kinesin. Disassembly and sliding both occur when an individual site is in the low-affinity ATP state, so their rates are independent of the binding energy in the high-affinity state. Thus the model combines the advantages of easy sliding and rapid disassembly with those of a high-affinity interaction, which respects the polarity of the lattice. Selective interaction with microtubules of the correct polarity (plus-end proximal) could be important for correct spindle morphogenesis.

I thank all the friends in the mitosis field who have contributed useful discussion, Lynn Williams for drawing Fig. 1, Pat Magrath for preparing the manuscript and the Medical Research Council for financial support.

REFERENCES

ALLEN, R. D., ALLEN, N. S. & TRAVIS, J. L. (1981). Video enhanced contrast differential interference microscopy (AVEC-DIC): a new method capable of analysing microtubule related motility in the reticulopodal networks of *Allogromia laticollaris*. *Cell Motil.* **1**, 291–302.

AMOS, L. A., LINCK, R. W. & KLUG, A. (1976). Molecular structure of cytoplasmic microtubules. In *Cell Motility* (ed. R. Goldman, T. Pollard & J. Rosenbaum), pp. 847–868. NY: Cold Spring Harbor Laboratory Press.

BERGEN, L. G. & BORISY, G. G. (1980). Head to tail polymerisation of microtubules *in vitro*. *J. Cell Biol.* **84**, 141–150.

BERGEN, L. G., KURIYAMA, R. & BORISY, G. G. (1980). Polarity of microtubules nucleated by centrosomes and chromosomes of Chinese hamster ovary cells *in vitro*. *J. Cell Biol.* **84**, 151–159.

CHALFIE, M. & THOMSON, J. N. (1979). Organisation of neuronal microtubules in the nematode *Caenorhabditis elegans*. *J. Cell Biol.* **82**, 278–289.

COHEN, C. HARRISON, S. C. & STEPHENS, R. E. (1971). X-ray diffraction from microtubules. *J. molec. Biol.* **59**, 375–380.

EUTENEUER, V. & McINTOSH, J. R. (1981*a*). Polarity of some motility related microtubules. *Proc. natn. Acad. Sci. U.S.A.* **78**, 372–376.

EUTENEUER, V. & McINTOSH, J. R. (1981*b*). Structural polarity of kinetochore microtubules in PtK₁ cells. *J. Cell Biol.* **89**, 338–345.

EVANS, L., MITCHISON, T. J. & KIRSCHNER, M. W. (1985). Influence of the centrosome on the structure of nucleated microtubules. *J. Cell Biol.* **100**, 1185–1191.

GIBBONS, I. R. (1981). Cillia and flagella of eukaryotes. *J. Cell Biol.* **91**, 107–124.

GRAFSTEIN, B. & FORMAN, D. S. (1980). Intracellular transport in neurons. *Physiol. Rev.* **60**, 1167–1282.

HAIMO, L. T., TELZER, B. R. & ROSENBAUM, J. L. (1979). Dynien binds to and cross bridges cytoplasmic microtubules. *Proc. natn. Acad. Sci. U.S.A.* **76**, 5759–5763.

HEIDEMANN, S. R., LANDERS, J. M. & HAMBORG, M. A. (1981). Polarity orientation of axonal microtubules. *J. Cell Biol.* **91**, 661–665.

HEIDEMANN, S. R. & MCINTOSH, J. R. (1979). Visualisation of the structural polarity of microtubules. *Nature, Lond.* **286**, 517–519.

HILL, T. L. (1985). Theoretical problems related to the attachment of microtubules to kinetochores. *Proc. natn. Acad. Sci. U.S.A.* **82**, 4404–4408.

INOUE, S. & SATO, H. (1967). Cell motility by labile association of macromolecules. The nature of spindle fibres and their role in chromosome movement. *J. gen. Physiol.* **50**, 259–292.

KIRSCHNER, M. W. (1978). Microtubule assembly and nucleation. *Int. Rev. Cytol.* **54**, 1–70.

MANDELKOW, E. M., SCHULTHEISS, R., RAPP, R. & MANDELKOW, E. (1986). On the surface lattice of microtubules: Helix starts, protofilament number, seam and handedness. *J. Cell Biol.* **102**, 1067–1073.

MARGOLIS, R. L. & WILSON, L. (1981). Microtubule treadmills – possible molecular machinery. *Nature, Lond.* **293**, 705–711.

MCNIVEN, M. A., WANG, M. & PORTER, K. R. (1984). Microtubule polarity and the direction of pigment transport reverse simultaneously in surgically severed melanophore arms. *Cell* **37**, 753–765.

MITCHISON, T. J., EVANS, L., SCHULZE, E. S. & KIRSCHNER, M. W. (1986). Sites of microtubule assembly and disassembly in the mitotic spindle. *Cell* **45**, 515–527.

MITCHISON, T. J. & KIRSCHNER, M. W. (1984*a*). Microtubule assembly nucleated by isolated centrosomes. *Nature, Lond.* **312**, 232–236.

MITCHISON, T. J. & KIRSCHNER, M. W. (1984*b*). Dynamic instability of microtubule growth. *Nature, Lond.* **312**, 237–241.

MITCHISON, T. J. & KIRSCHNER, M. W. (1985*a*). Properties of the kinetochore *in vitro*. I. Microtubule nucleation and tubulin binding. *J. Cell Biol.* **101**, 755–765.

MITCHISON, T. J. & KIRSCHNER, M. W. (1985*b*). Properties of the kinetochore *in vitro*. II. Microtubule capture and ATP dependent translocation. *J. Cell Biol.* **101**, 766–777.

NICKLAS, R. B. (1971). Mitosis. *Adv. Cell Biol.* **2**, 225–297.

PICKETT-HEAPS, J. D., TIPPET, D. H. & PORTER, K. R. (1982). Rethinking mitosis. *Cell* **29**, 729–744.

PORTER, K. R. (1966). Cytoplasmic microtubules and their functions. In *Ciba Fdn Symp. Principles of Biomolec. Org.* London: Churchill.

SALE, W. S. & SATIR, P. (1977). The direction of active sliding of microtubules in *Tetrahymena* cilia. *Proc. natn. Acad. Sci. U.S.A.* **74**, 2045–2049.

SCHOLEY, J. M., PORTER, M. E., GRISSON, P. M. & MCINTOSH, J. R. (1985). Identification of kinesin in sea urchin eggs, and evidence for its localisation in the mitotic spindle. *Nature, Lond.* **318**, 483–486.

TELZER, B. R., MOSES, M. J. & ROSENBAUM, J. (1975). Assembly of microtubules onto kinetochores of isolated mitotic chromosomes of HeLa cells. *Proc. natn. Acad. Sci. U.S.A.* **72**, 4023–4027.

VALE, R. D., REESE, T. S. & SHEETZ, M. P. (1985*a*). Identification of a novel force generating protein, kinesin, involved in microtubule base motility. *Cell* **42**, 39–50.

VALE, R. D., SCHNAPP, B. J., MITCHISON, T. J., STEUER, E., REESE, T. S. & SHEETZ, M. P. (1985*b*). Different axoplasmic proteins generate movement in opposite directions along microtubules *in vitro*. *Cell* **43**, 623–632.

VALE, R. D., SCHNAPP, B. J., REESE, T. S. & SHEETZ, M. P. (1985*c*). Organelle, bead and microtubule translocations promoted by soluble factors from the squid giant axon. *Cell* **40**, 559–569.

J. Cell Sci. Suppl. 5, 129–144 (1986)
Printed in Great Britain © The Company of Biologists Limited 1986

ANALYSIS OF PSEUDOPODIAL STRUCTURE AND ASSEMBLY WITH VIRAL PROJECTIONS

RENATO A. MORTARA* AND GORDON L. E. KOCH†

*Medical Research Council, Laboratory of Molecular Biology, Hills Rd,
Cambridge CB2 2QH, England*

SUMMARY

The mechanisms by which cells extend motile pseudopodial projections are still poorly understood. Several fundamental mechanisms have been proposed on the basis of hydrostatic pressure, membrane addition and microfilament reorganization. A common focus of all such mechanisms is the growing tip of a pseudopodium. Yet some basic questions about the nature of the tip in natural pseudopodia remain obscure. However, one class of structure, the virus-tipped projections, often contains a well-defined particle, both morphologically and biochemically, and therefore provides a useful model system for the examination of the tips of cellular projections.

In P815 cells the virus-tipped projections are long, thin structures closely resembling filopodia in other cells. The apical virus particle is a retrovirus particle produced by the chronic infection existing in this cell line. In demembranated filopodia, the virus particle retains a tight association with a single actin microfilament. Biochemical analyses indicate that the major retroviral structural polypeptide Pr65 is an actin-binding protein that could provide the anchorage site for the actin filament.

The existence of a solid virus particle tethered by an actin filament to the cytoskeleton makes it very unlikely that these projections grow by membrane addition at the tip. The major positive implication is that the apex of a projection does not relinquish its interaction with the submembranous cytoskeleton during growth. Such an arrangement would be compatible with either a hydrostatic-pressure-driven or a cytoskeleton-driven mechanism of filopodial growth.

INTRODUCTION

Motile cells from a wide variety of sources produce a group of surface projections commonly referred to as pseudopodia (Vasiliev, 1981). Morphologically, these projections can appear very different, ranging from the stout, rounded projections, lobopodia, of phagocytic cells (Yin *et al.* 1981; Boyles & Bainton, 1981), through the thin, long filopodia of growing neurites (Bray & Bunge, 1973; Albrecht-Buehler, 1976), to the broad, flat, sheet-like lamellipodia (Abercrombie *et al.* 1970) of moving fibroblasts. Consideration of such diverse structures within a common classification is based on the existence of a number of fundamental similarities (Vasiliev, 1981). They all represent highly motile and impermanent cellular extensions. Their motile characteristics are related to the existence of a very dense cytoplasmic arrangement of

*Present address: Depto. de Parasitologia, Escola Paulista de Medicina, Rua Botucatu 740, 04023 Sao Paulo S.P., Brazil.
† Author for correspondence.

microfilaments. It is commonly characteristic for most cellular organelles to be excluded from these pseudopodial regions, irrespective of morphology. In some cases, interconversion of the lamellipodial and filopodial structures has been observed (Edds, 1980), further emphasizing their intrinsic similarity.

One of the fundamental problems in cell biology concerns the mechanism by which cells extend their margins during the formation of the pseudopodial projections. Two of the intuitively simple concepts that have been advanced as providing a motive force for membrane extension have been a localized increase in hydrostatic pressure (Taylor *et al.* 1973) and membrane addition (Abercrombie *et al.* 1970; Harris, 1973), respectively. In the former the local increase in hydrostatic pressure could be generated by a contraction in one region accompanied by a herniation in the region of pseudopodial growth (Taylor & Fecheimer, 1982). Recently, an alternative based on a local increase in osmotic pressure has been proposed (Oster, 1984). Membrane addition as a basis for pseudopodial growth could operate by the fusion of membrane vesicles at the tip of the growing projection. Compensatory internalization of membrane in the cell body coupled *via* recycling through the cell to the site of addition would provide the basic mechanism for pseudopodial growth by membrane addition.

An alternative type of model, which is intrinsically more complex, for pseudopodial growth, is based on the invariable presence in such structures of very high concentrations of actin-rich microfilaments. Mechanisms of pseudopodial growth based on actin polymerization (Tilney *et al.* 1973, 1981), re-organization of actin filaments (Tilney, 1975; De Rosier *et al.* 1980) or even actomyosin-driven membrane extension have been proposed. Although there are some difficulties in visualizing how filaments could actually push out the membrane (Wessells *et al.* 1973), a major advantage of this type of mechanism is that the existence of the putative motive elements, the microfilaments, is clearly established. This contrasts with models such as membrane addition, which suffer from a lack of evidence for the basic elements such as vesicles, which are presumed to provide the membrane added at the growing end of the pseudopodium.

Resolution of this issue is severely limited by the lack of understanding of some basic structural features of pseudopodia. Of particular relevance are the structure and composition of the proximal tip of the projections. Most models accept that the focus of growth is the region most remote from the cell body. Thus the hydrostatic-pressure model requires that pressure should be applied at the apex, and an actin-driven model requires that actin polymerization, for example, should originate from that site. From the analytical standpoint, the type of projection most amenable to structural examination is the thin, long filopodium that has a relatively restricted and defined tip compared with the grosser lobopodia and lamellipodia. Thus the analysis of filopodia is a major area of interest in current examinations of this problem. Of particular relevance is the elucidation of the relationship between the internal structural elements, i.e. the microfilaments, and the membrane at the tips of the projections.

STRUCTURE OF TIPS OF FILOPODIA

Surprisingly little is known about the tips of cellular projections. Generally speaking, one of the most intensively analysed surface projections is the gut microvillus, where it is established that there is a distinct dense zone at the tip of the projection and that the microfilaments that make up the core insert into this dense body (Mooseker & Tilney, 1975). It is generally assumed that there are binding proteins for the microfilaments in this apical region, but they have not been identified. The claim that α-actinin is present in this dense body (Mooseker & Tilney, 1975) has not been confirmed (Bretscher & Weber, 1978).

The presence of dense material at the tips of cellular projections appears to be relatively common, although it cannot be concluded that they are obligatory. Sea-urchin coelomocyte filopodia, which can be isolated and analysed, also show a dense apical structure that remains associated with the microfilament bundle after de-membranation (Otto & Bryan, 1981). However, no biochemical characterization of these apical structures has been performed. Similarly, the fertilization tube of *Chlamydomonas*, which is also an actin-rich projection, exhibits an apical dense body (Detmers *et al*. 1983). It has frequently been reported that normal filopodia or microspikes on the surfaces of cells such as fibroblasts appear to possess an additional morphological specialization at the tip. Little is known about the structure or composition of these apical specializations.

It is clear from the above that a major constraint upon progress towards elucidating what happens at the tip of a growing projection is the lack of projections with adequately characterized apices.

INDUCTION OF SURFACE PROTEINS BY BUDDING VIRUSES

Many viruses are produced as a result of the budding of a particle from the plasma membrane. In many cases this involves the formation of a bud, which seals off and separates from the cell. However, in some cases the assembly of virus particles at the plasma membrane appears to be accompanied by the formation of surface projections resembling normal microvilli and filopodia. An example of this capacity of viruses to induce the formation of surface projections is observed in studies with vaccinia virus. When cultured cells are infected with myxoviruses such as vaccinia or Newcastle disease virus (NDV), they are induced to form projections (Stokes, 1976) very reminiscent of the normal microvilli on cells, with the exception that each projection contains a single virus particle at its tip. The fact that the expression of these projections is contingent upon viral infections strongly implicates the virus itself in the formation of the projections.

The capacity of myxoviruses to induce surface projections was originally described in the classical study by Marcus (1962). When HeLa cells were infected with NDV, the viral haemagglutinin was first detected at the tips of microvillus-like projections. These projections move centripetally towards the centre and the viral haemagglutinin remains permanently attached to the projection during this process. Parenthetically, it has been claimed that this experiment proves that the viral haemagglutinin is inserted at the cell margin (TIBS, 1985). However, the haemagglutination assay is very sensitive to valency changes (Morawiecki & Lisowska, 1965). Thus the margin might simply be the site of microvillus and viral assembly and not the site of haemagglutinin insertion.

Numerous other examples of virus-tipped surface projections have been described (Iwasaki & Tsuchida, 1978; Wang *et al.* 1976; Damsky *et al.* 1977). Several of these involve retrovirus particles. In one of the classical studies of virus production, strong evidence was obtained that the virus actually induced the formation of filament-rich projections (Yuen & Wong, 1977).

A less-direct line of evidence, namely, the presence of actin within a number of purified viruses, has led to the suggestion that viruses might commonly bud from the apices of surface projections (Wang *et al.* 1976; Damsky *et al.* 1977). The corrollary of this is that the ability of virus particles to induce surface projections is a relatively general phenomenon. However, studies with cytochalasin B have suggested that, even in such cases, the induction of actin-rich projections might not be obligatory (Genty & Bussereau, 1980).

RETROVIRUS-TIPPED PROJECTIONS ON P815 CELLS

The P815 cell line was one of the first murine cell lines to be established in permanent culture (Dunn & Potter, 1957). It is commonly believed that the cell line was derived from a cell of the mast cell lineage. However, several studies have shown that the cell line expresses several markers associated with the macrophage lineage and more that are diagnostic of mast cells. Thus it is probable that the P815 cell is itself a derivative of the macrophage lineage.

Some years ago it was shown that the P815 cell, or at least one of the many sub-lines derived from it, exfoliated large amounts of actin-rich material from its surface (Koch & Smith, 1978). Analysis of this material revealed a stable association between a membrane protein, the H-2 antigen and the microfilaments in these structures. It was suggested that the exfoliate was derived from surface microvilli.

Electron microscopy of the exfoliate shows that it consists of thin ($0 \cdot 1 \mu$m) long ($>10 \mu$m) membrane projections (Fig. 1). Under the currently accepted terminology, such projections cannot be derived from microvilli since this usually refers to relatively short projections. When intact P815 cells are examined by either scanning or transmission electron microscopy (Fig. 2), it is found that the surface is covered with large numbers of thin, long projections resembling the filopodia on other types of cells. The filopodia appear to be very fragile with a tendency to pull away from the cell body in large numbers, yielding material very similar in appearance to the exfoliate. Therefore, it appears that the exfoliate consists of detached filopodia and provides a convenient system for the analysis of these structures.

A particularly interesting feature of the P815 cells was revealed upon close examination of the electron micrographs (Fig. 3). At the tips of most of the projections a definite, dense structure was found. The apical dense body has the characteristic morphology of an immature C-type retrovirus particle. Analysis of the

Fig. 1. Morphology of P815 exfoliates by transmission electron microscopy (TEM). P815 cells were subjected to mechanical shearing, the exfoliates released to the supernatant were fixed *in situ*, and stained with 1 % (w/v) aqueous uranyl acetate. The tendency of the exfoliates to break, entangle and vesiculate is apparent. Bar, 0·5 μm.

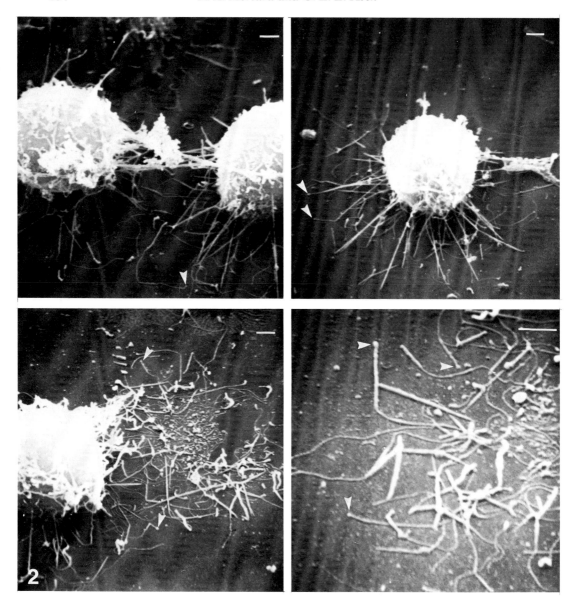

Fig. 2. Expression of filopodia at the surface of P815 cells. Scanning electron micrographs (SEM) of *in situ* fixed P815 cells attached to poly-L-lysine-coated coverslips. Arrowheads indicate the bulbous tips on some filopodia. The tendency of the surface filopodia to entangle, detach from the cell body, to break and vesiculate, as well as the lack of uniformity in the diameter of individual projections is apparent in these micrographs. Bars, 1 μm.

Fig. 3. Retrovirus-tipped filopodia of P815 cells. P815 cells fixed *in situ* were absorbed onto poly-L-lysine/carbon/collodion-coated electron microscope (EM) grids, allowed to attach and stained with uranyl acetate for TEM examination. Note the presence of the electron-dense tips with the appearance of immature C-type retrovirus particles. Bars, 2 μm (top); 0·5 μm (bottom left), and 0·1 μm (bottom right).

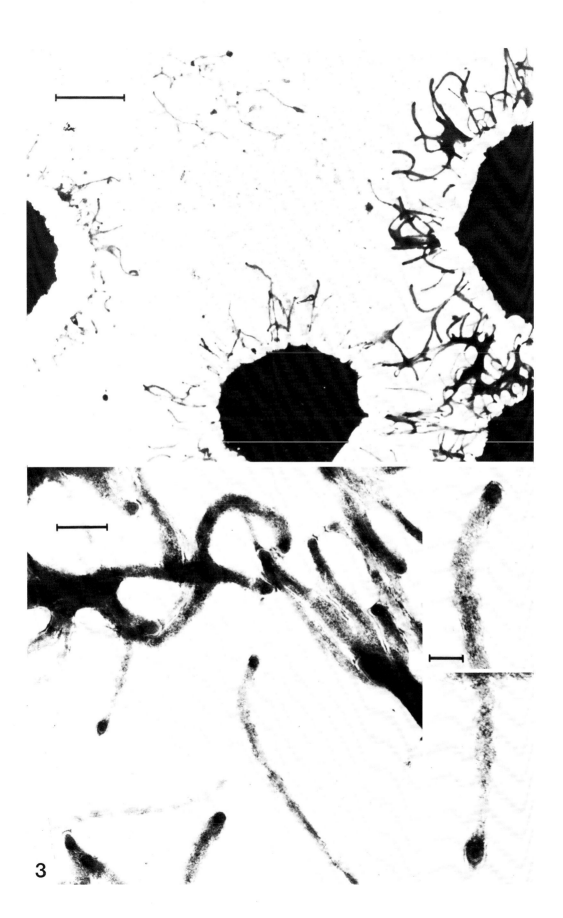

3

exfoliate confirmed the presence of substantial amounts of murine C-type retrovirus proteins, and direct immunogold labelling with monospecific antibody to murine retrovirus proteins such as P30, confirmed the identity of these as C-type retrovirus particles.

The fact that the apical particle is a retrovirus is particularly convenient since these viruses have a relatively simple structure and composition; and quite a lot is understood about their assembly (Bolognesi *et al.* 1978). This, together with the facility with which they can be isolated, makes P815 filopodia a useful system for the analysis of the events occurring at the tip of a pseudopodium.

The formation of virus-tipped filopodia is not unique to the P815 cell line. We have found that three other murine cell lines derived from the macrophage lineage produce retroviral filopodia, which can be isolated in the same way as those from the P815 cell. In fact many of the studies described below for P815 filopodia have also been carried out with projections isolated from the other cell lines.

ATTACHMENT OF ACTIN TO THE APICAL RETROVIRUS PARTICLE OF P815 FILOPODIA

Demembranation of P815 filopodia is readily effected with a non-ionic detergent such as Nonidet P40. Examination of this material by electron microscopy (Fig. 4) shows that it consists of filaments and spherical particles resembling the nucleocapsid 'cores' of murine retrovirus particles. The filaments were identified as actin filaments by classical myosin subfragment 1 (S1) decoration and the particles as cores by immunogold labelling. The striking feature of these preparations was the high incidence (30%) of viral cores that contained a single actin filament attached end-on to the core structure. No clear examples of more than one filament attached to a viral core has been observed so far.

Decoration of filament by myosin S1 fragments confirmed that it was an actin filament. Under the condition of staining that yield reasonable detail of the core structure, the polarity of the filament is not clear because the arrowhead pattern is not easily discernible. However, under the more conventional negative staining procedures, which give less detail of the core structures, the arrowhead pattern is clearer and points away from the viral core (Fig. 5).

Associations between a single actin filament and viral cores were also detected in the demembranated exfoliate from the other macrophage tumour cell lines mentioned above. Thus the arrangement observed in the P815 filopodia does not appear to be unique to this particular cell line.

ACTIN-ASSOCIATED VIRAL POLYPEPTIDES

The existence of actin filaments attached to the viral cores suggested that viral components might actually interact with actin itself. Co-sedimentation studies with the demembranated filopodia showed that some of the viral polypeptides, particularly Pr65, did indeed co-sediment with filamented actin. A more rigorous test of

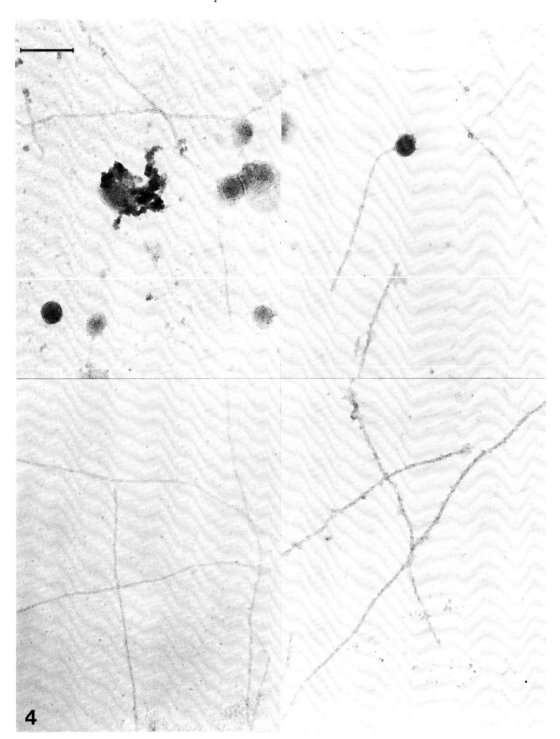

Fig. 4. Attachment of actin filaments to virus nucleocapsids of demembranated P815 filopodia. TEM of demembranated filopodia and actin filaments decorated with myosin S1 fragments. Top left, demembranated filopodia (DF); top right, DF after S1 treatment; bottom left, rabbit muscle actin filaments; bottom right, actin filaments treated with S1. DF filaments and rabbit muscle actin filaments show similar morphology before and after S1 decoration. Bar, 0·2 μm.

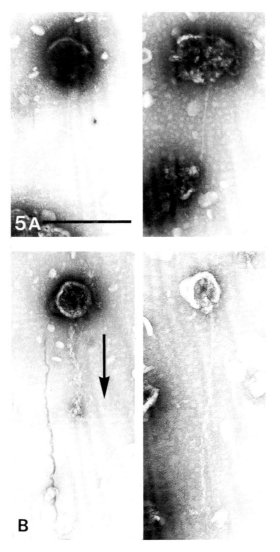

Fig. 5. Actin filaments attach the 'barbed' end to the virus capsid of P815 filopodia. TEM of negatively stained demembranated P815 filopodia before (A) and after (B) myosin S1 fragment decoration. Note in B the S1 arrowheads pointing away from the capsid (shown by arrow). Bar, 0·2 μm.

such associations is the myosin affinity technique, developed previously (Koch & Smith, 1978). When the actin is extracted from detergent-treated filopodia all of the Pr65 and some of its proteolytic fragments, notably P30, are specifically extracted with the actin (Fig. 6). The binding of Pr65 is completely inhibited by pre-saturating the myosin with actin showing that Pr65 extraction is mediated through actin. The extraction of P30 is more complex because only a fraction is extractable with myosin and only a part of this is prevented from binding by actin saturation.

ACTIN-BINDING VIRAL POLYPEPTIDES

To examine the possibility that viral polypeptides could serve as binding sites for actin filaments, they were tested for the ability to bind actin in an overlay assay (Snabes *et al.* 1983). When filopodia or cores are fractionated by sodium dodecyl sulphate–polyacrylamide gel electrophoresis (SDS–PAGE) and developed with ^{125}I-labelled F actin, two major actin-binding species are detected (Fig. 7). One of these has been identified tentatively as a gelsolin-type protein. The other co-migrates exactly with Pr65 and is also present in highly purified RNA tumour virus preparations. When Pr65 is purified by standard procedures and examined by the overlay assay, it also binds actin. It has been shown that this assay is subject to artefacts of unknown origin (Brown, 1985). However, under the conditions used in our studies, general binding to proteins did not occur, so the binding of Pr65 by actin appears to at least be specific. Similar binding assays using purified Pr65 in a plate binding assay were also positive. The major limitation of all these studies is that Pr65 has to be denatured in order to be isolated and analysed. Thus the theoretical possibility that the binding is unique to the denatured protein cannot be overcome.

The Pr65 molecule is a polyprotein which is cleaved during virus maturation, yielding a number of polypeptide domains. Thus it is possible to examine whether actin-binding is associated with a particular domain of the polyprotein. Direct binding studies indicated that actin binding could be detected with the purified P15 domain. This is a particularly hydrophobic species and advantage was taken of this to examine a possible association between the two proteins. P15 partitions quantitatively into the detergent phase during Triton X-114 separation (Bordier, 1981), whereas actin partitions quantitatively into the aqueous phase. However, when mixed, some of the actin co-purifies with the P15, indicating that complexing has occurred. Although these studies are still only preliminary, they do suggest that the Pr65 molecule can bind actin filaments at least *in vitro*.

GENERAL DISCUSSION

The major point to emerge from this study is that at least one actin filament forms a stable connection to the tip of the P815 filopodium by way of a retrovirus particle situated at the tip of the projection. The reason for the apparent preference for a single attached filament is not clear, but two possibilities are obvious. First, the attachment of a single filament could actually provide the stimulus for the growth of the projection. Subsequent attachment of other filaments could be precluded by changes in the virus particle during maturation. Alternatively, attachment sites for the actin filament may only become exposed at the most terminal stages of viral assembly, whereupon, for steric reasons, only one filament could be accommodated. This latter possibility is consistent with the known mechanism of retrovirus assembly (Bolognesi *et al.* 1978). Since this proceeds with the Pr65 polyprotein in direct attachment to the membrane, only at the latest stages of the process can a small set of Pr65 molecules that are incorporated into the nucleocapsid, but still not inserted into the membrane, become available for attachment to actin filaments. By this stage only

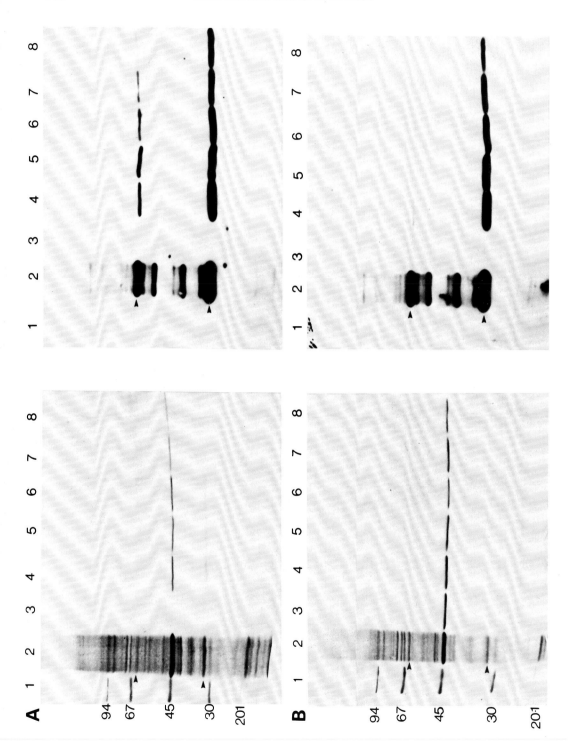

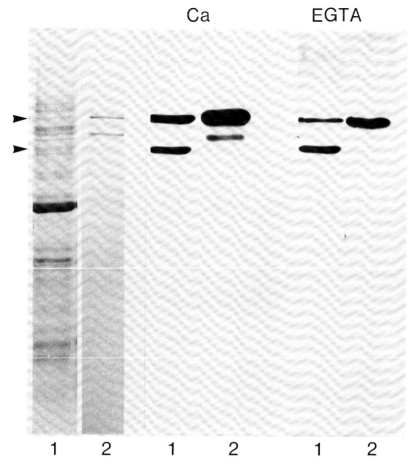

Fig. 7. ^{125}I-labelled actin gel overlay on P815 filopodia and plasma gelsolin. P815 filopodia (lanes 1) and pig plasma gelsolin (lanes 2) were fractionated by SDS–PAGE in 10/14% polyacrylamide gels and processed for ^{125}I-labelled actin overlay (Snabes *et al.* 1983). The lanes on the left show Coomassie-Blue-staining of the samples. The other lanes are autoradiographs after ^{125}I-labelled actin overlay of samples run on the same gel under EGTA or Ca^{2+} conditions (using buffers described by Snabes *et al.* 1983) as indicated. Arrowheads indicate: top, the calcium-sensitive binding protein (plasma) gelsolin; and bottom, the calcium-insensitive binding protein, which co-migrates with $Pr65^{gag}$.

Fig. 6. Myosin affinity precipitation of P815 filopodia lysates. Approximately 50 μg of P815 filopodia were lysed in 1% NP40/phosphate-buffered saline/1 mM-phenylmethyl-sulphonyl fluoride and: A, precipitated with 100 μg of pre-fixed myosin filaments; or B, precipitated with 100 μg of pre-fixed filaments pre-incubated with 100 μg of rabbit muscle F-actin. Left-hand panels: Coomassie-Blue-stained (10/12·5% polyacrylamide) gels. Right-hand panels: equivalent gels, probed by immunoblotting with rabbit anti-P30 antiserum. Arrowheads indicate Pr65 and P30, respectively. Lane 1, molecular weight markers ($\times 10^{-3}$); lane 2, filopodia lysates; lane 3, myosin or myosin pre-incubated with F-actin; lanes 4–8, myosin precipitates of serially diluted lysates.

enough Pr65 molecules to accommodate a single actin filament may be available. Testing of those hypotheses should be possible with the Gazdar strain of murine retrovirus, which does not undergo proteolytic processing and provides a homogeneous source of immature retrovirus particles consisting only of unprocessed Pr65 polyprotein (Pinter & de Harven, 1979).

What then are the consequences of this association between apical retrovirus particles and actin filaments on the mechanism of filopodial growth? The first is a negative one. In order that a projection can grow *via* membrane addition, the process must occur by way of vesicle fusion at the growing tip. Since the tip of the P815 filopodium is occupied by a virus particle, vesicle fusion cannot occur by the generally accepted process. The fact that the virus particle, and therefore the growing tip, is anchored to the cytoplasmic matrix by an actin filament makes it unlikely that, even if vesicle fusion could occur, it would provide a motive force of sufficient magnitude to overcome this anchorage.

Although this is a somewhat unusual system, it provides one of the first lines of evidence that microfilaments actually attach to the tip of a filopodium. Previously this was only inferred from the apparent proximity of filaments to the tip and the consistent polarity of the actin filaments with the preferred end for growth at the apical end. However, it was never clear whether a binding site of significant affinity existed at the tips for the filaments. Taken together with the above-mentioned circumstantial evidence, it is possible that this is a general characteristic of filopodia.

The existence of apex–filament interactions adds further support to the idea that actin filaments actually participate in the growth of projections. It is frequently suggested that actin polymerization at the tip effectively pushes it out and thereby growth is derived. However, the problem with such a mechanism is that extension of the membrane must precede actin polymerization, and therefore the ultimate force must come from elsewhere.

A model for filopodial growth that appeals to us is one involving microfilament capture. Thus at the site of growth, binding sites would develop for the attachment of actin filaments from the cortical meshwork. Once some filaments have become attached at the membrane by their ends, cross-linking proteins would start to maximize contacts between actin filaments (although tight bundling such as that of structures such as microvilli may not be essential) as well as lateral attachments to the membrane. As a result a co-ordinated configurational change of cytoplasmic matrix and membrane would have to occur to accommodate these interactions, and the formation of a projection, and its extension, would provide an arrangement that would maximize the interactions. This type of model requires an initial nucleation step that could be readily emulated by viral particles, thereby generating virus-tipped projections. Thus the major factor determining the propensity towards the formation of projections would be the state of the cytoplasmic matrix.

The presence of apically anchored microfilaments in a growing filopodium would not preclude the operation of a mechanism of growth involving a local increase in pressure such as that proposed recently (Oster, 1984). However, it is worth emphasizing that models based on hydrostatic-pressure effects might also require apically anchored microfilaments. Such an arrangement will ensure that the tip does not herniate out of control, but remains linked to the cytoplasmic matrix throughout the growth of the projection. However, in such a case the pressure exerted at the tip would not only extend the membrane outwards, but also carry some structural elements with it.

These studies have clarified one aspect of structure in one type of filopodium. Clearly, they only represent a small step towards the elucidation of the mechanism of growth of such projections. A process as complicated as this must depend on a large number of interactions. An understanding of precisely which components interact with one another will provide the structural basis for the elucidation of the mechanisms involved.

REFERENCES

ABERCROMBIE, M., HEAYSMAN, J. E. M. & PEGRUM, S. M. (1970). The locomotion of fibroblasts in culture. III. Movements of particles on the dorsal surface of the leading lamella. *Expl Cell Res.* **62**, 389–398.

ALBRECHT-BUEHLER, G. (1976). Filopodia in spreading 3T3 cells. Do they have a substrate-exploring function? *J. Cell Biol.* **69**, 275–286.

BOLOGNESI, D. P., MONTELARO, R. C., FRANK, H. & SCHAFER, W. (1978). Assembly of type-C oncornaviruses: A model. *Science* **199**, 183–186.

BORDIER, C. (1981). Phase separation of integral membrane proteins in Triton X-114 solutions. *J. biol. Chem.* **256**, 1604–1607.

BOYLES, J. & BAINTON, D. F. (1981). Change in plasma-membrane associated filaments during endocytosis and exocytosis in polymorphonuclear leukocytes. *Cell* **24**, 905–914.

BRAY, D. & BUNGE, M. B. (1973). The growth cone in neurite extension. In *Locomotion of Tissue Cells, Ciba Fdn Symp.* vol. 14, (new series). Amsterdam: Elsevier.

BRETSCHER, A. & WEBER, K. (1978). Localization of actin and microfilament-associated proteins in the microvilli and terminal web of intestinal brush border cells by immunofluorescence microscopy. *J. Cell Biol.* **79**, 839–842.

BROWN, S. S. (1985). The linkage of actin to non-erythroid membranes. *Bioessays* **3**, 65–67.

DAMSKY, C. H., SHEFFIELD, J. P., TUSZYNSKI, G. P. & WARREN, L. (1977). Is there a role for actin in virus budding? *J. Cell Biol.* **75**, 593–605.

DE ROSIER, D., TILNEY, L. G. & FLICKER, P. (1980). A change in the twist of the actin-containing filaments occurs during the extension of the actosomal process in *Limulus* sperm. *J. molec. Biol.* **137**, 375–389.

DETMERS, P. A., GOODENOUGH, W. V. & CONDEELIS, J. (1983). Elongation of the fertilization tube in *Chlamydomonas*: new observations on the core microfilaments and the effect of transient intracellular signals of their structural integrity. *J. Cell Biol.* **97**, 522–532.

DUNN, T. O. & POTTER, M. (1957). A transplantable mast cell neoplasm in the mouse. *J. natn. Cancer Inst.* **18**, 587–601.

EDDS, K. T. (1980). The formation and elongation of filopodia during transformation of sea urchin coelomocytes. *Cell Motil.* **1**, 113–130.

GENTY, N. & BUSSEREAU, F. (1980). Is cytoskeleton involved in vesicular stomatitis virus reproduction? *J. Virol.* **34**, 777–781.

HARRIS, A. K. (1973). Cell surface movements related to cell locomotion. In *Locomotion of Tissue Cells, Ciba Fdn Symp.* vol. 14 (new series). Amsterdam: Elsevier.

IWASAKI, Y. & TSUCHIDA, N. (1978). Transmission electron microscopy surveillance of retroviruses in tissue culture cells prepared by the critical-point drying method. *J. natn. Cancer Inst.* **61**, 431–436.

KOCH, G. L. E. & SMITH, M. J. (1978). An association between actin and the major histocompatibility antigen H-2. *Nature, Lond.* **273**, 274–278.

MARCUS, P. I. (1962). Dynamics of surface modification myxovirus-infected cells. *Cold Spring Harbor Symp. quant. Biol.* **27**, 351–365.

MOOSEKER, M. S. & TILNEY, L. S. (1975). Organization of an actin filament–membrane complex. Filament polarity and membrane attachment in the microvilli of intestinal epithelial cells. *J. Cell Biol.* **67**, 725–743.

MORAWIECKI, A. & LISOWSKA, E. (1965). Polymerised orosomucoid: An inhibitor of influenza virus haemagglutination. *Biochem. biophys. Res. Commun.* **18**, 606–610.

OSTER, G. F. (1984). On the crawling of cells. *J. Embryol. exp. Morph.* **83**, 329–364.

OTTO, J. J. & BRYAN, J. (1981). The incorporation of actin and fascin into the cytoskeleton of filopodial sea urchin coelomocytes. *Cell Motil.* **1**, 179–192.

PINTER, A. & DE HARVEN, E. (1979). Protein composition of a defective murine sarcoma virus particle possessing the enveloped type-A morphology. *Virology* **99**, 103–110.

SNABES, M. C., BOYD, A. E. III & BRYAN, J. (1983). Identification of G-actin binding proteins in rat tissues using a gel overlay technique. *Expl Cell Res.* **146**, 63–70.

STOKES, G. V. (1976). High-voltage electron microscope study of the release of vaccinia virus from whole cells. *J. Virol.* **18**, 636–643.

STRAUSS, E. G. & STRAUSS, J. H. (1985). Assembly of enveloped aminal viruses. In *Virus Structure and Assembly* (ed. S. Casjens). Boston, U.S.A.: Jones and Bartlett.

TAYLOR, D. L., CONDEELIS, J. S., MOORE, P. L. & ALLEN, R. D. (1973). The contractile basis of amoeboid movement. I. The chemical control of motility in isolated cytoplasm. *J. Cell Biol.* **59**, 378–394.

TAYLOR, D. L. & FECHEIMER, M. (1982). Cytoplasmic structure and contractility: The solation–contraction coupling hypothesis. *Phil. Trans. R. Soc. Lond.* B **229**, 185–197.

TILNEY, L. G. (1975). Actin filaments in the acrosomal reaction of *limulus* sperm. Motion generated by alterations in the packing of filaments. *J. Cell Biol.* **64**, 289–310.

TILNEY, L. G., BONDER, E. M. & DE ROSIER, D. J. (1981). Actin filaments elongate from their membrane-associated ends. *J. Cell Biol.* **90**, 485–494.

TILNEY, L. G., HATANO, S., ISHIKAWA, H. & MOOSEKER, M. S. (1973). The polymerization of actin. Its role in the generation of the acrosomal process of certain echinoderm sperm. *J. Cell Biol.* **59**, 109–126.

Trends Biochem. Sci. (1985). **10**, 464.

VASILIEV, J. M. (1981). The role of pseudopodial reactions in the attachment of normal and transformed cells. In *Internat. Cell Biol.* (ed. H. G. Schweiger). Berlin: Springer-Verlag.

WANG, E., WOLF, B. A., LAMB, R. A., CHOPPIN, P. W. & GOLDBERG, A. R. (1976). The presence of actin in enveloped virus. In *Cell Motility* (ed. R. Goldman, T. D. Pollard & J. Rosenbaum), pp. 589–600. NY: Cold Spring Harbor Laboratory Press.

WESSELLS, N. K., SPOONER, B. S. & LUDUENA, M. A. (1973). Surface movements, microfilaments and cell locomotion. In *Locomotion of Tissue Cells, Ciba Fdn Symp.* vol. 14 (new series). Amsterdam: Elsevier.

YIN, H. L., ALBRECHT, J. H. & FATT, A. (1981). Identification of gelsolin, a Ca^{2+}-dependent regulatory protein of actin gel–sol transformation and its intracellular distribution in a variety of cells and tissues. *J. Cell Biol.* **91**, 901–906.

YUEN, P. H. & WONG, P. K. Y. (1977). A morphological study on the ultrastructure and assembly of murine leukaemia virus using a temperature-sensitive mutant restricted in assembly. *Virology* **80**, 260–274.

J. Cell Sci. Suppl. 5, 145–159 (1986)
Printed in Great Britain © The Company of Biologists Limited 1986

RETICULOMYXA: A NEW MODEL SYSTEM OF INTRACELLULAR TRANSPORT

MICHAEL P. KOONCE, URSULA EUTENEUER AND
MANFRED SCHLIWA
Department of Zoology, University of California, Berkeley, CA 94720, USA

SUMMARY

Reticulomyxa is a large multinucleated freshwater protozoan that provides a new model system in which to study intracellular transport and cytoskeletal dynamics. Within the cell body and reticulopodial network, rapid, visually striking saltatory organelle motility as well as bulk cytoplasmic streaming can be readily observed. In addition, the cytoskeletal elements within these strands undergo dynamic splaying and fusing rearrangements, which can be visualized by video-enhanced light microscopy. A reactivatable lysed cell model has been developed that appears to preserve, and therefore permits examination of, these three forms of motility in a more controlled environment. Individual organelle movements are microtubule-based and have similarities to, but also differences from, the recently described kinesin-based transport. This lysed cell model can be further manipulated to provide native, ordered, completely exposed networks of either microtubules or microfilaments, or a combination of both, and thus may serve as a versatile motility assay system in which to examine the movement of exogenously added isolated organelles or latex beads.

INTRODUCTION

The transport of organelles from one subcellular region to another is a fundamental process of nearly every eukaryotic cell. Many pharmacological and correlative light- and electron-microscopical studies have demonstrated that microtubules and microfilaments play an integral role in this phenomenon (reviewed by Schliwa, 1984). In general, the directed, often saltatory, movement of individual organelles is representative of microtubule-based transport systems in animal cells including neurons (Allen *et al.* 1982; Brady & Lasek, 1982; Smith *et al.* 1975), chromatophores (Murphy & Tilney, 1974; Schliwa, 1982), cultured cells (Hayden *et al.* 1983) and protozoans (Travis *et al.* 1983). Recent detailed studies of organelle–microtubule interactions in the squid giant axon have resulted in the identification and isolation of at least one novel microtubule-associated translocator, kinesin (Vale *et al.* 1985a). On the other hand, microfilament (or actomyosin)-based transport is most common in plant cells as an often rapid bulk streaming of cytoplasm (Kamiya, 1981). The characean green algae have served as especially useful models for such transport (Sheetz & Spudich, 1983; Kachar, 1985). There is not, however, a simple dichotomy between plant and animal organelle transport systems, since examples of microtubule-based movements in plants (Gunning & Hardham, 1982; Menzel & Schliwa, 1986) and the involvement of microfilaments in these processes in animal cells (Brady *et al.* 1984) have been reported. However, little is known regarding the association and possible interaction of these two transport systems within the same cell (see, however, Burnside & Nagle, 1983; Menzel & Schliwa, 1986). Can they act together in a coordinate fashion or do they always mediate separate and distinct forms of motility? If the two mechanisms are usually separate, can one act in a role that is supportive of the other? In addition, are transport mechanisms universal and in what ways might they be tailored to a particular cell type? Here we describe a new, versatile model system of intracellular transport that will permit examination of these questions.

Reticulomyxa is a giant freshwater protozoan with striking intracellular transport. Both directed saltatory organelle movements and bulk cytoplasmic streaming are found within the cell body and a peripheral reticulopodial network of fine strands (Koonce *et al.* 1986). The large size of this organism, the speed and extent of these two forms of organelle movement, and the structural simplicity and order of the cytoskeleton make *Reticulomyxa* a good candidate for studies not only on the mechanisms of intracellular transport, but also on the interactions between, and functions of, the two organelle transport systems within the same cell. This paper reviews some of the unique morphological and structural features of this organism and describes the development of a reactivatable lysed cell model that preserves both saltatory and streaming-like forms of motility. With this model system, it is possible to address questions about the independent functions of each cytoskeletal system as well as their cumulative action in organelle transport.

MATERIALS AND METHODS

Reticulomyxa *culture*

Reticulomyxa (Nauss, 1949) was found growing on the sides and bottom of a freshwater aquarium. It is easily maintained and can be grown to large amounts (several ml of packed cells per week) in Petri dishes on a diet of either flaked fish food (TetraMin) or wheat germ. Twice weekly, dishes are cleaned of debris and refilled with fresh tap water. Food is added as needed. Under crowded conditions, organisms stream up the sides of dishes and onto the undersurface of the air–water interface, where they continue to thrive.

Light microscopy

For light-microscopic experiments, small pieces of cell body were placed on coverslips in Petri dishes containing either tap water or 10 mM-Hepes, 2 mM-MgCl$_2$, pH 7·0 and permitted to attach and extend networks (usually <1 h). The coverslips were then inverted onto slides with coverslip pieces as spacers. The longitudinal sides of this sandwich were sealed with VALAP, leaving the ends open for perfusion of solutions. Preparations were viewed in a Zeiss Photomicroscope III equipped with phase-contrast, polarization, or differential interference contrast (DIC) optics. For video enhancement, images were projected into a Dage-MTI series 67 videocamera (Dage-MTI Inc., Michigan City, IN) and further manipulated with an Interactive Video Image 1 processor (Interactive Video, Concord MA) as described elsewhere (Koonce & Schliwa, 1986). Low light level images were obtained with a Dage-MTI ISIT camera. Real time recordings were made with a Panasonic VHS recorder (nv-8050) and photographs of the enhanced images were taken directly from the video monitor with a 35 mm camera and Kodak Plus-X film. For lysis, preparations were perfused with 5% hexylene glycol, 1 mM-sodium orthovanadate, and 0·15% Brij 58 in a buffer consisting of 30 mM-Pipes, 12·5% Hepes, 4 mM-EGTA, and 1 mM-MgCl$_2$ (50% PHEM; Schliwa & van Blerkom, 1981), at pH 7·0. Movement was immediately arrested, and thin regions of network were completely lysed within 1 min. Preparations were then rinsed with buffer alone followed by the experimental solutions. All experiments were performed at room temperature.

Immunofluorescence

Lysed preparations were fixed with 1% glutaraldehyde, rinsed with buffer, and processed as described (Koonce *et al.* 1986). Monoclonal tubulin antibodies made against *Drosophila* alpha tubulin were kindly provided by Dr Margaret Fuller. Microfilaments were visualized with rhodamine–phalliodin, kindly provided by Dr T. Wieland.

Electron microscopy

For whole-mount preparations, networks extended on Formvar-coated gold finder grids were either fixed directly, or lysed and then fixed with 1% glutaraldehyde in 50% PHEM, pH 7·0, and processed as described (Koonce & Schliwa, 1986). Preparations were viewed in a Kratos high-voltage electron microscope (National Center For Electron Microscopy, Lawrence Berkeley Laboratories) operated at 1500 kV. Stereo pairs were taken with tilt angles of 12°.

Bead experiments

Reticulomyxa supernatant was prepared by homogenization of cell bodies at 0°C in a Dounce homogenizer in PHEM buffer supplemented with 40 mM-beta-glycerophosphate, 20 μg ml^{-1} DNase I, 2 mM-ATP, and a protease inhibitor cocktail of 40 μg ml^{-1} soybean trypsin inhibitor II, 40 μg ml^{-1} L-1-tosylamide-2-phenyl-ethylchloromethyl ketone (TAME), 40 μg ml^{-1} benzyl arginyl-methyl ester (BAME), 4 μg ml^{-1} leupeptin, 4 μg ml^{-1} pepstatin, 200 μg ml^{-1} antipain, 1 mM-phenyl-methylsulphonyl fluoride (PMSF), and 0·2 TI units ml^{-1} aprotinin. The homogenate was spun for 15 min at 80 000$\boldsymbol{g}$ in a Beckman airfuge at 2°C. The clear supernatant was removed by aspiration, avoiding both the pellet and the floating layer of lipid. Protein concentration of this supernatant was approximately 1·2 mg ml^{-1}. Carboxylated latex beads 0·19 μm in diameter (Polyscience Inc., Warrington, PA) were incubated in this supernatant for 15 min at 0°C and either added directly to the lysed–stripped networks (including supernatant), or first rinsed twice in buffer alone, then added. Beads were also incubated in 1 mg ml^{-1} bovine serum albumin as a control.

RESULTS

Reticulomyxa is a giant multinucleated protozoan (Class Rhizopoda, Order Granuloreticulosea; Levine *et al.* 1980) consisting of a large naked cell body of thick interconnected strands 50–200 μm in diameter (Fig. 1A,B) surrounded by a dynamic, highly reticulate network of fine strands (Fig. 1C). Typical individuals cover an area from 1–4 cm^2 but often form contiguous arrays many times larger. Conspicuous within both the cell body and reticulopodial network are rapid organelle movements. Constant bulk cytoplasmic streaming, which carries organelles, vacuoles and nuclei at rates of up to 20 μm s^{-1} is prominent within, though not confined to, the cell body. Streaming is bidirectional, often with several 'lanes' of countercurrent flow in a given strand. Within the network, individual organelles (predominantly mitochondria and small clear vesicles) move in a 'saltatory' fashion in close association with cytoskeletal linear elements (Fig. 1D). These individual movements occur in a bidirectional fashion along a given linear element at rates averaging 12–13 μm s^{-1} but may reach 25 μm s^{-1}. Saltatory movements are also seen in the cell body but, owing to the dominant bulk flow, are difficult to distinguish. Neither form of motility (streaming or saltations) is affected by extracellular addition of microtubule (10 μg ml^{-1} nocodazole or 2·5 mM-colchicine) or microfilament (10 μg ml^{-1} cytochalasin D) inhibitors but can be reversibly arrested, without affecting the network integrity, by 20 mM-MgCl$_2$, uncouplers of electron transport

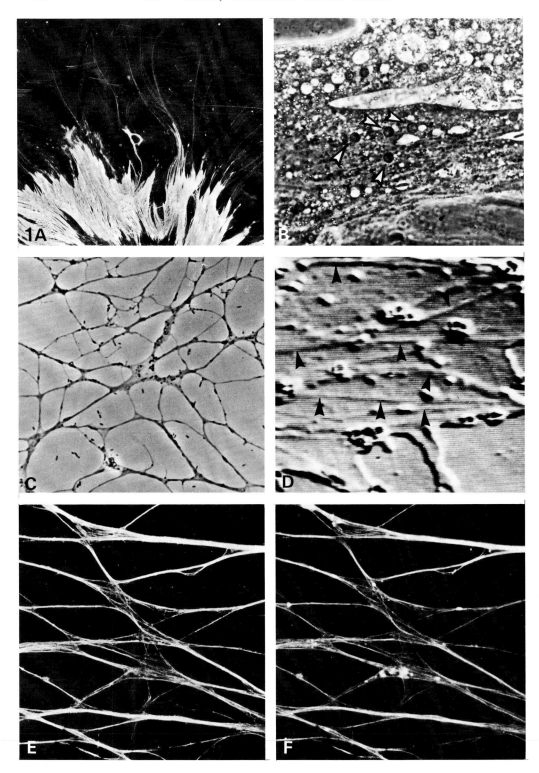

(100 μM-dinitrophenol, 10 μM-carbonylcyanide-4-trifluoromethoxyphenylhydrazone (FCCP), or, surprisingly, 1 mM-vanadate.

The cytoskeletal backbone of this organism consists primarily of long colinear bundles of microtubules and microfilaments. Within the network of double-labelled preparations, the immunofluorescent staining patterns of these two cytoskeletal elements often appear nearly identical (Fig. 1E,F). In the cell body, most of the microtubule antibody and rhodamine–phalloidin labelling occurs near the strand's cortex, though a strong background staining is seen uniformly throughout the thick strands. This colinear association is also confirmed by thin-section and whole-mount electron microscopy (see Koonce *et al.* 1986). Thin filaments not only bind rhodamine–phalloidin, but are also decorated with the S1 fragment of myosin, confirming their actin-like nature.

In addition to supporting rapid organelle movements, the peripheral network itself is a highly dynamic structure. Moderate diameter (1–10 μm) strands (Fig. 2) can be seen to extend from the ends of the cell body at rates exceeding 100 μm min^{-1}. The driving force for such elongation does not depend on contact with the substrate as strands can be extended upwards into the medium. It is not clear to what extent microtubule and microfilament sliding or polymerization contribute to this process, but a highly birefringent cytoskeletal rod can always be found continuous to the tips of these filopodia (Fig. 3). Large amounts of membrane must also be rapidly inserted along the sides or tips of these strands. Often, at a random distance proximal to the extending tip, a side branch will extend laterally, away from the direction of primary growth. If these branches contact another strand, they immediately fuse and begin common transport. Branches can be as small as 100 nm in diameter and minimally contain a single microtubule. Small strands and branches continuously splay, fuse, or 'zip' back and forth between larger strands. Within flattened coalesced regions of the network, cytoskeletal linear elements can be readily seen to exhibit analogous behaviour, suggesting that the splaying and zipping of small strands is probably based upon cytoskeletal interactions rather than membrane flow.

To study the physiological requirements of the various forms of *Reticulomyxa* motility, a gentle lysis procedure was developed, which completely removes the plasma membrane of the reticulopodial network's fine strands and flattened areas without visibly affecting cytoskeletal structure. A whole-mount electron micrograph

---

Fig. 1. Light microscopy of *Reticulomyxa*. A. Low-power overview of a portion of a single organism. Visible are the thick interconnected veins comprising the cell body and some of the larger reticulopodial strands radiating outwards. ×2·5. B. Higher-magnification phase-contrast micrograph of the cell body showing many organelles, vacuoles and nuclei (arrowheads). ×500. C. Phase-contrast micrograph of the highly anastomosed reticulopodial network. Not only do organelles rapidly move within these strands, but the strands themselves fuse, branch and 'zip' back and forth. ×500. D. High-magnification video-enhanced DIC micrograph of a flattened portion of the network showing the cytoskeletal linear elements (arrowheads) upon which organelles translocate. Each linear element is composed of a colinear bundle of both microtubules and micro-filaments. ×3500. E. Tubulin antibody; and F, rhodamine–phalloidin staining pattern of a double-labelled network. Note the close correspondence in staining between the two images. ×820.

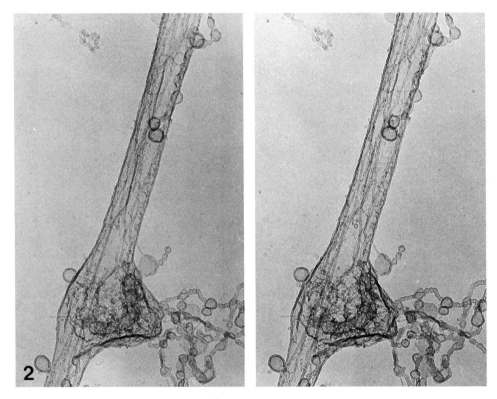

Fig. 2. High-voltage electron micrograph stereo pair of a whole-mount strand about 250 nm in diameter. Microtubules are prominent in these preparations but actin filaments are difficult to distinguish. ×63 000.

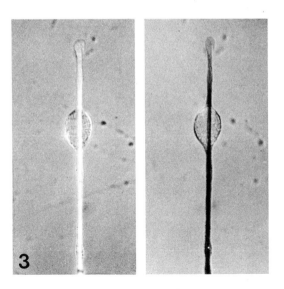

Fig. 3. Polarization micrograph of an extending strand demonstrating the birefringence of the cytoskeletal core at opposite compensator settings. Extending strands nearly always have a slightly bulbous tip and often have expanded 'droplets' of cytoplasm along their lengths. These droplets also move up and down these strands. ×560.

of the lysed preparation is shown in Fig. 4. Many organelles remain attached to the cytoskeletal framework and resume *in-vivo*-like movements if ATP is added (Fig. 5). Individual organelles move in a saltatory fashion along cytoskeletal elements with rates up to $20\,\mu\mathrm{m\,s^{-1}}$ (average $= 10\,\mu\mathrm{m\,s^{-1}}$ at pH 7·5). Movement is primarily unidirectional along a given element, though bidirectional motility and reversals of direction of single organelles are commonly seen. In addition, aggregates of organelles can move together in a smooth, streaming-like fashion visibly distinct from the saltatory movements, at rates of $1-5\,\mu\mathrm{m\,s^{-1}}$. These two forms of movement (saltations and streaming) are most prominent in the first 5 min of reactivation but motility can still be seen at least 1 h later. Motility is not reactivated with other nucleotide triphosphates, is only completely inhibited by concentrations of vanadate $100\,\mu\mathrm{M}$ or greater, and is not affected by up to 5 mM-erythro-9-(3-(2-hydroxynonyl))-adenine (EHNA). The sulphydryl reagent N-ethylmaleimide will inhibit reactivated motility at concentrations higher than $100\,\mu\mathrm{M}$.

4

Fig. 4. High-voltage electron micrograph stereo pair of a whole-mount lysed preparation demonstrating the attachment of organelles to the microtubules and the complete absence of a plasma membrane. The large organelles are mitochondria and the smaller ones (arrowheads) correspond to small vesicles seen *in vivo* (unknown identity). Actin filaments in these preparations are difficult to preserve for electron microscopy and thus are not prominent here. However, S1-myosin-decorated filaments are much more stable and significant numbers of filaments can be seen throughout the preparations (not shown). ×22 000.

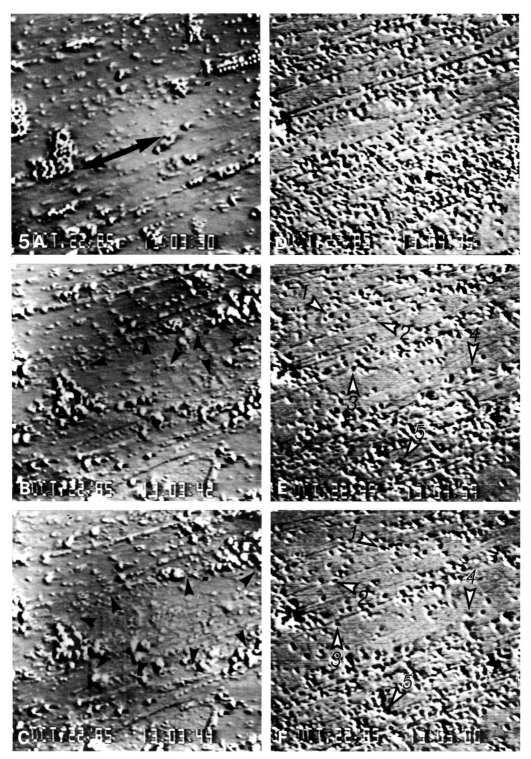

Fig. 5. Video-enhanced DIC sequence of the lysis and reactivation process. A. A flattened region of network before lysis. Organelles are moving bidirectionally as indicated by the arrow. B,C. Same region as in A, during lysis. The lysis buffer immediately arrests motility and the membrane often can be seen to peel off the cytoskeleton. The arrowheads here outline the expanding holes in the membrane. D. Same region after lysis and contrast enhancement. E,F. Two frames 1 s apart, of reactivated motility after ATP addition. Numbered arrowheads follow the movement of a few organelles. Time is given in seconds. ×2000.

In addition to the organelle movements, reactivation of the lysed network causes an active bending and splaying of microtubule bundles, usually resulting in a random dense meshwork of what appear to be single microtubules or small bundles of two to three microtubules (Fig. 6). Organelles still move along the fibres of this meshwork, sometimes switching from one microtubule to another. In contrast to the behaviour of microtubules, rhodamine–phalloidin-labelled actin filaments visualized with low light level, video fluorescence microscopy slowly condense from long linear bundles into discrete foci (Fig. 7). These foci usually show slow but smooth movements towards other fluorescent aggregates.

The lysed network is very stable. Reactivation as long as 1 h after lysis does not appear to differ from an immediate reactivation. This stability permits further manipulation of the lysed network. Most organelles can be removed (solubilized) by perfusion of buffer containing 1% Triton X-100, yielding a relatively 'clean' cytoskeleton (Fig. 8). The organization of neither microtubules nor microfilaments appears to be disturbed by this treatment. Reactivation at this point yields little microtubule bundle splaying, prominent only in areas where a few hardy organelles remain and move.

Microtubules in this lysed network are insensitive to 1 mM free calcium (>15 min), even in the presence of $1 \, \text{mg ml}^{-1}$ calmodulin. However, 0·5 M-KCl causes a slow endwise microtubule depolymerization visible in video-enhanced preparations. Microtubule ends can be seen to recede at rates of $0·98 \pm 0·24 \, \mu\text{m s}^{-1}$ ($n = 15$, 3 preparations). Rhodamine–phalloidin staining of high-salt-washed networks devoid of any visible microtubules still reveals a relatively undisturbed actin filament pattern. Alternatively, actin filaments can be selectively removed from this lysed cell model by incubation with $20 \, \mu\text{g ml}^{-1}$ gelsolin (kindly provided by Drs R. Ezzell,

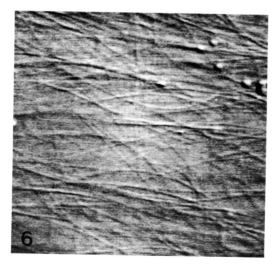

Fig. 6. Video-enhanced DIC micrograph of a random microtubule meshwork. Compare this image with either Fig. 5D or Fig. 8. This micrograph was taken approximately 5 min after reactivation. ×2000.

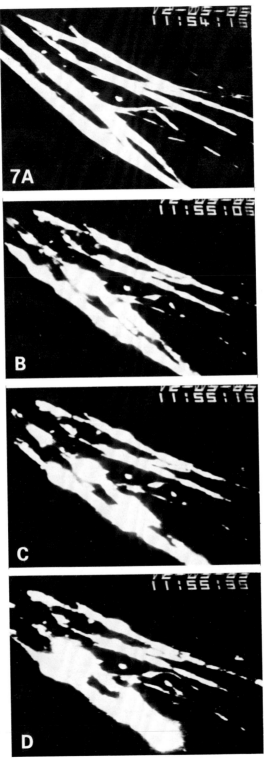

Fig. 7. Low light level, video fluorescence sequence of rhodamine–phalloidin-labelled microfilaments during reactivation. A. Labelling pattern after lysis but before ATP addition. B–D. After ATP addition, time is displayed in seconds. Note the formation of foci and the movement of these foci towards each other. ×1100.

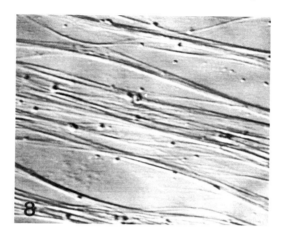

Fig. 8. Video-enhanced DIC micrograph of a lysed network stripped of most endogenous organelles with 1% Triton X-100. Compare with Fig. 5D. ×1700.

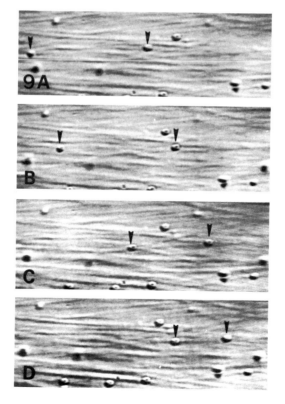

Fig. 9. Video-enhanced DIC sequence of latex bead motility at 5-s intervals. Two beads (arrowheads) are moving along a small microtubule bundle at a rate of approximately $4\,\mu\mathrm{m\,s}^{-1}$. Beads added to lysed-stripped networks can be readily distinguished from the few remaining organelles. ×2000.

H. Yin and T. Stossel) in the presence of 10 μM free calcium. No actin fluorescence can be detected after a 10-min treatment. Reactivation yields relatively normal organelle movements and bundle splaying, but the streaming-like movements are much less apparent. Reactivation of control preparations incubated in 10 μM free calcium alone (no gelsolin) did not appear to differ from normal.

This system is also amenable to studying interactions with inert latex beads. Beads coated with a high-speed *Reticulomyxa* supernatant, and added to the lysed–stripped network in the presence of this supernatant move along the framework at rates of up to 4·5 μm s^{-1} (Fig. 9). Supernatant-coated beads in buffer alone, uncoated beads, or beads coated with bovine albumin are not transported. The nature of the motility component in the high-speed supernatant is currently under investigation.

DISCUSSION

Reticulomyxa, first described by Nauss (1949) and recently re-discovered in this laboratory (Schliwa *et al.* 1984) as well as by Hulsmann (1984), is an extremely large fresh-water protozoan with rapid and pervasive intracellular motility. Several features make this organism attractive for studies of intracellular transport: (1) it is easy to work with, requiring no elaborate maintenance or preparation; (2) the motility *in vivo*, consisting of two distinct forms of polarized cytoplasmic transport, is among the fastest ever reported (and can be readily observed in the light microscope); (3) *Reticulomyxa* contains an extensive but highly ordered cytoskeleton, which can be visualized *in situ* with the aid of a computer-enhanced video system: (4) the large size and rapid growth makes *Reticulomyxa* amenable to biochemical analysis of the cytoskeletal and motility components; (5) last but not least, a reactivatable *in vitro* model has been developed, which retains both forms of organelle transport and itself can be further manipulated.

Using the combination of a non-ionic detergent (to solubilize the plasma membrane), hexylene glycol (to stabilize cytoskeletal components; Kane, 1965) and vanadate (to arrest *in vivo* movements and perhaps to cross-link organelles to the cytoskeleton, providing stability during membrane removal), a seemingly intact, completely open cytoskeletal framework can be obtained from the reticulopodial strands of *Reticulomyxa* that retains the ability to support organelle motility. Electron microscopy and immunofluorescence demonstrate that this framework consists predominantly of parallel bundles of long microtubules and microfilaments with many attached organelles (mainly mitochondria and small clear vesicles). Addition of ATP reactivates three forms of motility associated with this framework: individual organelle movements, a streaming-like movement of organelle aggregates, and a splaying of microtubule bundles into a meshwork.

Individual organelle movements are always associated with microtubules that are visible by video-enhanced light microscopy. Their motility is not greatly affected by the removal of microfilaments with gelsolin, demonstrating that the saltatory organelle movements are microtubule-based. Similar *in vitro* movements in extruded squid axoplasm (Allen *et al.* 1986; Vale *et al.* 1985c) have also been shown to be microtubule-based. This finding confirms and extends our previous demonstration of bidirectional organelle movement *in vivo* in *Reticulomyxa* strands containing single microtubules (Koonce & Schliwa, 1985).

Gelsolin-induced actin filament fragmentation does, however, appear to reduce the occurrence of streaming-like movements. In addition, there is a striking resemblance between this streaming and the observed condensation into, and subsequent movement of, microfilament foci in the reactivated model. Whether a contractile system mediates streaming, or whether a microfilament meshwork simply entangles organelles that still move along microtubules, is not yet known. Myosin can be detected with antibodies in Western blots of *Reticulomyxa* cytoplasm (Schliwa & Spudich, unpublished observations), and its organization in the lysed network is being investigated. Addition of ATP to lysed networks from which microtubules were removed by high salt treatment does not visibly alter the microfilament pattern, but high salt is also known to dissociate myosin filaments. Re-addition of myosin to these lysed and salt-treated networks in an attempt to reactivate the contractile system should help shed some light on its function.

The active splaying of microtubule bundles appears to be partially due to the reactivated organelle motility. Without a confining plasma membrane, the movement of just the organelles might indirectly push or pull bundles apart. Yet it is difficult to conceive that this action alone would result in such a dense meshwork or could account for the apparent active bending of microtubule bundles, especially in areas of little organelle motility. It is reasonable to speculate that some sort of inter-microtubule sliding and bundling process is important in the rapid *in vivo* extension of reticulopodial filaments or the zipping and unzipping of whole strands or cytoskeletal linear elements. The reactivatable model system, in combination with biochemical fractionation of extracts or monoclonal antibodies, should help identify the factors responsible for microtubule splaying and bending.

As with kinesin-based organelle transport, individual organelle movements in *Reticulomyxa* are also microtubule-based and share a similar relative insensitivity to vanadate (Vale *et al.* 1985*a*). However, the rate of motility is nearly an order of magnitude faster in *Reticulomyxa*, cannot be reactivated by GTP, and is much more sensitive to *N*-ethylmaleimide than kinesin-based transport (Vale *et al.* 1985*a*). More detailed comparisons are not yet possible owing to the limited information on these two systems at this time. Even if *Reticulomyxa* transport contains a kinesin-like component, the data suggest it will be different enough to warrant further analysis.

Reticulomyxa shares many morphological features with the better-known marine foraminiferan *Allogromia* (McGee-Russell & Allen, 1971; Travis & Allen, 1981; Travis *et al.* 1983). Both organisms possess a highly dynamic reticulate network of strands characterized by rapid organelle movements and a structural backbone of colinear microtubules. In addition, the organelle movements in *Allogromia* also appear to be microtubule-based. Disruption of microtubules with cold, colchicine or nocodazole blocks both motility and strand extension (Travis & Bowser, 1986). Actin filaments are also found in *Allogromia* but their distribution is mainly centred in focal adhesion-like plaques and some linear arrays, though not nearly as extensive as seen in *Reticulomyxa*. It is interesting that neither nocodazole, colchicine, nor cytochalasin D has an effect upon *in vivo* motility in *Reticulomyxa*, but it is not clear whether these compounds are able to cross this organism's plasma membrane. Even though the reticulopodial networks of *Reticulomyxa* and *Allogromia* are almost indistinguishable in the light microscope (except for the large size of the *Reticulomyxa* network), there are functional differences between these two organisms in network withdrawal, translocation, reproduction, and perhaps prey capture. It should be interesting to examine the structural and functional similarities and differences between these two organisms, especially in the context of environmental adaptations.

We thank Dr W. Z. Cande for many stimulating discussions, Drs M. Fuller and T. Wieland for providing tubulin antibodies and rhodamine–phalloidin, respectively, and Drs R. Ezzell, H. Yin and T. Stossel for a generous gift of gelsolin. This work was supported in part by NIGMS grant 31041.

REFERENCES

ALLEN, R. D., METUZALS, J., TASAKI, I., BRADY, S. T. & GILBERT, S. P. (1982). Fast axonal transport in giant squid axon. *Science* **218**, 1127–1129.

ALLEN, R. D., WEISS, D. G., HAYDEN, J. H., BROWN, D. T., FUJIWAKE, H. & SIMPSON, M. (1986). Gliding movement of and bidirectional transport along single native microtubules from squid axoplasm: evidence for an active role of microtubules in cytoplasmic transport. *J. Cell Biol.* **100**, 1736–1752.

BRADY, S. T. & LASEK, R. J. (1982). Axonal transport: a cell biological method for studying proteins associated with the cytoskeleton. *Meth. Cell Biol.* **25**, 365–398.

BRADY, S. T., LASEK, R. J., ALLEN, R. D., YIN, H. L. & STOSSEL, T. P. (1984). Gelsolin inhibition of fast axonal transport indicates a requirement for actin filaments. *Nature, Lond.* **310**, 56–58.

BURNSIDE, B. & NAGLE, B. (1983). Retinomotor movements of photoreceptors and retinal pigment epithelium: mechanisms and regulation. In *Progress in Retinal Research* (ed. N. Osborn & G. Chader), vol. 2, pp. 67–109. New York: Pergamon.

GUNNING, B. E. S. & HARDHAM, A. R. (1982). Microtubules. *A. Rev. Pl. Physiol.* **33**, 651–698.

HAYDEN, J. H., ALLEN, R. D. & GOLDMAN, R. D. (1983). Cytoplasmic transport in keratocytes: direct visualization of particle transport along microtubules. *Cell Motil.* **3**, 1–19.

HULSMANN, N. (1984). Biology of the genus *Reticulomyxa* (Rhizopoda). *J. Protozool.* **34**, 55a.

KACHAR, B. (1985). Direct visualization of organelle movement along actin filaments dissociated from characean algae. *Science* **227**, 1355–1357.

KAMIYA, N. (1981). Physical and chemical basis of cytoplasmic streaming. *A. Rev. Pl. Physiol.* **32**, 205–236.

KANE, R. E. (1965). The mitotic apparatus. Physical-chemical factors controlling stability. *J. Cell Biol.* **25** (Suppl.), 137–144.

KOONCE, M. P., EUTENEUER, U., McDONALD, K. L., MENZEL, D. & SCHLIWA, M. (1986). Cytoskeletal architecture and motility in a giant freshwater amoeba *Reticulomyxa. Cell Motil. Cytoskeleton* (in press).

KOONCE, M. P. & SCHLIWA, M. (1985). Bidirectional organelle transport can occur in cell processes that contain single microtubules. *J. Cell Biol.* **100**, 322–326.

KOONCE, M. P. & SCHLIWA, M. (1986). Reactivation of organelle movements along the cytoskeletal framework of a giant freshwater amoeba. *J. Cell Biol.* **103** (in press).

LEVINE, N. D., CORLISS, I. O., COX, F. E. G., DEROUX, G., GRAIN, J., HONIGBERG, B. M., LEEDALE, G. F., LOEBLICH, A. R., LOM, I., LYNN, D., MERINFIELD, E. G., PAGE, F. C., POLJANSKI, G., SPRAGUE, V., VAVARA, J. & WALLACE, F. G. (1980). A newly revised classification of the protozoa. *J. Protozool.* **27**, 37–58.

McGEE-RUSSELL, S. M. & ALLEN, R. D. (1971). Reversible stabilization of labile microtubules in the reticulopodial network of *Allogromia*. *Adv. cell. molec. Biol.* **1**, 153–184.

MENZEL, D. & SCHLIWA, M. (1986). Motility in the siphonous green alga *Bryopsis*. II. Chloroplast movement requires organized arrays of both microtubules and actin filaments. *Eur. J. Cell Biol.* **40**, 286–295.

MURPHY, D. B. & TILNEY, L. G. (1974). The role of microtubules in the movement of pigment granules in teleost melanophores. *J. Cell Biol.* **61**, 757–779.

NAUSS, R. N. (1949). *Reticulomyxa filosa* Gen. ET SP. NOV., a new primitive plasmodium. *Bull. Torrey bot. Club* **76**, 161–174.

SCHLIWA, M. (1982). Chromatophores: their use in understanding microtubule-dependent intracellular transport. *Meth. Cell Biol.* **25**, 285–312.

SCHLIWA, M. (1984). Mechanisms of intracellular transport. In *Cell and Muscle Motility* (ed. J. Shay), vol. 5, pp. 1–82. New York: Plenum.

SCHLIWA, M., McDONALD, K. L., KOONCE, M. P. & EUTENEUER, U. (1984). *Reticulomyxa*, a new model system for the study of intracellular organelle transport. *J. Cell Biol.* **99**, 239a.

SCHLIWA, M. & VAN BLERKOM, J. (1981). Structural interactions of cytoskeletal components. *J. Cell Biol.* **90**, 222–235.

SHEETZ, M. P. & SPUDICH, J. A. (1983). Movement of myosin-coated beads on actin cables *in vitro*. *Nature, Lond.* **303**, 31–35.

SMITH, D. S., JARLFORS, U. & CAMERON, B. F. (1975). Morphological evidence for the participation of microtubules in axonal transport. *Ann. N.Y. Acad. Sci.* **263**, 472–506.

TRAVIS, J. L. & ALLEN, R. D. (1981). Studies on the motility of the Foraminifera. I. Ultra-structure of the reticulopodial network of *Allogromia laticollaris* (Arnold). *J. Cell Biol.* **90**, 211–221.

TRAVIS, J. L. & BOWSER, S. S. (1986). A new model of reticulopodial motility and shape: evidence for a microtubule-based motor and an actin skeleton. *Cell Motil.* (in press).

TRAVIS, J. L., KENEALLY, J. F. X. & ALLEN, R. D. (1983). Studies on the motility of Foraminifera. II. The dynamic cytoskeleton of the reticulopodial network of *Allogromia laticollaris*. *J. Cell Biol.* **97**, 1668–1676.

VALE, R. D., REESE, T. S. & SHEETZ, M. P. (1985a). Identification of a novel force-producing protein, kinesin, involved in microtubule-based motility. *Cell* **42**, 39–50.

VALE, R. D., SCHNAPP, B. J., MITCHISON, T., STEUER, E., REESE, T. S. & SHEETZ, M. P. (1985b). Different axoplasmic proteins generate movement in opposite directions along micro-tubules *in vitro*. *Cell* **43**, 623–632.

VALE, R. D., SCHNAPP, B. J., REESE, T. S. & SHEETZ, M. P. (1985c). Movement of organelles along filaments dissociated from the axoplasm of the squid giant axon. *Cell* **40**, 449–454.

J. Cell Sci. Suppl. 5, 161–179 (1986)
Printed in Great Britain © *The Company of Biologists Limited 1986*

POLYMER SLIDING IN AXONS

RAYMOND J. LASEK

Bio-architectonics Center, Medical School, Case Western Reserve University, Cleveland OH 44106, USA

SUMMARY

In axons the cytoskeletal polymers are transported by slow axonal transport. Microtubules, microfilaments and neurofilaments move at different rates in the axon. On the basis of their transport rates, two populations of polymers can be distinguished: SCb polymers are transported at 2–4 mm day^{-1} and SCa polymers are transported at 0.25–1 mm day^{-1}. As they move within the axon, the faster moving SCb polymers must pass the slower moving SCa polymers. This observation and others indicate that polymers slide in the axon. A model of polymer sliding is presented. This model provides a dynamic architectural framework for studies of the mechanisms of slow axonal transport.

INTRODUCTION

Each differentiated cell type in a metazoan organism has one or more specialization that distinguishes that cell type. These specializations are derived from a repertoire of basic mechanisms that are present in most eukaryotic cells. In highly specialized cells, one or more of these basic mechanisms can be exaggerated and amplified to such a degree that they dominate the workings of the cell. For example, in striated muscle cells the actomyosin-based system of cell motility dominates the structure of the cytoplasm. For this reason, muscle cells are particularly useful for studying the mechanisms of actomyosin-based motility.

Like muscle cells, neurones have something special to offer the biologist who is interested in cell motility. Neurones are characterized by their ability to extend long processes, the axons. Axons are proportional to the size of an animal, and in large animals, like humans and dinosaurs, many axons are more than a metre long. To extend and maintain the cytoplasm in axons, neurones synthesize proteins in the cell body and convey these materials to the outlying regions of the axon.

Neurones have two systems for intracellular transport: the fast and slow axonal transport systems (Grafstein & Forman, 1980). Fast transport conveys vesicles through the axon at rates of 1–$4\,\mu\text{m s}^{-1}$ (Brady *et al.* 1985). Slow transport conveys the cytoskeletal polymers and their associated cytomatrix components through the axon at rates of 0.01–$0.04\,\mu\text{m s}^{-1}$ (1–4 mm day^{-1}). Although these two forms of intracellular motility are present in many metazoan cells, they are particularly well developed in neurones. Thus, neurones are particularly useful for studying vesicle transport mechanisms and cytoskeletal polymer transport mechanisms.

SLOW AXONAL TRANSPORT

The slow transport system for translocating cytoskeletal polymers is well developed in axons (Brady & Lasek, 1982a). This transport system translocates all of the cytoskeletal materials required for generating and maintaining the axonal cytoskeleton (Lasek et al. 1984). In addition to supplying cytoskeletal materials to the axon, the mechanisms of slow transport contribute directly to the locomotion of the axon during growth and regeneration (Lasek, 1982; Katz et al. 1984).

Whether the axon is growing or not, the slow transport mechanisms operate continuously within axons (Lasek & Hoffman, 1976). Essentially all of the axonal polymers are continuously moving within axons; in long axons, the slow transport system must move large amounts of cytoskeletal materials. For example, in axons one metre long, the slow transport system translocates one metre of axonal cytoskeleton 1–4 mm every day.

How does the slow transport system accomplish this remarkable feat of intracellular motility? Studies of the structural organization and dynamics of the axonal cytoskeleton indicate that the slow transport mechanisms operate by moving individual polymers or clusters of polymers within the axon (Lasek & Hoffman, 1976). That is, the mechanisms apparently operate locally on the individual polymers. The net result of the collective movements of the polymers throughout the axon is the translocation of the entire cytoskeleton from the cell body toward the axon terminal (Lasek & Hoffman, 1976).

The movement of polymers in axons has not been observed directly. Nonetheless, a reasonably detailed image of polymer movement in axons can be infered by combining detailed information from static electron-microscopic images of axonal cytoskeletons with information about the dynamics of cytoskeletal protein transport in axons.

THE ARCHITECTURE OF THE AXONAL CYTOSKELETON

The cytoplasm of axons can be relatively simple and uniform. Many of the structures that add complexity to the cytoplasm of other cells, such as fibroblasts, are not present in the axon. Notably, polysomes are contained within the neurone cell body and they rarely enter the axon (Peters et al. 1976).

Fig. 1 shows electron micrographs of a longitudinal section taken from a single axon in tissue culture. This section encompasses 130 μm of the axon and illustrates the uniformity of the axonal cytoplasm. Except for the distal end of the axon, each axonal segment is like the others. That is, the architectural pattern that is established in the axon near the cell body is maintained throughout the axon (Peters et al. 1976).

The basic building blocks of the axonal cytoskeleton are microtubules, neurofilaments and microfilaments. Microtubules and neurofilaments are easily visualized using conventional electron microscopic methods and much is known about their distribution in the axon. Fig. 2 shows that the microtubules and neurofilaments occupy a large part of the axonal volume. These polymers, which are of the order of 10–100 μm long, define the long axis of the axon.

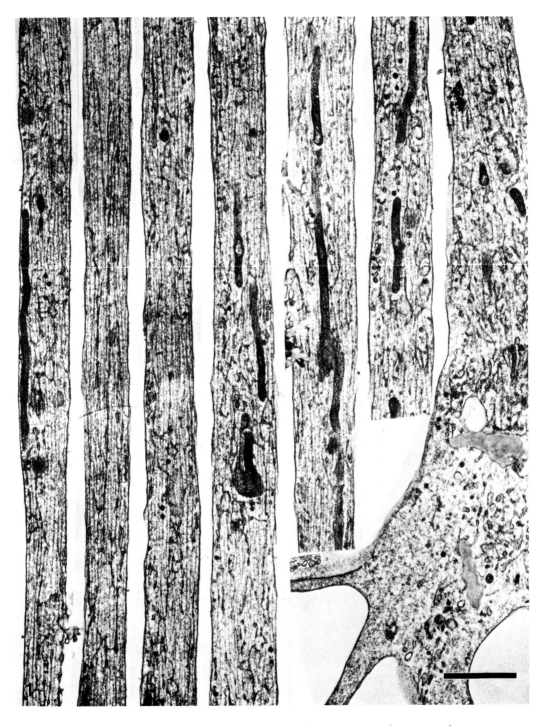

Fig. 1. Electron micrographs showing consecutive segments of an axon from an embryonic sensory ganglion cell cultured *in vitro*. The proximal end of the axon is at the upper left of the figure and the distal end of the axon including the growth cone is on the right. The axon increases in width at its distal end but otherwise is relatively uniform. Bar, $1.0\,\mu$m.

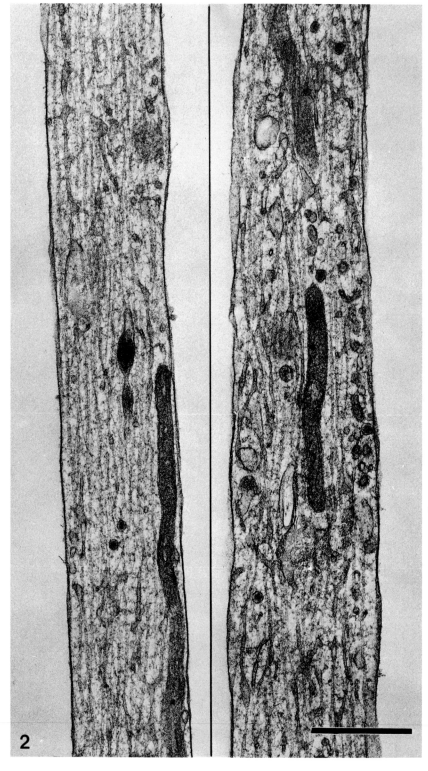

Fig. 2. Higher-magnification electron micrographs of the axon shown in Fig. 1. The cytoskeleton occupies most of the volume of the axon. Microtubules and neurofilaments are present throughout the axon. Bar, 0·5 μm.

Progress in understanding the detailed organization of the polymers in the axon has benefited significantly from studies of the squid giant axon. Except for its large diameter, the basic structure of the squid giant axon is like that of other molluscan and vertebrate axons (Lasek, 1984). Studies of the giant axon show that the axonal cytoskeleton has two regions: a thin outer *cortical region* that is associated directly with the plasma membrane and the *inner cytoskeleton* that occupies most of the axon (Metuzals & Tasaki, 1978; Tsukita *et al.* 1986; Hodge & Adelman, 1980).

Cortical cytoskeleton

The cortical region of the cytoskeleton is directly associated with the plasma membrane (Metuzals & Tasaki, 1978). Apparently, the inner surface of the plasma membrane has binding sites that have a high affinity for certain proteins and cytoskeletal structures. Through these binding sites, the plasma membrane concentrates structures in the axonal cortex.

In particular, the cortical region contains a dense meshwork of short microfilaments that line the inside surface of the plasma membrane (Tsukita *et al.* 1986). The dense microfilament network occupies a thin region that is usually less than $0 \cdot 1 \, \mu$m thick. Proteins that bind to microfilaments are also concentrated in the cortical cytoskeleton (Tsukita *et al.* 1986). For example, brain spectrin binds to microfilaments and it is more concentrated in the cortical region than in the inner cytoskeleton (Levine & Willard, 1981).

Though the microfilaments are concentrated in the cortical cytoskeleton, more than 90 % of the total axonal microfilaments and spectrin are present in the inner cytoskeleton of large diameter axons (Lasek, 1984; Fath & Lasek, unpublished). Moreover, microtubules and neurofilaments from the inner cytoskeleton also course through the cortical region and in some cases these polymers are closely associated with the plasma membrane. Thus, the cortical region and inner cytoskeleton often grade into each other.

Inner cytoskeleton

The inner cytoskeleton encompasses most of the volume of the axon (Schnapp & Reese, 1982; Hirokawa, 1982; Lasek, 1984). Fig. 3 illustrates the basic organization of the inner cytoskeleton in large axons. The microtubules form bundles among the neurofilaments. This tendency of the microtubules to segregate from the neurofilaments generates two domains in the axonal cytoskeleton: microtubule domains and neurofilament domains.

Microtubule domains. The microtubule domains consist of bundles of long microtubules interspersed with short microfilaments ($\approx 0 \cdot 5 \, \mu$m in length) (Fath & Lasek, unpublished). In addition, a dense matrix of filamentous and globular proteins surrounds the microfilaments. Some of these proteins, such as brain spectrin, apparently attach directly to binding sites on the surface of the microfilaments. Through these attachments the microfilaments contribute to the organization of the matrix proteins in the microtubule domains.

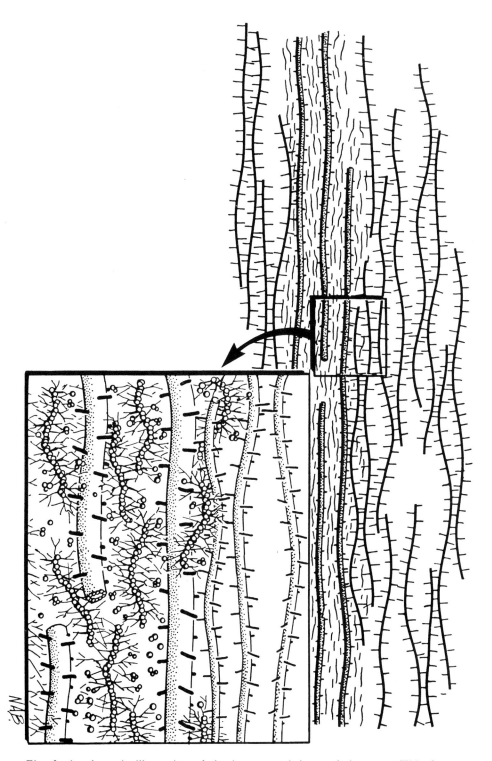

Fig. 3. A schematic illustration of the inner cytoskeleton of the axon. This figure summarizes a number of studies on the squid giant axon (see the text for more details). In the low-magnification drawing a microtubule domain is shown between two neuro-filament domains. The microtubule domain contains short microfilaments. In the inset, the substructure of the microfilaments is illustrated. A feltwork of filamentous and granular proteins surrounds the microfilaments and these proteins add to the density of the microtubule domains.

Microfilaments are more numerous than microtubules in the squid giant axon, and the total length of the microfilaments in the inner cytoskeleton is approximately twice that of the microtubules. Remarkably, the importance of microfilaments in the architecture of the inner cytoskeleton has been recognized only recently.

Through their large surface area and their binding sites for cytomatrix proteins, the microfilaments organize a multitude of cytomatrix proteins into a dense structural complex within the microtubule domains (Fath & Lasek, unpublished). Proteins, such as brain spectrin, clathrin, calmodulin and various enzymes of intermediary metabolism bind either directly or indirectly to the microfilaments. Because these proteins associate with the microfilaments they are transported with the microfilaments by the slow axonal transport mechanisms (Lasek *et al.* 1984).

Axonal microtubules have sidearms composed of microtubule-associated proteins (MAPs) (Vallee *et al.* 1984). These sidearms project from the surface of the microtubules and may link the microtubules to neighbouring structures, such as the microfilaments and neurofilaments. Furthermore, these structural associations between the microtubules and their neighbouring polymers may contribute to the dynamic mechanisms that coordinate polymer translocation in the axon (Tytell *et al.* 1983; Liem *et al.* 1985).

Neurofilament domains. In contrast to the dense matrix surrounding the microfilaments and microtubules in the microtubule domains, the region surrounding the neurofilaments can be relatively open in appearance (Metuzals *et al.* 1983). The neurofilament domains have few microfilaments by comparison with the microtubule domains and cortical region (Fath & Lasek, unpublished). For this reason, the numerous cytomatrix proteins that bind to microfilaments are also more concentrated in the microtubule domains and cortical regions than in the neurofilament domains.

Like the microtubules, the neurofilaments have sidearms that project from their surface (Hodge & Adelman, 1980; Hirokawa, 1982; Metuzals *et al.* 1983). These neurofilament sidearms are constructed from a specialized region of the neurofilament proteins that extends away from the backbone of the neurofilaments (Hirokawa, 1982). Through the sidearms, the neurofilaments can interact with neighbouring neurofilaments and microtubules (Shelanski *et al.* 1981; Hirokawa, 1982). These interactions between neighbouring polymers can have an important role in the coordination of the movement of the neurofilaments and microtubules in slow axonal transport (Lasek & Hoffman, 1976; Lasek, 1981).

CYTOSKELETAL PROTEIN TRANSPORT IN AXONS

The construction of a dynamic image from the static images of the cytoskeleton obtained with the electron microscope requires methods that provide information about the dynamics of these structures. An important method that has proved particularly useful for studying cytoskeletal dynamics in axons is to pulse-label the cytoskeletal proteins *in situ* (Brady & Lasek, 1982*b*). The pulse-labelled proteins can then be followed within the axons by analysing the distribution of the labelled proteins at different times after pulse-labelling. This approach provides detailed kinetic information about the movement of the cytoskeletal polymers in axons.

SCa and SCb in hypoglossal axons

Pulse-labelling experiments demonstrate that labelled axonal cytoskeletal proteins are transported in two separate and distinct waves, SCa and SCb. Fig. 4 illustrates the SCb and SCa waves of radioactivity in hypoglossal axons. The waves are completely separated by their rates of transport, at 15 days after pulse-labelling. The rates of the peaks of SCb and SCa are 2·7 and 1 mm day^{-1}, respectively.

The hypoglossal axons illustrate the detailed kinetics of the slowly transported structures more clearly than some other axons that have been used for these studies. In the hypoglossal axons, the SCa and SCb waves are both sharp and well separated. Separation of the waves in a population of axons is related to the amount of diversity of transport rates in the population. In hypoglossal axons the range of slow transport rates is relatively small. In contrast, in other axon populations, such as those of ventral motor neurones and dorsal root ganglion cells, the transport waves are much broader. In these cases, the SCa and SCb waves overlap, sometimes reducing the distinction between the two different waves (McQuarrie et al. 1986).

Protein composition of SCa and SCb

The kinetics of individual transported cytoskeletal proteins can be analysed by separating the proteins on sodium dodecyl sulphate–polyacrylamide gel electrophoresis(SDS)–PAGE and visualizing the labelled proteins with fluorography. Figs 5 and 6 show fluorographs that illustrate the distribution of individual slowly transported proteins at 15 and 27 days after pulse-labelling the hypoglossal neurones. At 15 days both the SCb and SCa waves are present in the axons. At 27 days the SCb wave has reached the ends of the axons (not shown) and only the SCa wave is present.

The protein composition of the SCa wave differs from that of SCb. The composition of the SCa wave is clearly illustrated at 27 days after labelling (Fig. 5). SCa consists primarily of the neurofilament proteins and tubulin. Other proteins that are associated with the neurofilaments and microtubules are also present in SCa (Tytell et al. 1983; Liem et al. 1985).

The composition of SCb is much more complex than SCa. Analyses of the proteins on two-dimensional SDS–PAGE indicate that more than 100 different proteins are transported coordinately with the SCb wave (Tytell et al. 1981; Brady & Lasek, 1982a). Actin is one of the major components of the SCb wave. In addition a significant amount of tubulin is transported with SCb in hypoglossal axons. This is clearly illustrated in a preparation in which[^{35}S]methionine was used to label the proteins (Fig. 6).

In addition to actin and tubulin, a variety of proteins that are components of the cytomatrix are present in SCb (Lasek et al. 1984). These proteins include clathrin, brain-spectrin, calmodulin, pyruvate kinase and enolase. The observation that these proteins are transported coordinately with actin in SCb has led to the proposal that these proteins bind to a 'carrier structure' that is the transport vehicle for the cytomatrix proteins (Lasek *et al.* 1984). Actin microfilaments appear to be part of this carrier structure.

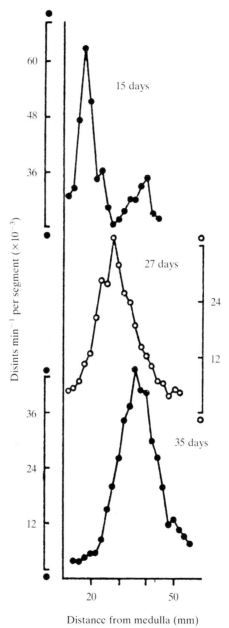

Fig. 4. The two subcomponents of slow axonal transport, SCa and SCb, are illustrated in these radioactive profiles of axonally transported proteins in the hypoglossal nerve of guinea pigs. SCa and SCb are separate waves at 15 days after labelling. At 27 and 35 days, SCb travelling at 2–3 mm day^{-1} has left the axons and the SCa wave travelling at 1 mm day^{-1} has progressed along the axons. The results are reproduced with permission from M. Black (Black, 1978).

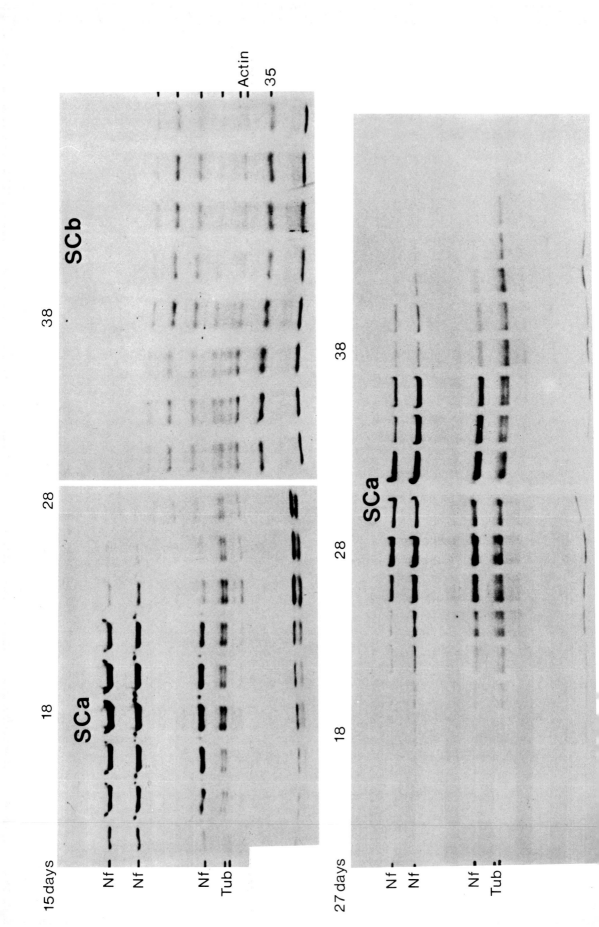

Kinetic relationships of the cytoskeletal proteins

The kinetic relationships of the proteins in hypoglossal axons at 15 and 27 days after injection is illustrated quantitatively in Fig. 7. These graphs show the amount of radioactivity in cytoskeletal protein bands excised from fluorographs like those shown in Figs 5 and 6. At 15 days both the SCb and SCa waves are present and at 27 days only the SCa wave is present.

The actin wave has a leading front and a peak that corresponds to SCb. In addition, some of the actin trails behind the SCb wave. The neurofilament proteins are distributed in a symmetrical bell-shaped wave that corresponds to SCa. The tubulin waveform is much more complex than that of the neurofilaments. The main wave of tubulin envelops the neurofilament protein wave and this wave has two peaks: one that coincides with the neurofilament peak and a larger one that moves more rapidly than the neurofilament peak. In addition, the tubulin waveform has an SCb component that overlaps the front of the actin wave.

To obtain these detailed transport kinetics, the pulse-labelled structures that are transported in the axon must be disrupted and their constituent proteins solubilized. By separating the transported structures into proteins, these analytical methods focus on the individual protein molecules. Nonetheless, biochemical analyses of the transported proteins strongly indicate that it is the structures and not their constituent proteins that are the natural units of axonal transport.

POLYMERS ARE THE NATURAL UNITS OF SLOW AXONAL TRANSPORT

The concept that cytological structures are the natural units of axonal transport is called the 'structural hypothesis' of axonal transport (Lasek & Brady, 1981; Lasek *et al.* 1984). This hypothesis holds that proteins are actively transported in the axon either as an integral part of a moving cytological structure or in association with one or more of these structures. The transport structures for membrane proteins are the membranous organelles and the transport structures for cytoskeletal proteins are the cytoskeletal polymers.

Stably assembled cytoskeletal polymers

The proposal that cytoskeletal proteins are transported in polymers was first established for the neurofilament proteins. In axons, the neurofilament proteins are stably assembled into neurofilaments and little, if any, of the neurofilament protein is free to diffuse (Morris & Lasek, 1982). This observation indicates that the radiolabelled neurofilament proteins in the axonal transport experiments correspond to assembled neurofilaments.

Fig. 5. Fluorographs of slowly transported proteins in guinea pig axons at 15 and 27 days after labelling the hypoglossal neurones with a mixture of [³H]proline and [³H]lysine. The labelled proteins in consecutive 2-mm segments of the hypoglossal nerve were analysed by SDS–PAGE. Actin and the $35 \times 10^3 M_r$ protein are transported with SCb. The neurofilament proteins (Nf) and tubulin (Tub) are transported with SCa. The results are reproduced with permission from M. Black (Black, 1978).

R. J. Lasek

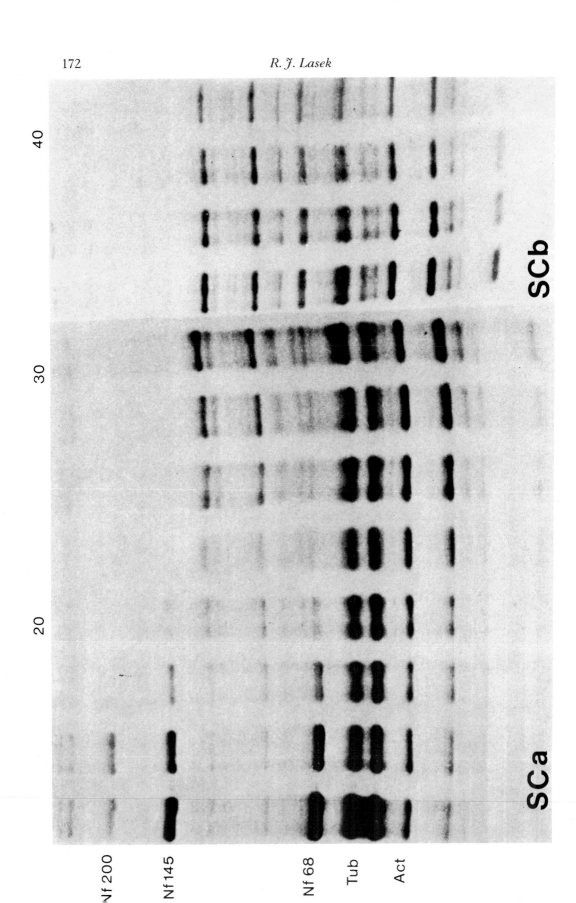

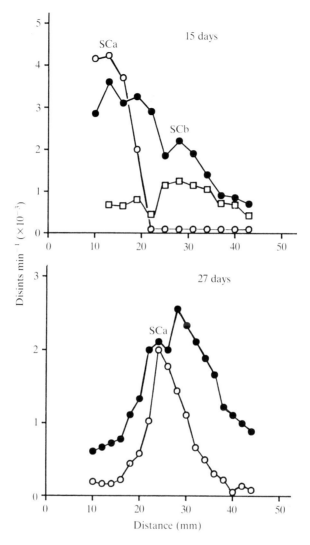

Fig. 7. Quantitative analyses of labelled cytoskeletal proteins at 15 days (rabbit) and 27 days (guinea pig) after labelling hypoglossal neurones obtained from fluorographs like those in Figs 5 and 6, respectively. Actin (□———□) travels with the SCb wave. Tubulin (●———●) has a complex waveform. The leading part of the wave travels with actin in SCb (15 days) and the bulk of the tubulin travels with the neurofilament proteins in SCa.

Fig. 6. Fluorographs of slowly transported proteins in rabbit axons at 15 days after labelling the hypoglossal neurones with [35S]methionine. The labelled proteins in consecutive 3-mm segments of the hypoglossal nerve were analysed by SDS–PAGE. Actin (Act) and the $35 \times 10^3 M_r$ protein are transported with SCb. The neurofilament proteins (Nf) and tubulin (Tub) are transported with SCa. Comparison of this fluorograph with those in Fig. 5 shows that [35S]methionine labels tubulin much more than the mixture of [3H]proline and [3H]lysine. The results are reproduced with permission from K. Heriot (Heriot, 1981).

Like the neurofilament proteins, a substantial fraction of the tubulin and actin in axons is stably bound in microtubules and microfilaments (Morris & Lasek, 1984). For example, in retinal ganglion cells 60% of the tubulin that is undergoing transport is stably polymerized in microtubules (Brady *et al.* 1984; Sahenk & Brady, 1983). The observation that these transported cytoskeletal proteins are stably assembled into polymers supports the hypothesis that the polymers are the transport vehicles for the cytoskeletal proteins.

Photobleaching experiments provide evidence for polymer transport

Important additional evidence that tubulin is axonally transported in the structured form of microtubules has been provided recently by experiments using the fluorescence photobleaching method to study the microscopic behaviour of tubulin in axons (Keith, 1986). In these experiments fluorescent tubulin was microinjected into PC12 neurones before the neurones extended neurites in tissue culture. After 12–18 h the neurones had extended neurites that were brightly fluorescent.

To examine the behaviour of the tubulin in the axons, a small region of the axon was photobleached. Recovery of fluorescence in the photobleached region requires that unbleached fluorescent protein enters this region. For example, if the tubulin in the axon was free to diffuse, the photobleached spot should recover at a rate equal to the diffusion of tubulin in the axon.

Observation of the photobleached region showed that the edges of the band remained sharp and that it was not compressed. This observation indicates that most of the tubulin was not free to diffuse. Instead, most of the tubulin in the axons appears to be contained in microtubules. Furthermore, the photobleached band moved anterogradely in the axon and split into two bands that moved at 0·3 and $2 \, \mathrm{mm \, day^{-1}}$.

These results from the photobleaching experiments are similar to those that have been obtained by the pulse-labelling method. They indicate that axons contain two classes of microtubules: one that is transported primarily with SCa and another that is transported with SCb. In addition to the differences in their transport rate, the SCa and SCb microtubules differ with regard to their chemistry. Notably, analyses by two dimensional SDS–PAGE demonstrate that the isoforms of tubulin in the SCa and SCb microtubules differ (Brady & Black, 1985).

These observations and others indicate that in the pulse-labelling experiments the radiolabelled cytoskeletal proteins are transported in polymers. That is, the distributions of radiolabelled proteins are directly related to the distributions of radiolabelled polymers. Because of this relationship between the radiolabelled proteins and polymer transport, the pulse-labelling method can be used to study polymer transport in the axon.

THE POLYMER SLIDING HYPOTHESIS

The radiolabelled transport profiles in Fig. 7 indicate that cytoskeletal polymers are transported at different rates. Most of the microfilaments are transported with

SCb at 2–4 mm day^{-1}. In contrast, the neurofilaments are transported exclusively with SCa at 0·25–1 mm day^{-1} (McQuarrie *et al.* 1986). The microtubules have a broad distribution of rates that includes at least two and possibly three populations of microtubules. One population moves with the microfilaments in the SCb wave and another population moves with the neurofilaments in the SCa wave. In the hypoglossal axons the waveform of the SCa microtubules has two peaks: one that coincides with the neurofilament peak and another that moves somewhat faster than the neurofilaments but slower than SCb (Fig. 7; and McQuarrie *et al.* 1986).

Because SCb polymers move faster than SCa polymers, the SCb polymers must pass slower moving SCa polymers as they move within the axon. This capacity of faster-moving polymers to pass slower-moving polymers indicates that polymers are able to slide past adjacent polymers in axons.

This hypothesis that polymers can slide in the axon is supported by studies of sinusoidal shortening in tissue culture (George, 1985). Sinusoidal shortening occurs in axons that have been grown on a poorly adhesive substrate. If these axons are cut, the segment of the axon distal to the cut slowly shortens and pulls the cut end of the axon segment toward the stationary growth cone.

Sinusoidal shortening requires metabolic energy and occurs at the rate of slow axonal transport. On the basis of these observations and others, George & Lasek (1983) have proposed that sinusoidal shortening can be used as an experimental model to study the detailed mechanisms of cytoskeletal transport in axons. Electron microscopic studies of sinusoidal shortening support this proposal and indicate that the cytoskeletal polymers translocate toward the growth cone during the shortening process (George, 1985).

Notably, the microtubules advance toward the stationary growth cone more quickly than the neurofilaments and the neurofilaments remain behind at the proximal end of the shortened axons. These observations indicate that microtubules can slide past neurofilaments in axons and provide direct support for the polymer sliding hypothesis.

POLYMER SLIDING IN OTHER MOTILE SYSTEMS

A precedent for polymer sliding in cells is provided by studies of motility in muscle and cilia. In muscle, the thick myosin filaments slide against the thin actin microfilaments during both contraction and relaxation, and in cilia, the dynein-bearing A microtubule slides against its neighbouring B microtubule during flexion and re-extension of the cilia.

In muscle and cilia, the sliding movement is bidirectional and the motility cycle produces no net translocation of the polymers. In these systems, the polymers are tied firmly to a stable fixture in the cell, the Z line in muscle and the basal body in cilia. The force produced during polymer sliding is applied against either the Z line or the basal body and this is translated either into movement of the cell in relation to its environment (e.g. muscle contraction) or movement of the environment in

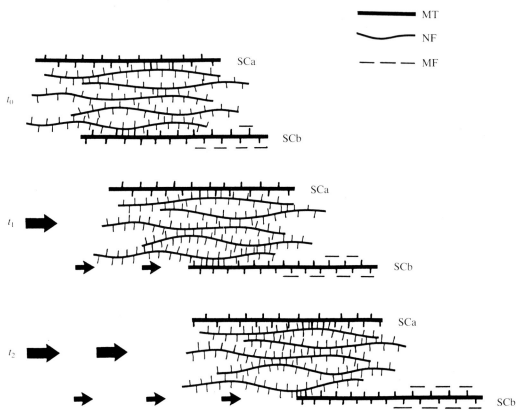

Fig. 8. A polymer sliding model. Microtubules (MT), neurofilaments (NF) and micro-filaments (MF) are illustrated schematically in a segment of an axon. One SCb micro-tubule, which is surrounded by microfilaments, is shown with a bundle of neurofilaments and an SCa microtubule. During the interval t_0–t_2, the polymers advance in the axon. The SCb polymers move together and slide in relationship to the slower-moving SCa polymers.

relation to the cell (e.g. translocation of mucus by ciliated epithelial cells in the trachea).

In contrast to the bidirectional movements of the polymers in muscle and cilia, the polymers in axons undergo net translocation in one direction. This suggests that the polymers in axons are not stably bound to fixed structures in the axon, such as the plasma membrane. Instead, the axonal polymers are relatively free to move within the axon and translocate unidirectionally toward the axon terminal.

CONCLUSION: A POLYMER SLIDING MODEL

How might we translate these observations into a simple and biologically plausible model? Fig. 8 schematically illustrates a model for polymer sliding in hypoglossal axons. For simplicity a small region of an axon that contains SCa and SCb polymers is illustrated. The polymers are shown at three consecutive time points (t_0–t_2).

During the interval between t_0 and t_2, the polymers translocate toward the end of the axon.

The SCb polymers move more rapidly than the SCa polymers. This requires that the SCb polymers slide in relation to adjacent SCa polymers. In Fig. 8, an SCb microtubule with its associated microfilaments is shown sliding past a bundle of neurofilaments. SCb microtubules may also slide past adjacent SCa microtubules (not illustrated).

During the sliding movements of the SCb polymers past the SCa polymers, the polymer sidearms interact. Through these interactions, the SCb polymers may transfer force to the SCa polymers and contribute to their movement. Furthermore, because of these interactions, the SCa polymers offer resistance to the forward movement of the SCb polymers and this resistance will tend to slow the rate of the SCb polymers. In this way interactions between the slow moving SCa neurofilaments and the SCb microtubules may produce the large population of slow moving microtubules that lags behind the SCb wave. In the hypoglossal axons these slow moving microtubules form a distinct population that is intermediate in rate between SCb and the neurofilament wave (Fig. 7).

The SCb microfilaments and SCb microtubules move together in the axon. The movements of these polymers may be coordinated by crosslinks between adjacent polymers. Likewise, neurofilaments form bundles that move coordinately with the SCa microtubules. The movements of these polymers may also be coordinated by the interaction of their sidearms.

This is the first and most basic version of the polymer sliding model. The detailed mechanisms of slow axonal transport are not represented. Many of the molecular mechanisms of slow axonal transport have not been elucidated. For example, the force-generating mechanism for polymer translocation in axons has not been identified. As these mechanisms are found, the polymer sliding model can be expanded and these detailed mechanisms added.

REFERENCES

BLACK, M. M. (1978). Axonal transport of cytoskeletal proteins. Thesis, Case Western Reserve University. Cleveland, Ohio, USA.

BLACK, M. M. & LASEK, R. J. (1979). Axonal transport of actin: Slow Component b is the principal source of actin for the axon. *Brain Res.* **171**, 401–413.

BRADY, S. T. & LASEK, R. J. (1982a). The slow components of axonal transport: movements, composition and organization. In *Axoplasmic Transport* (ed. D. G. Weiss), pp. 207–217. Berlin: Springer-Verlag.

BRADY, S. T. & LASEK, R. J. (1982b). Axonal transport: a cell biological method for studying proteins that associate with the cytoskeleton. In *Methods in Cell Biology*, vol. 25 (ed. L. Wilson), pp. 365–398. New York: Academic Press.

BRADY, S. T., LASEK, R. J. & ALLEN, R. D. (1985). Videomicroscopy of fast axonal transport in extruded axoplasm: A new model for study of molecular mechanisms. *Cell Motil.* **5**, 81–101.

BRADY, S. T., TYTELL, M. & LASEK, R. J. (1984). Axonal tubulin and axonal microtubules: Biochemical evidence for cold stability. *J. Cell Biol.* **99**, 1716–1724.

GEORGE, E. B. (1985). The role of microtubules in axonal transport and growth. Thesis, pp. 210, Case Western Reserve University, Cleveland, USA.

GEORGE, E. B. & LASEK, R. J. (1983). Contraction of isolated neural processes: A model for studying cytoskeletal translocation in neurons. *J. Cell Biol.* **97**, 267a.

GRAFSTEIN, B. & FORMAN, D. S. (1980). Intracellular transport in neurons. *Physiol. Rev.* **60**, 1167–1282.

HERIOT, K. (1981). Definition of the granulo-filamentous complex of the axon. Thesis, Case Western Reserve University, Cleveland, Ohio, USA.

HIROKAWA, N. (1982). Cross-linker system between neurofilaments, microtubules, and membranous organelles in frog axons revealed by the quick freeze deep-etching method. *J. Cell Biol.* **94**, 129–142.

HODGE, A. J. & ADELMAN, W. J. (1980). The neuroplasmic network in *Loligo* and *Hermissenda* neurons. *J. Ultrastruct. Res.* **70**, 220–241.

KATZ, M. J., GEORGE, E. B. & GILBERT, L. J. (1984). Axonal elongation as a stochastic walk. *Cell Motil.* **4**, 351–370.

KEITH, C. H. (1986). Slow axonal transport of tubulin in cultured cells. *Trans. Am. Soc. Neurochem.* **17**, 163 (abstr.).

LASEK, R. J. (1981). The dynamic ordering of neuronal cytoskeletons. *Neurosci. Res. Prog. Bull.* **19**, 7–32.

LASEK, R. J. (1982). Translocation of the cytoskeleton in neurons and axonal growth. *Phil. Trans. R. Soc. Lond.* B, **299**, 313–327.

LASEK, R. J. (1984). The structure of axoplasm. *Curr. Top. Membr. Transport*: The squid axon. **22**, 39–53.

LASEK, R. J. & BRADY, S. T. (1981). The structural hypothesis of axonal transport: Two classes of moving elements. In *Axoplasmic Transport* (ed. D. G. Weiss), pp. 397–405. Berlin: Springer-Verlag.

LASEK, R. J., GARNER, J. A. & BRADY, S. T. (1984). Axonal transport of the cytoplasmic matrix. *J. Cell Biol.* **99**, 212s–221s.

LASEK, R. J. & HOFFMAN, P. N. (1976). The neuronal cytoskeleton, axonal transport and axonal growth. In *Cell Motility, Cold Spring Harbor Conf. Cell Proliferation*, vol. 3, pp. 1021–1049. New York: Cold Spring Harbor Laboratory Press.

LEVINE, J. & WILLARD, M. (1981). Fodrin. Axonally transported polypeptides associated with the internal periphery of many cells. *J. Cell Biol.* **90**, 631–643.

LIEM, R. J. K., PACHTER, J. S., NAPOLITANO, CHIN, MORARU, S. S. M. & HEIMANN, R. (1985). Associated proteins as possible cross-linkers in the neuronal cytoskeleton. *Ann. N. Y. Acad. Sci.* **455**, 492–508.

MCQUARRIE, I. G., BRADY, S. T. & LASEK, R. J. (1986). Diversity in the axonal transport of structural proteins: Major differences between optic and spinal axons in the rat. *J. Neurosci.* (in press).

METUZALS, J., HODGE, A. J., LASEK, R. J. & KAISERMAN-ABRAMOF, I. R. (1983). Neurofilamentous network and filamentous matrix preserved by different techniques from squid giant axon. *Cell Tiss. Res.* **228**, 415–432.

METUZALS, J. & TASAKI, I. (1978). Subaxolemmal filamentous network in the giant nerve fiber of the squid (*Loligo pealei*) and its possible role in excitability. *J. Cell Biol.* **78**, 597–621.

MORRIS, J. R. & LASEK, R. J. (1982). Stable polymers of the axonal cytoskeleton: the axoplasmic ghost. *J. Cell Biol.* **92**, 192–198.

MORRIS, J. R. & LASEK, R. J. (1984). Monomer–polymer equilibria in the axon: direct measurement of tubulin and actin as polymer and monomer in axoplasm. *J. Cell Biol.* **98**, 2064–2076.

PETERS, A., PALAY, S. L. & WEBSTER, H. DEF. (1976). *The Fine Structure of the Nervous System: The Neurons and Supporting Cells*. Philadelphia: Saunders.

SAHENK, Z. & BRADY, S. T. (1983). Morphologic evidence for stable regions on axonal microtubules. *J. Cell Biol.* **97**, 210a.

SCHNAPP, B. J. & REESE, T. S. (1982). Cytoplasmic structure in rapid-frozen axons. *J. Cell Biol.* **94**, 667–679.

SHELANSKI, M., LETERRIER, J.-F. & LIEM, R. K. (1981). Evidence for interactions between neurofilaments and microtubules. *Neurosci. Res. Prog. Bull.* **19**, 32–43.

TSUKITA, S., TSUKITA, S., KOBAYASHI, T. & MATSUMOTO, G. (1986). Subaxolemma cytoskeleton in squid axon. II. Morphological identification of microtubule- and microfilament-associated domains of axolemma. *J. Cell Biol.* **102**, 1710–1726.

TYTELL, M., BLACK, M. M., GARNER, J. A. & LASEK, R. J. (1981). Axonal transport: Each rate component reflects the movement of distinct macromolecular complexes. *Science* **214**, 179–181.

TYTELL, M., BRADY, S. T. & LASEK, R. J. (1983). Axonal transport in a subclass of tau proteins: evidence for the regional differentiation of microtubules in neurons. *Proc. natn. Acad. Sci. U.S.A.* **81**, 1570–1574.

VALLEE, R. B., BLOOM, G. S. & THEURKAUF, W. E. (1984). Microtubule-associated proteins: Subunits of the cytomatrix. *J. Cell Biol.* **99**, 38s–44s.

J. Cell Sci. Suppl. 5, 181–188 (1986)
Printed in Great Britain © The Company of Biologists Limited 1986

VESICLE MOVEMENTS AND MICROTUBULE-BASED MOTORS

MICHAEL P. SHEETZ[1], RONALD VALE[2], BRUCE SCHNAPP[2], TRINA SCHROER[1] AND THOMAS REESE[2]

[1]*Department of Cell Biology and Physiology, Washington University Medical School, 660 S. Euclid Avenue, St Louis, MO 63110, USA*

[2]*NINCDS at Woods Hole, Marine Biological Laboratory, Woods Hole, MA, USA*

SUMMARY

The movements of many cytoplasmic vesicles follow the paths of microtubules, some moving in one direction and others moving in the opposite direction on the same microtubule. Recently we have isolated one cytoplasmic motor, kinesin, and defined another, the axoplasmic retrograde factor, both of which are capable of powering anionic latex beads in both directions along polar microtubule arrays. Evidence summarized here supports but does not prove the hypothesis that kinesin and the retrograde motors are indeed responsible for powering vesicle movements.

INTRODUCTION

There have been many observations of organelle movements within different cells under a wide variety of conditions and many movements have been linked to microtubule integrity (Schliwa, 1984). Although some movements may be diffusion-dependent and will be altered by microtubule depolymerization in secondary ways, there are clearly ATP-dependent vesicle movements within axoplasm and in other extensive cell processes that normally follow the paths of microtubules. Fast axo-plasmic transport within the squid giant axon provides an excellent model system both for viewing vesicle transport and for obtaining sufficient quantities of material for biochemical measurements. With the application of new video technologies to light microscopy it was possible to view directly the abundant bidirectional organelle traffic within the axon (Allen *et al.* 1982). Previous microscopic studies had revealed only a portion of the organelle traffic measured in biochemical studies (Grafstein & Forman, 1981). The abundant movements of organelles upon 'single filaments' in both directions were seen not only within axons and isolated axoplasm (Brady *et al.* 1982), but also in regions of dissociated axoplasm where single filaments had become disentangled from the bulk of the axoplasm (Allen *et al.* 1985). With a reproducible method of preparing active dissociated axoplasm it was possible to explore the exact nature of the single filaments, which could have been microtubules, actin filament bundles or a complex of both (Vale *et al.* 1985a). Sequential examination of the same single filaments in the light and electron microscopes revealed that a single filament was a single microtubule (Schnapp *et al.* 1985a) and no actin was found associated with the filaments (Schnapp *et al.* 1985b).

Further proof that the organelles could move on microtubules came from the reconstitution of organelle movement with semi-purified organelles and purified microtubules (Vale *et al.* 1985*b*) or axonemal microtubules (Gilbert *et al.* 1985).

Purification of a microtubule motor involved in organelle movements was aided by the serendipidous observation that purified microtubules would move on glass coated with an axoplasmic supernatant fraction free of organelles (Vale *et al.* 1985*b*). Using microtubule movement on glass as an assay, it was possible to purify the motor. A major affinity purification step for the isolation of the motor was suggested by the observation that the non-hydrolysable analogue of ATP, AMP-PNP, would not only inhibit organelle movement but also would cause the microtubules to become decorated with organelles (Lasek & Brady, 1985). The possibility that the motor was trapped in a high-affinity state for microtubules was borne out since AMP-PNP caused the motor activity to pellet with microtubules. Subsequent purification steps yielded a protein that was a complex of 110, 65 and 70 ($\times 10^3$) M_r polypeptides in a 4:1:1 ratio and chromatographed on a gel filtration column with an apparent native molecular weight of $660 \times 10^3 M_r$. The subunit molecular weight and relative insensitivities to both vanadate ion and the sulphhydryl reagent, N-ethylmaleimide, differentiated this protein from the other known microtubule-based motor, dynein (Gibbons, 1981). It was, therefore, named 'kinesin' from the Greek verb 'to move' because of its ability to power the movement of beads on microtubules and microtubules on glass, and to increase vesicle movement on microtubules (Vale *et al.* 1985*c*).

Microtubules supported the movement of organelles in both directions in axons and dissociated axoplasm. With purified kinesin, movement in only one direction was observed using beads or organelles. An assay system was needed to determine the direction of kinesin movement relative to the microtubule polarity, which is defined by the direction of preferred microtubule polymerization. In the chosen assay centrosomes were used to seed microtubule growth and provided a radial array with all of the fast growing (plus) ends away from the centre (Mitchison & Kirschner, 1985). When kinesin-coated beads were added to the centrosomal microtubule arrays, they always moved away from the centre towards the plus end of the microtubule (Vale *et al.* 1985*d*).

IDENTIFICATION OF A RETROGRADE FACTOR

When crude supernatants from axoplasm were applied to beads, the beads were found to move towards the minus as well as the plus ends of microtubules (Vale *et al.* 1985*d*). Thus, a component was lost in the purification of kinesin, which enabled beads to move towards the minus end of the microtubule. To determine if kinesin was also involved in movements towards the minus end, an anti-kinesin antibody bound to agarose was used to extract the kinesin from the crude axoplasmic supernatant, which moved beads in both directions. When kinesin was removed, the supernatant-coated beads would only move in the minus direction. Further indications that the minus moving component was distinct from kinesin came from the finding that treatment with the sulphhydryl reagent, N-ethylmaleimide, or low concentrations of vanadate would inactivate the minus moving factor but not kinesin. There is thus a motor other than kinesin that will move objects in the minus direction on microtubules.

Within axons the polarity of microtubules is such that the plus ends are oriented towards the synapse (Burton & Paige, 1981; Heidemann *et al.* 1981). Kinesin would be expected to drive organelle movements in the anterograde direction from the cell body to the synapse; whereas a distinctly different factor would be responsible for moving organelles in a retrograde direction. There are many questions that remain to be answered including the following. How do the motors become attached to the organelle surface since they can exist in a soluble form? How does the retrograde factor reach the synapse? What happens to the kinesin when it reaches the synapse?

The central question is: do kinesin and the retrograde factor actually power vesicle movements *in vivo*? In this paper we will summarize the findings that support the hypothesis that they are the motors and discuss some of the major difficulties with that hypothesis.

FIDELITY OF THE DIRECTIONALITY OF ORGANELLE MOVEMENTS ON MICROTUBULES

The signal for the movement of vesicles from the cell body to the axon must be programmed into the vesicle and a different program must exist for vesicles moving from the synapse to the cell. If this were the case, then the vesicles from axoplasm that are moving should move unidirectionally on microtubules. In studies of dissociated axoplasm, which maintains activity for hours, the movement of smaller vesicles with the apparent sizes of 0.2–$0.6\,\mu$m on single microtubules was unidirectional with only three observations of direction reversals out of several thousand vesicle movements. Another test of the fidelity of the direction of movement is suggested by the switching of vesicles from one filament to another. As illustrated in Fig. 1 vesicles will occasionally switch from one filament to another and move on that second filament. When an organelle is moving upward (see X in Fig. 1), and switches filaments and moves to the right, then all of the subsequent vesicles that are moving up will move to the right if they switch. If a vesicle is capable of moving in only one direction on a microtubule, then those vesicles moving down on the vertical microtubule should move to the left on the horizontal microtubule (see Y in Fig. 1). In all observations of vesicle switching the vesicles moving in the opposite direction on the first microtubule moved in the opposite direction on the second filament (Fig. 1). The vesicles thus appear to move in a polar fashion on microtubules and maintain the polarity of movement even after switching from one microtubule to another.

VESICLES CONTAIN MOTORS ON THEIR SURFACE

In the dissociated axoplasm discussed above the microtubules could be coated with motor proteins or, more probably, the vesicles could contain the motors. When vesicles were purified from axoplasm by sucrose density gradient centrifugation, some vesicles did move on purified microtubules (Vale *et al.* 1985*b*) and as well on axonemal tubules (Gilbert *et al.* 1985). The number of moving vesicles per micrometre of microtubule length was significantly lower with purified vesicles than with similar vesicle concentrations in dissociated axoplasm. There was also considerable variability in the percentage of organelles that moved towards the plus end *versus* the minus end of microtubules in a centrosome assay from one experiment to the next.

In order to determine if the vesicles brought with them a significant concentration of motor proteins into the gradient, the sucrose gradient was fractionated and each fraction was analysed for its ability to promote bead movement on microtubules. To avoid problems with vesicle membranes Triton X-100 was added to each fraction prior to assay. When the gradients were analysed for the amount of motile activity *versus* fraction from the gradient, a peak of motile activity was indeed found (Fig. 2). Since the centrifugation time and gravitational(g) force were such that only very large particles could travel this far into the gradient, it was necessary for the motors to be attached to larger structures such as vesicles. Vesicles isolated from these fractions were capable of moving on purified microtubules. These data support the concept that motors can remain bound to vesicles and copurify with them.

If motor proteins were bound to vesicles and kinesin was one of the motors, then it should be possible to find kinesin on the purified vesicles. Purification of organelles from squid optic lobes was accomplished by initial density gradient sedimentation followed by addition of sucrose and flotation through a second density gradient. The final vesicle fraction from a 12% sucrose layer did have kinesin as determined by Western immunoblot analysis with an anti-kinesin antibody. Furthermore, when

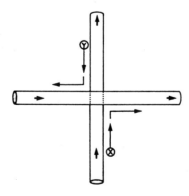

Fig. 1. This diagram illustrates the switching of vesicles from one filament to another, which occurs in dissociated preparations of axoplasm (Vale *et al.* 1985*a*). In over 300 observations when the first vesicle (such as X) turned in one direction the subsequent vesicles always followed that path. If vesicles were moving in the opposite direction on the first filament (such as Y) and switched filaments, then they would move in the opposite direction on the second filament (no exceptions in 25 observations).

intact vesicles (12 % to 18 % sucrose layers) were incubated with monoclonal anti-kinesin antibody bound to agarose approximately 50 % of the vesicle kinesin was bound to the resin. Thus one of the cytoplasmic microtubule motors, kinesin, copurifies with vesicles and is available externally for binding to antibodies.

IS MOTOR BINDING TO VESICLES REVERSIBLE?

Purification of vesicles by sucrose gradient sedimentation may cause decreased motility on microtubules *in vitro*, for a variety of reasons. One possibility is that motor binding to the vesicles is reversible and motors come off the vesicles in the gradient. If this were the case, then the addition of purified motors should increase vesicle motility. As seen in Table 1, increases in vesicle motility were observed after the addition of purified kinesin in four out of five experiments. In all cases stimulation of purified organelle movement was observed when a crude supernatant was added. The possibility exists that a supernatant enzyme activity, which is a contaminant of the kinesin preparations, causes the stimulation of vesicle movement. These findings, however, are consistent with the hypothesis that kinesin is reversibly bound to the vesicle surface.

KINESIN AND VESICLE MOVEMENTS

Although the circumstantial evidence strongly suggests that kinesin moves vesicles towards the plus ends of microtubules (anterograde direction) *in vivo*, there are a number of problems that remain unexplained. The majority of kinesin is found in a soluble form in dissociated axoplasm and not on vesicle surfaces. What prevents it from attaching to retrograde vesicles or other cytoplasmic constituents and moving them all away from the cell body? Preliminary studies of the kinesin–vesicle interaction have shown that the binding of kinesin to vesicles can occur and yet those

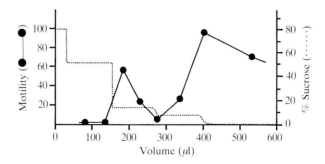

Fig. 2. The motility of fractions of a sucrose gradient sedimentation of dissociated axoplasm reveals a peak of activity at the 50 %–15 % sucrose interface. The axoplasm dissociation and sucrose gradient procedures have been described by Vale *et al.* (1985*d*). Gradients were centrifuged at 135 000 ***g*** for 2 h at 4 °C and the graph shows the data from a typical experiment. Motility (number of bead movements per 10 min) was assayed with a standard density of microtubules using carboxylated latex beads and Triton, as described by Vale *et al.* (1985*d*).

vesicles will not move on microtubules (Schroer *et al.* unpublished results). This finding suggests that in addition to attachment to a vesicle an activation of bound kinesin must occur. Anionic latex beads are, therefore, somewhat unusual in their ability to bind kinesin in an active form.

Another implication of the large amount of soluble kinesin and the findings in Table 1 is that kinesin may be binding to the vesicles reversibly. If the ratio of free to bound kinesin in Fig. 2 reflects the true affinity constant, then there is obviously a low-affinity binding of kinesin to the vesicles. A weak interaction will have difficulty transmitting force from kinesin to the vesicle since the force of movement will be likely to break the kinesin–vesicle interaction. An obvious alternative explanation is that there are both strong and weak interactions of kinesin with vesicles and that the strong form a minority of the total.

There is a problem of what to do with kinesin when it reaches the synapse. Is it degraded there or transported back to the cell body? In smaller cells kinesin can easily diffuse from the periphery back to the cell centre as a soluble molecule. Because axonal processes are so long a diffusion mechanism is impractical, but a weak binding to retrograde vesicles could move kinesin towards the cell without inhibiting retrograde movement.

There are many other practical problems to be solved by experimentation before it is possible to state that kinesin does indeed power vesicle movements on microtubules *in vivo*. To consider the role of the retrograde axoplasmic motor in retrograde vesicle movements is even more speculative at this point.

Table 1. *Movements supported by squid and bovine translocators*

Sample	Organelle movement†
Buffer	+
S2, axoplasmic supernatant*	+ + + to + + + +
Squid, gel filtration	+ + to + + + +
Squid, hydroxyapatite	+ + to + + + +
Bovine, gel filtration	+ to + +

Microtubule, bead and organelle movements promoted by S2 axoplasmic supernatant or purified squid or bovine translocator; movement occurred consistently in preparations. Squid gel filtration peak fractions ($n = 7$; equivalent to lane 30 in fig. 4 of Vale *et al.* 1985c) and hydroxyapatite peak fractions ($n = 3$; equivalent to lane 40, 41 in fig. 5) were tested in motility buffer or 100 mM-KCl, 50 mM-Tris (pH 7·6), 5 mM-MgCl$_2$, 0·5 mM-EDTA, 2 mM-ATP at final protein concentrations between 10 and 150 μg ml^{-1}. Bovine gel filtration peak fractions ($n = 3$; equivalent to lane 30 in fig. 7) were tested in KCl/Tris buffer at protein concentrations between 20 and 50 μg ml^{-1}. Organelle movement was assessed by viewing a 20 μm × 20 μm field of microtubules for 2·5–15 min and counting the number of different organelles that made directed movements along microtubules. The following rating system was employed: −, no movement in all preparations; +, 0–3 movements/min; + +, 3–7 movements/min; + + +, 7–15 movements/min; + + + +, 15–34 movements/min. The range of organelle movement in different preparations is reported. Microtubule, bead or organelle movement assays are described in the text.

  * Values from Vale *et al.* (1985a).
  † The velocity of organelle movement in all samples was approximately $1·64 \pm 0·24\ \mu$m s^{-1}.

GENERALITY OF KINESIN-DEPENDENT MOVEMENTS

One of the important controlling elements in cell form and polarity is the radial microtubule array emanating from the centrosome. Since kinesin would be expected to move objects to the periphery of the cell on those microtubules, it could be very useful in building and maintaining polar distributions of materials within cells. Material analogous to kinesin has been isolated from a variety of sources, including kidney, liver, eggs (Scholey *et al.* 1985) and cultured cells. Also, polyclonal antibodies to squid kinesin ($110 \times 10^3 M_r$) crossreacted on Western blots with a 95–140 ($\times 10^3$) M_r component in every cell tested. It is therefore likely that kinesin or a close analogue acts similarly in all cell systems to power objects along microtubules.

CONCLUSIONS

Recent studies of organelle movements and the definition of motor proteins from axoplasm have suggested a simple model to explain vesicle movements on microtubules. Since microtubule polarity and position are tightly regulated within cells it is possible, with two microtubule-based motors, kinesin and the axoplasmic retrograde motor, to explain directed vesicle movements by attachment of the appropriate active motor protein to the vesicle. Some of the practical problems in implementing such a mechanism call for further experimentation.

This work was supported in part by NIH grants GM-33352 and NS-14576 to M.P.S. M. Sheetz is an established investigator of the American Heart Association. T. Schroer is supported by a Muscular Dystrophy Association postdoctoral fellowship.

REFERENCES

ALLEN, R. D., METUZALS, J., TASAKI, I., BRADY, S. T. & GILBERT, S. P. (1982). Fast axonal transport in squid giant axon. *Science* **218**, 1127–1128.

ALLEN, R. D., WEISS, D. G., HAYDEN, J. H., BROWN, D. T., FUJIWAKE, H. & SIMPSON, M. (1985). Gliding movement of and bidirectional organelle transport along single native microtubules from squid axoplasm: evidence for an active role of microtubules in cytoplasmic transport. *J. Cell Biol.* **100**, 1736–1752.

BRADY, S. T., LASEK, R. J. & ALLEN, R. D. (1982). Fast axonal transport in extruded axoplasm from squid giant axon. *Science* **218**, 1129–1131.

BURTON, R. R. & PAIGE, J. L. (1981). Polarity of axoplasmic microtubules in the olfactory nerve of the frog. *Proc. natn. Acad. Sci. U.S.A.* **78**, 3269–3273.

GIBBONS, I. R. (1981). Cilia and flagella of eukaryotes. *J. Cell Biol.* **91**, 107–124.

GILBERT, S. P., ALLEN, R. D. & SLOBODA, R. D. (1985). Translocation of vesicles from squid axoplasm on flagellar microtubules. *Nature, Lond.* **315**, 245–248.

GRAFSTEIN, B. & FORMAN, D. S. (1980). Intracellular transport in neurons. *Physiol. Rev.* **60**, 1167–1283.

HEIDEMANN, S. R., LANDERS, J. M. & HAMBORG, M. A. (1981). Polarity orientation of axonal microtubules. *J. Cell Biol.* **91**, 661–665.

LASEK, R. J. & BRADY, S. T. (1985). Attachment of transported vesicles to axonal microtubules is faciliated by AMP-PNP. *Nature, Lond.* **316**, 645–647.

MITCHISON, T. & KIRSCHNER, M. (1984). Microtubule assembly nucleated by isolated centrosomes. *Nature, Lond.* **312**, 232–237.

SCHLIWA, M. (1984). Mechanisms of intracellular organelle transport. In *Cell Muscle Motility*, vol. 5 (ed. J. W. Shaw), pp. 1–81. New York: Plenum.

Schnapp, B. J., Vale, R. D., Sheetz, M. P. & Reese, T. S. (1985*a*). Single microtubules from squid axoplasm support bidirectional movement of organelles. *Cell* **40**, 455–462.

Schnapp, B. J., Vale, R. D., Sheetz, M. P. & Reese, T. S. (1985*b*). Filamentous actin is not a component of transport filaments isolated from squid axoplasm. *J. Cell Biol.* **99**, 351a.

Scholey, J. M., Porter, M. E., Grissom, P. M. & McIntosh, J. R. (1985). Identification of kinesin in sea urchin eggs, and evidence for its localization in the mitotic spindle. *Nature, Lond.* **318**, 483–486.

Vale, R. D., Reese, T. S. & Sheetz, M. P. (1985*c*). Identification of a novel force generating protein (kinesin) involved in microtubule-based motility. *Cell* **41**, 39–50.

Vale, R. D., Schnapp, B. J., Mitchison, T., Steuer, E., Reese, T. S. & Sheetz, M. P. (1985*d*). Different axoplasmic proteins generate movement in opposite directions along microtubules *in vitro*. *Cell* **43**, 623–632.

Vale, R. D., Schnapp, B. J., Reese, T. S. & Sheetz, M. P. (1985*a*). Movement of organelles along filaments dissociated from the axoplasm of the squid giant axon. *Cell* **40**, 449–454.

Vale, R. D., Schnapp, B. J., Reese, T. S. & Sheetz, M. P. (1985*b*). Organelle, bead and microtubule translocations promoted by soluble factors from the squid giant axon. *Cell* **40**, 559–569.

J. Cell Sci. Suppl. 5, 189–196 (1986)
Printed in Great Britain © The Company of Biologists Limited 1986

DYNEIN STRUCTURE AND FUNCTION

KENNETH A. JOHNSON, SILVIO P. MARCHESE-RAGONA,
DANIEL B. CLUTTER, ERIKA L. F. HOLZBAUR
AND TAMIE J. CHILCOTE
*Department of Molecular and Cell Biology, Pennsylvania State University,
University Park, PA 16802, USA*

SUMMARY

The structure of dynein isolated from several sources follows the pattern first observed with *Tetrahymena* 22 S dynein, which has three globular heads attached by three flexible strands to a root-like base. Recent biochemical data indicate that there is one ATPase site on each dynein head and that all three heads interact with microtubules in an ATP-sensitive manner. Accordingly, images of dynein *in situ* can be interpreted in terms of a model for crossbridge action where the roots of the bouquet anchor the dynein to the A-tubule and all three heads reach out to interact with the B-tubule in an ATP-dependent reaction to produce a force for sliding.

REVIEW

The structure of dynein has been examined by a variety of electron-microscopic techniques, but none has been as powerful or provided as much new information as scanning transmission electron microscopy (STEM). The STEM is unique in its ability to examine unstained biological macromolecules and to derive molecular weight estimates from images of single particles (Wall, 1979). This information, combined with the high-resolution structural data, has served to establish un-equivocally the structure and molecular weight of dynein (Johnson & Wall, 1982, 1983). In this review, I will summarize new structural data on dynein isolated from several sources and show how the structure of the isolated dynein relates to the biochemical data and provides a rational basis for understanding the images of dynein seen *in situ*. In addition, models for force production by dynein will be discussed in terms of the detailed structural and biochemical information that is available (Johnson, 1985).

Over the past 20 years a great deal of evidence from several laboratories established that the dynein is structurally attached to the A-tubule and interacts transiently with the B-tubule in an ATP-dependent reaction to produce a force for sliding (reviewed by Gibbons, 1981). The first detailed examination of images of fixed, embedded and thin-sectioned cilia indicated that dynein had a hook-shaped, asymmetric structure, which was thinner at its point of attachment to the A-tubule (Allen, 1968). However, analysis of negatively stained axonemes suggested that dynein was a rod-shaped molecule consisting of three or four globular subunits, 9 nm in diameter (Warner *et al.* 1977). Witman & Minervini (1982) presented a refined analysis of negatively stained axonemes and described a 'spur', which appeared to connect the dynein arm to the base of the adjacent arm. This spur was again observed in images of rapidly frozen, deep-etched, rotary-shadowed axonemes but was called the 'interdynein linker' (Goodenough & Heuser, 1982). In this study, the dynein arm was described as having two 'feet' associated with the A-tubule, which supported a body that was connected to the B-tubule *via* a thin projection. Thus, the images obtained with shadowed axonemes were quite confusing and, in fact, first led the authors to propose that existing models for the dynein arm were backwards and that the dynein was actually attached to the B-tubule rather than the A-tubule (Heuser & Goodenough, 1981).

The confusion resulting from examination of the intact axoneme was resolved by examination of isolated dynein using the Brookhaven STEM (Johnson & Wall, 1982, 1983). It was shown that *Tetrahymena* dynein consisted of a bouquet of three globular heads attached by three flexible strands to a base, and had a net M_r of $1 \cdot 9 \times 10^6$ (see Fig. 1). It thus immediately appeared reasonable that the roots of the bouquet anchored the dynein to the A-tubule and the three heads interacted with the B-tubule in the ATP-dependent reaction. The spur or interdynein linker then actually consisted of the stems of the bouquet connecting the heads to the base, and what appeared previously as the rod-like arm was, in fact, the three dynein heads. The growing evidence in support of this working hypothesis will be described below.

The view of dynein as a three-headed molecule was confirmed by examination of 18S and 12S dyneins isolated from *Chlamydomonas* and known to be both components of the outer dynein arm (Piperno & Luck, 1979). The larger 18S dynein was shown to be a two-headed particle with $1 \cdot 25 \times 10^6 M_r$ and the smaller 12S dynein was shown to be a one-headed particle with $470 \times 10^3 M_r$ as shown in Fig. 1 (Witman *et al.* 1982). The two *Chlamydomonas* dyneins sum to be approximately equal to the *Tetrahymena* dynein in terms of the number of heads, the polypeptide composition, and the net M_r. Two years later, it was shown that three-headed particles could also be seen in shadowed preparations of *Tetrahymena* dynein; it was also reported that a three-headed particle could be found in crude extracts of *Chlamydomonas* (Goodenough & Heuser, 1984), although no one has ever isolated a three-headed particle from *Chlamydomonas*.

Sea-urchin 21S dynein has two heads and $1 \cdot 25 \times 10^6 M_r$ (Gibbons & Fronk, 1979; Johnson *et al.* unpublished results; Sale *et al.* 1985). We have also examined dyneins isolated from bull sperm (Marchese-Ragona *et al.* 1984) and from porcine oesophagial cilia (Hastie *et al.* unpublished). In each case an 18–19S, two-headed ATPase was observed in addition to a single-headed, 12S ATPase. These results correspond to the case of the *Chlamydomonas* dyneins, but further work will be required to establish definitively whether the 12S ATPase was derived from the inner or the outer dynein arm. Preliminary data indicate that the 12S ATPase was derived from the outer arm; and so, in each case except sea-urchin, the data argue for a three-headed outer arm. The sea-urchin dynein is the only two-headed outer arm indicated to date and further work will be required to establish whether this is due to a real species difference or whether a third head remains associated with the axoneme following the extraction. It was originally thought that perhaps the difference of two *versus* three heads was a characteristic of flagella *versus* cilia; accordingly, the third head may have been required for the generation of an asymmetric ciliary wave. This does not appear to be reasonable because mutants of *Chlamydomonas* lacking the outer arm are capable of swimming forward with a normal, but slower, ciliary waveform (Kamiya & Okamoto, 1985; Mitchell & Rosenbaum, 1985).

A large body of evidence suggests that the base of the bouquet is attached to the A-tubule and the three heads reach out to interact with the B-tubule in an ATP-dependent reaction to produce a force for sliding (see Johnson, 1985). This was initially suggested from the structure of the isolated dynein and the previous description of an ATP-sensitive association of dynein with the B-tubule and a protease-sensitive attachment to the A-tubule (Takahashi & Tonomura, 1978). Moreover, this assignment is consistent with the observation that the ATP-sensitive association site was broader than the ATP-insensitive attachment site (Haimo *et al.*

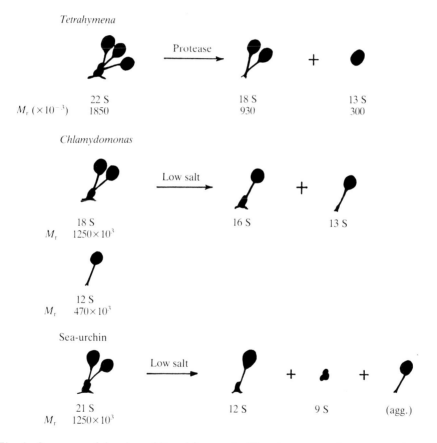

Fig. 1. Summary of dynein and its subfragments. The structures and masses are shown for purified dynein particles and subfragments isolated from *Tetrahymena* (Johnson & Wall, 1982, 1983; Clutter & Johnson, unpublished), *Chlamydomonas* (Witman *et al.* 1982; Pfister & Witman, 1985) and sea-urchin (Sale *et al.* 1985). The structures of the *Chlamydomonas* subfragments are tentative assignments based upon the polypeptide composition and sedimentation coefficients of the particles. The structure of the second sea-urchin subfragment is not definitively known because it aggregates (agg.) and sediments at 15–30 S.

1979). The first direct evidence in support of the identification of the dynein heads as the ATP-sensitive site came from an analysis of the radial mass distribution of dynein bound to microtubules; it was shown that the mass due to the dynein heads was close to the microtubule wall when the dynein was bound in an ATP-sensitive manner (Johnson & Wall, 1983). Subsequent titrations established that there were three ATP binding sites per dynein (Johnson, 1983) and that three molecules of ATP were required to dissociate the dynein from the microtubule (Shimizu & Johnson, 1983*b*), thus indicating that all three heads were bound to the microtubule.

More recently, numerous experiments have confirmed the rule that there is one ATPase site per dynein head. For example, there is one heavy chain per head and reaction with azido-ATP labels all heavy chains for each species of dynein examined, including *Chlamydomonas* (Pfister *et al.* 1984*a,b*), *Tetrahymena* (Chilcote & Johnson, unpublished) and sea-urchin (Ow & Gibbons, 1985). In addition, subfragments of dynein can be obtained and each head fragment has been shown to possess ATPase activity. Sea-urchin 21 S dynein can be fractionated into two ATPases as shown in Fig. 1 (see also Tang *et al.* 1981). It was originally thought that these two ATPases corresponded to the two *Chlamydomonas* ATPases; however, the STEM images and mass indicated that the sea-urchin dynein was similar to the *Chlamydomonas* 18 S dynein (Witman *et al.* 1982). This was directly confirmed by Pfister & Witman (1984), who showed that the 18 S dynein could be fractionated to yield two ATPases corresponding to the two sea-urchin ATPases, and by Sale *et al.* (1985), who examined the structure of the sea-urchin dynein subfragments as summarized in Fig. 1. In addition, *Tetrahymena* dynein can be digested with proteases to yield several fragments (Clutter & Johnson, 1985, unpublished). Extended digestion produces single head fragments with ATPase activity. Mild digestion produces two stable fragments: a two-headed fragment with $930 \times 10^3 M_r$ and a single globular head with $300 \times 10^3 M_r$. Each fragment has ATPase activity and will rebind to microtubules in an ATP-sensitive manner. These data establish that there are at least two and probably three ATP-sensitive, microtubule-binding domains on the *Tetrahymena* dynein. In addition, there may be something special about the structure of dynein in terms of its organization as two heads plus one, because *Tetrahymena* and *Chlamydomonas* dyneins subfractionate as a two-headed particle plus a third head.

Little is known about the functional differences between the three dynein heads. Tests with monoclonal and monospecific, affinity-purified polyclonal antibodies indicate that all three heavy chains are immunologically distinct (King *et al.* 1985; Clutter & Johnson, unpublished). However, there do not appear to be any significant kinetic differences between the three dynein heads. The time course of the ATP-induced dissociation of dynein from the microtubule is potentially complicated by the fact that all three heads interact with the microtubule and three ATP molecules must bind to the dynein to induce dissociation. Nonetheless, the dissociation reaction follows a single exponential, indicative of a single kinetic step (Porter & Johnson, 1983). This could be due to cooperative interactions between the three dynein heads, such that the binding of ATP to the first head causes a more rapid binding to the remaining two heads, or due to a kinetic difference between the heads, such that the rate of ATP binding to the third head was slower than the binding to the first two heads. Alternatively, a rapidly reversible binding of ATP to each head could account for the data if the dynein did not dissociate from the microtubule until all three heads were occupied by ATP. The latter possibility is the most plausible working hypothesis because it can account quantitatively for the interaction of dynein with microtubules (Johnson, 1986).

There is considerable evidence that all three heads interact functionally with the microtubule in the ATP-sensitive complex. For example, dynein is activated by microtubules at low ATP concentration under conditions where dynein remains tethered to the microtubule by association *via* one or more of the heads and any dissociated head detects a high local concentration of microtubules and is activated (Omoto & Johnson, 1985). This dynamic activation of the ATPase occurs as the dynein 'twiddles' on the microtubule surface, as the heads go off and then back on the microtubule with the binding and hydrolysis of each ATP. The binding and hydrolysis of ATP without dissociation of the dynein from the microtubule was first described in terms of a loss of signal amplitude for the dissociation reaction at low ATP concentration (Shimizu & Johnson, 1983*b*). The addition of vanadate led to full recovery of the signal because it tied up each active site after the hydrolysis of only one ATP, thereby making the binding of ATP to each site irreversible (Shimizu & Johnson, 1983*a,b*). Moreover, the kinetics suggested a multi-step reaction due to the sequential dissociation of the three dynein heads from the microtubule. All of these observations support the conclusion that each of the three dynein heads directly associates with the microtubule in an ATP-sensitive reaction and that the rates of ATP binding and hydrolysis at each site are similar.

Because existing models of dynein crossbridge action are based solely upon morphology and ignore the biochemical evidence (Satir *et al.* 1981; Goodenough & Heuser, 1982, 1984), they can be eliminated from serious consideration. The major point of disagreement between the crossbridge models and the biochemical evidence is that the models postulate a single point of attachment to the B-tubule. Existing models for crossbridge motion are based upon an interpretation of relatively low-resolution images of the dynein arm *in situ*, and are subject to considerable error in interpretation because of the lack of definitive data to relate directly the elements of the bouquet seen in isolated dynein to the structures seen *in situ*. There is additional confusion because the length of the stems connecting the heads to the base equals the linear repeat of the dynein along the microtubule; and so, the heads of the dynein overlap the base of the adjacent molecule (Johnson *et al.* 1984; Goodenough & Heuser, 1984). The morphological data must be re-interpreted in order to construct the most reasonable model for crossbridge action that accounts for the biochemical data indicating that all three dynein heads interact with the B-tubule.

A second major flaw with existing models of dynein crossbridge action is in the identification of the structure of the rigor complex. In every case, the rigor complex has been defined as that structure seen in the absence of ATP. However, it is not that simple because placing an axoneme in the absence of ATP does not ensure that the crossbridges will be attached in rigor. On the contrary, most of the images obtained in the absence of ATP indicate that the arm is not crossbridged to the B-tubule. This is exactly what is predicted from a knowledge of the mechanochemistry of the axoneme. Unlike muscle, there must be some mechanism to prevent the interaction of most dynein arms so that only a small fraction of the dynein arms may be able to interact with the B-tubule at any given time in order to propagate a wave (Brokaw, 1980). Thus, even in the absence of ATP, one should expect that less than 10% of the dynein arms will be crossbridged to the B-tubule. This explains the observation that the dynein heads appear to be associated with the A-tubule in the absence of ATP (Goodenough & Heuser, 1982, 1984); the thin connections from the base to the dynein heads are quite flexible and will allow the heads to collapse back onto the A-tubule during the freeze-etching procedure. The numerous, imaginative crossbridge models based upon this definition of the rigor complex cannot be correct.

If existing models of dynein crossbridge action can be eliminated, then what can be said about the conformational changes responsible for force production? In concrete structural terms, very little is known with certainty. The kinetic and thermodynamic data are indicative of a model based upon two conformational states, a tight-microtubule-binding state predominates in the absence of ATP and a second, weak-microtubule-binding conformation is induced by ATP binding (Johnson, 1985; Holzbaur & Johnson, 1986). Nucleotide binding energy establishes the crossbridge pathway thermodynamically and kinetically by inducing a change in conformation to switch the dynein from one state to the other, coupled to dissociation and re-formation of the crossbridge. Because of the close kinetic and thermodynamic similarities between dynein and myosin, crossbridge models based upon the myosin crossbridge cycle form the best working hypothesis for dynein at present. However, as outlined above, the major weakness in the available data is in terms of defining the structure of the microtubule–dynein complex in the absence of nucleotides. Future work is required to obtain the needed high-resolution, three-dimensional reconstruction of the microtubule–dynein complex.

This work was done during the tenure of an Established Investigatorship of the American Heart Association with funds contributed in part by the Pennsylvania Affiliate. Support was also given by the National Institutes of Health, grants GM26726 and GM32023.

REFERENCES

ALLEN, R. D. (1968). A re-investigation of cross-sections of cilia. *J. Cell Biol.* **37**, 825–830.
BROKAW, C. J. (1980). Theoretical models for oscillation and bend propagation by sperm flagella. In *Testicular Development, Structure, and Function* (ed. A. Steinberger & E. Steinberger), pp. 417–430. New York: Raven.
CLUTTER, D. B. & JOHNSON, K. A. (1985). Characterization of *Tetrahymena* dynein fragments produced by proteolytic digestion. *Biophys. J.* **47**, 216a.
GIBBONS, I. R. (1981). Cilia and flagella of eukaryotes. *Cell Biol.* **91**, 107s–124s.
GIBBONS, I. R. & FRONK, E. (1979). A latent ATPase form of dynein-1 from sea urchin sperm. *J. biol. Chem.* **254**, 187–196.
GOODENOUGH, U. W. & HEUSER, J. E. (1982). Substructure of the outer dynein arm. *J. Cell Biol.* **95**, 798–815.

GOODENOUGH, U. W. & HEUSER, J. E. (1984). Structural comparison of purified dynein proteins with *in situ* dynein arms. *J. molec. Biol.* **180**, 1083–1118.

HAIMO, L. T., TELZER, B. R. & ROSENBAUM, J. L. (1979). Dynein binds to and crossbridges cytoplasmic microtubules. *Proc. natn. Acad. Sci. U.S.A.* **76**, 5759–5763.

HEUSER, J. E. & GOODENOUGH, U. W. (1981). Three-dimensional structure of axonemal dynein. *J. Cell Biol.* **91**, 49a.

HOLZBAUR, E. L. F. & JOHNSON, K. A. (1986). Rate of ATP synthesis by dynein. *Biochemistry* **25**, 428–434.

JOHNSON, K. A. (1983). The pathway of ATP hydrolysis by dynein: kinetics of a presteady state phosphate burst. *J. biol. Chem.* **258**, 13 825–13 832.

JOHNSON, K. A. (1985). Pathway of the microtubule–dynein ATPase and the structure of dynein: A comparison with actomyosin. *A. Rev. biophys. biophys. Chem.* **14**, 161–188.

JOHNSON, K. A. (1986). Kinetics of the ATP-induced dissociation and reassociation of the microtubule–dynein complex. *Biochemistry* **24**, 426–427.

JOHNSON, K. A., PORTER, M. E. & SHIMIZU, T. (1984). Mechanism of force production for microtubule-dependent movements. *J. Cell Biol.* **99**, 132s–136s.

JOHNSON, K. A. & WALL, J. S. (1982). Structural and mass analysis of dynein by scanning transmission electron microscopy. *J. submicrosc. Cytol.* **15**, 181–186.

JOHNSON, K. A. & WALL, J. S. (1983). Structure and molecular weight of the dynein ATPase. *J. Cell Biol.* **96**, 669–678.

KAMIYA, R. & OKAMOTO, M. (1985). A mutant of *Chlamydomonas reinhardtii* that lacks the flagellar outer dynein arm but can swim. *J. Cell Sci.* **74**, 181–192.

KING, S. M., OTTER, T. & WITMAN, G. B. (1985). Characterization of monoclonal antibodies against *Chlamydomonas reinhardtii* flagellar dynein by high resolution protein blotting. *Proc. natn. Acad. Sci. U.S.A.* **82**, 4717–4721.

MARCHESE-RAGONA, S. P., BELLES ISLES, M., GAGNON, C., WALL, J. S. & JOHNSON, K. A. (1984). Structures and masses of 14S dynein from *Tetrahymena* and 19S dynein from bull sperm. *J. Cell Biol.* **99**, 45a.

MITCHELL, D. R. & ROSENBAUM, J. L. (1985). A motile *Chlamydomonas* flagellar mutant that lacks outer dynein arms. *J. Cell Biol.* **100**, 1228–1234.

OMOTO, C. K. & JOHNSON, K. A. (1986). Activation of the dynein ATPase by microtubules. *Biochemistry* **25**, 419–427.

OW, R. A. & GIBBONS, I. R. (1985). Polypeptide origin of dynein fragment 1A and the localization of its ATP-binding site. *J. Cell Biol.* **101**, 276a.

PFISTER, K. K., HALEY, B. E. & WITMAN, G. B. (1984a). The photoaffinity probe 8-azido ATP selectively labels the heavy chain of *Chlamydomonas reinhardtii* 12S dynein. *J. biol. Chem.* **259**, 8499–8504.

PFISTER, K. K., HALEY, B. E. & WITMAN, G. B. (1984b). Labelling of *Chlamydomonas* 18S dynein polypeptides by 8-azido ATP, a photoaffinity analog of ATP. *J. biol. Chem.* **260**, 12 844–12 850.

PFISTER, K. K. & WITMAN, G. B. (1984). Subfractionation of *Chlamydomonas* 18S dynein into two unique subunits containing ATPase activity. *J. biol. Chem.* **259**, 12 072–12 080.

PIPERNO, G. & LUCK, D. J. L. (1979). ATPases from flagella of *Chlamydomonas reinhardtii*. *J. biol. Chem.* **254**, 3804–3900.

PORTER, M. E. & JOHNSON, K. A. (1983). Transient state kinetic analysis of the ATP-induced dissociation of the dynein–microtubule complex. *J. biol. Chem.* **258**, 6582–6587.

SALE, W. S., GOODENOUGH, U. W. & HEUSER, J. E. (1985). The substructure of isolated and *in situ* outer dynein arms of sea urchin sperm flagella. *J. Cell Biol.* **101**, 1400–1412.

SATIR, P., WAIS-STEIDER, J., LEBDUSKA, S., NASR, A. & AVOLIO, J. (1981). The mechanochemical cycle of the dynein arm. *Cell Motil.* **1**, 303–327.

SHIMIZU, T. & JOHNSON, K. A. (1983a). Presteady state kinetic analysis vanadate-induced inhibition of the dynein ATPase. *J. biol. Chem.* **258**, 13 833–13 840.

SHIMIZU, T. & JOHNSON, K. A. (1983b). Kinetic evidence for multiple dynein ATPase sites. *J. biol. Chem.* **258**, 13 841–13 848.

TAKAHASHI, M. & TONOMURA, Y. (1979). Binding of 30S dynein with the B-tubule of the outer doublet of axonemes from *Tetrahymena pyriformis* and ATP-induced dissociation of the complex. *J. Biochem.* **84**, 1339–1355.

TANG, W. Y., BELL, C. W., SALE, W. S. & GIBBONS, I. R. (1981). Structure of the dynein-1 outer arm in sea urchin sperm flagella. *J. biol. Chem.* **257**, 508–515.

WALL, J. S. (1979). Biological scanning transmission electron microscopy. In *Introduction to Electron Microscopy* (ed. J. J. Hren, J. I. Goldstein & D. C. Joy), pp. 333–342. New York: Plenum.

WARNER, F. D., MITCHELL, D. R. & PERKINS, C. R. (1977). Structural conformation of the ciliary ATPase dynein. *J. molec. Biol.* **114**, 367–384.

WITMAN, G. B., JOHNSON, K. A., PFISTER, K. K. & WALL, J. S. (1982). Fine structure and molecular weight of the outer arm dyneins of *Chlamydomonas*. *J. submicrosc. Cytol.* **15**, 193–197.

WITMAN, G. B. & MINERVINI, N. (1982). Dynein arm conformation and mechanochemical transduction in the eukaryotic flagellum. *Symp. Soc. exp. Biol.* **35**, 203–223.

J. Cell Sci. Suppl. 5, 197–204 (1986)
Printed in Great Britain © The Company of Biologists Limited 1986

CHARACTERIZATION OF THE SEA-URCHIN EGG MICROTUBULE-ACTIVATED ATPase

CHRISTINE A. COLLINS AND RICHARD B. VALLEE

Cell Biology Group, Worcester Foundation for Experimental Biology, 222 Maple Avenue, Shrewsbury, MA 01545, USA

SUMMARY

We have found that cytoplasmic extracts from unfertilized sea-urchin eggs contain a prominent microtubule-activated ATPase activity. This activity is induced by polymeric tubulin, but not by tubulin subunits. The activity cosediments with taxol-stabilized microtubules in an ATP-independent manner. We have separated the ATPase from cytoplasmic dynein and other ATPases on sucrose gradients. The sedimentation, enzymic and microtubule-binding properties of the microtubule-activated species show it to be distinct from cytoplasmic dynein, myosin and kinesin. Since the major function of microtubules in the early sea-urchin embryo is in mitosis, this enzyme represents a new candidate for a role in spindle motility.

INTRODUCTION

The unfertilized sea-urchin egg stores many of the proteins that will be used during the early stages of embryogenesis. This has been found, in particular, to be true for tubulin, which is present in the unfertilized egg at high concentration in an unpolymerized form (Raff & Kaumeyer, 1973; Pfeffer *et al.* 1976; Bestor & Schatten, 1981). Upon fertilization, microtubule assembly is initiated (Harris *et al.* 1980), and a series of synchronous, closely spaced mitotic divisions ensues.

The mitotic spindle is a complex organelle and presumably requires the interaction of many protein components to function in the separation of chromosomes. It has been the goal of our laboratory over the past four years to develop a procedure for the comprehensive identification of microtubule-binding components of the spindle. Rather than analyse isolated spindles, which are extremely complex in composition, our aim was to develop a procedure for the purification of microtubules from the unpolymerized protein pool present in the unfertilized egg. We reasoned that if tubulin is stockpiled in the egg, the same may be true for other spindle components, and these could, in principle, be identified by copurification with tubulin. A major difficulty encountered with this approach has been that microtubule self-assembly does not occur in sea-urchin egg cytosolic extracts (Kane, 1975; Kuriyama, 1977). Therefore, purification of microtubules by the traditional reversible assembly method was impossible.

We have succeeded, however, in purifying microtubules from sea-urchin eggs using an alternative procedure developed in this laboratory that takes advantage of the microtubule assembly-promoting activity of taxol (Vallee, 1982; Vallee & Bloom,

1983). The microtubules we obtain consistently show a number of polypeptides in addition to tubulin. We have raised monoclonal antibodies to five of these proteins so far. Using these antibodies we found that all five of these proteins were components of the mitotic spindle (Vallee & Bloom, 1983; Bloom *et al.* 1985). Like tubulin, these proteins were present in the unfertilized egg, apparently stockpiled as spindle precursors. The unfertilized egg, therefore, appears to be a promising system in which to search for further structural and functional components of the spindle.

ATPases IN THE SEA-URCHIN EGG

The dynamics of the mitotic spindle probably reflect both the reversible assembly of microtubules (Oakley & Morris, 1981; Cande *et al.* 1981) and the behaviour of associated mechanochemical enzymes (see below). In studies examining mitosis in permeabilized cells, a requirement for ATP in both chromosome separation and spindle elongation was found, though the nature of the ATP-utilizing machinery was uncertain (Cande & Wolniak, 1978; Cande, 1982). The presence of myosin in the spindle has been reported (Fujiwara & Pollard, 1978), but its functional importance was disputed by experiments involving microinjection of anti-myosin antibodies (Mabuchi & Okuno, 1977; Kiehart *et al.* 1982). Dynein-like activity in the spindle has been implied by the inhibitory effects of erythro-9-[3-(2-hydroxynonyl)]adenine (EHNA) and vanadate on mitotic movement (Cande & Wolniak, 1978; Cande, 1982). A cytoplasmic enzyme with dynein-like properties has, in fact, been found in the sea-urchin egg (Pratt, 1980). This enzyme, known as cytoplasmic dynein, has been reported to be present in spindle preparations (Weisenberg & Taylor, 1968; Pratt *et al.* 1980). It is not yet clear, however, whether it has a functional role in mitosis, or serves as a precursor for the cilia that are formed in the blastula-stage embryo.

We have examined our purified egg microtubule preparations for ATPase activity in the hope of identifying ATP-utilizing enzymes that might play a role in spindle function. We have, in fact, identified what appears to be a novel, prominent ATPase activity that is specifically and dramatically activated by assembled microtubules.

ACTIVATION OF CYTOPLASMIC ATPase ACTIVITY BY MICROTUBULES

In analysing the properties of fractions obtained during the course of microtubule purification, we found that the total ATPase activity in the microtubule pellet and post-microtubule supernatant always exceeded the initial cytosolic level. One explanation for this effect was that ATPase activity was stimulated by formation of the microtubules. In experiments performed by other investigators, it has been shown that a fraction of the cytoplasmic dynein present in the egg cosedimented with microtubules prepared according to our procedure (Scholey *et al.* 1984). However, this would not by itself account for the excess activity we observed.

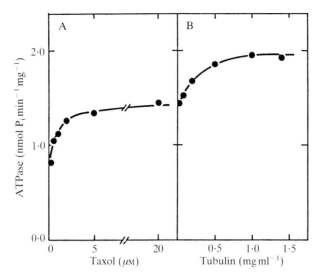

Fig. 1. Activation of cytosolic ATPase activity by microtubules. A. Increase in activity
due to endogenous tubulin assembly by taxol. Taxol was added at the concentrations
indicated to a cytosolic extract prepared from eggs of the sea-urchin *Strongylocentrotus
purpuratus* (Collins & Vallee, 1986). After incubation at 37°C for 5 min to assemble
microtubules, the treated extracts were assayed for ATPase activity (Collins & Vallee,
1986). B. Effect of additional microtubules on cytosolic ATPase activity. Pure calf brain
tubulin was assembled with taxol (as described by Collins & Vallee, 1986) and added at
the concentrations indicated to samples of the same extracts shown in A previously
treated with 10 μM-taxol to assemble endogenous tubulin. After a 5 min incubation at
37°C, the extracts were assayed for ATPase activity.

We performed several experiments to determine the mechanism accounting for the
excess ATPase activity measured in our preparations. In the experiment shown in
Fig. 1A, taxol was added to a cytosolic extract to evaluate the effect of microtubule
assembly on ATPase activity. As can be seen, the addition of taxol up to 2–5 μM led
to an increase in total ATPase activity. The concentration dependence of the taxol
effect reflected the concentration of the drug required for stoichiometric binding to
tubulin dimers present in the extract. Further activation was not observed in the
presence of higher taxol concentrations. In other experiments, the microtubules
formed in the presence of increasing taxol concentrations were sedimented from the
cytosolic extract (Collins & Vallee, 1986). All the newly induced activity was found
to cosediment with the microtubules.

Addition of exogenous microtubules to egg cytosolic extracts led to an activation of
the ATPase activity similar to that induced by taxol (Collins & Vallee, 1986).
Microtubules prepared from calf brain tubulin and flagellar axoneme outer doublet
microtubules were equally effective in activating the ATPase. Fig. 1B shows that the
addition of exogenous microtubules composed of taxol-stabilized pure brain tubulin
to an extract already treated with taxol resulted in a further increase in ATPase
activity. This additional activity saturated at about 0·5 mg ml^{-1} tubulin. The total
stimulation of activity due to the combined effects of endogenous tubulin assembly

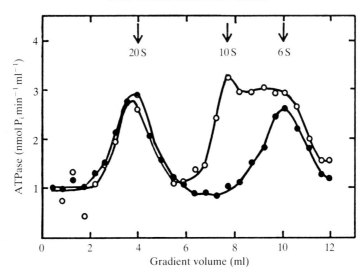

Fig. 2. Sucrose density-gradient analysis of egg cytosolic extract. Density-gradient centrifugation of unfertilized *S. purpuratus* egg cytosolic extracts was carried out on linear gradients of 5% to 20% sucrose. The effect of microtubules on enzymic activity was determined by addition to a final concentration of 0.25 mg ml^{-1} of purified calf brain tubulin that had been assembled into microtubules with taxol. Gradient fractions were assayed for ATPase activity at 30 °C in the presence (O——O) or absence (●——●) of microtubules (from Collins & Vallee, 1986).

and addition of exogenous microtubules was more than twofold over the untreated control.

To determine whether the increased activity reflected stimulation of an existing activity or activation of a new species, egg cytosolic extracts were analysed by sucrose density-gradient centrifugation (Collins & Vallee, 1986). In the absence of added microtubules, ATPase activity resolved into two peaks at sedimentation values of 20 S and 6 S (Fig. 2). The 20 S species had the properties reported for cytoplasmic dynein. This is larger than the 12–14 S species many investigators find for this enzyme (Pratt, 1980; Hisanaga & Sakai, 1980; Penningroth *et al.* 1985). We also find a dynein-like activity migrating at 12 S in some of our sucrose gradient experiments (Collins & Vallee, 1986). Both the 20 S and 12 S ATPases were inhibited by 100 μM-sodium vanadate and stimulated by non-ionic detergent. The relative abundance of the two dynein species in the gradient was found to be dependent on buffer conditions (Collins & Vallee, unpublished results).

To determine the gradient position of the microtubule-activated ATPase, microtubules assembled from pure calf brain tubulin with the aid of taxol were added to each fraction for enzyme assay. No effect of microtubules on the activity of cytoplasmic dynein was seen. This is consistent with observations made with axonemal dynein, the activity of which shows some stimulation by microtubules, but only at extremely high microtubule concentrations (Omoto & Johnson, 1986). A new major peak of ATPase activity was observed at a sedimentation value of 10 S. The size of this peak could account for the total stimulation of activity in the cytosolic extract. Thus, the enhancement of ATPase activity by microtubules seen in the extract appears to reflect the activation of a previously undetected enzyme.

ENZYMIC PROPERTIES OF MICROTUBULE-ACTIVATED ATPase

Table 1 summarizes several of the enzymic properties of the ATPase. Some of the data shown were obtained using the 10 S sucrose density-gradient fraction. Other data were obtained using purified egg microtubules, which contain primarily the microtubule-activated enzyme (Collins & Vallee, 1986), but some cytoplasmic dynein as well.

The enzyme requires divalent cations (either Mg^{2+} or Ca^{2+}), and in this regard differs from non-muscle myosins (Korn, 1978), including myosin from echinoderm eggs (Mabuchi, 1976). Non-muscle myosin activity also shows a marked increase in activity with increasing KCl in the presence of Ca^{2+}. This contrasts with the microtubule-activated enzyme, which showed a decrease in activity under these conditions.

The ATPase was unaffected by 100 μM-vanadate, an important distinction from cytoplasmic and other dyneins. Cytoplasmic dynein and sea-urchin flagellar 'latent activity' dynein have also been found to be stimulated two- to threefold by non-ionic detergents and by certain anions, including Cl^- (Hisanaga & Pratt, 1984; Asai & Wilson, 1985; Gibbons & Fronk, 1979; Gibbons *et al.* 1985; Collins & Vallee, 1986). In contrast, Triton X-100 showed only a small negative effect on the microtubule-activated ATPase, and 0·25 M-NaCl strongly suppressed activity. This salt concentration has been found sufficient to cause release of sea-urchin egg, mammalian brain and cultured cell microtubule-associated proteins from the tubulin polymer (Vallee,

Table 1. *Properties of egg microtubule-activated ATPase*

	Condition	Relative activity (%)
Control	2 mM-MgSO$_4$	100
Experiment I (microtubules)	2 mM-EDTA, 500 mM-KCl	2
	10 mM-CaCl$_2$	107
	10 mM-CaCl$_2$, 100 mM-KCl	88
	10 mM-CaCl$_2$, 200 mM-KCl	68
	10 mM-CaCl$_2$, 300 mM-KCl	67
Experiment II (10 S fraction)	100 μM-Na$_3$VO$_4$	107
	0·25 % Triton X-100	74
	2 mM-N-ethylmaleimide	12
	0·25 M-NaCl	11

For experiment I, data were obtained using whole purified sea-urchin microtubules. ATPase assays were conducted according to Collins & Vallee (1986) under the conditions indicated. Other pharmacological and co-sedimentation data indicate that ATPase in whole microtubule protein is primarily due to the activity of the 10 S microtubule-activated enzyme. In experiment II, the 10 S sucrose density-gradient peak was used. The data are taken from Collins & Vallee (1986) and represent the activity of the ATPase fraction in the presence of microtubules as a percentage of control activity with 2 mM-MgSO$_4$.

1982; Vallee & Bloom, 1983). Thus, a reasonable explanation for the observed effect of NaCl on activity is that it reflects the dissociation of the enzyme from micro-tubules. The microtubule-activated ATPase also showed efficient utilization of GTP as substrate (Collins & Vallee, 1986), again in contrast with dynein.

A protein with proposed mechanochemical functions has recently been identified in sea-urchin eggs (Scholey et al. 1985). This protein, kinesin, has been shown to induce bead movement along microtubules and sliding of microtubules on coverslips (Vale et al. 1985). Under appropriate conditions, kinesin has been shown to bind to microtubules (Vale et al. 1985; Scholey et al. 1985). In the presence of ATP, the bound kinesin is released from the microtubule and can be recovered in soluble form. The microtubule-activated ATPase described here was found to bind to micro-tubules even at high levels of ATP (Collins & Vallee, 1986), in contrast to kinesin. We have monitored the fate of kinesin in our preparations by using a polyclonal antibody (Scholey et al. 1985) and have confirmed that only a small amount of that protein co-sediments with microtubules under our microtubule purification conditions. Thus, the microtubule-activated ATPase activity cannot be attributed to kinesin, and represents a distinct species. In further support of this conclusion, 2 mM-N-ethylmaleimide inactivated the ATPase (Table 1). In contrast, kinesin-mediated motility is unaffected by this agent. We have also performed experiments similar to that shown in Fig. 2 with calf brain cytosol, which contains abundant

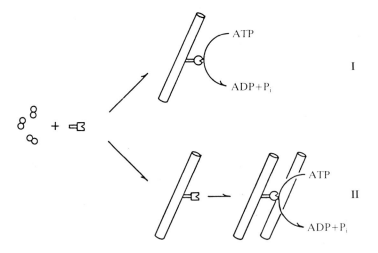

Fig. 3. Alternative schemes describing possible mechanisms for microtubule binding and microtubule activation of the sea-urchin egg cytosolic ATPase. Tubulin dimers are shown on the left in an unassembled state along with the inactive enzyme. Activation is envisaged to occur in two ways, each accounting in a distinct manner for the observed ATP-independence of microtubule binding. In scheme I, the enzyme binds to a microtubule via a non-catalytic site, and activation occurs by an allosteric mechanism. In scheme II, binding occurs at two sites on the enzyme (not necessarily in the sequence shown). Binding at a non-catalytic site would account for the ATP-independent binding that is observed. Binding at or near the catalytic site to a second microtubule would be responsible for activation of the catalytic activity.

kinesin (Vale *et al.* 1985). We observed no detectable microtubule stimulation of ATPase activity in brain cytosolic extracts.

A MODEL FOR MICROTUBULE-ACTIVATION OF THE ATPase

Two schemes to account for the ATP-independent binding of the enzyme as well as its activation by microtubules are presented in Fig. 3. In scheme I, the enzyme is shown to bind to a microtubule *via* a site independent of the ATPase catalytic site. Activation is envisaged to occur by an allosteric mechanism. While there is no existing counterpart for such a mechanism among the known mechanochemical enzymes, it does account for our existing data.

Alternatively (scheme II), the enzyme may bind to microtubules *via* two distinct sites. Binding at one site would be ATP-independent, and would account for the observed cosedimentation with microtubules in the presence or absence of ATP. Binding at a second site, at or near the catalytic site, would be responsible for activation of the enzyme. Binding here could be disrupted by ATP, but co-sedimentation would still occur due to binding at the first site. This scheme is based on our present understanding of the mechanism of action of myosin and dynein. It may imply a role for the new enzyme in microtubule sliding, and we are at present actively investigating this possibility.

FUNCTIONAL IMPLICATIONS OF A MICROTUBULE-ACTIVATED ATPase

We find that the microtubule-activated ATPase present in egg cytosolic extracts copurifies with microtubules assembled with taxol from these same extracts. Therefore the ATPase itself is likely to be a normal component of the microtubule, and to be one of the protein species we have already identified in microtubule preparations from several species of sea urchin. However, the precise molecular identification of the enzyme must await further work. We do not yet know the function of the ATPase in the cell. In view of its abundance in the egg, a particularly intriguing possibility is that it serves an important role in the mechanochemistry of the mitotic spindle.

REFERENCES

ASAI, D. J. & WILSON, L. (1985). A latent activity dynein-like cytoplasmic magnesium adenosine triphosphatase. *J. biol. Chem.* **260**, 699–702.
BESTOR, T. H. & SCHATTEN, G. (1981). Anti-tubulin immunofluorescence microscopy of microtubules present during the pronuclear movements of sea urchin fertilization. *Devl Biol.* **88**, 80–91.
BLOOM, G. S., LUCA, F. C., COLLINS, C. A. & VALLEE, R. B. (1985). Use of multiple monoclonal antibodies to characterize the major microtubule-associated protein in sea urchin eggs. *Cell Motil.* **5**, 431–446.
CANDE, W. Z. (1982). Inhibition of spindle elongation in permeabilized mitotic cells by erythro-9-[3-(2-hydroxynonyl)]adenine. *Nature, Lond.* **295**, 700–703.
CANDE, W. Z., McDONALD, K. & MEEUSEN, R. L. (1981). A permeabilized cell model for studying cell division: a comparison of anaphase chromosome movement and cleavage furrow constriction in lysed PtK$_1$ cells. *J. Cell Biol.* **88**, 618–629.

CANDE, W. Z. & WOLNIAK, S. M. (1978). Chromosome movement in lysed mitotic cells is inhibited by vanadate. J. Cell Biol. **79**, 573–580.

COLLINS, C. A. & VALLEE, R. B. (1986). A microtubule activated ATPase from sea urchin eggs distinct from cytoplasmic dynein. Proc. natn. Acad. Sci. U.S.A. **83**, 4799–4803.

FUJIWARA, K. & POLLARD, T. D. (1978). Simultaneous localization of myosin and tubulin in human tissue culture cells by double antibody staining. J. Cell Biol. **77**, 182–195.

GIBBONS, I. R. & FRONK, E. (1979). A latent adenosine triphosphatase form of dynein 1 from sea urchin sperm flagella. J. biol. Chem. **254**, 187–196.

GIBBONS, B. H., TANG, W.-J. Y. & GIBBONS, I. R. (1985). Organic anions stabilize the reactivated motility of sperm flagella and the latency of dynein 1 ATPase activity. J. Cell Biol. **101**, 1281–1287.

HARRIS, P., OSBORN, M. & WEBER, K. (1980). Distribution of tubulin containing structures in the egg of the sea urchin Strongylocentrotus purpuratus. J. Cell Biol. **84**, 668–679.

HISANAGA, S. & SAKAI, H. (1980). Cytoplasmic dynein of the sea urchin egg. I. Partial purification and characterization. Dev. Growth Differ. **22**, 373–384.

KANE, R. E. (1975). Preparation and purification of polymerized actin from sea urchin egg extracts. J. Cell Biol. **66**, 305–315.

KIEHART, D. P., MABUCHI, I. & INOUE, S. (1982). Evidence that myosin does not contribute to force production in chromosome movement. J. Cell Biol. **94**, 165–178.

KORN, E. D. (1978). Biochemistry of actomyosin-dependent cell motility (a review). Proc. natn. Acad. Sci. U.S.A. **75**, 588–599.

KURIYAMA, R. (1977). In vitro polymerization of marine egg tubulin into microtubules. J. Biochem., Tokyo **81**, 1115–1125.

MABUCHI, I. (1976). Myosin from starfish egg: properties and interaction with actin. J. molec. Biol. **100**, 569–582.

MABUCHI, I. & OKUNO, M. (1977). The effect of myosin antibody on the division of starfish blastomeres. J. Cell Biol. **74**, 251–263.

OAKLEY, B. R. & MORRIS, N. R. (1981). A β-tubulin mutation in Aspergillus nidulans that blocks microtubule function without blocking assembly. Cell **24**, 837–845.

OMOTO, C. K. & JOHNSON, K. A. (1986). Activation of the dynein adenosine triphosphatase by microtubules. Biochemistry **25**, 419–427.

PENNINGROTH, S. M., ROSE, P., CHEUNG, A., PETERSON, D. D., ROTHACKER, D. Q. & BERSHAK, P. (1985). An EHNA-sensitive ATPase in unfertilized sea urchin eggs. Cell Motil. **5**, 61–75.

PFEFFER, T. A., ASNES, C. F. & WILSON, L. (1976). Properties of tubulin in unfertilized sea urchin eggs. J. Cell Biol. **69**, 599–607.

PRATT, M. M. (1980). The identification of a dynein ATPase in unfertilized sea urchin eggs. Devl Biol. **74**, 364–378.

PRATT, M. M., OTTER, T. & SALMON, E. D. (1980). Dynein-like ATPase in mitotic spindles isolated from sea urchin embryos (Strongylocentrotus droebachiensis). J. Cell Biol. **86**, 738–745.

RAFF, R. A. & KAUMEYER, J. F. (1973). Soluble microtubule proteins of the sea urchin embryo: partial characterization of the proteins and behavior of the pool in early development. Devl Biol. **32**, 309–320.

SCHOLEY, J. M., NEIGHBORS, B., McINTOSH, J. R. & SALMON, E. D. (1984). Isolation of microtubules and a dynein-like MgATPase from unfertilized sea urchin eggs. J. biol. Chem. **259**, 6516–6525.

SCHOLEY, J. M., PORTER, M. E., GRISSOM, P. M. & McINTOSH, J. R. (1985). Identification of kinesin in sea urchin eggs, and evidence for its localization in the mitotic spindle. Nature, Lond. **318**, 483–486.

VALE, R. D., REESE, T. S. & SHEETZ, M. P. (1985). Identification of a novel force-generating protein, kinesin, involved in microtubule-based motility. Cell **42**, 39–50.

VALLEE, R. B. (1982). A taxol-dependent procedure for the isolation of microtubules and microtubule-associated proteins (MAPs). J. Cell Biol. **92**, 435–442.

VALLEE, R. B. & BLOOM, G. S. (1983). Isolation of sea urchin egg microtubules with taxol and identification of mitotic spindle microtubule-associated proteins with monoclonal antibodies. Proc. natn. Acad. Sci. U.S.A. **80**, 6259–6263.

WEISENBERG, R. & TAYLOR, E. W. (1968). Studies on ATPase activity of sea urchin eggs and the isolated mitotic apparatus. Expl Cell Res. **53**, 372–384.

J. Cell Sci. Suppl. 5, 205–227 (1986)
Printed in Great Britain © The Company of Biologists Limited 1986

COMPARISON OF SPINDLE ELONGATION *IN VIVO* AND *IN VITRO* IN *STEPHANOPYXIS TURRIS*

K. L. McDONALD, K. PFISTER, H. MASUDA, L. WORDEMAN, C. STAIGER AND W. Z. CANDE*

Departments of Botany and Zoology, University of California, Berkeley, CA 94720, USA

SUMMARY

The spindle in dividing cells of the diatom *Stephanopyxis turris* contains three distinct classes of microtubules: central spindle microtubules, which slide over each other and grow during anaphase spindle elongation; kinetochore-attached microtubules, which are located on the outer surface of the central spindle; and peripheral microtubules, which fan out from the spindle poles in astral-like arrays. The poles are multilayered structures, which remain attached to the spindle after isolation. *In vitro*, after addition of ATP, central spindles elongate and the two half-spindles slide completely apart with a concurrent decrease in the extent and magnitude of the zone of microtubule overlap. Spindle elongation takes place in spindles whose chromatin has been removed by enzymic digestion and the extent of elongation *in vitro* is increased by the addition of neurotubulin. After ATP addition the arrays of interdigitating microtubules in the zone of overlap become disordered and selectively depolymerize from the overlap zone polewards. In some reactivated spindles an unusual structure, a striated fibre, can be seen running from the pole plates part of the way towards the spindle midzone. The fibre has no precedent in mitotic ultrastructure and its function is unclear. These results demonstrate that we can duplicate the essential elements of anaphase B *in vitro* and that this system will be useful for further studies of the molecular basis of spindle elongation.

INTRODUCTION

Our understanding of cellular mechanochemistry has been aided by the development of *in vitro* model systems that mimic the key elements of cellular movements that occur *in vivo*. These model systems have provided the bridge between ultrastructural and physiological analysis of the whole system and biochemical analysis of individual components. For example, cinematic analysis of *in vitro* flagellar models combined with selective extraction of component parts (i.e. cross-bridges) and analysis by electron microscopy was essential for understanding the mechanochemistry of flagellar beat (reviewed by Gibbons, 1981). Although the ATP-induced sliding of flagellar microtubules could be seen in the light microscope, the corresponding analysis by electron microscopy gave detailed information about the dynein arms and how they behaved under different reactivation conditions (Summers & Gibbons, 1971; Sale & Satir, 1977).

Until now, the mitosis field has not had a functional *in vitro* model that can be used for correlated physiological and ultrastructural studies of spindle function. In recent publications (Cande & McDonald, 1985, 1986) we have described the conditions for isolating functional central spindles from diatoms, an assay for studying reactivation of spindle elongation with immunofluorescence and light microscopy, and the ultrastructural changes that occur *in vitro* after reactivation with ATP. We have used

*Author for correspondence.

diatom spindles as starting material because the unique attributes of these spindles make them more amenable to structural analysis than spindles prepared from other commonly used sources such as mammalian tissue culture cells or sea-urchin eggs. As described in this paper and elsewhere (Wordeman *et al.* 1986), the spindles from the centric diatom *Stephanopyxis turris* contain three classes of microtubules: central spindle microtubules, which appear to slide over each other during spindle elongation and also grow longer during this process; kinetochore-attached micro-tubules, which are located on the outer surface of the central spindle and are in-volved in chromosome-to-pole movement; and peripheral microtubules, which may function like astral microtubules in animal cells to position the spindle in the cell (Wordeman *et al.* 1986). At least two of the three classes, the central spindle microtubules and the peripheral microtubule bundles, are readily resolved using indirect immunofluorescence and antibodies against tubulin. As we show here changes in peripheral or central spindle microtubule distribution due to experimental manipulation are easily detected even at the light-microscopic level.

In this paper we describe the process of spindle elongation *in vivo* and *in vitro* and summarize the ultrastructural changes that occur during reactivation. With the addition of ATP, the two half-spindles slide completely apart with a concurrent decrease in the extent and magnitude of the zone of microtubule overlap. This process can even take place in spindles whose chromatin has been removed by enzymic digestion. ATP also initiates a depolymerization of microtubules similar to changes *in vivo* (Sorrano & Pickett-Heaps, 1982). In the presence of neurotubulin and taxol, tubulin is incorporated into the central spindle and the extent of spindle elongation *in vitro* is increased. Spindle reactivation requires ATP hydrolysis and is highly specific for ATP, and elongation is inhibited by vanadate, sulphhydryl reagents, and equimolar mixtures of AMPPNP and ATP (Cande & McDonald, 1986). We interpret these results to mean that spindle elongation in diatoms is effected by a dynein-like mechanochemical ATPase operating in the zone of overlap and that ATP is also required for controlled disassembly of spindle microtubules. For this system we can conclusively eliminate mechanisms of spindle elongation that are based solely on forces pulling at the poles (Aist & Berns, 1981) or assembly of continuous microtubules (reviewed by Inoue, 1981). However, the importance of these mechanisms in other systems and as possible auxiliary motors in spindles with sliding microtubule mechanochemistry is discussed.

MATERIALS AND METHODS

Materials

Nucleotides, non-hydrolysable nucleotide analogues, drugs and enzymes were obtained from Sigma Chemical Co. (St Louis, MO) or Boehringer–Mannheim Biochemicals (Federal Republic of Germany). Vanadate was obtained from Accurate Chemical & Scientific Corp. (Hicksville, NY). Taxol was a gift from Dr Matthew Suffness, Natural Products Branch, Division of Cancer Treatment, National Cancer Institute, Bethesda, MD. Tubulin was prepared as described by Hollenbeck *et al.* (1984).

Methods

Cell culture and synchronization. Stephanopyxis turris (stock no. L1272) was obtained from the Culture Collection of Marine Phytoplankton, Bigelow Laboratory for Ocean Sciences, West Boothbay, Maine. Cells were grown in F/2 medium (Guillard, 1975) in a suspension culture on a 6·5-h day, 17·5-h night schedule at 19°C. At 3 h before harvest cells were drugged with 2×10^{-8} M-nocodazole and 20 min before harvest cells were collected on 60 μm mesh Nitex filters and washed extensively to remove the drug (Cande & McDonald, 1986; Wordeman *et al.* 1986). At 20 min after drug reversal all cells undergoing mitosis are at a similar stage, that is the central spindles are 6–8 μm long and the cells are in metaphase–early anaphase.

Spindle isolation and reactivation. Cells were suspended in homogenization medium on ice (50 mM-PIPES, pH 7·0, 40 mM-sodium glycerophosphate, 10 mM-MgSO$_4$, 10 mM-EGTA, 0·2 % Brij 58, 30 % glycerol, 1 mM-dithiothreitol (DTT), 0·5 mM-phenylmethylsulphonyl fluoride (PMSF), 10 ml l^{-1} soyabean trypsin inhibitor, 10 mg l^{-1} L-1-tosylamide-2-phenyl-ethylchloromethyl ketone, 10 mg l^{-1} benzylarginylmethyl ester, 1 mg l^{-1} leupeptin, 1 mg l^{-1} pepstatin), then homogenized on ice with two strokes of a Kontes dounce homogenizer, β pestle. The homogenate was filtered once through 60 μm mesh and then through 25 μm mesh Nitex filters, then centrifuged for 10 min, 0°C at 2000 $\boldsymbol{g}$ onto coverslips. The coverslips were placed in fresh homogenizing medium in plastic dishes and briefly swirled to remove adhering chloroplasts, then stored on ice until use.

For spindle reactivation studies, coverslips were transferred to reactivation medium (50 mM-PIPES, pH 7·0, 5 mM-MgSO$_4$, 10 mM-EGTA, 1 mM-DTT, with or without proteolytic inhibitors, and nucleotide) and incubated at room temperature or in a water bath at 20°C. Reactivation was terminated by addition of fixative, usually 0·2 % glutaraldehyde.

In order to prevent chromatin from unravelling during isolation and reactivation, in some experiments homogenization medium was altered to include 1 mM-spermidine, 0·5 mM-spermine and no Mg^{2+} salts, and reactivation medium included 0·1 mM-spermidine, 0·05 mM-spermine and 10 mM-MgSO$_4$. In order to remove chromatin from the spindles, after they were centrifuged onto coverslips the spindles were incubated in normal (i.e. minus spermidine) isolation medium with 10 % glycerol and 300 units ml^{-1} DNase I.

Spindles used in tubulin incorporation experiments were handled slightly differently than described above or previously (Cande & McDonald, 1985, 1986). Spindles were homogenized in a modified medium with 50 mM-HEPES, pH 7·5, as a buffer including in addition 80 mM-sodium glycerophosphate and 50 μM-ATPγS. After homogenization, spindles were centrifuged through a 40 % sucrose cushion containing the above medium (minus glycerol) and a 60 % sucrose cushion containing the above medium (minus glycerol) and 10 μM-taxol. For reactivation, spindles were incubated in 75 mM-HEPES, pH 7·5, 2·5 mM-MgSO$_4$, 5 mM-EGTA, 40 mM-sodium glycerophosphate, 25 μM-ATPγS, 0·1 mM-ATP, 0·1 mM-GTP, proteolytic inhibitors, 1 mM-DTT, 20 μM-taxol with or without 25 μM-neurotubulin.

Microscopy

Video recordings of spindle birefringence were made on a Zeiss standard microscope equipped with polarization optics as described previously (Cande & McDonald, 1985). Micrographs of fluorescent or phase images were made on a Zeiss Universal or photomicroscope equipped with epi-fluorescence optics and a 100× Neofluar or 25× Plan-neofluar lens. Unless otherwise indicated spindle lengths were measured from a TV monitor using a DAGE-MTI low light level TV camera and all metaphase spindles on a transect of the preparation were used for length measurements (Cande & McDonald, 1986). Intact cells and isolated spindles were prepared for electron microscopy using standard procedures as described previously (Cande & McDonald, 1985, 1986).

Indirect immunofluorescence. The antibody against tubulin (a monoclonal antibody against sea-urchin flagellar tubulin) was kindly provided by Dr David Asai (Department of Biology, Purdue University) and its preparation and characterization have been described previously (Asai *et al.* 1982). Spindles or whole cells were fixed in glutaraldehyde and handled as described (Cande & McDonald, 1986; Wordeman *et al.* 1986). Chromatin was stained by adding 200 ng ml^{-1} DAPI (4′,6-diamidino-2-phenylindole dihydrochloride) to the isolation or reactivation medium.

Electron microscopy. Dividing cells and isolated spindles were prepared for electron microscopy by two slightly different methods. Intact cells were fixed in 0·5 % glutaraldehyde in F/2 medium

(Guillard, 1975) for 30 min at 23 °C (unless otherwise stated, all remaining steps were at 23 °C). Spindles were rinsed for 5 min in phosphate-buffered saline (PBS: 137 mM-NaCl, 2·68 mM-KCl, 8 mM-Na$_2$HPO$_4$·7H$_2$O, 1·47 mM-KH$_2$PO$_4$) at pH 7·3, fixed in 0·2 % OsO$_4$+0·3 % K$_3$Fe(CN)$_6$ in PBS for 15 min at 4 °C, rinsed twice in PBS for 5 min each, rinsed in distilled water for 5 min, incubated in 2 % aqueous uranyl acetate for 90 min, dehydrated in acetone by 10 % steps for 10 min each and embedded in Epon–Araldite (3·1 g Epon 812, 2·2 g Araldite 502, 6·1 g DDSA, 0·2 g DMP-30). Some isolated spindles were prepared by the same method and others were fixed in 0·5 % glutaraldehyde in PBS, pH 7·3, rinsed in PBS, fixed in 0·5 % OsO$_4$+0·5 % K$_3$Fe(CN)$_6$ in 0·1 M-cacodylate buffer, pH 7·2, rinsed in cacodylate buffer for 5 min, then in distilled water three times for 5 min each, then into 2 % aqueous uranyl acetate for 90 min, then dehydrated and embedded as above. Coverslips were flat-embedded on slides sprayed with release agent (MS-122; Miller-Stephenson, Sylmar, CA). After the resin had cured, coverslips were removed from the resin by dissolving them in HF for 15–20 min (Moore, 1975).

Spindles were sectioned in known orientation and serial sections of approximately 75 nm thickness were picked up on slot grids. Sections were stained for 10–15 min in 1 % aqueous uranyl acetate and for 5 min in lead citrate (Reynolds, 1963). Sections were viewed and photographed on a JEOL 100S electron microscope at 80 kV. Magnifications were determined from negatives of a calibration grid (Polysciences catalogue no. 1732) taken at the appropriate magnification step on the microscope.

RESULTS

Mitosis in vivo

Light microscopy. In the hours preceding mitosis, the nucleus migrates from its interphase position at the end wall to the centre of the cell (Fig. 1). The newly formed prophase spindle is apparent in the centred nucleus as a birefringent square or rectangle (Fig. 2) and a zone of overlap appears shortly thereafter (Fig. 4A). The later stages of mitosis are hard to distinguish in living cells because individual, condensed chromosomes are difficult to see. However, the shape of the chromatin mass and length of the spindle offer some clues. Fig. 4B is probably a metaphase spindle because the chromatin is still mostly equatorial in position. The movement of chromosomes to the poles (anaphase A) causes the chromatin mass to assume a dumbbell shape around the central spindle (Fig. 4C), which then starts to elongate (anaphase B). Fig. 4D,E shows the final stages of spindle elongation by which time the spindle length has increased about twofold over the metaphase length. A sequence similar to that in Fig. 4B–E is shown in Fig. 5 by immunofluorescence staining with an antibody to tubulin. In addition to the brightly staining central spindle microtubules one can also see the network of peripheral microtubules and how their position changes during anaphase. Initially the peripheral microtubules point inward towards the metaphase chromosomes (Fig. 5A), but as anaphase proceeds they become rearranged to point away from the spindle, so that by telophase (Fig. 5D) they form a radial array around the decondensing chromatin of the daughter nuclei. Shortly after this stage, the broad cleavage furrow (Fig. 3) separates the daughter nuclei and they come to lie at the end wall of the cell. Remnants of the central spindle can be detected up to an hour after cleavage.

We have looked at the rate and extent of spindle elongation in several cells monitored by video microscopy (Fig. 6). After the spindle sinks through the nuclear envelope into the chromatin mass it continues to increase in length and breadth

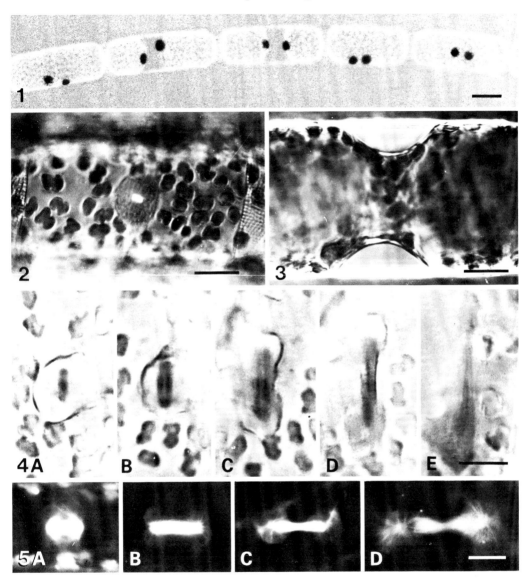

Fig. 1. A strand of DAPI-stained cells in different stages of mitosis. The first, fourth and fifth cells from the left are in anaphase, and the second and third cells have just undergone cleavage. Bar, 50 μm.

Figs 2–4. Polarization micrographs (with positive or negative compensation) showing cells undergoing mitosis and cleavage. Fig. 2. The cell is in prophase and the spindle, the bright birefringent bar, rests on top of the nucleus. Bar, 10 μm. Fig. 3. The cell is cleaving in two and the nuclei are not in the plane of focus. Bar, 10 μm. Fig. 4A–E. The central spindle is shown undergoing spindle elongation: A, prometaphase; B, metaphase (0 min); C, early anaphase (2 min); D, mid-anaphase (4 min); E, late anaphase or telophase (8 min). The zone of microtubule overlap is apparent in A–C as a region of increased birefringence. Bar, 10 μm.

Fig. 5. Anti-tubulin immunofluorescence micrographs of the central spindle in intact, fixed cells showing: A, metaphase; B, mid-anaphase; C–D, late anaphase or telophase. C–D are different cells photographed at different focal planes to show the central spindle (C) and the elaborate peripheral microtubule arrays (D). Bar, 10 μm.

(Fig. 4A,B). During prophase–prometaphase the zone of microtubule overlap increases in size from 2 μm to 3 μm while the spindle increases in size from 5 μm to 10 μm at a rate of about 0·7 μm min^{-1}. There is a prolonged but variable metaphase

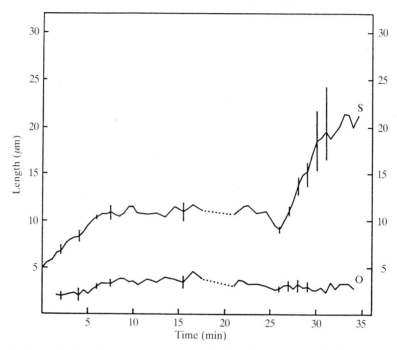

Fig. 6. A graph of the length changes *versus* time for the central spindle (S) and the zone of microtubule overlap (O) during mitosis in *S. turris*. This graph is a composite and an average of eight separate video time-lapse recordings made with polarization optics. Four recordings were used for the prophase–metaphase length changes (before the break) and four different recordings were used for the metaphase–anaphase length changes (after the break). No cell went completely through mitosis while under observation; hence, the duration of metaphase is an estimate. During prophase–prometaphase, spindles elongated at a rate of 0·7 μm min^{-1} (range 0·5–0·9 μm min^{-1}) and during anaphase spindles elongated at a rate of 1·7 μm min^{-1} (range 1·4–3·2 μm min^{-1}). The bars on the graph depict the range of measurements. The irregularities in the graph are due to movements of the spindles into and out of the plane of focus, and changes in focus during recordings. Fig. 4A corresponds to 3 min on this graph, 4B to 8–25 min, 4C to 27 min, 4D to 29 min and 4E to 32 min.

Fig. 7. Low-magnification view of spindle (*s*) formation outside the nucleus (*n*) and just beneath the cell wall (*w*). ×6300. Bar, 2 μm.

Fig. 8. Later stage of spindle formation showing the spindle sinking into the nucleus (*n*). An elaborate membrane system (*m*) surrounds the spindle, which now shows a distinct zone of overlap (*o*). ×9800. Bar, 1 μm.

Fig. 9. Median longitudinal section through a forming spindle showing the laminated plates (*pl*) on the inside of the recurved pole organelle (*p*). The vacuoles on the concave side of the spindle pole are always present. ×36 500. Bar, 0·5 μm.

Fig. 10. High-magnification view of the spindle in Fig. 8D. The pole organelle (*p*) is more recurved than in earlier stages and now contains a single vacuole (*v*). A remnant of the laminated plate can be seen on one pole (arrow) and peripheral microtubules (*t*) are now evident. ×28 500. Bar, 5 μm.

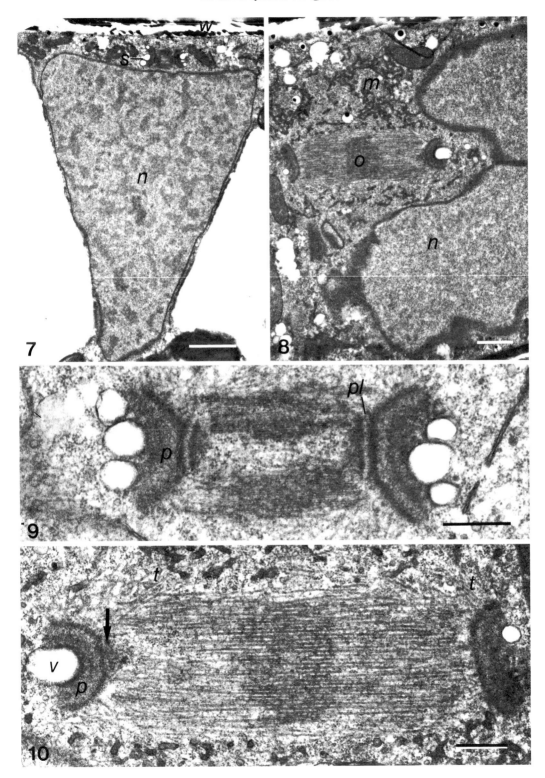

period before the cell enters anaphase. Some of this delay may be due to the
sensitivity of the cells to conditions required for video recording since most cells
monitored from early prophase die before going through anaphase. Cells monitored
from metaphase will persist through telophase but not always through cleavage.
During anaphase the spindle elongates at an average rate of about $1·7\,\mu m\,min^{-1}$.
During this period there is little or no change in the size of the zone of overlap.

Electron microscopy. As in other diatoms, the spindle of *S. turris* forms outside
the nucleus (Fig. 7), then sinks into an opening in the nuclear envelope at prometaphase (Fig. 8). Figs 7 and 8 are comparable to the light-microscopic views
shown in Figs 2 and 4A, respectively. A higher-magnification image of a developing
spindle (Fig. 9) shows that the spindle poles have a complex morphology. The
principal structure is a recurved polar organelle, which has a laminated plate on its
inside convex face and several small vesicles on the outside concave surface. The
microtubules extending between the inner plates appear to be embedded in an
osmiophilic material. At a later stage (Fig. 10) the zone of overlap is apparent
and the poles have lost most of the laminated plate structure. Peripheral microtubules are also evident at this stage. By metaphase the structure of the polar
organelle has changed still further. It is now nearly spherical, contains a single
vacuole (Figs 11, 13) and is displaced to one side of the place where most microtubules end (Figs 13, 14). Some microtubules end at kinetochore-like dense areas
(Figs 11, 12), which form a ring around the outside of the central spindle. The dense
bodies are particularly clear in these preparations because the chromatin does not
pick up much stain and is more electron-transparent than the rest of the cytoplasm.
Fig. 14 shows that the polar organelle is retained in isolated spindle preparations.

Spindle elongation in vitro

Light microscopy. Spindle elongation *in vitro* can be studied on-line in one spindle
at a time using polarization optics and time-lapse video (Fig. 15), or with populations of spindles using indirect immunofluorescence and antibodies against tubulin
(Figs 16–18). The central spindle is readily identified as a birefringent or fluorescent
bar embedded in chromatin. As shown in Fig. 15, perfusion of ATP leads to an
increase in spindle length and a concurrent decrease in the magnitude and extent of
birefringence in the zone of overlap. The rate of spindle elongation observed *in vitro*
depends on the method of spindle preparation. Using the method described in this
paper, spindles elongate at a rate of $0·1–0·5\,\mu m\,min^{-1}$, but if spindles are prepared
in 40–80 mM-sodium glycerophosphate and preincubated in $50\,\mu M$-ATPγS spindle
elongation may be considerably faster, up to $1\,\mu m\,min^{-1}$ (see Wordeman *et al.* 1985).

When monitored by indirect immunofluorescence we find that over 85 % of the
spindles on a coverslip have undergone striking structural changes equivalent to
those observed with polarization optics (Figs 16, 17). After ATP addition, there is a
distinct gap between the two half-spindles and the phase-dense material in the

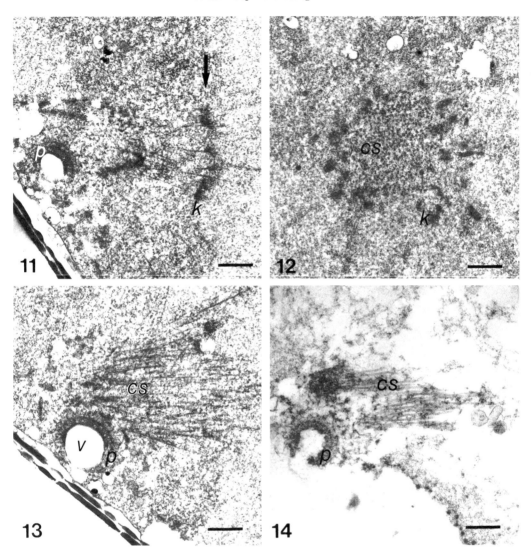

Fig. 11. Oblique longitudinal section through the pole of a metaphase–early anaphase spindle showing the pole organelle (*p*) and presumed kinetochores (*k*) on the leading edge of the chromatin. The arrow shows the plane of section of Fig. 12. ×19 000. Bar, 0·5 μm.

Fig. 12. Cross-section through the ring of kinetochores (*k*) surrounding the central spindle (*cs*). ×19 000. Bar, 0·5 μm.

Fig. 13. Longitudinal section through the pole region of metaphase–early anaphase central spindle (*cs*). The polar structure (*p*) is spherical, off to one side of the microtubule bundle, and encloses a single vacuole (*v*). ×19 000. Bar, 0·5 μm.

Fig. 14. Longitudinal section through the pole region of an isolated spindle (*cs*) showing that the pole organelle (*p*) is retained through the spindle isolation and that little cytoplasm projects beyond the pole. ×19 000. Bar, 0·5 μm.

spindle midzone has been dispersed (Cande & McDonald, 1986; and Fig. 18A,C). Spindles that display these structural changes (i.e. gaps) are longer than control populations of spindles, and those spindles that do not show altered midzones after ATP addition are often the shortest in the population (Fig. 19).

Alterations in the chromatin shell that surrounds the spindle do not appear to contribute to the spindle elongation process. Spindles prepared and reactivated in spermine/spermidine have condensed chromosomes, and after ATP addition these spindles elongate and display altered midzones (Fig. 16). After DNase I digestion little or no chromatin remains attached to the central spindle and with the addition of ATP these spindles also elongate and show gaps in the midzone (Figs 17, 19).

In the absence of exogenous tubulin, the extent of elongation observed *in vitro* is equivalent to the size of the original zone of microtubule overlap. That is, after isolation spindles are about 8 μm long with overlap zones 1·5–2·0 μm in size. The average increase in length seen *in vitro* either on-line or by indirect immunofluorescence is about 1·5–2·0 μm. In preliminary experiments we incubated spindles with neurotubulin, taxol, ATP and GTP (Fig. 18). After several minutes incubation, the spindles contain many more microtubules than spindles incubated in tubulin alone. These spindles are wider and have many new peripheral microtubule bundles. Many spindles have almost doubled in length and the length increase is equivalent to several times the original overlap zone size. Spindle elongation but not tubulin incorporation requires ATP. Although spindles incubated in GTP alone become 'hairy', demonstrating new microtubule incorporation and growth, there is no dramatic increase in length in the absence of ATP (H. Masuda, unpublished data).

Electron microscopy. At the ultrastructural level, the formation of gaps seen in the light microscope is revealed as a decrease in number and a rearrangement of microtubules in the overlap region (Fig. 20). In the absence of ATP, spindle overlap-zone microtubules are stable for a long time. After 10 min (Fig. 20A) there are as many microtubules as in an intact spindle. In fact, this number will remain high for up to several hours in the absence of ATP. However, as soon as ATP is added the microtubules begin to depolymerize in the midzone. After 5 min (Fig. 20B) there are fewer than half the original number, and by 10 min (Fig. 20C) fewer than one-sixth. At longer times in ATP, the midzone microtubules may disappear altogether (Fig. 21).

In isolated, ATP-treated spindles we also see some structural changes within the half-spindle, outside the zone of overlap. Some, but not all, ATP-treated spindles have a striated fibre among the half-spindle microtubules (Figs 21–23). We have not seen such structures in spindles *in vivo* and only faintly in one isolated spindle without ATP. Longitudinal sections (Figs 21, 22) show that the fibre is composed of layered plates connected by fine fibres. The repeat distance between plates is about 225 nm. The fibre/plates are rectangular in cross-section and are embedded within the microtubule bundle, not at its surface (Fig. 23). In ATP-treated spindles we also see between microtubules some fine fibres and osmiophilic material, which is not organized into striated fibres (Fig. 23).

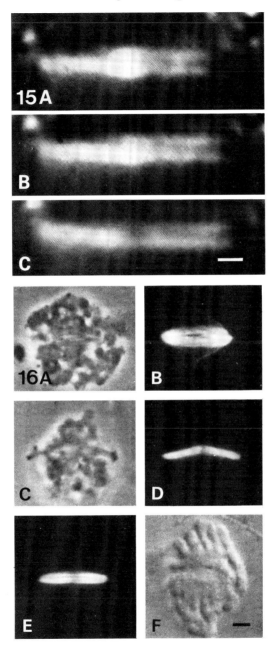

Fig. 15. The change in spindle structure after reactivation as monitored by polarization optics and time-lapse video. A. The central spindle just after addition of 1 mM-ATP; B, after 5 min in ATP; C, after 13 min in ATP. Bar, 1 μm.

Fig. 16. Phase-contrast, Nomarski and immunofluorescent (anti-tubulin) micrographs of isolated spindles with and without addition of 1 mM-ATP. The spindles were isolated in spermidine/spermine to maintain condensed chromosomes. A,B. A spindle incubated without ATP; C,D, a spindle incubated in ATP for 10 min; E,F, different spindles incubated in ATP for 10 min; F was taken with Nomarski optics. In B, the micrograph was overexposed to show the peripheral microtubules. In D,E, there is a gap between the half-spindles. Bar, 2 μm.

DISCUSSION

Comparison of spindle elongation in vivo *and* in vitro

Anaphase chromosome movement is a complex process that involves several discrete phases (Inoue, 1981; Ris, 1949): chromosome-to-pole movement (anaphase A), pole-from-pole movement (spindle elongation or anaphase B) and, in some cells,

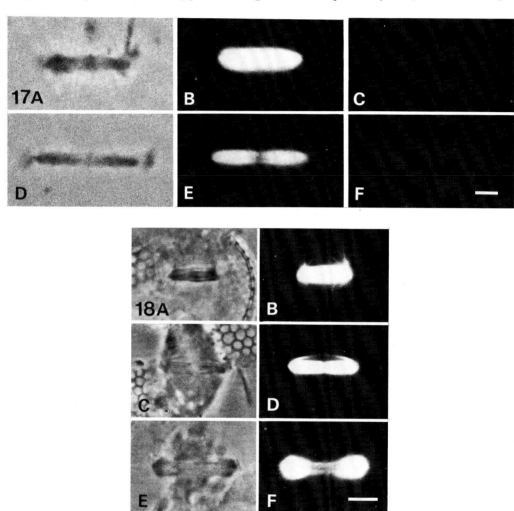

Fig. 17. Phase-contrast and fluorescent micrographs of isolated spindles treated with DNase I to remove chromatin before reactivation. A,D. Phase-contrast micrographs; B,E, fluorescent micrographs to show anti-tubulin distribution; C,F, fluorescent micrographs to show DAPI staining of chromatin. A–C. A spindle after incubation for 10 min without ATP; D–F, a spindle after 10 min in 1 mM-ATP. The pole complexes are still attached to these spindles. Bar, 2 μm.

Fig. 18. Phase-contrast and fluorescent (anti-tubulin) micrographs of isolated spindles incubated in 20 μM-taxol and 25 μM-neurotubulin during reactivation. A,B. A spindle incubated for 10 min in taxol but no tubulin or ATP; C,D, a spindle incubated in taxol and ATP; E,F, a spindle incubated in taxol, neurotubulin and ATP. Bar, 5 μm.

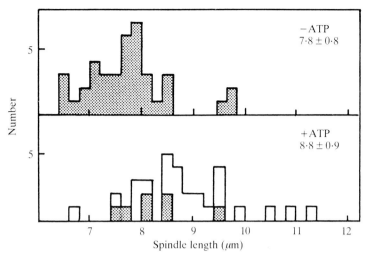

Fig. 19. Histograms of the lengths of spindles after 10 min, with or without ATP. Before reactivation, the chromatin was removed from these spindles by digestion with DNase I. Average spindle lengths (±s.D.) are given in the upper right-hand corner of each panel. Spindles with prominent zones of microtubule overlap are shown as shaded areas while those with midzone structural alternations (gaps) are not shaded.

further movement of the poles and chromosomes during late anaphase/telophase generated by interactions between the cytoplasm and the re-forming nuclei. All of these categories of movement contribute to chromosome separation during anaphase in *Stephanopyxis*. Early in anaphase chromosomes move polewards, the central spindles undergo a twofold increase in length and, finally, as cytokinesis is initiated, peripheral microtubules may be involved in repositioning the separated chromosome masses so that they are properly aligned with the plane of cleavage (Wordeman *et al.* 1986; Heunert, 1975*a,b*).

Stephanopyxis is an excellent organism for studying the mechanisms of spindle elongation *in vitro*. As in other diatom spindles, in this organism the classes of microtubules responsible for anaphase A and B are spatially separated and the central spindle consists of a paracrystalline array of microtubules in the overlap zone. The central spindle is constructed of two sets of about 300 microtubules, which originate from plate-like poles and interdigitate in the zone of microtubule overlap.

In vivo microtubule growth must make an enormous contribution to the changes in central spindle length that occur during anaphase. Hence, this is a good system for studying the relative roles of microtubule polymerization *versus* mechanical rearrangements of microtubules in generating the forces required for spindle elongation. Since the overlap zone is never more than about 25 % of the overall spindle length, sliding apart of the two half-spindles could never contribute more than this amount of length to overall spindle elongation during anaphase if microtubules did not grow. Moreover, *in vivo* the overlap zone size changes little even when the spindle is undergoing its maximum extent of elongation. Does the mechanical rearrangement of microtubules contribute at all to the process of spindle elongation *in vivo*? To answer this question it is necessary to know where tubulin incorporation takes place during anaphase. Indirect evidence gained from studying the structure of the *Dictyostelium* spindle (McIntosh *et al.* 1985) suggests that tubulin subunits add on to elongating, interdigitating microtubules at their pole distal ends. The newly added tubulin must then slide through the overlap zone for anaphase spindle elongation to occur (Margolis *et al.* 1978; McIntosh *et al.* 1969). If on the other hand, tubulin is incorporated into microtubules primarily at the poles,

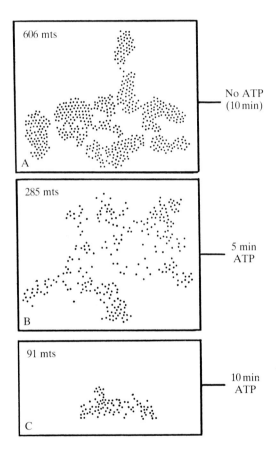

Fig. 20. Diagrammatic representation of the number and arrangement of microtubules (mts, represented by small dots) in cross-sections of the overlap regions of isolated central spindles after 10 min with no ATP (A), 5 min in ATP (B), and 10 min in ATP (C).

Fig. 21. Longitudinal section through an isolated spindle after reactivation of elongation by ATP. The half-spindles have disengaged completely and the microtubule ends distal to the poles are abnormally curved (large arrow). Each half-spindle contains striated fibres (small arrows). ×10 500. Bar, 1 μm.

Fig. 22. Details of a striated fibre showing layered structures (*l*) connected by fine fibres (arrows). ×67 000. Bar, 0·2 μm.

Fig. 23. A–C. Adjacent serial cross-sections through a striated fibre (*s*). Other osmiophilic material (large arrow) and fine fibres (small arrows) can be seen between microtubules in Fig. 18A. ×84 000. Bar, 0·2 μm.

as suggested by Pickett-Heaps *et al.* (1986) or throughout the spindle (Inoue & Sato, 1967), then sliding would not be required for spindles to elongate. As shown by our studies using isolated spindles, it is possible to answer these questions *in vitro*.

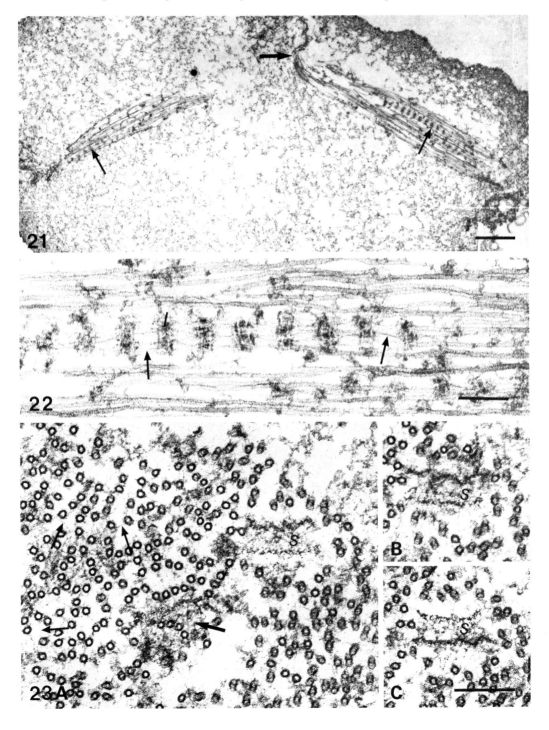

As demonstrated on-line by video microscopy, spindle elongation *in vitro* is due to the sliding apart of the two half-spindles and a concomitant decrease in the zone of microtubule overlap (Cande & McDonald, 1985, 1986). The process of spindle elongation that we observed *in vitro* is consistent with models of force generation that postulate that mechanochemical interactions in the zone of microtubule overlap play a major role in generating the forces required for spindle elongation (Margolis *et al.* 1978; McDonald *et al.* 1977, 1979; McIntosh *et al.* 1969; Nicklas, 1971). Our results can best be interpreted by imagining that the microtubules of one half-spindle push off against the microtubules of the other half-spindle, generating sliding forces between them. We predict and can show that the maximum extent of spindle elongation *in vitro* is limited to the length of the overlap zone. Spindle elongation cannot be due to the autonomous swimming apart of the half-spindles since they always remain associated with each other even in the absence of chromatin. After digestion with DNase I, during reactivation we see spindles that are bent almost in two and with one half-spindle or the overlap zone not attached to the coverslip (Cande, unpublished data). These morphologies could develop only if (1) the forces responsible for spindle elongation are developed in the overlap zone and (2) one half-spindle uses the other half-spindle as a substrate for mechanochemical interactions.

As described recently by Cande & McDonald (1986) the process of microtubule sliding during spindle elongation requires ATP hydrolysis and is inhibited by vanadate and sulphhydryl reagents. The physiology of this process resembles that of reactivation of flagellar beat (Gibbons, 1981), suggesting that a dynein-like ATPase, but with some unique properties, may be involved. It is not consistent with the involvement of a kinesin-like motor since kinesin is not affected by sulphhydryl reagents or low concentrations of vanadate (Vale *et al.* 1985). Since DNase I binds to actin with high affinity and can be used to depolymerize actin in extracts (Hitchcock *et al.* 1976), our observation that spindles will elongate after digestion of chromatin reinforces our view that actomyosin is not involved in this process (Cande, 1982). This observation also eliminates the possibility that passive swelling of chromatin during reactivation could artificially make the half-spindles move apart.

When neurotubulin is incorporated into the isolated central spindles, the extent of spindle elongation *in vitro* is no longer limited to the size of the overlap zone and some spindles elongate two to three times the length of the overlap zone. Is the motive force for this extra elongation derived from the microtubule polymerization process, as predicted by Inoue & Sato (1967), or does the new growth merely permit more elongation to take place (McIntosh *et al.* 1969; Margolis *et al.* 1978)? This question cannot be answered with certainty until we understand the pattern of neurotubulin incorporation into the spindle *in vitro*. However, our preliminary physiological studies show that spindle elongation can be uncoupled from microtubule incorporation into the spindle. Spindles incubated with neurotubulin in the absence of ATP are wider and contain many more microtubules than normal, yet these spindles have not elongated to any significant extent (Masuda, unpublished observations). This observation is consistent with the hypothesis that new neurotubulin is incorporated onto pre-existing diatom microtubules in the overlap zone distal to the poles and that these new microtubule lengths slide past each other using the 'old motor'. As discussed below, in the absence of neurotubulin ATP leads to selective microtubule loss starting from the overlap zone and working poleward. This finding is also consistent with the idea that the overlap zone is the site of addition of new tubulin.

Comparing spindle structure in vitro *and* in vivo

The methods used to isolate central spindle microtubules from *S. turris* (Cande & McDonald, 1985, 1986) are sufficiently gentle for the arrangement and number of microtubules to be essentially the same as those of central spindles *in vivo*. The pole structure is retained during isolation, but the peripheral, non-central spindle microtubules are retained in only about one-third of the metaphase spindles and in none of the spindles at later stages (Cande & McDonald, 1986). Also, membranous components of the spindle are lost or drastically altered by treatments with detergent and glycerol during isolation. This suggests that membranes may not be important in the initial phases of spindle elongation though they may be important for other aspects of spindle elongation that we do not see *in vitro*, such as growth of half-spindle microtubules. The association of membranes with the developing spindle shown in Figs 7–10 also suggests that they may have a role in spindle formation. Finally, the kinetochore-like structures seen *in vivo* (Figs 11, 12) are not seen in isolated spindle preparations viewed by electron microscopy. However, when populations of spindles are stained with an antibody against mitosis-specific phosphory-lated proteins (Wordeman *et al.* 1985) a similar distribution of kinetochore-like structures is seen. This suggests that they are still present but in a modified form.

The pattern of microtubule loss after ATP addition

After addition of ATP, the isolated spindle structure changes in ways that are similar overall to changes *in vivo* but are different in detail. *In vivo* and *in vitro* the half-spindles separate, resulting in spindle elongation. The differences are seen in the detailed structure of the overlap zone. *In vivo* the extent of overlap decreases as the spindle elongates and at the end of elongation there is a dense midbody-like structure enclosing the few remaining microtubules in the midzone (McDonald *et al.* 1977). *In vitro* the half-spindles tend to disengage completely and nothing is left in the overlap zone. This difference between behaviour *in vivo* and *in vitro* may be related to the osmiophilic matrix material between microtubules in the overlap, which may function to keep the overlapping microtubule ends together (McDonald *et al.* 1979).

Our results show that microtubule depolymerization in isolated spindles is an ATP-dependent phenomenon. Without ATP isolated spindles show no loss of birefringence over a 10-min period (Cande & McDonald, 1986) and electron microscopy (EM) shows no reduction in microtubule number. However, within minutes of ATP addition, microtubules begin to depolymerize from the overlap region back towards the poles and then the spindle begins to elongate. The same pattern of microtubule depolymerization is seen *in vivo* (Sorrano & Pickett-Heaps, 1982) and when free ends are created artificially with an ultraviolet (u.v.) microbeam

(Leslie & Pickett-Heaps, 1984). While there is probably a correlation between the creation of free ends due to half-spindle sliding and microtubule depolymerization, as Tippi *et al.* (1984) have suggested, the process of regulating spindle microtubule depolymerization must be more complicated than just having a microtubule end free in the cytoplasm.

The striated fibre

The striated fibre is a difficult structure to interpret because it has no precedent in mitotic spindle ultrastructure and its disposition in the diatom central spindle gives no clue to a possible function. Structures of similar appearance have been described from a variety of non-mitotic sources, including striated flagellar rootlet fibres (Salisbury *et al.* 1984), myonemes of *Acantharia* (Febvre & Febvre-Chevalier, 1982), paracrystals of myosin (Burridge & Bray, 1975) and, most similarly, para-crystals of high molecular weight actin binding protein (HMWP) from HeLa cells (Weihing & Franklin, 1983). It is unlikely that the fibrous structure we see is biochemically identical to any of the above. However, this literature survey does show that a variety of motility-related proteins will form banded fibres under appropriate conditions. And just as HMWP is not organized into a striated fibre *in vivo*, we believe that the components of the diatom striated fibre are probably also dispersed among central spindle microtubules in intact cells. For one thing, we never see the striated fibre in spindles *in vivo* and have only seen a faint hint of a fibre in one isolated spindle without ATP. Whatever the disposition of striated fibre molecules *in vivo*, it is difficult to imagine a function for them with the available data. But these results suggest that the diatom central spindle contains fibrous elements, perhaps distributed along microtubules, which are not normally seen under conditions of conventional EM preparation. In this regard, it is worth noting the observations of Leslie & Pickett-Heaps (1983) on u.v.-irradiated diatom spindles. When metaphase central spindles of *Hantzschia* are severed with a microbeam the poles collapse inwards, suggesting that they were under compressive forces. To explain this they suggest that "it is possible that a contractile or elastic component permeates the microtubules of the central spindle and is allowed to contract when the microtubules are locally destroyed" (Leslie & Pickett-Heaps, 1983, p. 556). If the striated fibre components are dispersed among the microtubules as we believe, then perhaps they are the agents responsible for the contraction seen by these investigators.

Current popular models of anaphase spindle elongation

The two models that have received the most attention with regard to the mechanism of anaphase spindle elongation are the pole-pulling model of Aist & Berns (1981), which implies that spindle poles and their associated chromatin are pulled apart by cytoplasmic forces acting on astral microtubules, and the sliding filament model described by McIntosh *et al.* (1969, 1976), which suggests that poles/chromatin are pushed apart as the result of microtubule–microtubule interactions in the zone of half-spindle overlap. Another model, which is no less important but harder to test experimentally, is the microtubule polymerization model described by Inoue & Sato

(1967), which assumes that growth of non-kinetochore microtubules provides the force to move the poles apart. There are other models (Snyder *et al.* 1984), but unlike those mentioned above there is little or no independent evidence supporting or refuting them so they will not be discussed in detail here.

Although there were earlier suggestions (Girbardt, 1968) that cytoplasmic pulling forces might be involved in mitotic spindle movements the most specific and positive statement of the pole-pulling model and the most conclusive evidence is found in the study by Aist & Berns (1981). On the basis of laser microbeam studies of *Fusarium* central spindles, Aist & Berns (1981) postulated a pole-pulling force generated by an interaction between a stationary cytoplasmic microfilament system (possibly located at the plasma membrane) with astral microtubules of opposite polarity. According to this model the function of the central spindle is to provide the bipolar axis for chromosome separation and to act as a mechanical governor that regulates the rate of spindle elongation. The model does not exclude the possibility that microtubule–microtubule sliding is also taking place, but if it is the rate is slower than the pulling forces and the net result is a braking action caused by the microtubule bridges. Heath *et al.* (1984) came to similar conclusions from their detailed morphological studies of *Saprolegnia* and reconsidered (Girbardt, 1968) the important point that many fungal nuclei migrate extensively during their life cycles. It makes sense, as they suggest, that this machinery for nuclear migration could easily be adapted to pull poles apart during the later stages of spindle elongation. Nevertheless, physiological evidence concerning the nature of the molecular motor for pulling is non-existent and whether it is actomyosin interacting with astral microtubules or something else remains to be determined.

Although now considered incorrect in some details (Nicklas, 1971; see also McIntosh *et al.* 1976), the origin of the sliding-filament model of anaphase spindle elongation is the theoretical paper of McIntosh *et al.* (1969). This model contends that microtubules of opposite polarity (called antiparallel microtubules) overlap in the spindle midzone and are connected by bridges with ATPase activity. During spindle elongation the bridges walk over antiparallel microtubules in such a way that the spindle poles are pushed apart and, if there is no microtubule growth, the extent of overlap decreases. Serial-section reconstructions of diatom central spindles during elongation (McDonald *et al.* 1977; Tippit *et al.* 1980) showed rearrangement of spindle microtubules that was consistent with the predictions of the model. Other reconstructions have shown spindle elongation with little (McIntosh *et al.* 1985; Tippit *et al.* 1984) or no (Tippit *et al.* 1980) decrease in overlap. However, these can be explained by a sliding mechanism coupled with microtubule growth. Another line of evidence concerns the spacing and arrangement of antiparallel microtubules in the zone of overlap. Near-neighbour analyses of microtubule distributions in a variety of cell types have shown that antiparallel microtubules are preferentially associated in the overlap zone and that the spacing is compatible with a dynein-like bridge molecule (McDonald *et al.* 1977; McDonald & Euteneuer, 1983; McIntosh *et al.* 1985; Tippit *et al.* 1983). However, other reconstructions (Heath, 1974; Heath *et al.* 1984; Oakley & Heath, 1978) show spacings that are too great to be compatible with a dynein-like bridge. These spindles must elongate by some other mechanism, perhaps by a pulling force on the spindle poles, or by having an accessory fibre system connecting antiparallel microtubules that enables them to interact over longer distances (Oakley & Heath, 1978).

There are some experimental results that support a mechanism based on microtubule sliding. Leslie & Pickett-Heaps (1983) irradiated diatom central spindles with a u.v. microbeam and the resultant pattern of microtubule rearrangements during anaphase (severed half-spindles moving polewards with a reduction in overlap) were best explained by force generation in the zone of overlap. In a mammalian lysed cell model, Cande & Wolniak (1978) and Cande (1982) showed that spindle elongation was specifically inhibited by low concentrations of vanadate, suggesting the involvement of a dynein-like ATPase. Biochemical studies (Hollenbeck *et al.* 1984; Pratt *et al.* 1980) have shown that a dynein-like ATPase is present in sea-urchin cells and spindles. For a more detailed discussion of the physiological and biochemical evidence relevant to a microtubule sliding model of spindle elongation see Cande & McDonald (1986). The exact role of microtubule polymerization in anaphase spindle elongation is still obscure. Morphological studies show unequivocally that microtubules increase in length during spindle elongation (reviewed by Tippit *et al.* 1984); however, there are no experimental studies that demonstrate that microtubule assembly is the sole motive force pushing the poles apart. Information about the site of subunit addition would help resolve the question, since a model based solely on microtubule polymerization requires that subunits add on at the poles to explain the morphological data. If they were added anywhere else the extent of overlap would not decrease as the spindle elongated. For a more detailed discussion of this problem see McIntosh *et al.* (1985).

Comparison of our results with current models

It is gratifying that the results obtained by reactivating diatom central spindles *in vitro* (Cande & McDonald, 1985, 1986) confirm the speculations about mechanism based on morphological (McDonald *et al.* 1977) and microbeaming (Leslie & Pickett-Heaps, 1983) observations. Everything we know about diatom central spindles seems to suggest that the initial stages of spindle elongation are due to the sliding apart of the two half-spindles. The physiological results from Cande & McDonald (1986) are the first real evidence we have, for diatoms, that the process requires ATP and that the ATPase has characteristics similar to the flagellar ATPase, dynein. Similar physiological results have already been obtained in mammalian cells with the PtK_1 lysed cell model (Cande, 1982; Cande & Wolniak, 1978). Given the evolutionary distance between diatoms and mammals, it seems possible that microtubule sliding is of general significance as a mechanism of chromosome separation during anaphase.

Another consequence of our results is that they demonstrate that microtubule polymerization has a subsidiary role during spindle elongation and is not required to generate the forces responsible for moving the spindle poles apart. In the absence of exogenous tubulin, spindles elongate because the two half-spindles slide apart.

Microtubule assembly cannot be responsible for this increase in length. In the presence of neurotubulin and new microtubule formation spindles elongate more, but preliminary physiological experiments suggest that it is possible to block elongation while microtubule assembly continues. Although microtubule polymerization undoubtedly occurs *in vivo* during spindle elongation (reviewed by Tippit *et al.* 1984), our results from experiments *in vitro* support the idea that microtubule polymerization is an auxiliary process rather than the motor responsible for anaphase spindle elongation.

The morphological analysis of the *in vitro* spindles has shown that there are no cytoplasmic structures beyond the poles. This means that cytoplasmic pulling forces cannot account for the observed increase in spindle length *in vitro*. It does not mean that such forces are not operating *in vivo*. Because the nucleus in *S. turris* undergoes considerable migration during the cell cycle there is a possibility that the nuclear migration machinery is also involved in the later stages of elongation. However, we still believe that microtubule–microtubule sliding is the main motor for elongation, and in those cell types that have no nuclear migration it may be the only motor.

CONCLUSIONS

It is clear from the accumulated evidence that more than one force-generating system can operate to separate spindle poles during anaphase B. What is not clear is whether they can operate simultaneously or in tandem in the same spindle. It is also certain that microtubule growth can occur during spindle elongation, but it has not been shown that microtubule polymerization is an active force as opposed to being simply permissive. In the absence of evidence to the contrary, we assume that microtubule growth is permissive. As for the first question, we agree with those authors (Aist & Berns, 1981; Heath *et al.* 1984) who believe that both kinds of mechanochemistry could be operating at the same time. Although the evidence we have presented in this paper is strongly in favour of sliding, we have reason to believe from observation *in vivo*, and from immunofluorescence studies of cytoplasmic microtubule distributions during the cell cycle (Wordeman *et al.* 1986), that a pulling mechanism may also be involved in the later stages of spindle elongation in *Stephanopyxis*. Astral microtubules proliferate and are oriented away from the poles in a manner that suggests that they may be pulling the daughter nuclei. Also, microtubule inhibitors interfere with nuclear migration. It seems reasonable, in fact, to propose that any cell type that expresses post-mitotic nuclear migration is capable of adapting the migration machinery to pull poles apart in the later stages of mitosis. Likewise, it has not been demonstrated, even in those organisms with obvious pulling mechanisms for anaphase B (Aist & Berns, 1981), that the initial stages of pole separation are not due to a sliding mechanism. Our results suggest that an ATP-dependent event starts pole separation and the controlled disassembly of the spindle (see also Tippit *et al.* 1984). Whether this is characteristic of all spindles remains to be determined.

We thank Dan Coltrin, Ellen Dean and Doug Ohm for their technical assistance. This work was supported by NSF grant PCM8408594 and NIH grant GM23238.

REFERENCES

AIST, J. R. & BERNS, M. W. (1981). Mechanics of chromosome separation during mitosis in *Fusarium* (Fungi imperfecti): new evidence from ultrastructural and laser microbeam experiments. *J. Cell Biol.* **91**, 446–458.

ASAI, D. J., BROKAW, C. J., THOMSON, W. C. & WILSON, L. (1982). Two different monoclonal antibodies to tubulin inhibit the bending of reactivated sea urchin spermatozoa. *Cell Motil.* **2**, 599–614.

BURRIDGE, K. & BRAY, D. (1975). Purification and structural analysis of myosin from brain and other non-muscle tissues. *J. molec. Biol.* **99**, 1–14.

CANDE, W. Z. (1982). Nucleotide requirements for anaphase chromosome movement in permeabilized mitotic cells: anaphase B but not anaphase A requires ATP. *Cell* **28**, 15–22.

CANDE, W. Z. & McDONALD, K. L. (1985). *In vitro* reactivation of anaphase spindle elongation using isolated diatom spindles. *Nature, Lond.* **316**, 168–170.

CANDE, W. Z. & McDONALD, K. L. (1986). Physiological and ultrastructural analysis of elongating mitotic spindles reactivated *in vitro*. *J. Cell Biol.* (in press).

CANDE, W. Z. & WOLNIAK, S. M. (1978). Chromosome movement in lysed mitotic cells is inhibited by vanadate. *J. Cell Biol.* **79**, 573–580.

FEBVRE, J. & FEBVRE-CHEVALIER, C. (1982). Motility processes in *Acantharia* (Protozoa). 1 – Cinematographic and cytological study of the myonemes. Evidence for a helix–coil mechanism of the constituent filaments. *Biol. Cell* **44**, 283–304.

GIBBONS, I. R. (1981). Cilia and flagella of eukaryotes. *J. Cell Biol.* **91** (3, part 2), 107s–124s.

GIRBARDT, M. (1968). Ultrastructure and dynamics of the moving nucleus. In *Aspects of Cell Motility, 22nd Symp. Soc. Exp. Biol.*, pp. 249–259. Oxford: Cambridge University Press.

GUILLARD, R. R. L. (1975). Culture of phytoplankton for feeding marine invertebrates. In *Culture of Marine Invertebrate Animals* (ed. W. L. Smith & M. H. Chanley), pp. 29–60. New York: Plenum.

HEATH, I. B. (1974). Mitosis in the fungus *Thraustotheca clavata*. *J. Cell Biol.* **60**, 204–220.

HEATH, I. B., RETHORET, K. & MOENS, P. B. (1984). The ultrastructure of mitotic spindles from conventionally fixed and freeze-substituted nuclei of the fungus *Saprolegnia*. *Eur. J. Cell Biol.* **35**, 284–295.

HEUNERT, H.-H. (1975a). Diatoms from the sea. Methods of study and life cycle. I. Methods of vegetative reproduction. *Mikrokosmos* **64**, 357–386.

HEUNERT, H.-H. (1975b). Ungeschlechtliche Fortplanzung den Kieselalge *Stephanopyxis turris*: C982T. Göttingen: Institut fur den Wissenschaftlichen Film, Nonnensteig 72.

HITCHCOCK, S. E., CARLSSON, L. & LINDBERG, U. (1976). Depolymerization of F-actin by deoxyribonuclease 1. *Cell* **7**, 531–542.

HOLLENBECK, P. J., SUPRYNOWICZ, F. & CANDE, W. Z. (1984). Cytoplasmic dynein-like ATPase cross-links microtubules in an ATP-dependent manner. *J. Cell Biol.* **99**, 1251–1258.

INOUE, S. (1981). Cell division and the mitotic spindles. *J. Cell Biol.* **91** (3, part 2), 131s–147s.

INOUE, S. & SATO, H. (1967). Cell motility by labile association of molecules: the nature of mitotic spindle fibers and their role in chromosome movement. *J. gen. Physiol.* **50**, 259–292.

LESLIE, R. J. & PICKETT-HEAPS, J. D. (1983). Ultraviolet microbeam irradiation of mitotic diatoms. Investigation of spindle elongation. *J. Cell Biol.* **96**, 548–561.

LESLIE, R. J. & PICKETT-HEAPS, J. D. (1984). Spindle dynamics following ultraviolet microbeam irradiations of mitotic diatoms. *Cell* **36**, 717–727.

MARGOLIS, R. L., WILSON, L. & KIEFER, B. I. (1978). Mitotic mechanism based on intrinsic microtubule behaviour. *Nature, Lond.* **272**, 450–452.

McDONALD, K. L., EDWARDS, M. K. & McINTOSH, J. R. (1979). Cross-sectional structure of the central mitotic spindle of *Diatoma vulgare*. Evidence for specific interactions between antiparallel microtubules. *J. Cell Biol.* **83**, 443–461.

McDonald, K. L. & Euteneuer, U. (1983). Studies on the structure and organization of microtubule bundles in the interzone of anaphase and telophase PtK₁ cells. *J. Cell Biol.* **97**, 88a (Abst.).

McDonald, K. L., Pickett-Heaps, J. D., McIntosh, J. R. & Tippit, D. H. (1977). On the mechanism of anaphase spindle elongation in *Diatoma vulgare*. *J. Cell Biol.* **74**, 377–388.

McIntosh, J. R., Cande, W. Z., Lazarides, E., McDonald, K. & Snyder, J. A. (1976). Fibrous elements of the mitotic spindle. *Cold Spring Harbor Conf. Cell Prolifer.* **3C**, 1261–1272.

McIntosh, J. R., Hepler, P. K. & van Wie, D. G. (1969). Model for mitosis. *Nature, Lond.* **224**, 659–663.

McIntosh, J. R., Roos, U.-P., Neighbors, B. & McDonald, K. L. (1985). Architecture of the microtubule component of mitotic spindles from *Dictyostelium discoideum*. *J. Cell Sci.* **75**, 93–129.

Moore, M. J. (1975). Removal of glass coverslips from cultures flat embedded in epoxy resin using hydrofluoric acid. *J. Microsc.* **104**, 205–207.

Nicklas, R. B. (1971). Mitosis. In *Advances in Cell Biology* (ed. D. M. Prescott, L. Goldstein & E. McConkey), pp. 225–297. New York: Appleton-Century-Crofts.

Oakley, B. R. & Heath, I. B. (1978). The arrangement of microtubules in the serially sectioned spindles of the alga *Cryptomonas*. *J. Cell Sci.* **31**, 53–70.

Pickett-Heaps, J. D., Tippit, D. H., Cohn, S. A. & Spurck, T. P. (1986). Microtubule dynamics in the spindle. Theoretical aspects of assembly/disassembly reactions *in vivo. J. theor. Biol.* **118**, 153–169.

Pratt, M. M., Otter, T. & Salmon, E. D. (1980). Dynein-like Mg⁺⁺ ATPase in mitotic spindle isolated from sea urchin embryos (*Strongylocentrotus droebachiensis*). *J. Cell Biol.* **86**, 738–745.

Reynolds, E. S. (1963). The use of lead citrate at high pH as a electron-opaque stain in electron microscopy. *J. Cell Biol.* **17**, 208–212.

Ris, H. (1949). The anaphase movement of chromosomes in the spermatocytes of the grasshopper. *Biol. Bull. mar. Biol. Labs, Woods Hole* **96**, 90–106.

Sale, W. S. & Satir, P. (1977). Direction of active sliding of microtubules in *Tetrahymena* cilia. *Proc. natn. Acad. Sci. U.S.A.* **74**, 2045–2049.

Salisbury, J. L., Baron, A., Surek, B. & Melkonian, M. (1984). Striated flagellar roots: isolation and partial characterization of a calcium-modulated contractile organelle. *J. Cell Biol.* **99**, 962–970.

Snyder, J. A., Golub, R. & Berg, S. P. (1984). Sucrose-induced spindle elongation in mitotic PtK₁ cells. *Eur. J. Cell Biol.* **35**, 62–69.

Sorrano, T. & Pickett-Heaps, J. D. (1982). Directionally controlled spindle disassembly after mitosis in the diatom *Pinnularia*. *Eur. J. Cell Biol.* **26**, 234–243.

Summers, K. & Gibbons, I. R. (1971). Adenosine triphosphate-induced sliding of tubules in trypsin-treated flagella of sea-urchin sperm. *Proc. natn. Acad. Sci. U.S.A* **68**, 3092–3096.

Tippit, D. H., Fields, C. T., O'Donnell, K. L., Pickett-Heaps, J. D. & McLaughlin, D. J. (1984). The organization of microtubules during anaphase and telophase spindle elongation in the rust fungus *Puccinia*. *Eur. J. Cell Biol.* **34**, 34–44.

Tippit, D. H., Pillus, L. & Pickett-Heaps, J. D. (1983). Near-neighbor analysis of spindle microtubules in the alga *Ochromonas*. *Eur. J. Cell Biol.* **30**, 9–17.

Tippit, D. H., Schulz, D. & Pickett-Heaps, J. D. (1980). Analysis of the distribution of spindle microtubules in the diatom *Fragilaria*. *J. Cell Biol.* **86**, 402–416.

Vale, R. D., Reese, T. S. & Sheetz, M. P. (1985). Identification of a novel force-generating protein kinesin involved in microtubule-based motility. *Cell* **42**, 32–50.

Weihing, R. R. & Franklin, J. S. (1983). Striated paracrystals that contain HMWP, the homolog of actin-binding protein and filamin from HeLa cells. *Cell Motil.* **3**, 535–543.

Wordeman, L., McDonald, K. & Cande, W. Z. (1986). The distribution of cytoplasmic microtubules through the cell cycle of centric diatom *Stephanopyxis turris*: their role in nuclear migration and repositioning the mitotic spindle during cytokinesis. *J. Cell Biol.* **102**, 1688–1698.

Wordeman, L., McDonald, K. L., Cande, W. Z., Davis, F. M., Rao, P. N. & Salisbury, J. L. (1985). Functional mitotic spindles isolated from the diatom *Stephanopyxis turris* are phosphorylated structures. *J. Cell Biol.* **101**, 153a (Abst.).

J. Cell Sci. Suppl. 5, 229–241 (1986)
Printed in Great Britain © The Company of Biologists Limited 1986

GROWTH POLARITY AND CYTOKINESIS IN FISSION YEAST: THE ROLE OF THE CYTOSKELETON

JOHN MARKS, IAIN M. HAGAN AND JEREMY S. HYAMS*

Department of Botany & Microbiology, University College London, Gower Street, London WC1E 6BT, UK

SUMMARY

The distribution of F-actin in the fission yeast *Schizosaccharomyces pombe* was investigated by fluorescence microscopy using rhodamine-conjugated phalloidin. Fluorescence was seen either at the ends of the cell or at the cell equator. End staining was predominantly in the form of dots whilst equatorial actin was resolved as a filamentous band. The different staining patterns showed a close correlation with the known pattern of cell wall deposition through the cell cycle. In small, newly divided cells actin was localized at the single growing cell end whilst initiation of bipolar cell growth was coincident with the appearance of actin at both ends of the cell. As cells ceased to grow and entered cell division, a ring of actin was seen to anticipate the deposition of the septum at cytokinesis. The relationship between actin and cell wall deposition was further confirmed in three temperature-sensitive cell division cycle (*cdc*) mutants; *cdc*10, *cdc*11 and *cdc*13. Immunofluorescence microscopy of *S. pombe* with an anti-tubulin antibody revealed a system of cytoplasmic microtubules extending between the cell ends. The function of these was investigated in the cold-sensitive, benomyl-resistant mutant *ben*4. In cold-grown cells actin was seen to form conspicuous filamentous rings around the nucleus. The origin of these and the possible role of microtubules in the cell-cycle-dependent rearrangements of F-actin are discussed.

INTRODUCTION

The use of simple model systems to study complex problems is a familiar strategy in biological research. Recent developments in molecular genetics have reinforced the value of organisms such as yeasts in the study of fundamental cellular processes. This is particularly true in the case of the cytoskeleton. Although the small size of yeast cells and the presence of a cell wall present obstacles to traditional approaches to the organization of cytoplasmic filament systems such as immunofluorescence microscopy, these have now been largely overcome (Kilmartin & Adams, 1984; Adams & Pringle, 1984). Coupled with the analysis of cloned actin and tubulin genes (Thomas *et al.* 1984; Yanagida *et al.* 1985) this opens up a combination of approaches to cytoskeleton structure and function that is possible in few other organisms.

An additional attraction of yeasts as experimental systems is the availability of a large number and variety of mutants that affect the yeast cell division cycle (Pringle & Hartwell, 1981; Nurse, 1981). Thus, the relationship of the cytoskeleton to other cell cycle events is also open to direct study. Two yeasts in particular have been the focus of most attention, the budding yeast *Saccharomyces cerevisiae* and the fission

*Author for correspondence.

yeast *Schizosaccharomyces pombe*. Of the two, *S. pombe* may prove to be the better model, if only because its cell division cycle more closely resembles that of higher eukaryotes (Nurse, 1985).

Fission yeast cells grow only at their ends (Johnson, 1965; Streiblova & Wolf, 1972; Mitchison & Nurse, 1985). In newly divided cells growth occurs solely at the old end, that is, the end that existed prior to septation. At a point in the G_2 phase of the cell cycle termed NETO (new-end take off) bipolar growth is initiated. This is maintained until the end of G_2, at which point growth ceases and the sequence of mitosis, cytokinesis and cell separation begins. In this paper we describe the relationship of the cytoskeleton to these changes in growth polarity. We also address the role of the cytoskeleton in establishing the division plane in these simple eukaryotes, both in wild-type cells and in various cell division cycle (*cdc*) mutants.

MATERIALS AND METHODS

Wild-type *S. pombe* strain 972h⁻ and the mutant strains *cdc*10, 129h⁻, *cdc*11, 136h⁻ and *cdc*13, 117h⁻ (Nurse *et al.* 1976) were kindly supplied by Dr Paul Nurse; strain *ben*4, D3 (Roy & Fantes, 1982) was kindly supplied by Dr Peter Fantes. Cultures were grown as previously described (Marks & Hyams, 1985). Temperature-sensitive *cdc* strains were grown at 25 °C to mid-log phase prior to arrest at 36 °C for 5–7 h. The cold-sensitive mutant *ben*4 was grown at 36 °C to mid-log phase and blocked at 22·5 °C for 24 h. Intracellular F-actin distribution was determined by phalloidin staining (Wulf *et al.* 1979; Wieland & Govindan, 1974) according to Marks & Hyams (1985). Nuclear morphology, and thus the position of the cell in its mitotic cycle, was determined using DAPI (4′-6-diamidino-2-phenylindole; Williamson & Fennell, 1975). Calcofluor white was used to reveal both the cell wall and the septum (Darken, 1961). Tubulin staining of wild-type cells using the monoclonal antibody to yeast tubulin, YOL 1/34 (Kilmartin *et al.* 1982), was performed essentially after the method of Kilmartin & Adams (1984).

RESULTS

A field of *S. pombe* cells stained with rhodamine-conjugated phalloidin as a probe for F-actin is shown in Fig. 1B. Fluorescence is seen either at one end of the cell, at both ends or at the cell equator. End staining is mainly in the form of dots whereas equatorial actin is resolved as a filamentous ring. The different staining patterns may be ordered with respect to the cell cycle by reference to Fig. 1A, which shows the same field of cells stained with the cell wall stain Calcofluor and the DNA probe DAPI. Newly divided *S. pombe* cells grow only at the old end (Mitchison & Nurse, 1985). The two cell ends can be distinguished by their affinity for Calcofluor, the old (growing) end staining brightly whilst the new (non-growing) end appears as a dark, unstained hemisphere (Fig. 1A, cell *1*). When new-end growth is initiated (NETO) this dark region is internalized and appears as a birth scar on the cell surface (Fig. 1A, cell *2*). Comparison of the phalloidin staining patterns reveals that the distribution of actin coincides precisely with the polarity of cell growth; namely, actin resides at the single growing end before NETO and at both growing ends after NETO (compare cells *1* and *2* in Fig. 1B). The transition from one-end to two-end staining also sees the transient appearance of fine filaments of F-actin possibly extending the length of the cell (cell *3*, Fig. 1B).

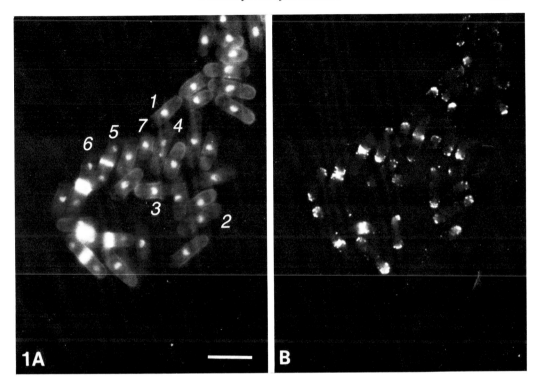

Fig. 1. Two views of the same field of asynchronous wild-type *S. pombe* cells: A, stained with Calcofluor–DAPI; B, stained with rhodamine-conjugated phalloidin. Numbers designate the staining patterns referred to in the text. Bar, 10 μm.

Double-end actin staining is maintained until the onset of mitosis (cell *4*, Fig. 1A), which coincides with the completion of end growth. Actin now disappears from the poles but reappears as a ring at the cell equator where it overlies the dividing nucleus (cell *4*, Fig. 1A,B). The position of the actin ring anticipates the deposition of the septum, which stains intensely with Calcofluor (cell *5*, Fig. 1A). As the septum grows centripetally the appearance of the equatorial actin changes from a filamentous ring to clusters of dots (cell *6*, Fig. 1B). At the completion of septation the remnants of the equatorial actin lie at the new ends of the two daughter cells (cell *7*, Fig. 1B). Since growth will be initiated at the opposite (old) end, actin must rapidly relocate to the other end of the cell before the next cell division cycle can begin. This transition is again accompanied by the transient appearance of fine actin fibres (not shown). The complete sequence of actin distribution through the *S. pombe* cell cycle is summarized in Fig. 2.

Further evidence for the relationship between actin and cell growth and division in fission yeast has been obtained from various temperature-sensitive *cdc* mutants. These become arrested at a specific point in the cell division cycle when grown at the restrictive temperature although their metabolic processes are maintained and they continue to elongate (Bonatti *et al.* 1972; Nurse *et al.* 1976). Fig. 3 shows Calcofluor and phalloidin images of *cdc*10, which arrests in G_1, i.e. prior to NETO. Intense actin staining is seen at the growing old end although a few dots are also seen at the new end (Fig. 3B). Correspondingly, although Calcofluor staining indicates that growth is predominantly at the old end, a small amount of cell wall deposition at the new end is also detectable (Fig. 3A). None of the cells display equatorial actin nor do they form septa. Similar images of *cdc* 13 are shown in Fig. 4. This mutant arrests in mitosis although under certain conditions a proportion of the cells leak through the temperature block and form multiple, aberrant septa (Fig. 4A). Growing cell ends (as judged by Calcofluor staining) again reveal intense actin fluorescence in the form of both dots and fibres (cells *1, 2* and *3* in Fig. 4B). Actin dots also occur in the region of the multiple septa in cell *4* whilst cells *5* and *6* reveal the equatorial actin ring, which anticipates the septum. The contiguous nature of the ring is particularly clearly seen in these cells. In cell *1*, the equatorial actin is largely dispersed following the formation of a septum and intense staining is again seen at the cell poles.

Fig. 5 shows the relationship of the equatorial actin ring to nuclear position in an early septation mutant *cdc* 11. These cells are unable to undergo cytokinesis at the restrictive temperature although nuclear division and cell elongation continue. At the first mitosis following the temperature block the daughter nuclei return to a point either side of the middle of the cell (cell *1*, Fig. 5B). Reinitiation of end growth is indicated by the bipolarity of actin staining (cell *1*, Fig. 5A). Although these cells do not form a septum, a pair of actin rings forms at the positions occupied by the two nuclei prior to mitosis (cell *2*, Fig. 5A). The nuclei do not appear to be physically connected to their respective actin rings since they are able to move away from their original position at the second mitotic division (cell *2*, Fig. 5A,B). At the next mitosis actin rings appear at the position occupied by each of the four daughter nuclei (not shown).

Although not excluding other possibilities, we have begun to investigate whether the changing patterns of actin described above are dependent on the presence of cytoplasmic microtubules. *S. pombe* cells stained with anti-tubulin antibody are shown in Fig. 6. During interphase, groups of microtubules extend between the two ends of the cell. As the cell enters mitosis, these cytoplasmic microtubules disappear, to be replaced by an intranuclear spindle. The precise details of the cell cycle rearrangements of tubulin in *S. pombe* will be presented elsewhere (I. M. Hagan, P. Nurse & J. S. Hyams, unpublished data). Since anti-microtubule drugs have only a limited effect on fission yeast (Burns, 1973; Walker, 1982; our unpublished results) we have attempted to destabilize cytoplasmic microtubules by genetic means. The cold-sensitive, benomyl-resistant mutant *ben*4 is unable to undergo cell division at 20°C (Roy & Fantes, 1982). When cold-grown cells are stained with phalloidin, a dramatic rearrangement of actin is observed. Instead of multiple small dots at the ends of the cells, a single large dot is frequently present. Most obviously, however, much of the cellular F-actin is seen to be associated with the nucleus. Predominantly, this is in the form of a continuous ring, although sometimes this is twisted to form a figure eight and often bears a tail like a hangman's noose (Fig. 7). These various perinuclear configurations are present in up to 90% of the cells.

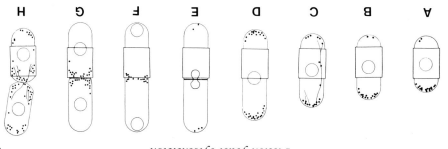

Fig. 2. Schematic representation of the structural rearrangements of F-actin through the cell division cycle of *S. pombe*. The old end of the cell is at the top of the figure. The open circle in the centre of the cell is the nucleus; dots show the position of actin. Because of the asymmetric nature of cell growth in *S. pombe*, the cell wall material inherited by each daughter cell from its mother is different. The cell depicted in A has a 'waistcoat' of old cell wall material, which acts as a useful marker for the directionality of new wall deposition. Note that at the end of the sequence (cell H) only one daughter inherits the waistcoat. The major transitions of actin distribution are seen in cell C, which is at NETO, where actin filaments are also transiently observed; cell E, which shows the completion of end growth and the initiation of the actin ring (note that the shape of the nucleus has changed to signify that these events are coincident with the initiation of mitosis); and cell H, where actin left at the cell equator by the breakdown of the actin ring must relocate to the opposite end of each daughter cell in order that new cell growth may be initiated. Fibres also appear transiently at this stage. (Redrawn from Marks & Hyams (1985).)

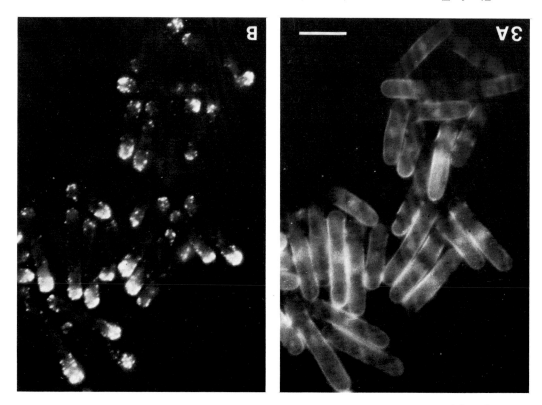

Fig. 3. Temperature-arrested cells of *cdc*10 double stained with: A, Calcofluor; and B, phalloidin. Note that as these cells block before NETO both growth and the location of actin are restricted largely to the old ends. Bar, 10 µm.

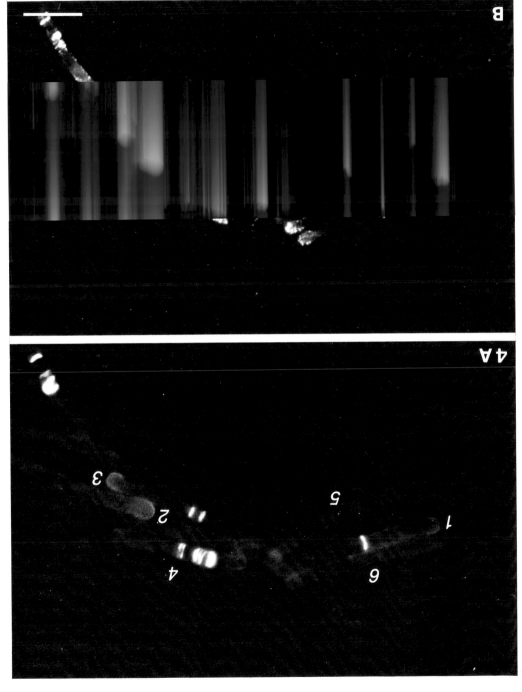

Fig. 4. Calcofluor (A) and phalloidin (B) images of temperature-arrested *cdc*13 cells. Note: the intense apical staining associated with the growing cell ends in cells *1*, *2* and *3*; the diffuse arrays of actin dots associated with the multiple septa in cell *4*; the actin ring preceding septum deposition in cells *5* and *6*. Bar, 10 μm.

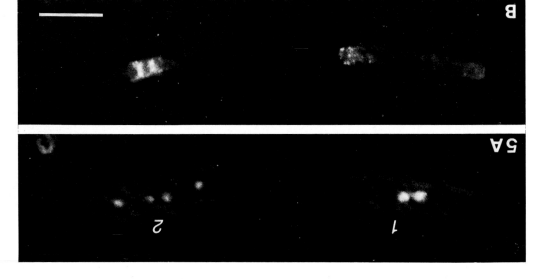

Fig. 5. Phase–DAPI (A) and phalloidin (B) images of two temperature-arrested *cdc*11 cells. At the restrictive temperature these cells undergo repeated nuclear divisions but do not divide. Following the first mitosis the daughter nuclei return to the middle of the cell and end growth is reinitiated (cell *1*). As the daughter nuclei synchronously enter the next mitotic division an actin ring appears at the site formerly occupied by the nuclei (cell *2*). The fact that cell *1* contains two interphase nuclei as opposed to a single mitotic nucleus is confirmed by the obvious difference in size between the nuclei in these two cells. Bar, 10 μm.

DISCUSSION

The precise manner of cell growth in *S. pombe* coupled with the availability of mutants affecting both the cytoskeleton and the cell division cycle make this a most attractive organism in which to investigate the structural rearrangements and inter-actions of cytoskeletal proteins through the cell cycle and the mechanisms whereby these are integrated with other cellular events. In this paper we have shown that the two major growth transitions in the *S. pombe* cell cycle, that is, from monopolar to bipolar cell growth early in G_2 (NETO), and the cessation of end growth and the initiation of cell division are accompanied by corresponding rearrangements of F-actin. These findings, which were originally established in wild-type cells (Marks & Hyams, 1985), have been confirmed here by the use of cell division cycle mutants arrested at different points of the cell cycle by growth at the restrictive temperature (Nurse *et al.* 1976). In *cdc*10 both actin and cell growth were predominantly mono-polar (consistent with the known execution point of this mutant before NETO). It was noticeable, however, that a small amount of actin staining, and a corresponding degree of Calcofluor staining, was always detectable at the opposite pole. A small amount of new-end growth prior to NETO has been detected in wild-type cells although its extent has been difficult to assess, partly because it represents only a minor contribution to total cell growth and also because the methods of analysis used to date are relatively crude (Mitchison & Nurse, 1985). The problem may be

resolved when more sophisticated methods for detecting zones of cell expansion in yeasts are applied to *S. pombe* (Staebell & Soll, 1985), or through the use of mutants such as *cdc*10, which can be held prior to NETO for extended periods. Preliminary observations of *cdc*11 have shown that the normal relationship between nuclear division and the formation and disappearance of the equatorial actin ring is maintained even in the absence of septation. Mitchison & Nurse (1985) noted that *cdc*11 showed pulses of cell growth interspersed with periods of quiescence. The fact that actin disappears from the cell ends with each cycle of ring formation provides an explanation for their observations. The relationship between the actin ring and septation is also clearly shown in *cdc*13, where the ring cycle and nuclear cycle become uncoupled and multiple septa are laid down in the absence of nuclear division.

At present we cannot distinguish whether the coincidence of actin and polarized cell growth is a cause or an effect relationship. In the case of septation, however, the situation is unambiguous, actin appearing at the cell equator prior to the

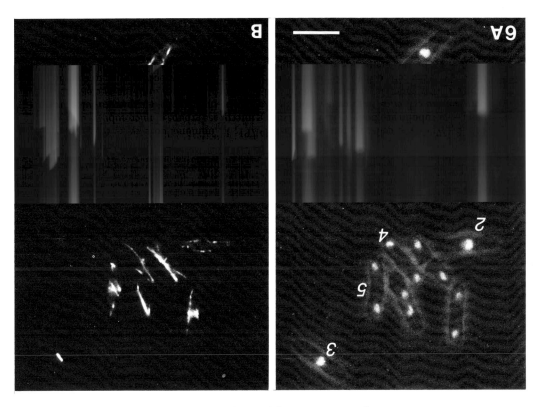

Fig. 6. Wild-type cells: A, phase-contrast–DAPI; B, immunofluorescence microscopy using anti-tubulin antibody YOL1/34. During interphase groups of microtubules extend between the cell ends (e.g. cells *1* and *2*). During mitosis the cytoplasmic microtubules are replaced by a short intranuclear spindle (cell *3*), which elongates until the nuclei reach the ends of the cell (cell *4*). Reinitiation of the interphase array occurs prior to spindle breakdown by the nucleation of microtubules at the cell equator (cells *4* and *5*). Bar, 10 μm.

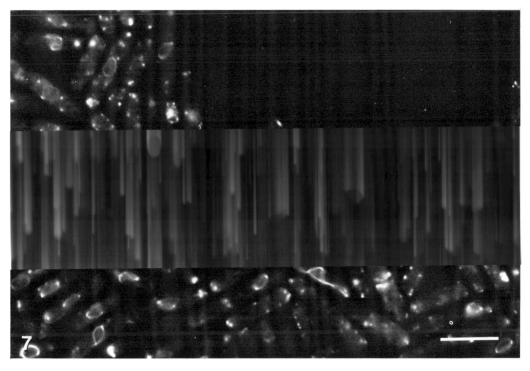

Fig. 7. Phalloidin staining of cold-treated *ben*4 cells. These contain fewer, larger actin dots and, in many cases, a conspicuous perinuclear ring. Bar, 10 μm.

deposition of Calcofluor-staining material. Both end growth and septation involve the deposition of new cell wall macromolecules, albeit of different chemical composition (Bush *et al.* 1974; Horisberger & Rouvet-Vauthey, 1985). In fungi this requires the mobilization of vesicles containing wall precursors to the growing region (McClure *et al.* 1968; Grove, 1978). Vesicles associated with the poles and septa of *S. pombe* cells have been reported (Oulevey *et al.* 1970; Johnson *et al.* 1973), and this suggests a possible explanation for the dot-like nature of actin staining. Although at present there is no evidence for the association of actin with cell wall vesicles in yeasts, vesicles coated with fine filaments of the approximate dimensions of F-actin have been observed in a filamentous fungus (Hoch & Howard, 1980). The role of actin in wall deposition may not be finally clarified until cell wall vesicles are available for biochemical study. The localization of myosin may also provide important clues (Watts *et al.* 1985) as will drugs that selectively interfere with cell wall morphology (Miyata *et al.* 1985, 1986), and experiments to these ends are in progress. Although the nature of the dot staining remains to be resolved, it is obviously a common feature of fungal cells, having been seen in three ascomycetous yeasts (*Sa. cerevisiae*, *Sa. uvarum* and *S. pombe*) (Kilmartin & Adams, 1984; Adams & Pringle, 1984; Marks & Hyams, 1985) and a filamentous basidiomycete (*Uromyces phaseoli*) (Hoch & Staples, 1983). This represents a broader sample than may initially be apparent, in view of the evolutionary divergence between budding and fission yeasts (Huysmans *et al.* 1983) and the fact that their mode of division is quite different. Cytokinesis in budding yeast is assymmetric and involves a chitin ring, whereas fission yeasts divide symmetrically and lack chitin (Bush *et al.* 1974).

The nature of actin staining as well as its position undergoes a marked change at the initiation of mitosis. Dot staining at the cell ends is replaced by a filamentous ring, which presumably occupies the thin layer of cytoplasm between the nucleus and the cell membrane (Streiblova & Girbardt, 1980). Our finding that a ring of actin anticipates the formation of the septum in *S. pombe* is consistent with earlier studies of cytokinesis in fungi, which have provided ultrastructural evidence for the presence of such a structure (Girbardt, 1979). The intimate relationship between the nucleus and the actin ring is most clearly demonstrated by *cdc*11, which can go through multiple nuclear divisions at the restrictive temperature without undergoing cytokinesis (Nurse *et al.* 1976). An actin ring forms in association with each daughter nucleus at the start of mitosis; however, as the nuclei divide this spatial relationship is lost. The fact that *cdc*11 forms apparently normal actin rings and yet fails to lay down any detectable septal material may well be of value in establishing the coupling of these two events.

The relationship between the nucleus and the actin ring may also be addressed by our findings with *ben*4. This mutant has the classic phenotype of a tubulin gene mutation, namely, it is benomyl-resistant and cold-sensitive (Roy & Fantes, 1982). Genetic studies have shown, however, that the *ben*4 gene is distinct from the known tubulin genes of *S. pombe* (P. Fantes, personal communication; see Yanagida *et al.* 1985). The exciting possibility therefore exists that *ben*4 codes for a protein that interacts with microtubules, i.e. a microtubule-associated protein (MAP). This is supported by immunofluorescence staining of *ben*4 cells with anti-tubulin antibody, which reveals an apparently normal array of cytoplasmic microtubules (our unpublished results). The most conspicuous cytological feature of cold-treated *ben*4 cells is the presence of a perinuclear F-actin ring, reminiscent of the rings of intermediate filaments that form around the nuclei of cultured cells treated with colchicine (Goldman, 1971). A possible explanation for the origin of these structures is that, like the β-tubulin mutant *nda*3 (Hiraoka *et al.* 1984), cold-treated *ben*4 cells arrest at mitotic prophase. Since this is the time at which the equatorial actin ring appears, the perinuclear rings in *ben*4 may be the equatorial ring displaced from its normal location. Although Roy & Fantes reported that *ben*4 does not exhibit classical cell cycle arrest, we have used a different temperature from that used in their study and this can have a profound effect on the phenotype (Hiraoka *et al.* 1984). Clearly, examination of the distribution of actin in known tubulin mutants of *S. pombe* will be of value in further establishing the nature of the *ben*4 mutation as well as clarifying the relationship between actin and tubulin in this organism.

Investigations of the role of microtubules in *S. pombe* will also be considerably aided by the introduction of the immunofluorescence techniques described here. Spindle microtubules have previously been demonstrated in this way (Hiraoka *et al.* 1984) but this is the first report of the visualization of cytoplasmic microtubules. These are much more abundant than has previously been appreciated from electron microscopy (Hereward, 1974; Streiblova & Girbardt, 1980; King & Hyams, 1982*a*,*b*; Tanaka & Kanbe, 1986) and extend from one end of the cell to the other. Cytoplasmic microtubules are clearly involved in the establishment and maintenance of cell morphology since treatment of fission yeast with anti-micro-tubule drugs results in a variety of morphological changes (Walker, 1982), as does the disruption of microtubules by means of tubulin gene mutations (Toda *et al.* 1983; Hiraoka *et al.* 1984). Whether microtubules are actively involved in the transport of

We thank Professor Th. Wieland and Dr John Kilmartin for the generous gifts of phalloidin and tubulin antibody, respectively. This work was supported by Action Research for the Crippled Child and the Science and Engineering Research Council.

REFERENCES

ADAMS A. E. M. & PRINGLE, J. R. (1984). Relationship of actin and tubulin distribution to bud growth in wild-type and morphogenetic mutant *Saccharomyces cerevisiae*. *J. Cell Biol.* **98**, 934–945.

BONATTI, S., SIMILI, M. & ABBONDANDOLO, A. (1972). Isolation of temperature sensitive mutants of *Schizosaccharomyces pombe*. *J. Bact.* **109**, 484–491.

BURNS, R. G. (1973). ^{3}H-Colchicine binding: Failure to detect any binding to soluble proteins from various lower organisms. *Expl Cell Res.* **81**, 285–292.

BUSH, D. A., HORISBERGER, M., HORMAN, I. & WURSCH, P. (1974). The wall structure of *Schizosaccharomyces pombe*. *J. gen. Microbiol.* **81**, 199–206.

DARKEN, M. A. (1961). Applications of fluorescent brighteners in biological techniques. *Science* **133**, 1704–1705.

GIRBARDT, M. (1979). A microfilamentous septal belt (FSB) during induction of cytokinesis in *Trametes versicolor* (L. ex Fr). *Expl Mycol.* **3**, 215–228.

GOLDMAN, R. D. (1971). The role of the three cytoplasmic fibres in BHK-21 cell motility. 1. Microtubules and the effect of colchicine. *J. Cell Biol.* **51**, 752–762.

GROVE, S. N. (1978). The cytology of hyphal tip growth. In *The Filamentous Fungi*, vol. 3 (ed. J. E. Smith & D. R. Berry), pp. 28–50. New York: John Wiley & Sons.

HAYLES, J. & NURSE, P. (1986). Cell cycle regulation in yeast. *J. Cell Sci. Suppl.* **4**, 155–170.

HEREWARD, F. V. (1974). Cytoplasmic microtubules in a yeast. *Planta* **117**, 355–360.

HIRAOKA, Y., TODA, T. & YANAGIDA, M. (1984). The *NDA3* gene of fission yeast encodes β-tubulin. A cold sensitive *nda3* mutation reversibly blocks spindle formation and chromosome movement in mitosis. *Cell* **39**, 349–358.

HOCH, H. C. & HOWARD, R. J. (1980). Ultrastructure of freeze-substituted hyphae of the basidiomycete *Laetisaria arvalis*. *Protoplasma* **103**, 281–297.

HOCH, H. C. & STAPLES, R. C. (1983). Visualization of actin *in situ* by rhodamine-conjugated phalloin in the fungus *Uromyces phaseoli*. *Eur. J. Cell Biol.* **32**, 52–58.

HORISBERGER, M. & ROUVET-VAUTHEY, M. (1985). Cell wall architecture of the fission yeast *Schizosaccharomyces pombe*. *Experientia* **41**, 748–750.

HUYSMANS, E., DAMS, E., VANDERBERGHE, A. & DE WATCHER, R. (1983). The nucleotide sequences of the 5 S rRNAs of four mushrooms and their use in studying the phylogenetic position of basidiomycetes among the eukaryotes. *Nucl. Acids Res.* **11**, 2871–2880.

JOHNSON, B. F. (1965). Autoradiographic analysis of regional cell wall growth of yeasts. *Expl Cell Res.* **39**, 613–624.

JOHNSON, B. F., YOO, B. Y. & CALLEJA, G. B. (1973). Cell division in yeasts: Movement of organelles associated with cell plate growth of *Schizosaccharomyces pombe*. *J. Bact.* **115**, 358–366.

KILMARTIN, J. V. & ADAMS, A. E. M. (1984). Structural rearrangements of tubulin and actin during the cell cycle of the yeast *Saccharomyces*. *J. Cell Biol.* **98**, 922–933.

KILMARTIN, J. V., WRIGHT, B. & MILSTEIN, C. (1982). Rat monoclonal antitubulin antibodies derived by using a new nonsecreting rat cell line. *J. Cell Biol.* **93**, 576–582.

KING, S. M. & HYAMS, J. S. (1982a). Synchronization of mitosis in a *cdc* mutant of *Schizosaccharomyces pombe* released from temperature arrest. *Can. J. Microbiol.* **28**, 261–264.

KING, S. M. & HYAMS, J. S. (1982b). Interdependence of cell cycle events in *Schizosaccharomyces pombe*. Terminal phenotypes of *cdc* mutants arrested during DNA synthesis and cell division. *Protoplasma* **110**, 54–62.

MARKS, J. & HYAMS, J. S. (1985). Localization of F-actin through the cell division cycle of *Schizosaccharomyces pombe*. *Eur. J. Cell Biol.* **39**, 27–32.

McCLURE, W. D., PARK, D. & ROBINSON, P. M. (1968). Apical organization in the somatic hyphae of fungi. *J. gen. Microbiol.* **50**, 177–182.

MITCHISON, J. M. & NURSE, P. (1985). Growth in cell length in the fission yeast *Schizosaccharomyces pombe*. *J. Cell Sci.* **75**, 357–376.

MIYATA, M., KANBE, T. & TANAKA, K. (1985). Morphological alterations in the fission yeast *Schizosaccharomyces pombe* in the presence of aculeacin A: Spherical wall formation. *J. gen. Microbiol.* **131**, 611–621.

MIYATA, M., MIYATA, H. & JOHNSON, B. F. (1986). Assymetric location of the septum in physiologically altered cells of the fission yeast *Schizosaccharomyces pombe*. *J. gen. Microbiol.* **132**, 883–891.

NURSE, P. (1981). Genetic analysis of the cell cycle. In *Genetics as a Tool in Microbiology*. SGM *Symp.* 31, pp. 291–315. Cambridge University Press.

NURSE, P. (1985). Cell cycle control genes in yeast. *Trends Genet.* **2**, 51–55.

NURSE, P., THURIAUX, P. & NASMYTH, K. (1976). Genetic control of the cell division cycle of the fission yeast *Schizosaccharomyces pombe*. *Molec. gen. Genet.* **146**, 167–178.

OULEVEY, N., DESHUSSES, J. & TURIAN, G. (1970). Étude de la zone septale de *Schizosaccharomyces pombe* en division a ses etapes succesives. *Protoplasma* **70**, 217–224.

PRINGLE, J. R., COLEMAN, K., ADAMS, A., LILLIE, S., HAARER, B., JACOBS, C., ROBINSON, J. & EVANS, C. (1984). Cellular morphogenesis in the yeast cell cycle. In *Molecular Biology of the Cytoskeleton* (ed. G. G. Borisy, D. W. Cleveland & D. B. Murphy). New York: Cold Spring Harbor Laboratory Press.

PRINGLE, J. R. & HARTWELL, L. H. (1981). The *Saccharomyces cerevisiae* cell cycle. In *The Molecular Biology of the Yeast* Saccharomyces (ed. J. N. Strathern, E. W. Jones & J. R. Broach). New York: Cold Spring Harbor Laboratory Press.

ROY, D. & FANTES, P. A. (1982). Benomyl resistant mutants of *Schizosaccharomyces pombe* cold-sensitive for mitosis. *Curr. Genet.* **6**, 195–201.

STAEBELL, M. & SOLL, D. R. (1985). Temporal and spatial differences in cell wall expansion during bud and mycelial formation in *Candida albicans*. *J. gen. Microbiol.* **131**, 1467–1480.

STREIBLOVA, E. & GIRBARDT, M. (1980). Microfilaments and cytoplasmic microtubules in cell division cycle mutants of *Schizosaccharomyces pombe*. *Can. J. Microbiol.* **26**, 250–254.

STREIBLOVA, E. & WOLF, A. (1972). Cell wall growth during the cell cycle of *Schizosaccharomyces pombe*. *Z. Allg. Mikrobiol.* **12**, 673–684.

TANAKA, K. & KANBE, T. (1986). Mitosis in fission yeast *Schizosaccharomyces pombe* as revealed by freeze-substitution electron microscopy. *J. Cell Sci.* **80**, 253–268.

THOMAS, J. H., NOVICK, P. & BOTSTEIN, D. (1984). Genetics of the yeast cytoskeleton. In *Molecular Biology of the Cytoskeleton* (ed. G. G. Borisy, D. W. Cleveland & D. B. Murphy). New York: Cold Spring Harbor Laboratory Press.

TODA, T., UMESONO, K. & HIRAOKA, A. (1983). Cold-sensitive nuclear division arrest mutants of the fission yeast *Schizosaccharomyces pombe*. *J. molec. Biol.* **168**, 251–270.

WALKER, G. M. (1982). Cell cycle specificity of certain antimicrotubular drugs in *Schizosaccharomyces pombe*. *J. gen. Microbiol.* **128**, 61–71.

WATTS, F. Z., MILLER, D. M. & ORR, E. (1985). Identification of myosin heavy chain in *Saccharomyces cerevisiae*. *Nature, Lond.* **316**, 83–85.

J. Cell Sci. Suppl. 5, 243–255 (1986)
Printed in Great Britain © *The Company of Biologists Limited 1986*

TUBULIN ISOTYPES: GENERATION OF DIVERSITY
IN CELLS AND MICROTUBULAR ORGANELLES

K. GULL[1], P. J. HUSSEY[1], R. SASSE[1], A. SCHNEIDER[2],
T. SEEBECK[2] AND T. SHERWIN[1]

protozoan, *Trypanosoma brucei*. The carrot plant expresses six, well-defined β-tubulin isotypes
that possess characteristic two-dimensional gel coordinates. These six β-tubulin isotypes are
differentially expressed during development of the flowering plant. In a similar manner, *Physarum*
expresses three separate β-tubulin isotypes during its life cycle; of the two $\beta1$ isotypes, one is
expressed solely in the myxamoeba whilst the other is expressed both in the myxamoeba and in the
plasmodium. A further β-tubulin isotype, $\beta2$, is expressed only in the plasmodium. In carrot and in
Physarum the generation of β-tubulin diversity appears, in the main, to be generated by the
differential expression of a β-tubulin multi-gene family. However, tubulin isotypes can also be
generated by post-translational modifications and *T. brucei* utilizes two different modifications
within one cell. First, the primary translation product, the $\alpha1$-tubulin isotype, can be acetylated to
produce the $\alpha3$ isotype. Second, both the $\alpha1$ and $\alpha3$ isotypes appear to exist in both tyrosinated
and detyrosinated forms. The generation of these α-tubulin isotypes within the same cell and their
presence in particular cellular domains, modulated throughout the cell cycle, reveals a complex
relationship between α-tubulin isotypes produced by post-translational modifications and the
dynamics of microtubule construction.

OVERVIEW

Microtubules represent one of the most readily observed components of the
cytoskeleton and as such their structure and organization has been extensively
documented during the past 20 years using a variety of electron-microscopic
techniques. They have been described as components of the cytoplasmic architecture
of most cells as well as providing the major structural elements of mitotic and meiotic
spindles, cilia and flagella. They also occur in a host of other specialized arrangements in cells as diverse as neurones and free-living flagellates. Despite the diversity
of these occurrences and structural arrangements it has become clear that the basic
biochemical unit used in their construction is a heterodimer of tubulin.

Early reports tended to emphasize the conserved nature of tubulin; however, the
introduction and application of more sophisticated techniques soon led to reports of
tubulin heterogeneity. These reports have now documented the existence of tubulin
multi-gene families in many organisms; however, the number of genes and their
arrangement in the genome varies considerably (Cowan & Dudley, 1983; Raff,

1984). In the yeast *Schizosaccharomyces pombe* two functional α-tubulin genes have been identified; the genes are dispersed within the genome, one having an intron and one being intronless (Toda *et al.* 1984). In unicellular organisms there appear to be no simple paradigms governing the number or arrangement of tubulin genes. *Chlamydomonas* and *Aspergillus* both possess two α and two β-tubulin genes (Weatherbee & Morris, 1984), *Physarum* has at least four α and three β-tubulin DNA sequences (Schedl *et al.* 1984), whilst *Naegleria* has been reported to possess eight α-tubulin DNA sequences (Lai *et al.* 1984). In most of the above cases the multi-tubulin gene sequences have been shown to be dispersed throughout the organism's genome. In a few cases, however, there is evidence of clustering of these sequences within the genome. In trypanosomes the tubulin genes are arranged in tightly packed clusters of tandemly repeated alternating α/β pairs (Thomashow *et al.* 1983; Seebeck *et al.* 1983), whilst in *Leishmania* there is a cluster of tandemly duplicated α-tubulin genes and a completely separate cluster of tandemly repeated β-tubulin genes (Landfear *et al.* 1983).

In metazoan organisms there is also excellent evidence for the existence of tubulin multi-gene families, although there is also some evidence for the presence of pseudogenes in certain of the organisms studied (Lee *et al.* 1983). The multi-tubulin DNA sequences observed in human, rat, mouse and chicken genomes are all dispersed, whilst there is some clustering within the sea-urchin genome. The molecular biology and genetics of these multi-tubulin gene families have been excellently analysed in a recent review (Cleveland & Sullivan, 1985).

In many cases where multiple tubulin DNA sequences have been observed in an organism's genome it has subsequently been shown that at least some (in the case of mammals), and more often many, of these DNA sequences do represent functional tubulin genes. In some cases these genes can be shown to be different and yet to code for the same tubulin polypeptide. For instance, in *Chlamydomonas* there are two different β-tubulin genes expressed, yet both genes encode an identical tubulin polypeptide (Youngblom *et al.* 1984). In chicken there may be around seven to nine different β-tubulin genes; DNA sequencing and other techniques have shown that at least five chicken β-tubulin genes encode different authentic polypeptides (Cleveland & Sullivan, 1985). In some cases a link has been made between individual tubulin genes and particular tubulin isotypes that can be resolved and recognized by two-dimensional gel electrophoresis. In *Aspergillus nidulans* there are two genes for α-tubulin, *tub*A and *tub*B, and two genes for β-tubulin, *ben*A and *tub*C. The *tub*A gene codes for two proteins, α1-tubulin and α3-tubulin, whilst the *tub*B gene codes for α2-tubulin. The *ben*A gene codes for two β-tubulin isotypes, β1-tubulin and β2-tubulin, whilst the *tub*C gene encodes a third β-tubulin isotype, β3-tubulin (May *et al.* 1985). Similar relationships between an individual tubulin gene and a particular, identifiable tubulin isotype have also been established in *Drosophila* (Raff & Fuller, 1984). These relationships are particularly useful in permitting links to be more easily established between investigations of the cell and molecular biology of the tubulin multi-gene family.

In this paper we will discuss the initial evidence that suggests that higher plants also contain multiple tubulin isotypes, and that these tubulin isotypes are differentially expressed within different parts of the mature plant. We will then discuss the generation and usage of different tubulin isotypes in two other organisms. First, the generation of multiple β-tubulin isotypes as the products of separate genes in *Physarum polycephalum*, and second the generation of α-tubulin isotypes *via* two separate post-translational modifications in *Trypanosoma brucei*.

amongst plant polypeptides separated by two-dimensional polyacrylamide gel electrophoresis. In early experiments root tip cell lysates of *Phaseolus vulgaris* were analysed by one-dimensional polyacrylamide gel electrophoresis (Hussey & Gull, 1985). The α-tubulin and β-tubulin polypeptides were then identified by Western blotting of the separated polypeptides onto nitrocellulose paper and probing with a panel of well-characterized monoclonal antibodies that recognize evolutionarily conserved epitopes. These initial experiments showed that the plant α-tubulin migrated ahead of the plant β-tubulin on Laemmli sodium dodecyl sulphate–polyacrylamide gels. This is the reverse migration to that characteristic of animal cell tubulins, where the β-tubulin is the faster-migrating species. This α/β inversion of the tubulins was first described in *Physarum* (Clayton *et al.* 1980) and has now been reported in *Dictyostelium*, *Paramecium*, *Tetrahymena* and *Crithidia*. The two-dimensional gel analysis of *Phaseolus* polypeptides revealed that both the α and β-tubulins of this organism could be separated into four discrete isotypes. We have recently concentrated our studies of plant tubulins on *Daucus carota*, the carrot, and have used monoclonal antibodies and immunoblotting protocols to reveal the presence of a complex family of β-tubulin isotypes within this plant. We have been able to detect six well-defined β-tubulin isotypes that are differentially expressed within various parts of the carrot plant. The β5 isotype is present in the vegetative phase of the flowering plant; it is expressed in the stem, the midrib and the leaf lamina. However, there is a marked increase in its relative abundance from stem to midrib, until it is found as the dominant β-tubulin isotype in the leaf lamina. All of the organs of the floret except pollen possess β1, β2 and β3-tubulin isotypes. However, in the stamen, where pollen is developing, a β4-tubulin isotype is detected that increases in relative abundance in the mature stamen. In the pollen the β4-tubulin is the major β-tubulin isotype. The β6-tubulin isotype is only expressed in seedlings.

There is, as yet, little detailed evidence available to link this complex expression of β-tubulin isotypes with the presence of a multi-tubulin family. However, preliminary evidence from *in vitro* translation of mRNA preparations from various tissues and organs of the plant suggests that the β-tubulin heterogeneity is a reflection of the presence of multiple β-tubulin mRNA species, and Southern blot analysis using a heterologous β-tubulin cDNA probe has revealed the presence of multiple restriction fragments.

GENERATION OF β-TUBULIN ISOTYPES AS THE PRODUCTS OF SEPARATE GENES IN *P. POLYCEPHALUM*

The slime mould *P. polycephalum* expresses two distinct isotypes of β-tubulin, separable by two-dimensional gel electrophoresis. These two electrophoretically separable β-tubulin isotypes, β1-tubulin and β2-tubulin, are differentially expressed within the life cycle of this eukaryotic microbe. The β1-tubulin is the only β-tubulin isotype expressed within the myxamoeba, whilst the macroscopic, syncytial plasmodium expresses both the β1-tubulin and the β2-tubulin isotypes. The tubulins from *Physarum* have been characterized as components of microtubules purified from both the myxamoeba and plasmodium by cycles of assembly/disassembly *in vitro*. Also, they have been extensively characterized by peptide mapping, reaction with well-characterized monoclonal antibodies and by *in vitro* translations of specific mRNAs selected by hybridization to cloned tubulin DNA sequences (Burland *et al.* 1983; Roobol *et al.* 1984).

Recently, Schedl *et al.* (1984) have provided an understanding of the number and arrangement of β-tubulin DNA sequences within the *Physarum* genome. These workers were able to use restriction-fragment length polymorphisms to analyse the multiple DNA sequences detected on Southern blots of *Physarum* DNA using heterologous β-tubulin-specific DNA probes. This mapping approach has revealed the presence of at least three β-tubulin loci, *bet*A, *bet*B and *bet*C; no linkage was detected between any of these three loci. What relationship exists between these three β-tubulin loci and the two electrophoretically defined β-tubulin isotypes, β1 and β2-tubulin?

The β1-tubulin isotype

The β1-tubulin is expressed in both myxamoebae and the plasmodium; however, a variety of types of evidence suggests that this apparently simple pattern of expression belies a more complex regulatory phenomenon. We have previously shown that neither growth of *Physarum* myxamoebae nor the *in vitro* assembly of *Physarum* myxamoebal tubulin is sensitive to the classical anti-microtubule agent, colchicine. However, both growth of the cells and polymerization of *Physarum* tubulin are extremely sensitive to inhibition by members of the benzimidazole carbamate group of drugs (Quinlan *et al.* 1981). Burland *et al.* (1984) have isolated and characterized a number of mutants that show resistance to the anti-microtubule fungicide MBC (methyl benzimidazole-2-yl-carbamate). Analogy with other systems suggested that at least some of these mutants would occur within the structural genes for β-tubulin. Burland and his colleagues were able to define two unlinked resistance loci, *ben*A and *ben*D, that appeared to cosegregate with some of the previously mentioned β-tubulin restriction fragments in meiotic analysis. Mutations in *ben*A cosegregate with the *bet*A locus and mutations in *ben*D cosegregate with the *bet*B locus. Thus, the general conclusion of this study is the suggestion that *ben*A and *ben*D each define a different β-tubulin structural gene. More direct evidence to confirm this proposal for *ben*D has come from the observation of Burland *et al.* that one mutation in *ben*D, *ben*D210, results in the production of a novel, electrophoretically altered β-tubulin

and the amino acid sequence of both the α and β subunits has been determined by Singhofer-Wowra and Little in Heidelberg. During the sequencing of the β-tubulin a very clear heterogeneity was detected at position number 283 in the polypeptide chain. The heterogeneity involved the detection of a double signal (alanine and serine) at this position. No other heterogeneities were detected during the sequencing of nearly the entire polypeptide chain, so providing direct evidence for the normal expression of two very similar β-tubulin isotypes in the *Physarum* myxamoeba and that these two isotypes are the products of different genes, presumably *ben*A and *ben*D.

The *ben*A and *ben*D genes exhibit differential expression during the life cycle of *Physarum*. The altered, electrophoretically novel *ben*D210 β-tubulin can be easily located on two-dimensional gels of polypeptides from the plasmodial form of this mutant. However, in plasmodia of such mutants Burland *et al.* were able to show that there was no wild-type β1-tubulin isotype. Thus, the *ben*D gene appears to be expressed in both the myxamoeba and the plasmodium, whilst the *ben*A gene appears to be expressed only in the myxamoebal stage of the life cycle. The initial view of the *Physarum* β1-tubulin isotype was that it was expressed in both the myxamoebae and the plasmodium. We can now see that a more complex scenario actually pertains: there are two β1-tubulin isotypes expressed in the myxamoeba, differing from each other in only one known amino acid and colocalizing to the same two-dimensional gel spot. They are encoded by two separate genes, only one of which is expressed in the plasmodium.

The β2-tubulin isotype

The β2-tubulin isotype is expressed only in the plasmodium. This β2-tubulin isotype is found when RNA extracted from the plasmodium is translated *in vitro* and, thus, the assumption is that this β2-tubulin isotype is also a direct gene product, presumably from the *bet*C locus. Since this β-tubulin gene(s) is expressed only in the plasmodium (a syncytium) it is not amenable to study by mutant selection. However,

1

Fig. 1. The tubulin isotypes of *T. brucei* separated by two-dimensional gel electrophoresis and detected by immunoblotting using monoclonal antibodies to α and β-tubulin (a mixture of DM1A and KMX). The blot shows the relationship between the α1, α3 and β-tubulin species.

when this gene is cloned it should be immediately recognizable by virtue of the unique nature of the region encoding the C-terminal sequence of the β2 polypeptide (Gull *et al.* 1985; Birkett *et al.* 1985).

GENERATION OF α-TUBULIN ISOTYPES AS THE PRODUCTS OF POST-TRANSLATIONAL MODIFICATIONS IN *T. BRUCEI*

The *T. brucei* genome contains a well-characterized tubulin multi-gene family of around 10 α and 10 β genes that comprise a clustered array of alternating α and β genes (Imboden *et al.* 1986). There is no evidence for the presence of heterogeneity within these gene clusters that might result in the production of multiple tubulin isotypes. However, our studies of the tubulin polypeptides of this organism clearly indicate that it does use two post-translational modification mechanisms in order to generate distinct isotypes of α-tubulin.

Acetylated α-tubulin

The effect of the first of these two post-translational modification systems is seen when total protein from procyclic forms of trypanosomes is analysed by two-dimensional gel electrophoresis and immunoblotted with well-characterized anti-α-tubulin monoclonal antibodies. This procedure detects the presence of two clearly separated α-tubulin isotypes (Fig. 1). In accordance with the nomenclature applied previously to the tubulins of *Chlamydomonas*, we have termed the more basic of the two proteins, α1-tubulin, and the apparently higher molecular weight, less-basic isotype, α3-tubulin. A large quantitative difference is seen between the two α-tubulin isotypes, the α3 isotype being the most abundant. In order to assess the probable relationship between these two isotypes we have selected α-tubulin mRNA by preparative hybridization and have analysed this α-tubulin mRNA by translation

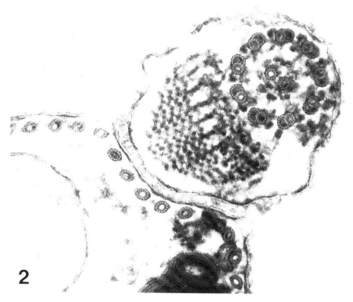

2

Fig. 2. Transmission electron micrograph (TEM) showing the cytoskeletal, sub-pellicular microtubules of *T. brucei*. The structure in the flagellum near to the axoneme is the paraflagellar rod.

in vitro. Two-dimensional gel analysis of the translation products revealed only a single α-tubulin electrophoretic species, the α1-tubulin isotype. Thus, α1-tubulin presumably represents the primary transcription product, whilst α3-tubulin is most probably a modified derivative of α1-tubulin. We have now been able to show that this is indeed the case and that the post-translational modification that produces the α3-tubulin isotype is an acetylation. The same post-translational modification has been described previously in *Chlamydomonas* by Rosenbaum's group (McKeithan *et al.* 1983; L'Hernault & Rosenbaum, 1983, 1985).

Trypanosome cells contain a precisely arranged microtubule cytoskeleton and we have determined the distribution of the α1 and α3-tubulin isotypes within the microtubular organelles of the interphase cell. The cytoplasmic pool of soluble tubulin contains almost exclusively the α1-tubulin isotype. In contrast, the membrane associated sub-pellicular microtubules (Figs 2, 3) contain both isotypes, α3-tubulin being the major isotype; whilst the flagellar axonemal microtubules are almost completely devoid of the α1-tubulin isotype. This pattern of generation of a distinct α-tubulin isotype *via* acetylation, a post-translational modification, is very similar to the patterns discovered in other eukaryotic microbes such as *Chlamydomonas reinhardtii*, *Polytomella agilis* (McKeithan *et al.* 1983) and *Crithidia fasciculata* (Russell *et al.* 1984; Russell & Gull, 1984). The role of the acetylated α3-tubulin isotype is still rather unclear. The post-translational modification is reversible in that the modification occurs either just before or just after the tubulin is deposited in the flagellar axonemal microtubules (L'Hernault &

K. Gull and others

Rosenbaum, 1983; Russell & Gull, 1984) and is deacetylated upon resorption of the flagellum (L'Hernault & Rosenbaum, 1985). Our studies with *T. brucei*, together with those recently reported by Piperno & Fuller (1985), argue that acetylation is not

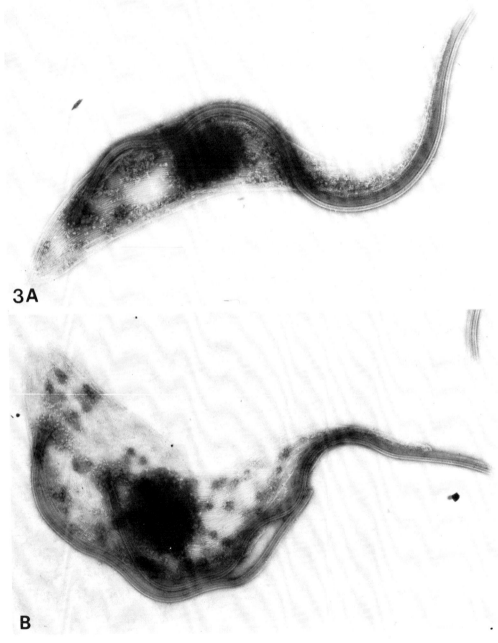

Fig. 3. TEM of negatively stained cytoskeletons of *T. brucei* showing a cell at an early stage in the cell cycle (A), and one at a later stage with one mature and one daughter flagellum (B). The arrangement of the sub-pellicular microtubules is seen in both cells.

a specific marker for flagellar tubulin. Rather, the production of tubulin isotypes by acetylation may provide a marker for stable microtubules. This is suggested by the very different ratios of $\alpha 1$ to $\alpha 3$-tubulin in the various trypanosomal microtubule types. The cytoplasmic pool of soluble tubulin contains very little or no $\alpha 3$-tubulin isotype, while the very stable microtubules of the flagellum axoneme contain almost exclusively $\alpha 3$-tubulin. The microtubules of the membrane-associated sub-pellicular array, which are of intermediate stability, are also intermediate in their content of $\alpha 3$-tubulin. It is clear that possession of the acetylated α-tubulin is not restricted to the microtubules of the flagellum and so appears not to be linked with the production of doublet (axonemal) or triplet (basal body) microtubules. The suggestion of a link with the more stable microtubules in a cell involves an experimental, operational definition of microtubule stability (resistance to drugs, etc.). There is, at present, no direct evidence to suggest a *causal* relationship between acetylation of α-tubulin and the production of stable microtubules. The true function of α-tubulin acetylation in the cell may well have nothing to do with inherent microtubule stability itself, but may just correlate with this observed property of these particular subsets of microtubules. However, it is clear that this particular modification occurs in many cells and, moreover, has an intimate association with the dynamics of microtubule polymerization in the cell.

Tyrosinated α-tubulin

Barra *et al.* (1973) first reported the post-translational addition of tyrosine to a brain protein that was subsequently identified as α-tubulin. This modification of what is now known to be the C-terminus of α-tubulin has been shown to occur in a number of cells, but is not the primary post-translational event in this complex scenario. Cloning and sequencing of α-tubulin genes and cDNAs has revealed that most α-tubulin polypeptides are translated with a tyrosine as their C-terminal amino acid (Tyr-tubulin; Cleveland & Sullivan, 1985). *In vivo* the initial post-translational modification is the removal of this tyrosine by a specific carboxy peptidase (Agarana *et al.* 1978), so exposing the penultimate glutamic acid residue (Glu-tubulin). It appears likely that this reaction occurs preferentially, whilst the α-tubulin is in a microtubule (Thompson, 1982; Kumar & Flavin, 1981). Such detyrosinated α-tubulin can then act as a substrate for a cytoplasmic tubulin tyrosine ligase, which restores a tyrosine residue to the C-terminus of the α-tubulin polypeptide (Raybin & Flavin, 1975, 1977; Thompson, 1982; Flavin & Murofushi, 1984). Recently, the presence of this α-tubulin modification cycle has been demonstrated in *T. brucei* (Stieger *et al.* 1984) by *in vivo* labelling with [^{3}H]tyrosine under conditions of stringent inhibition of protein synthesis. We have recently extended this initial observation by studying the pattern of radiolabelled products from such an experiment using two-dimensional gel electrophoresis. In the presence of protein synthesis inhibitors the incorporation of [^{3}H]tyrosine into tubulin reaches a plateau after 2 h. When a lysate from cells that have been labelled under these conditions is analysed by two-dimensional gel electrophoresis and fluorography, it is clear that radioactive tyrosine is incorporated exclusively into α-tubulin. Both $\alpha 1$ and $\alpha 3$-tubulins (see above) are labelled. Knowledge of the distribution of these tubulin isotypes in *T. brucei* cells and the results of various kinetics experiments suggest that it is the α1-tubulin isotype that is the true substrate for the tubulin tyrosine ligase. The soluble α1-tubulin then being incorporated into a cellular microtubule during the course of the experiment (being acetylated in the process) and so appearing as the α3 electromorph on two-dimensional gels. The specificity of the *in vivo* labelling experiments for α-tubulin is not a trivial result since the *T. brucei* β-tubulin gene is unusual in that it also encodes a tyrosine as the C-terminal amino acid of the β-tubulin polypeptide. Thus, the absence of labelling of the β-tubulin during these *in vivo* experiments shows that the tubulin tyrosine ligase-catalysed modification in *T. brucei* is, as with other organisms, restricted to α-tubulin. Unlike the acetylation described earlier, the detyrosination–tyrosination cycle does not result in shifts of two-dimensional gel coordinates that correlate with precursor–product species. However, it is clear that this α-tubulin terminal tyrosine cycle does operate within the *T. brucei* cell to produce α-tubulin isotypes with distinct cellular localizations.

Previous work with polyclonal antibodies raised against synthetic peptides representing the tyrosinated and detyrosinated C-terminus of α-tubulin have led to the general conclusion that these two α-tubulin isotypes may be differentially distributed amongst the individual microtubules of interphase and mitotic cells (Gundersen *et al.* 1984; Gundersen & Bulinski, 1986). In our studies we have used a monoclonal antibody (YL1/2) that is specific for tyrosinated tubulin (Kilmartin *et al.* 1982; Wehland *et al.* 1984) and have used immunofluorescence microscopy to reveal the changes in distribution of Tyr-tubulin during the *T. brucei* cell cycle. A distinct advantage of using *T. brucei* in these studies is that the position of a particular individual cell in the cell cycle can be estimated with reasonable accuracy, since there are particular structural landmarks that occur with distinct cell cycle timings. These landmarks include cell size and shape, the presence or absence of a daughter flagellum, the length of any such flagellum (Fig. 3), the position of the basal bodies and the position (and segregation) of nuclear and kinetoplast DNA as visualized by the intercalating dye, DAPI (4′6,diamidino-2-phenylindole). When trypanosome cells are viewed by immunofluorescence microscopy using an anti-β-tubulin monoclonal antibody, or an anti-α-tubulin monoclonal antibody whose epitope is not subject to post-translational modification, then the cell body is seen to be intensely fluorescent due to the massive numbers and homogeneous distribution of the subpellicular microtubules. The flagellum is seen as a wavy line attached to the side of the cell body. However, immunofluorescent staining with the YL1/2 antibody (Tyr-tubulin-specific) reveals a completely different pattern that is modulated throughout the cell cycle. The markers outlined above permit changes in the cell-cycle-related staining to be deduced from populations of asynchronous cells. Cells at the start of the cell cycle exhibit bright fluorescence at the posterior third of the cell; the flagellum is not stained. As the cell cycle progresses, a short daughter flagellum forms on the new basal body and this new flagellum stains very brightly with YL1/2. This bright fluorescence of the daughter flagellum is maintained as it continues to elongate, as is this generally brighter fluorescence of the posterior portion of the cell.

This pattern of fluorescence then changes, concomitant with separation of the kinetoplast DNA (as seen by DAPI double staining) and the separation of basal bodies. At this time the intensity of staining of the posterior third of the cell is reduced and the very bright staining of the daughter flagellum is lost almost completely. This point at which the daughter flagellum loses its ability to be recognized by the YL1/2 antibody correlates well with the point at which it has grown to its full length. Interestingly, the basal bodies of the trypanosome cell stain brightly with the YL1/2 antibody at all times during the cell cycle.

The staining pattern of the *T. brucei* flagellum permits a modulation of the tyrosination cycle to be observed in microtubules of known lineage and strongly suggests that the tyrosinated state of α-tubulin is a marker of newly formed microtubules. According to this view, the pool of soluble tubulin consists of the primary translation products containing the C-terminal tyrosine coded for by the mRNA, as well as the 'recycled' Glu-tubulin to which a new terminal tyrosine has been added by the tubulin tyrosine ligase. Tyr-tubulin is the species that actually participates in the polymerization into a microtubule, and once incorporated into the polymer it can be detyrosinated by the action of the microtubule-associated tubulin carboxy peptidase. The amount of Glu-tubulin that accumulates in a particular microtubule is dependent upon the residence time of subunits in that microtubule and such 'old' microtubules can be expected to possess an elevated proportion of Glu-tubulin.

The actual function of this unique detyrosination–tyrosination cycle as well as the α-tubulin acetylation, described earlier, remains poorly understood. However, our studies of these two post-translational modifications in *T. brucei* have revealed how each modification can produce particular tubulin isotypes whose existence and distribution are intimately linked to the formation of the precisely ordered microtubule cytoskeleton of this organism. We feel that the cytoskeleton of this simple, yet important, microorganism represents a highly suitable system for further investigations of tubulin isotype diversity and function.

We thank John Kilmartin for generous gifts of monoclonal antibody.

The work described in this paper was supported by grants to K.G. from the Science and Engineering Research Council, the Medical Research Council and the WHO/World Bank Special Programme for Research and Training in Tropical Diseases. The carrot tubulin project was supported by an SERC CASE award to K.G. and to Dr C. W. Lloyd, Norwich.

REFERENCES

AGARANA, C. E., BARRA, H. S. & CAPUTTO, R. (1978). Release of [^{14}C]tyrosine from tubulinyl-[^{14}C]-tyrosine by brain extract. Separation of a carboxy peptidase from tubulin tyrosine ligase. *Molec. Cell. Biochem.* **19**, 17–22.

BARRA, H. S., RODRIQUEZ, J. A., ARCE, C. A. & CAPUTTO, R. (1973). A soluble preparation from rat brain that incorporates into its own proteins [^{14}C]-arginine by a ribonuclease-sensitive system and [^{14}C]-tyrosine by a ribonuclease-insensitive system. *J. Neurochem.* **20**, 97–108.

BIRKETT, C. R., FOSTER, K. E. & GULL, K. (1985). Evolution and patterns of expression of the *Physarum* multi-tubulin family analysed by the use of monoclonal antibodies. In *Molecular Genetics of the Filamentous Fungi* (ed. W. Timberlake). New York: A. R. Liss.

BURLAND, T. G., GULL, K., SCHEDL, T., BOSTON, R. S. & DOVE, W. F. (1983). Cell type-dependent expression of tubulins in *Physarum*. *J. Cell Biol.* **97**, 1852–1859.

BURLAND, T. G., SCHEDL, T., GULL, K. & DOVE, W. F. (1984). Genetic analysis of resistance to benzimidazoles in *Physarum*: Differential expression of β tubulin genes. *Genetics* **108**, 123–141.

CLAYTON, L., QUINLAN, R. A, ROOBOL, A., POGSON, C. I. & GULL, K. (1980). A comparison of tubulins from mammalian brain and *Physarum polycephalum* using SDS polyacrylamide gel electrophoresis and peptide mapping. *FEBS Lett.* **115**, 301–305.

CLEVELAND, D. W. & SULLIVAN, K. F. (1985). Molecular biology and genetics of tubulin. *A. Rev. Biochem.* **54**, 331–365.

COWAN, N. J. & DUDLEY, L. (1983). Tubulin isotypes and the multigene tubulin families. *Int. Rev. Cytol.* **85**, 147–173.

FLAVIN, M. & MUROFUSHI, H. (1984). *Meth. Enzym.* **106**, 223–237.

GULL, K., BIRKETT, C. R., BLINDT, A. R., DEE, J., FOSTER, K. E. & PAUL, E. C. A. (1985). Expression of a multi-tubulin family and the *in vivo* assembly of microtubular organelles in *Physarum polycephalum*. In *Microtubules and Microtubule Inhibitors* (ed. M. De Brabander & J. De Mey). Amsterdam: Elsevier.

GUNDERSEN, G. G. & BULINSKI, J. C. (1986). Distribution of tyrosinated and nontyrosinated α-tubulin during mitosis. *J. Cell Biol.* **102**, 1118–1126.

GUNDERSEN, G. G., KALNOSKI, M. H. & BULINSKI, J. C. (1984). Distinct populations of mictrotubules: Tyrosinated and Nontyrosinated alpha tubulin are distributed differently *in vivo. Cell* **38**, 779–789.

HUSSEY, P. J. & GULL, K. (1985). Multiple isotypes of α and β tubulin in the plant *Phaseolus vulgaris*. *FEBS Lett.* **181**, 113–118.

IMBODEN, M., BLUM, B., DELANGE, T., BRAUN, R. & SEEBECK, T. (1986). Tubulin mRNAs of *Trypanosoma brucei*. *J. molec. Biol.* **188**, 393–402.

KILMARTIN, J. V., WRIGHT, B. & MILSTEIN, C. (1982). Rat monoclonal antitubulin antibodies derived using a new non-secreting rat cell line. *J. Cell Biol.* **93**, 576–582.

KUMAR, N. & FLAVIN, M. (1981). Preferential action of a brain detyrosinating carboxypeptidase on polymerised tubulin. *J. biol. Chem.* **256**, 7678–7686.

LAI, E. Y., REMILLARD, S. P. & FULTON, C. (1984). Tubulin and actin; Yin-Yang gene expression during *Naegleria* differentiation. In *Molecular Biology of the Cytoskeleton* (ed. G. G. Borisy, D. W. Cleveland & D. B. Murphy). New York: Cold Spring Harbor Laboratory Press.

LANDFEAR, S. M., MCMAHON-PRATT, D. & WIRTH, D. F. (1983). Tandem arrangement of tubulin genes in the protozoan parasite *Leishmania enriettii*. *Molec. Cell. Biol.* **3**, 1070–1076.

LEE, M. G. S., LEWIS, S. A., WILDE, C. D. & COWAN, N. J. (1983). Evolutionary history of a multi-gene family: an expressed human β tubulin gene and three processed pseudogenes. *Cell* **33**, 477–487.

L'HERNAULT, S. W. & ROSENBAUM, J. L. (1983). *Chlamydomonas* alpha tubulin is post-translationally modified in the flagella during flagellar assembly. *J. Cell Biol.* **97**, 256–263.

L'HERNAULT, S. W. & ROSENBAUM, J. L. (1985). *Chlamydomonas* α-tubulin is post-translationally modified by acetylation on the ε-amino group of a lysine. *Biochemistry* **24**, 473–478.

MAY, G. S., GAMBINO, J., WEATHERBEE, J. A. & MORRIS, N. R. (1985). Identification and functional analysis of β tubulin genes by site specific integrative transformation in *Aspergillus nidulans*. *J. Cell Biol.* **101**, 712–719.

MCKEITHAN, T. W., LEFEBVRE, P. A., SILFLOW, C. D. & ROSENBAUM, J. L. (1983). Multiple forms of tubulin in *Polytomella* and *Chlamydomonas*: evidence for a precursor of flagellar α tubulin. *J. Cell Biol.* **96**, 1056–1063.

PIPERNO, G. & FULLER, M. T. (1985). Monoclonal antibodies specific for an acetylated form of α tubulin recognise the antigen in cilia and flagella from a variety of organisms. *J. Cell Biol.* **101**, 2085–2094.

QUINLAN, R. A., ROOBOL, A., POGSON, C. I. & GULL, K. (1981). A correlation between *in vivo* and *in vitro* effects of the microtubule inhibitors colchicine, parbendazole and nocodazole on myxamoebae of *Physarum polycephalum*. *J. gen. Microbiol.* **122**, 1–6.

RAFF, E. C. (1984). Genetics of microtubule systems. *J. Cell Biol.* **98**, 1–10.

RAFF, E. C. & FULLER, M. T. (1984). Genetic analysis of microtubule function in *Drosophila*. In *Molecular Biology of the Cytoskeleton* (ed. G. G. Borisy, D. W. Cleveland & D. B. Murphy). New York: Cold Spring Harbor Laboratory Press.

RAYBIN, D. & FLAVIN, M. (1975). An enzyme tyrosylating alpha tubulin and its role in microtubule assembly. *Biochem. biophys. Res. Commun.* **60**, 1384–1390.

ROOBOL, A., WILCOX, M., PAUL, E. C. A. & GULL, K. (1984). Identification of tubulin isoforms in the plasmodium of *Physarum polycephalum* by *in vitro* microtubule assembly. *Eur. J. Cell Biol.* **33**, 24–28.

RUSSELL, D. G. & GULL, K. (1984). Flagellar regeneration of the trypanosome *Crithidia fasciculata* involves post-translational modification of cytoplasmic alpha tubulin. *Molec. Cell. Biol.* **4**, 1182–1185.

RUSSELL, D. G., MILLER, D. & GULL, K. (1984). Tubulin heterogeneity in the trypanosome *Crithidia fasciculata. Molec. Cell. Biol.* **4**, 779–790.

SCHEDL, T., OWENS, J., DOVE, W. F. & BURLAND, T. G. (1984). Genetics of the tubulin gene families of *Physarum. Genetics* **108**, 143–164.

SEEBECK, T., WHITTACKER, P. A., IMOBODEN, M., HARDMAN, N. & BRAUN, R. (1983). Tubulin genes of *Trypanosoma brucei*: A tightly clustered family of alternating genes. *Proc. natn. Acad. Sci.* **80**, 4634–4638.

STIEGER, J., WYLER, T. & SEEBECK, T. (1984). Partial purification and characterisation of microtubular protein from *Trypanosoma brucei. J. biol. Chem.* **259**, 4596–4602.

THOMASHOW, L. S., MILHAUSEN, M., RUTTER, W. J. & AGABIAN, N. (1983). Tubulin genes are tandemly linked and clustered in the genome of *Trypanosoma brucei. Cell* **32**, 35–43.

THOMPSON, W. C. (1982). The cyclic tyrosination/detyrosination of alpha tubulin. *Meth. Cell Biol.* **24**, 235–255.

TODA, T., ADACHI, Y., HIRAOKA, Y. & YANAGIDA, M. (1984). Identification of the pleiotropic cell division gene *NDA2* as one of the two different α tubulin genes in *Schizosaccharomyces pombe. Cell* **37**, 233–242.

WEATHERBEE, J. A. & MORRIS, N. R. (1984). *Aspergillus* contains multiple tubulin genes. *J. biol. Chem.* **259**, 15 452–15 459.

WEHLAND, J., SCHRODER, H. C. & WEBER, K. (1984). Amino acid sequence requirements in the epitope recognised by the α-tubulin specific monoclonal antibody YL1/2. *EMBO J.* **3**, 1295–1300.

YOUNGBLOM, H., SCHLOSS, J. A. & SILFLOW, C. D. (1984). The two β tubulin genes of *Chlamydomonas reinhardtii* code for identical proteins. *Molec. Cell. Biol.* **4**, 2686–2696.

J. Cell Sci. Suppl. 5, 257–271 (1986)
Printed in Great Britain © The Company of Biologists Limited 1986

MUTATIONS AFFECTING MICROTUBULE STRUCTURE IN *CAENORHABDITIS ELEGANS*

MARTIN CHALFIE[1,*], ELLEN DEAN[1], EVELYN REILLY[1], KAY BUCK[2,†] AND J. NICHOL THOMSON[2]

[1]*Department of Biological Sciences, Columbia University, New York, NY 10027, USA*
[2]*MRC Laboratory of Molecular Biology, Hills Road, Cambridge CB2 2QH, UK*

SUMMARY

Three types of microtubules are seen in the neuronal processes of the nematode *Caenorhabditis elegans*. Single cytoplasmic microtubules of most neurones have 11 protofilaments whereas those of six touch receptor cells have 15 protofilaments. The axonemes of sensory cilia have nine outer doublets with a variable number (up to seven) of singlet microtubules. Mutations in 11 genes affect the appearance of these microtubules.

INTRODUCTION

More is known about the cellular development and structure of the nematode *Caenorhabditis elegans* than about that of any other multicellular organism. For example, White *et al.* (1986) have described the detailed structure (position, shape and connections) of each of the animal's 302 neurones. The development and structure of the *C. elegans* neurones are remarkably constant from animal to animal, but can be disrupted by mutation (for reviews, see Chalfie, 1984; Sternberg & Horvitz, 1984). Detailed examination of *C. elegans* neurones has led to the observation of multiple forms of neuroneal microtubules. In this paper we describe these different microtubule forms and discuss insight that has been gained into their function from observations on a number of *C. elegans* mutants.

STRUCTURE OF NEURONEAL MICROTUBULES IN *C. ELEGANS*

Three types of neuroneal microtubules have been described in *C. elegans*. The most common form, found in almost all neurones, is a cytoplasmic microtubule that is indistinguishable from cytoplasmic microtubules in other *C. elegans* cells. These *C. elegans* microtubules differ from those commonly found in other eucaryotes in that they contain 11, rather than 13, protofilaments (Fig. 1; Chalfie & Thomson, 1982).

The second most prevalent microtubule structure is that of the axonemes of sensory cilia (Fig. 2). Fifty neurones in the hermaphrodite contain these structures (White *et al.* 1986), which usually consist of nine outer doublet microtubules and a variable number (up to seven have been seen) of inner singlet microtubules (Ward

* Author to whom reprint requests should be addressed.
† Deceased.

et al. 1975; Ware *et al.* 1975; Perkins *et al.* 1986). The doublet microtubules have A subfibres with 13 protofilaments and B subfibres with 11 protofilaments; the singlet microtubules have 11 protofilaments (Chalfie & Thomson, 1982). Dynein arms, nexin links and radial spokes are not seen.

Perkins *et al.* (1986) have described the sensory cilia in great detail. The axonemes in adults have three structurally identifiable regions (Fig. 3). In the most proximal region, the transition zone, the doublets are attached to the plasma membrane by Y-shaped links; the singlet microtubules are attached to the inside of a central cylinder that also links the doublets. There is no associated basal body in adults. In the next axonemal region, the middle segment, the diameter of the ring of doublets is larger, and the doublets are directly associated with the plasma membrane. The singlets appear unattached in the centre of the axoneme. In the most distal, or terminal, segment there are no doublets; only the A subfibres and the singlets remain. Perkins *et al.* (1986) noted differences among the axonemes of different neurones. In some axonemes only four or five of the doublets extend through the length of the cilium; in others the doublets are filled with electron-dense material. Still other axonemes are associated with supernumerary microtubules or striated rootlets. The significance of these structural differences and of the variable number of inner singlet microtubules is not known.

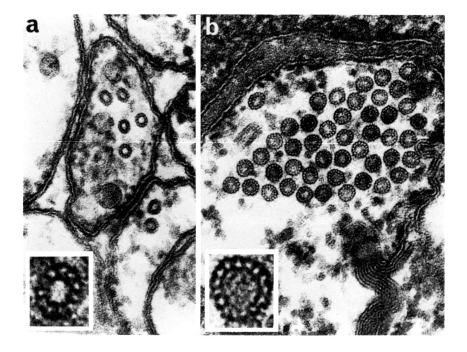

Fig. 1. Electron micrographs of cytoplasmic microtubules in *C. elegans*. Preparations were stained with tannic acid to reveal the protofilament structure of microtubules in a ventral cord neurone (a) and a touch cell (b). ×160 000. Inset, ×600 000. (Reproduced from *J. Cell Biol.* **93**, 15–23, by copyright permission of The Rockefeller University Press.)

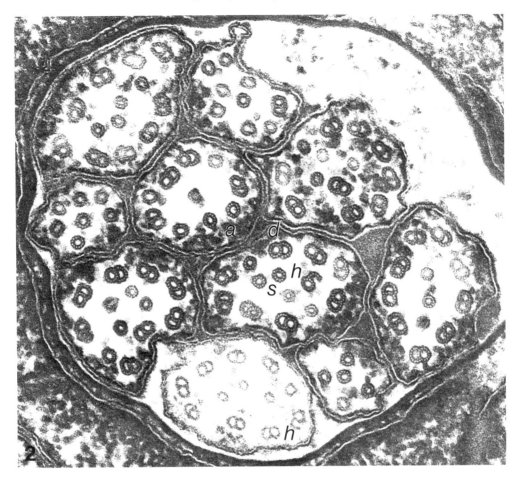

Fig. 2. Tannic acid fixation of the ciliated endings of amphidial neurones. These neurones are putative chemosensory cells in the head of the nematode. Doublet (d) and singlet (s) microtubules as well as microtubules with hooks (h) are seen. These latter microtubules are doublets that are in the process of losing their B subfibres. The resulting microtubule after the loss of the B subfibre has 13 protofilaments (a). ×270000. (Reproduced from *J. Cell Biol.* **93**, 15–23, by copyright permission of The Rockefeller University Press.)

The third microtubule form, a cytoplasmic microtubule with 15 protofilaments, is found only in the six neurones that serve as receptors for gentle touch (Fig. 1; Chalfie & Thomson, 1982). Only rarely (about one in 450) is an 11-protofilament microtubule seen in the processes of these touch cells. The 15-protofilament microtubules differ from the 11-protofilament microtubules in several respects: (1) they are less cold-labile; (2) they are stable during osmium fixation; (3) they are differentially sensitive to anti-microtubule drugs; and (4) they are differentially disrupted by mutation (see below). Moreover, the arrangement of the 15-protofilament microtubules within the cell is more orderly than that of the 11-protofilament microtubules. The larger microtubules form bundles in which each microtubule maintains its relative position. The smaller microtubules found in other *C. elegans* neurones do not associate with one another and do not maintain a set spatial relationship with each other.

Because of their orderly arrangement, the 15-protofilament microtubules can be followed easily in electron micrographs of serial sections. These microtubules do not span the entire length of the neuroneal process: the touch cell process is $400-500\,\mu m$ long whereas the microtubules are $10-20\,\mu m$ long (Chalfie & Thomson, 1982). (The 11-protofilament microtubules are also short compared to the length of the neuroneal processes that contain them.) We have postulated that such short microtubules could slide relative to each other and thus permit stable microtubule organization in the face of changes in cell length (such as those that probably occur during the sinusoidal bending of the animal). Interestingly, the end of the 15-protofilament microtubule that is distal to the cell body is always found on the outside of the bundle of microtubules; the proximal end is preferentially found within the bundle. The proximal and distal ends also differ structurally (Fig. 4). The significance of the closeness of the distal microtubule end to the plasma membrane is not known.

DRUGS AFFECTING NEURONAL MICROTUBULES IN *C. ELEGANS*

A number of anti-mitotic drugs have been tested on *C. elegans*. A striking effect is seen when animals are grown in the presence of benomyl or other benzamidazole carbamates. Such animals are paralysed, contorted, and grow slowly (Fig. 5; Chalfie & Thomson, 1982). The ventral nerve cords of these animals have fewer neuroneal processes than those of untreated animals. Presumably the drugs interfere with microtubule stability and, thereby, prevent process extension. Experiments with benomyl-resistant mutants (see below) support this view. In contrast, the 15-proto-filament microtubules of the touch cells appear to be unaffected by benomyl at concentrations that cause great reduction in process outgrowth in the ventral cord neurones.

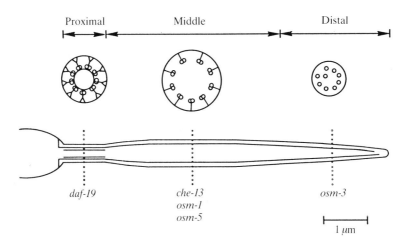

Fig. 3. Diagram of a *C. elegans* cilium. Cross-sections at three intervals are shown. See the text for details. Dotted lines indicate the extent of axonemes in various mutants.

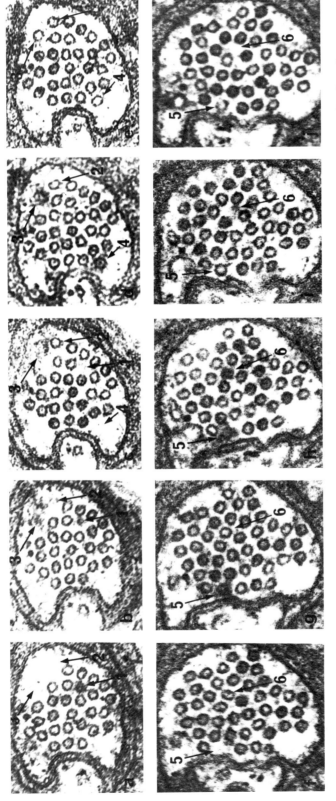

Fig. 4. Arrangement of microtubules in the touch cell process. Two sets (a–e and f–k) of serial sections are shown, anterior (distal) to the right. Distal ends of the microtubules (2–5) are always found on the outside of the microtubule bundle and are often associated with diffusely staining material that appears to contact the plasma membrane. Proximal ends of the microtubules (1 and 6) are found preferentially within the microtubule bundle and often have a filled appearance. ×116 000. (Reproduced from *J. Cell Biol.* **93**, 15–23, by copyright permission of The Rockefeller University Press.)

Colchicine has a strikingly different effect on *C. elegans*. Animals grown in 0·5–2·0 mM-colchicine are completely touch insensitive and their touch cells lack microtubules, yet these animals develop at the same rate and have as many progeny as untreated controls (Chalfie & Thomson, 1982). (In these experiments, animals were exposed to the drug after they hatched from the egg shell, which is after the touch cell processes have reached their targets.) At higher concentrations of colchicine, progeny counts are reduced, but uncoordination like that associated with benomyl-sensitivity is not seen. Thus, the touch cell microtubules appear to be selectively sensitive to colchicine, at least at lower concentrations of the drug. Podophyllotoxin, a drug thought to have the same tubulin binding site as colchicine (Wilson & Bryan, 1974), has a similar (but more reversible) effect on touch sensitivity and microtubule structure to that of colchicine; lumicolchicine, the ultraviolet light-inactivated derivative of colchicine, has none of these effects (Chalfie & Thomson, 1982).

MUTATIONS AFFECTING MICROTUBULE STRUCTURE AND FUNCTION

Mutations affecting sensory cilia

The functions of the neurones with ciliated dendrites are unknown, but the pattern of synapses they make suggests that they are sensory receptors (White *et al.* 1986). A number of the cells have cilia that project through the cuticle and are thus in

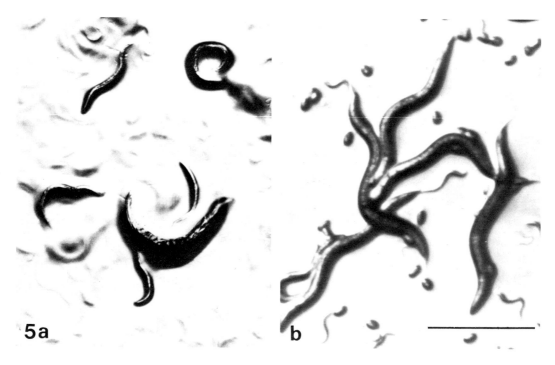

5a   **b**

Fig. 5. Appearance of wild-type animals (a) and *ben-1* mutants (b) grown in the presence of 7 μM-benomyl. Bar, 500 μm.

Table 1. *Genes affecting microtubule structure*

Gene	Phenotype
daf-19	No sensory cilia
che-13 *osm-1* *osm-5* *osm-6*	Transition zone normal; axoneme shortened (*osm-6* phenotype less severe)
osm-3	Terminal segment of axoneme missing in amphidial neurones
cat-6	Supernumerary microtubules of mechanosensory cilia extend the entire length of the axoneme
mec-7	Touch cells lack 15-protofilament microtubules
mec-12	Reduced touch cell processes; fewer microtubules
ben-1	Benzimidazole carbamates resistance; probable β-tubulin defect
unc-33	Supernumerary microtubules in sensory processes, some with abnormal structures

contact with the external environment. These cells are presumed to be chemosensory receptors (Ward *et al.* 1975; Ware *et al.* 1975). Other cells have cilia that are embedded in or near the cuticle and are thought to be mechanosensory receptors.

Mutations affecting cilia have been identified in screens for animals with defects in behaviours such as chemotaxis (Dusenbery *et al.* 1975; Lewis & Hodgkin, 1977), osmotic avoidance (Culotti & Russell, 1978), dauer larvae formation (Riddle *et al.* 1981; Albert *et al.* 1981 (the dauer is an alternative third larval stage that arises during periods of starvation; it can be initiated by a pheromone released by the worm; Golden & Riddle, 1982)), and male-mating (Hodgkin, 1983). Mutants isolated by one of these schemes are often defective in more than one type of behaviour (Lewis & Hodgkin, 1977; Dusenbery, 1980; Perkins *et al.* 1986). For example, mutations in the gene *che-3* have been identified in screens for chemotaxic and osmotic avoidance mutants, and mutations in *daf-10* have been found in screens for chemotactic and dauer-formation mutants (Perkins *et al.* 1986). Such pleiotropic phenotypes could result from defects in cells that are required for several types of behaviour or from defects in features shared by these cells, such as the sensory cilia.

Hedgecock *et al.* (1985) have found that some of the presumed chemosensory cells can be stained when living animals are exposed to fluorescein isothiocyanate (FITC). FITC vital staining permits the visualization of the entire cell including the cell body and axon. Using this procedure, these workers examined previously isolated behavioural mutants for abnormal staining patterns and screened for additional mutants (Perkins *et al.* 1986). The new mutants with FITC-staining abnormalities were also defective in chemotaxis. In their examination of mutants with FITC-labelling defects Perkins *et al.* (1986) identified seven genes required for the normal structure of microtubules of the cilia (Table 1; Fig. 3). The most pronounced effect is seen in *daf-19* mutants: all sensory dendrites lack cilia although some centriole-like structures remain. Mutations in three other genes (*che-13*, *osm-1*, *osm-5*) result in shortened axonemes with normal transition zones but little else. It is intriguing that the axonemes of one set of sensory neurones, the IL2 cells, which never have nine doublets in wild-type adults, have nine doublets in these mutants. Ectopic doublets are often seen in the sensory dendrites of many cells of these animals. Animals with defects in the gene *osm-6* show many of the same abnormalities but to a lesser degree, i.e. their axonemes are not as severely shortened. Even less severe is the abnormality in *osm-3* mutants. The axonemes in these animals are normal except that they are missing the terminal segment with its A subfibres and singlet microtubules. This defect is more selectively expressed than the above mutations: the only sensory cells affected in the heads of *osm-3* animals are in a pair of sensilla, the amphids. The action of the gene *cat-6* is also selective, as it affects only the supernumerary microtubules seen at the ends of the cilia of the supposed mechanosensory cells CEP and OLL. In these mutants the rods of microtubules and their associated matrix material are not restricted to the end of the axoneme as in wild-type animals but extend through its entire length. Perkins *et al.* (1986) identified two other genes that affect ciliary structure but not the microtubules. In *che-11* mutants there is an accumulation of ground substance amongst the microtubules, and in *che-10* mutants there is the loss of the striated rootlet associated with some of the axonemes (the axonemes, however, appear normal).

Mutations affecting touch cell microtubules

Over 300 mutations in 16 genes have been identified that render *C. elegans* insensitive to gentle touch (Chalfie & Sulston, 1981; M. Chalfie & M. Au, unpublished data). Mutations in two of these genes, *mec-7* and *mec-12*, affect the production of 15-protofilament microtubules normally seen in the touch cells.

The *mec-7* mutations have been the more extensively studied (Chalfie & Thomson, 1982; M. Chalfie, unpublished). Most of the 33 *mec-7* mutations are recessive, but some express a dominant or semidominant phenotype with regard to touch sensitivity. Some alleles of *mec-7* are dominant at high temperature (25 °C) but recessive at low temperature (15 °C). (This temperature-sensitive dominance is also seen for some alleles of the *mec-12* and *ben-1* genes described below.) The temperature-sensitive period exhibited by these mutants extends from hatching to the last larval stage. During this time the microtubules in the touch cells, which have already reached their targets and formed functional synapses, increase in length and number.

mec-7 mutants exhibit normal touch cell processes, but these processes are devoid of 15-protofilament microtubules. These are replaced by a smaller number of 11-protofilament microtubules (Fig. 6). (Normally there are about 450 15-protofilament microtubules and very few, if any, 11-protofilament microtubules in touch cell processes of adults; in the touch cells of the *mec-7* mutants there are about 100 11-protofilament microtubules.) Thus *mec-7* appears to be required for the presence of 15-protofilament microtubules in the touch cells. Because the microtubule structure is changed and the temperature-sensitive period for *mec-7* corresponds to the time at which the microtubule number increases in the touch cells, we proposed the hypothesis that the *mec-7* product may be needed to alter the nucleation sites of touch cell microtubules so that 15-protofilament structures are made (Chalfie &

Thomson, 1982). (The protofilament number of microtubules polymerized *in vitro* is dependent on nucleation material, whether it is the A subfibres of flagellar axonemes (Scheele *et al.* 1982) or centrosomes (Evans *et al.* 1985).)

The 11-protofilament microtubules found in the *mec-7* touch cells have unusual drug sensitivities. In the mutants, both colchicine and benomyl prevent the outgrowth of the touch cell process, whereas only colchicine affects the microtubules in wild-type touch cells. The colchicine effect signifies that a sensitive component is retained in the touch cells despite the change in microtubule structure. The benomyl effect is difficult to interpret as it could mean that the touch cell microtubules are sensitive to the drug because they have the 11-protofilament structure or because they utilize a drug-sensitive component in compensation for the *mec-7* defect.

Mutations in the *mec-12* gene also affect touch sensitivity and the touch cell microtubules (Chalfie & Sulston, 1981; M. Chalfie & K. Buck, unpublished data). Phenotypes vary in an allele-specific manner. Some alleles are recessive and result in a slight loss of touch sensitivity; others are recessive and result in complete touch insensitivity; still others are semidominant and also produce complete touch insensitivity. In animals displaying the weakest phenotype, the touch cell microtubules

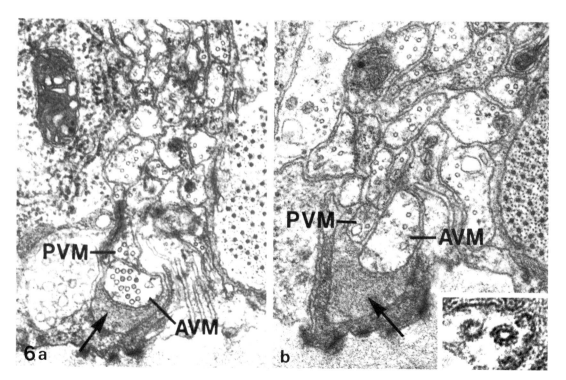

Fig. 6. Touch cell microtubules in wild-type (a) and *mec-7* (b) animals. The ventral cord touch cells (AVM and PVM) in *mec-7* mutants have microtubules that appear the same as those in other ventral cord neurones. These unusual microtubules in the mutant touch cells have 11 protofilaments (inset). The arrows point to the extracellular material that is characteristic of the touch cells. ×60 000. Inset, ×300 000. (Reproduced from *J. Cell Biol.* **93**, 15–23, by copyright permission of The Rockefeller University Press.)

look normal, i.e. they have the same diameter as the 15-protofilament microtubules do in the wild type. Electron micrographs of serial sections of anterior touch cells in these animals, however, reveal that the cells are incomplete. In the wild type, the touch cells have a long anteriorly directed process that has a distal branch. In these mutants, this terminal branch is missing. In the more severe recessive mutants, the processes have a reduced number of microtubules, although the microtubules appear to be of the correct size. The touch cell processes of the semidominant mutants are considerably truncated and are severely depleted of microtubules. Because an extreme loss of microtubules is seen before the reduction in the length of the axonal process, it is possible that the *mec-12* product is necessary for the proper production of the touch cell microtubules and that the shortening of the process is a secondary consequence.

Observations on *mec-7* and *mec-12* mutants and on animals treated with anti-microtubule drugs suggest that the 15-protofilament microtubules of the touch cells serve at least two functions: process elongation, where protofilament number is not particularly important, and sensory transduction, where the 15-protofilament structure appears to be crucial. We have hypothesized that one role of the large microtubules might result from their ability to associate to form a bundle of microtubules; this bundle could provide a rigid cytoskeleton against which the cell might be deformed by the touch stimulus (Chalfie & Thomson, 1982). Fifteen-protofilament microtubules in cells of other organisms also appear to be arranged in bundles (Burton *et al.* 1975; Nagano & Suzuki, 1975; see also Eichenlaub-Ritter & Tucker, 1984). Perhaps the 15-protofilament structure facilitates crosslinking among the microtubules.

Mutations affecting other cytoplasmic microtubules

Benomyl-induced paralysis provides a convenient basis for the isolation of resistant mutants. Benomyl resistance, as shown in a number of lower eucaryotes (Sheir-Neiss *et al.* 1978; Neff *et al.* 1983; Burland *et al.* 1984; Schedl *et al.* 1984), can result from mutations in genes for β-tubulin. As indicated below, this appears to be the case in *C. elegans*. We have identified 23 non-complementing mutations that convey benomyl resistance (M. Chalfie, E. Dean & E. Reilly, unpublished data). The resistant mutants were identified by their wild-type movement among the F2 progeny of mutagenized nematodes that were grown in 7 μM-benomyl (see Fig. 5). All 23 mutations map to the same locus, *ben-1*, on the third chromosome. Nineteen of the mutations were isolated after mutagenesis with ethyl methanesulphonate (EMS; Brenner, 1974) and arose at a frequency of 10^{-3} (this is similar to the average mutation rate for *C. elegans* genes; Brenner, 1974; Greenwald & Horvitz, 1980). Three other *ben-1* mutations arose spontaneously in the strain TR679 (kindly provided by P. Anderson, University of Wisconsin). This strain produces spontaneous mutations at a high rate; many of these mutations appear to be the result of transpositional events (J. Collins & P. Anderson, personal communication). DNA from all three of the spontaneous *ben-1* mutants shows the same size insert into a restriction fragment that hybridizes to β-tubulin DNA (Fig. 7). Thus, it is likely that *ben-1* codes for a β-tubulin. Interestingly, the *ben-1* mutations, including the insertional mutations, are dominant or semidominant. For most alleles this dominance is temperature dependent, i.e. it is only seen at high temperature (25 °C; complementation tests were done at 15 °C).

Homozygous *ben-1* mutants are extremely resistant to benomyl and other benzamidazole carbamates. For the most severe alleles, the only effect of these drugs is a slight slowing of growth rate at saturating concentrations of the drugs. In the absence of benomyl, the mutants appear wild type. The *ben-1* effect is specific in that the mutants are not resistant to colchicine.

The *ben-1* mutations prevent the effects of benomyl on neuroneal process development. The ventral cord in mutants grown in the presence of benomyl are wild type in appearance. Moreover, the touch cell processes are present when *ben-1 mec-7* double mutants are grown on benomyl.

It has been difficult, however, to determine the null phenotype of the *ben-1* gene. The high frequency of mutation with EMS, the virtual abolition of the response to benomyl and other benzamidazole carbamates, and the occurrence of insertional mutants all suggest that benomyl resistance results from the absence of the *ben-1* β-tubulin. Since *ben-1* mutants resemble wild-type animals, it may be that this β-tubulin is not essential and that other β-tubulin genes are expressed in the same cells as *ben-1* (see Greenwald & Horvitz, 1980, for a discussion of this point). However, the temperature-sensitive dominance displayed by most of the *ben-1* alleles is difficult to interpret. This dominance does not seem to be the result of haplo-insufficiency at the *ben-1* locus, since animals that are heterozygous for a deficiency of the region are not resistant to benomyl at either high or low temperatures. An alternative explanation is that the *ben-1* mutations lead not to a loss of a drug-sensitive β-tubulin but to an overproduction of a benomyl-resistant β-tubulin. A precedent for this interpretation is seen in the *sup-3* gene of *C. elegans*. *sup-3* mutations, which suppress several mutations affecting thick filaments in muscle, arise at high frequency with EMS, and are dominant (Riddle & Brenner, 1978) and increase levels of myosin in their body wall muscle cells (Waterston *et al.* 1982).

Hedgecock *et al.* (1985) have identified a second gene, *unc-33*, that affects cytoplasmic microtubules in nerve cells. Mutations of *unc-33* cause animals to be severely uncoordinated. Numerous neuronal processes are misdirected in these mutants (presumably the underlying cause of the uncoordinated phenotype). Examination of the sensory structures of the head in these mutants revealed an increase in the number of microtubules in the sensory dendrites proximal to the cilia and in the non-neuroneal supporting cells. Moreover, a number of anomolous microtubule forms including large-diameter microtubules, doublet and triplet microtubules, and microtubules with hooks, are present. Such forms are similar to those seen when microtubules are decorated *in situ* with exogenous tubulin (e.g. see Euteneuer & McIntosh, 1980), but the nature of the *unc-33* defect is unknown. The effect of *unc-33* mutations is somewhat specific in that abnormal microtubules are not seen in muscle cells or in the hypodermis of the mutants. It is not known whether neuronal processes of other neurones are similarly affected.

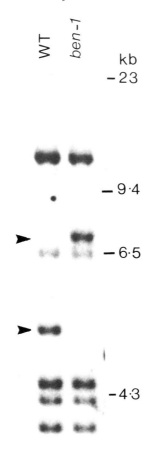

Fig. 7. Southern blot analysis of DNA from wild type (WT) and *ben-1(u347)*. DNA was digested with *Xba*I and probed with β-tubulin DNA generously provided by L. Gremke & J. Culotti, Northwestern University. Animals with the spontaneous *ben-1* mutation *u347* have an insert of approximately 1·7 kb (10^3 base-pairs) into one of the hybridizing bands (arrowheads). Relevant λ *Hin*dIII size standards (kb) are given to the right of the figure.

FUTURE PROSPECTS

All three of the major microtubule forms in *C. elegans* neurones can be altered by mutation. Many of these mutations cause the elimination or reduction of the microtubules, but some, such as those in *unc-33*, appear to cause an increase in microtubules. Mutations in *mec-7* (and similarly *unc-33*), are of particular interest because they apparently cause a change in the number of microtubular proto-filaments. Because the mutations discussed in this paper also affect cell shape and function, their study may help us understand how different microtubule forms are generated and function within different nerve cells.

The characterization of these genes is incomplete; in particular it will be necessary to define more fully the null phenotypes of the genes. Some genes are represented by a single mutant allele. Characterization of additional alleles coupled with exper-iments examining dosage effects of these loci should help to clarify the actions of the various gene products.

The 11 genes listed in Table 1 are probably not the only ones required for proper microtubule structure in *C. elegans*. It is unlikely that additional genes acting selectively on the 15-protofilament microtubules will be identified by the isolation of new touch-insensitive mutants, since that collection of genes appears saturated (Chalfie & Sulston, 1981; M. Chalfie & M. Au, unpublished data). However, the search for genes affecting ciliary microtubules is not complete, and it is likely that additional genes affecting sensory cilia will be identified. Moreover, little has been done to revert any of these strains in order to identify extragenic suppressors. Such suppressors may identify other components required for microtubule assembly and structure.

In addition, relatively little is known about the biochemistry and molecular biology of microtubules in *C. elegans*. A number of investigators are beginning to examine tubulin proteins (E. Byard, personal communication) and microtubule-associated proteins (E. Aamodt & J. Culotti, personal communication) and the cloning of various tubulins from *C. elegans* is in progress (L. Gremke & J. Culotti, personal communication). These studies will certainly be augmented by use of the mutants derived from the mutator strain TR679 (see above). If insertional mutants with defects in the genes discussed in this paper can be isolated, their transposon-tagged DNA can be used to begin a molecular analysis of these genes (see, e.g., Eide & Anderson, 1985; Greenwald, 1985; Moerman *et al.* 1986). Molecular analysis will refine the level of genetic dissection of the role of microtubules in *C. elegans* and will make available biochemical probes of microtubule function.

We thank Ed. Hedgecock for commenting on the manuscript and generously providing Fig. 3. We are also grateful to our colleagues at Columbia for their comments and Donna Schwartz for typing the manuscript. Research in the Columbia laboratory is funded by grants from the US Public Health Service (GM30997 and A19399) and the US Department of Agriculture (85-CRCR-1-1806).

REFERENCES

ALBERT, P. S., BROWN, S. J. & RIDDLE, D. L. (1981). Sensory control of dauer larva formation in *Caenorhabditis elegans*. *J. comp. Neurol.* **198**, 435–451.
BRENNER, S. (1974). The genetics of *Caenorhabditis elegans*. *Genetics* **77**, 71–94.
BURLAND, T. G., SCHEDL, T., GULL, K. & DOVE, W. F. (1984). Genetic analysis of resistance to benzimidazoles in *Physarum: Differential expression of β-tubulin genes. Genetics* **108**, 123–141.

BURTON, P. R., HINKLEY, R. E. & PIERSON, G. B. (1975). Tannic acid-stained microtubules with 12, 13, and 15 protofilaments. *J. Cell Biol.* **65**, 227–233.

CHALFIE, M. (1984). Neuronal development in *Caenorhabditis elegans. Trends Neurosci.* **7**, 197–202.

CHALFIE, M. & SULSTON, J. (1981). Developmental genetics of the mechanosensory neurons of *Caenorhabditis elegans. Devl Biol.* **82**, 358–370.

CHALFIE, M. & THOMSON, J. N. (1982). Structural and functional diversity in the neuronal microtubules of *Caenorhabditis elegans. J. Cell Biol.* **93**, 15–23.

CULOTTI, J. G. & RUSSELL, R. L. (1978). Osmotic avoidance defective mutants of the nematode *Caenorhabditis elegans. Genetics* **90**, 243–256.

DUSENBERY, D. B. (1980). Chemotactic behavior of mutants of the nematode *Caenorhabditis elegans* that are defective in osmotic avoidance. *J. comp. Physiol.* **137**, 93–96.

DUSENBERY, D. B., SHERIDAN, R. E. & RUSSELL, R. L. (1975). Chemotaxis defective mutants of the nematode *Caenorhabditis elegans. Genetics* **80**, 297–310.

EICHENLAUB-RITTER, E. & TUCKER, J. B. (1984). Microtubules with more than 13 protofilaments in the dividing nuclei of ciliates. *Nature, Lond.* **307**, 60–62.

EIDE, D. & ANDERSON, P. (1985). Transposition of Tc*1* in the nematode *Caenorhabditis elegans. Proc. natn. Acad. Sci. U.S.A.* **82**, 1756–1760.

EUTENEUER, U. & MCINTOSH, J. R. (1980). Polarity of midbody and phragmoplast microtubules. *J. Cell Biol.* **87**, 509–515.

EVANS, L., MITCHISON, T. & KIRSCHNER, M. (1985). Influence of the centrosome on the structure of nucleated microtubules. *J. Cell Biol.* **100**, 1185–1191.

GOLDEN, J. W. & RIDDLE, D. L. (1982). A pheromone influences larval development in the nematode *Caenorhabditis elegans. Science* **218**, 578–580.

GREENWALD, I. S. (1985). *lin-12*, a nematode homeotic gene, is homologous to a set of mammalian proteins that includes epidermal growth factor. *Cell* **43**, 583–590.

GREENWALD, I. S. & HORVITZ, H. R. (1980). *unc-93(e1500)*: a behavioral mutant of *Caenorhabditis elegans* that defines a gene with a wild-type null phenotype. *Genetics* **96**, 147–164.

HEDGECOCK, E. M., CULOTTI, J. G., THOMSON, J. N. & PERKINS, L. A. (1985). Axonal guidance mutants of *Caenorhabditis elegans* identified by filling sensory neurons with fluorescein dyes. *Devl Biol.* **111**, 158–170.

HODGKIN, J. (1983). Male phenotypes and mating efficiency in *Caenorhabditis elegans. Genetics* **103**, 43–46.

LEWIS, J. A. & HODGKIN, J. A. (1977). Specific neuroanatomical changes in chemosensory mutants of the nematode *Caenorhabditis elegans. J. comp. Neurol.* **172**, 489–510.

MOERMAN, D. G., BENIAN, G. M. & WATERSTON, R. H. (1986). Molecular cloning of the *unc-22* gene in *Caenorhabditis elegans* by Tc*1* transposon-tagging. *Proc. natn. Acad. Sci. U.S.A.* **83**, 2579–2583.

NAGANO, T. & SUZUKI, F. (1975). Microtubules with 15 subunits in cockroach epidermal cells. *J. Cell Biol.* **64**, 242–245.

NEFF, N. F., THOMAS, J. H., GRISAFI, P. & BOTSTEIN, D. (1983). Isolation of the β-tubulin gene from yeast and demonstration of its essential function *in vivo. Cell* **33**, 211–219.

PERKINS, L. A., HEDGECOCK, E. M., THOMSON, J. N. & CULOTTI, J. G. (1986). Mutant sensory cilia in *Caenorhabditis elegans. Devl Biol.* (in press).

RIDDLE, D. L. & BRENNER, S. (1978). Indirect suppression in *Caenorhabditis elegans. Genetics* **89**, 299–314.

RIDDLE, D. L., SWANSON, M. M. & ALBERT, P. S. (1981). Interacting genes in nematode dauer larva formation. *Nature, Lond.* **290**, 668–671.

SCHEDL, T., OWENS, J., DOVE, W. F. & BURLAND, T. G. (1984). Genetics of the tubulin gene gamilies of physarum. *Genetics* **108**, 143–164.

SCHEELE, R. B., BERGEN, L. F. & BORISY, G. G. (1982). Control of structural fidelity of microtubules by initiation sites. *J. Cell Biol.* **154**, 485–500.

SHEIR-NEISS, G., LAI, M. H. & MORRIS, N. R. (1978). Identification of a gene for β-tubulin in *Aspergillus nidulans. Cell* **15**, 639–647.

STERNBERG, P. W. & HORVITZ, H. R. (1984). The genetic control of cell lineage during nematode development. *A. Rev. Genet.* **18**, 489–524.

WARD, S., THOMSON, N., WHITE, J. G. & BRENNER, S. (1975). Electron microscopical reconstruction of the anterior sensory anatomy of the nematode *Caenorhabditis elegans*. *J. comp. Neurol.* **160**, 313–338.

WARE, R. W., CLARK, D., CROSSLAND, K. & RUSSELL, R. L. (1975). The nerve ring of the nematode *Caenorhabditis elegans*: Sensory input and motor output. *J. comp. Neurol.* **162**, 71–110.

WATERSTON, R. H., MOERMAM, D. G., BAILLIE, D. L. & LANE, T. R. (1982). Mutations affecting myosin heavy chain accumulation and function in the nematode *Caenorhabditis elegans*. In *Diseases of the Motor Unit* (ed. D. M. Schotland), pp. 747–760. New York: J. Wiley and Sons.

WHITE, J. G., SOUTHGATE, E., THOMSON, J. N. & BRENNER, S. (1986). The structure of the nervous system of the nematode *Caenorhabditis elegans*. *Phil. Trans. R. Soc. Lond. (Biol.)* (in press).

WILSON, L. & BRYAN, J. (1974). Biochemical and pharmacological properties of microtubules. *Adv. Cell molec. Biol.* **3**, 21–72.

J. Cell Sci. Suppl. 5, 273–291 (1986)
Printed in Great Britain © The Company of Biologists Limited 1986

SUPRACELLULAR MICROTUBULE ALIGNMENTS IN CELL LAYERS ASSOCIATED WITH THE SECRETION OF CERTAIN FISH SCALES

P. J. DANE AND J. B. TUCKER

Department of Zoology and Marine Biology, Bute Buildings, St Andrews University, St Andrews, Fife KY16 9TS, UK

SUMMARY

Intercellularly aligned microtubule arrays are present in cell layers associated with the growth and secretion of scales in the zebra fish *Brachydanio rerio* and the neon tetra fish *Hyphessobrycon innesi*. The layers in question are: the osteoblast layer that covers the ossified outer surface of a scale, and the layer of fibroblasts that is situated immediately underneath the inner collagenous surface of a scale's fibrillary plate.

In certain osteoblasts, the proximal portions of microtubules (with respect to centrosomes) run closely alongside the anterior margin of each cell where it flanks one of a scale's ridge-shaped circuli. These osteoblasts and microtubule portions are arranged in aligned rows that are parallel to circuli. However, the distal portions of the microtubules curve into an orientation that is approximately at right angles to circuli and they are aligned with each other and similar microtubule portions in adjacent osteoblasts. Such microtubule alignments only occur in osteoblasts that are associated with circuli. In *Hyphessobrycon* osteoblasts situated elsewhere on a scale's surface, microtubules radiate from cell centres but their distal portions curve into alignment with each other and are oriented alongside cell margins.

The proximal portions of fibroblast microtubules radiate from centrally positioned centrosomes but the distal portions curve into alignment with each other and distal microtubule portions in neighbouring fibroblasts. The overall pattern of microtubule alignment is similar to that of collagen fibres, which these fibroblasts are secreting onto the fibrillary plate.

The immunofluorescence protocol that was used to demonstrate the microtubule alignments described above did not reveal such alignments in the osteoblast and fibroblast layers associated with scales of the brown trout *Salmo trutta fario*.

These findings are assessed in terms of intra- and inter-cellular control of microtubule alignment, and decentralized reorientation of microtubules at distances of several micrometres from centrosomal microtubule-organizing centres. The functional significance of the relationships between microtubule alignment and supracellular patterns of alignment that take place as collagen deposition and ossification proceed during scale formation is also considered.

INTRODUCTION

There are substantial indications that intercellular coordination of cytoskeletal deployment (and its mechanical consequences) sometimes make an important contribution during the supracellular control of animal tissue growth and form (Tucker, 1981). Progress in evaluating control of cytoskeletal deployment and performance in intact tissues is hindered by the difficulty of monitoring overall cytoskeletal distribution. Light microscopical examination of cytoskeletal deployment after decoration with fluorescently conjugated antibodies is currently one of the most effective ways of surveying cytoskeletal layout. This approach has been especially rewarding for cells 'spread' on coverslips in tissue culture (see Weber & Osborn, 1979; Brinkley *et al.* 1980). However, it has not often been successfully applied to unsectioned tissue cells fixed *in situ*. This is because the relatively large thickness of tissue portions usually interferes with antibody penetration, and/or elution of non-specifically bound antibody (Gorbsky & Borisy, 1985). Hence, our understanding of cytoskeletal deployment in tissue cells that are actually functioning and interacting in their usual somatic environments is scanty compared with that available for cells isolated in tissue culture. How close is the relationship between *in vivo* and *in vitro* cytoskeletal behaviour? Is cytoskeletal configuration and co-ordination in tissues very different from that which occurs in tissue culture? The answers to these questions are crucial for progress in evaluating cytoskeletal contributions to embryogenesis and tissue organization. In spite of the problems outlined above, immunofluorescence microscopy can be rewardingly exploited for such evaluations on occasion. For example, Byers *et al.* (1980) and Byers & Fujiwara (1982) have shown that immunofluorescence microscopy can be used to examine the arrangement of microtubules and actin filaments in sheets of fibroblasts that remain *in situ* on the inner surfaces of the scales of certain teleosts after removal of scales from the organisms. The transparent scales and associated cell layers are then prepared for immunofluorescence microscopy in much the same way as a coverslip with attached cells.

The present study shows that the immunofluorescence procedure can be used equally successfully to demonstrate decorated microtubules in the osteoblast layer on the other (outer) surfaces of certain fish scales. This paper deals mainly with the marked examples of intercellular microtubule alignment that have been found in the fibroblast and osteoblast layers associated with the scales of two cypriniform teleosts. The spatial relationships of these microtubule alignments with respect to the location of centrosomal microtubule-organizing centres and supracellular patterns of extra-cellular matrix deposition have been explored.

MATERIALS AND METHODS

Juvenile zebra fish (*Brachydanio rerio*), neon tetra fish (*Hyphessobrycon innesi*) and brown trout (*Salmo trutta fario*) with body lengths of 3, 2 and 9 cm, respectively, have been used in this study. Fish were killed by decapitation and shallow grazing cuts were made through the dermis with scissors to remove small portions of skin and their associated scales.

For immunofluorescence studies, scales were separated from the portions of skin by prising them out of scale pouches using fine tungsten needles. Then the procedure described by Byers *et al.* (1980) was used with the following modifications. A solution of 3 % formaldehyde in teleost phosphate-buffered saline (TPBS) (Grimstone & Skaer, 1972) was used for fixation. Microtubules were decorated with a monoclonal rat anti-yeast-tubulin (YOL 1/34) (Serotec Ltd, Bicester, UK), which was used in conjunction with fluorescein isothiocyanate (FITC)-conjugated sheep anti-rat immunoglobulin (Serotec Ltd) as secondary antibody. Scales were mounted in a mixture of 9 parts glycerol:1 part TPBS (v/v) (with diazobicyclo-octane at a final concentration of 2 mg ml^{-1} added to reduce the rate of photobleaching) for examination with a Leitz Ortholux fluorescence microscope using a ×50 water immersion objective (n.a. 1·0). Kodak Tri-X film was used for photography.

Portions of *Brachydanio* skin and its scales were prepared for electron microscopy using procedures outlined elsewhere (Dane & Tucker, 1985) except that scales were fixed using the method described by Baird *et al.* (1967) and then decalcified for 72 h (Waterman, 1970) prior to dehydration. In addition, each portion of skin and its scales was sandwiched within a strip (3 cm×0·75 cm) of copper gauze (0·4 mm mesh-spacing) that was folded around it before fixation and remained until dehydration was completed. This was to prevent the marked curling up of skin portions, which otherwise occurs during fixation.

RESULTS

General organization of the scales and associated cell layers of Brachydanio

Each scale is an approximately circular sheet of extracellular matrix material. An outer osseous layer covers a more interiorly situated fibrillary plate (Fig. 1). This plate mainly consists of layers of collagen fibres stacked in an 'orthogonal cross-ply' configuration (Fig. 4). Cells that form a layer covering the outer osseous surface of a scale will be referred to as osteoblasts (Van Oosten, 1957) in this account, and cells in the layer that is situated against a scale's inner fibrillary surface will be called fibroblasts (Onozato & Watabe, 1979) (Fig. 1). Osteoblasts and fibroblasts have also been termed scleroblasts (e.g. see Byers & Fujiwara, 1982) or described as episquamal and hyposquamal cells (Waterman, 1970), respectively, by previous investigators. Several layers of epidermal cells cover the osteoblast layer, and layers of dermal cells and pigment cells are situated inside and against the fibroblast layer (Waterman, 1970). They have not been examined in detail in this study. The osseous layer of each scale exhibits a polarized pattern of ridges (circuli) and grooves (radii) on its outer surface that is oriented with respect to the anterior/posterior axis of the organism (Fig. 2).

Microtubule alignments in the osteoblast layer of Brachydanio

Osteoblasts are arranged in rows, which are parallel to circuli in the regions where circuli occur. Each inter-circulus space is one osteoblast wide (Waterman, 1970) (Fig. 1). The anterior and posterior margins of adjacent osteoblasts run alongside each other close to the crests of the ridge-like circuli (Figs 1, 3). The anterior portion of an osteoblast contains its nucleus (Fig. 3) and juxtanuclear centrosome. Each osteoblast flattens out posteriorly into an extremely thin (about 0·2 μm thick) lamella-like cell portion (Figs 1, 3).

Most of the microtubules close to the anterior margins of these osteoblasts are aligned with, and run alongside, the steep posterior flanks of adjacent circuli (Fig. 3). In immunofluorescent preparations the decorated microtubules contribute to fluorescent bands and strands that spatially coincide with the positions and alignments of circuli (Figs 5, 6). However, in the remaining more posteriorly situated portions of these cells most of the microtubules are oriented approximately at right angles to circuli and some of them span inter-circulus spacings (Figs 5, 6). Examination of thin sections revealed microtubules concentrated along the anterior margins of these osteoblasts (Fig. 3, short arrows). However, profiles of microtubules were rarely encountered in the more posterior lamelliform portions of the

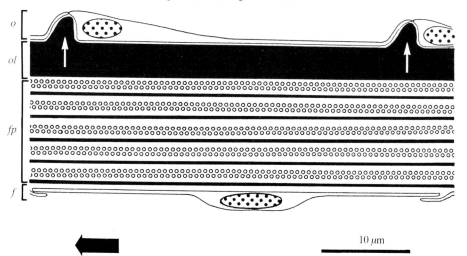

10 μm

Fig. 1. Schematic diagram showing the shapes and arrangements of osteoblasts (*o*) and fibroblasts (*f*), which cover a scale's osseous layer (*ol*) and fibrillary plate (*fp*), respectively. The diagram is based on sections cut near the anterior ends of *Brachydanio* scales and at right angles to the plane of each scale and the longitudinal axes of their circuli. The positions of the scarp-shaped cross-sectional profiles of the osseous circuli are indicated by arrows. Nuclei are stippled. The number of layers of collagen fibres represented in the fibrillary plate is approximately 70% of that found in the scales examined.

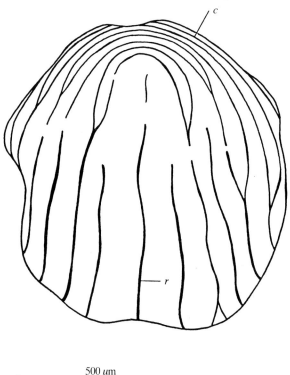

500 μm

Fig. 2. Schematic diagram showing the arrangement of circuli (*c*) and radii (*r*) on the outer surface of the osseous layer of a *Brachydanio* scale. The anterior edge of the scale is oriented towards the top of the figure.

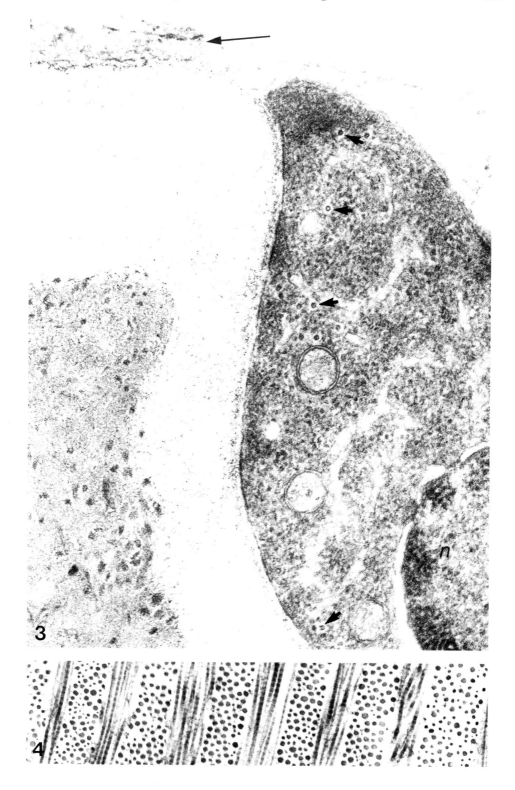

cells where immunofluorescence microscopy demonstrates the presence of aligned microtubule portions with an average spacing of 4 μm. Most of these microtubule portions were apparently not preserved during preparation for electron microscopy.

Microtubule arrangement varies in ways that are correlated with the spacing of circuli and whether osteoblasts are located in regions where circuli or radii occur. For example, the alignment of microtubules at right angles to circuli is most marked for osteoblasts located close to the anterior edge of a scale (within about 100 μm) where the circuli are more closely spaced (10–15 μm apart) than elsewhere (Fig. 5). Microtubules are less precisely aligned with respect to each other, and at a wider range of angles with respect to circuli in slightly more posterior regions of scales where circuli are spaced about 50 μm apart (compare Figs 5, 6). In regions where circuli and radii approach each other, circuli are most widely spaced (60–80 μm apart) and they sometimes exhibit discontinuities. As far as these osteoblasts are concerned, microtubule arrangement only approximates to the orderly patterns described above for regions where circuli are closest together (compare Figs 5, 7). In the central and posterior portions of scales where radii occur well-defined circuli were not detected. Adjacent radii are separated by distances of up to 150 μm. This spacing is several times greater than the major dimensions of individual osteoblasts. Microtubules do not exhibit any well-defined patterns of alignment in osteoblasts that are situated between radii; in general, most microtubules radiate out from the central nucleus-containing portions of the cells (Fig. 8). Strips of weak fluorescence coincided with the location of radii (Fig. 8). This is apparently due to non-specific binding of the fluorescently labelled secondary antibody in the grooved radii, or to components that run closely alongside them, because it occurred in control preparations in which the primary antibody (antitubulin) was omitted.

Fig. 3. Section through part of the osseous layer and layer of osteoblasts of a decalcified *Brachydanio* scale cut in the same plane as that described for Fig. 1. The steep posteriorly directed 'scarp-face' of a circulus is towards the left of the micrograph. The posterior margin of an osteoblast (long arrow) is situated near the crest of the circulus. The anterior margin of an adjacent osteoblast flanks the scarp face of the circulus and cross-sectional profiles of microtubules (short arrows) are present in the cytoplasmic region situated between this margin and the nucleus (*n*). ×63 000.

Fig. 4. Section through part of the fibrillary plate of a decalcified *Brachydanio* scale cut in the same plane as that described for Fig. 1 showing the orthogonal cross-ply arrangement of its layers of collagen fibres. The plane of the scale is oriented parallel to the sides of the page. ×22 500.

Fig. 5. Immunofluorescence micrograph showing part of the osteoblast layer near the anterior edge of a *Brachydanio* scale. Circuli are oriented across the micrograph (from top left to bottom right). The more anterior regions of the scale are towards the top of the micrograph. Some microtubule portions (arrows) are aligned parallel to and alongside circuli; others are aligned and oriented more or less at right angles to circuli. ×900.

Fig. 6. Immunofluorescence micrograph of part of a *Brachydanio* osteoblast layer oriented as in Fig. 5 in a region where circuli are more widely spaced than they are in Fig. 5. Microtubules are not as precisely aligned at right angles to circuli as they are in the osteoblasts shown in Fig. 5. ×900.

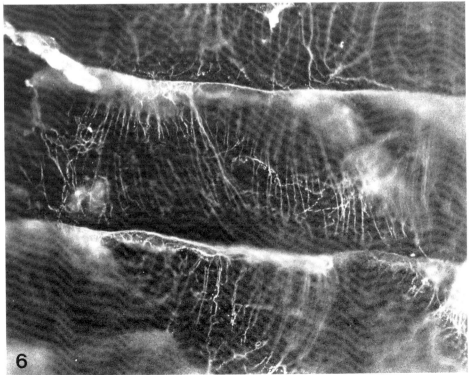

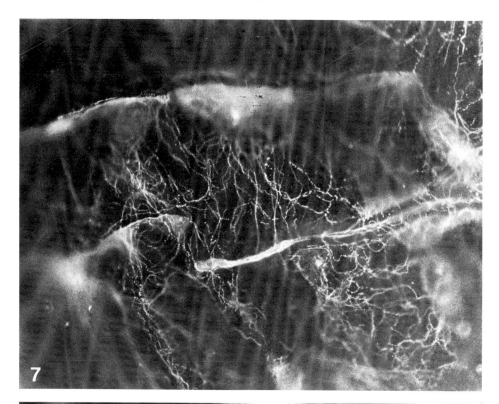

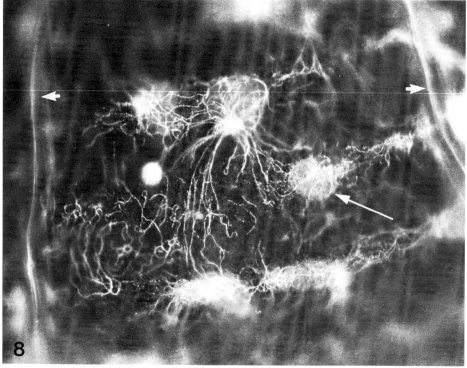

Microtubule alignment in the fibroblast layer of Brachydanio

Microtubules are arranged radially with respect to a fairly central site in each fibroblast. However, most microtubules curve into alignment with each other, and those in neighbouring cells, at distances of up to 15 μm from the central site (Fig. 9). The aligned portions of microtubules have lengths of 10–50 μm. Examination of thin sections revealed that centrosomes are situated near the centres of cells and close to their nuclei. Hence, centrosomes probably occupy the central sites referred to above. The central nucleus-containing regions of the cells have thicknesses of up to 1·5 μm but the peripheral regions, which contain most of the aligned microtubule portions, are extremely thin and mainly have thicknesses of about 0·2 μm (Figs 1, 10). As was the case for osteoblasts, very few microtubule profiles were encountered in thin sections of the lamelliform portions of fibroblasts.

In some regions of scales the aligned portions of microtubules trace out a set of arc-like alignments across the fibroblast layer (Fig. 9); in others, they are oriented straight across the layer. Phase-contrast and differential interference contrast examinations of unfixed scales showed that the aligned collagen fibres in fibrillary plates exhibit a similar pattern of 'arcs' and 'straights'. Direct comparison between the alignment of microtubules, and collagen fibres in the layer closest to the upper secretory surfaces of fibroblasts, was not achieved. This was because it was not possible to differentiate between fibres at the level in question from those at other levels in the fibrillary plates of scales prepared for immunofluorescence microscopy.

Microtubule alignments and the scales of Hyphessobrycon

Hyphessobrycon innesi and *Brachydanio rerio* are both members of the Order Cypriniformes. In addition, the patterns of circuli and radii on the surfaces of the osseous layers of their scales are very similar. Correlated with this is the finding that microtubule arrangements and alignments in the osteoblast and fibroblast layers associated with scales of these two species are also very similar. For example, in both species microtubule portions are most exactly aligned, and oriented most precisely at right angles to circuli, in regions where circuli are most closely spaced (compare Figs 11, 12 and Figs 5, 6). Furthermore, in some *Hyphessobrycon* osteoblasts that are associated with circuli it is evident that individual microtubules (or small groups of microtubules) curve fairly abruptly through about 90° out of alignment with circuli at many points along the anterior margin of an osteoblast (Fig. 15). The portions of microtubules oriented at right angles to circuli are thus likely to be the distal portions of the microtubules that are aligned with circuli and are closest to the anteriorly

Fig. 7. Immunofluorescence micrograph of part of a *Brachydanio* osteoblast layer oriented as in Fig. 5 in a region where the scale's circuli are relatively widely spaced and exhibit discontinuities. There are few instances of microtubule portions that are precisely aligned and oriented at right angles to circuli. ×900.

Fig. 8. Immunofluorescence micrograph of part of a *Brachydanio* osteoblast layer in a region situated between radii (short arrows). Most of the microtubules in these osteoblasts radiate from the central portions of cells where weakly fluorescent osteoblast nuclei (long arrow) are sometimes apparent. ×900.

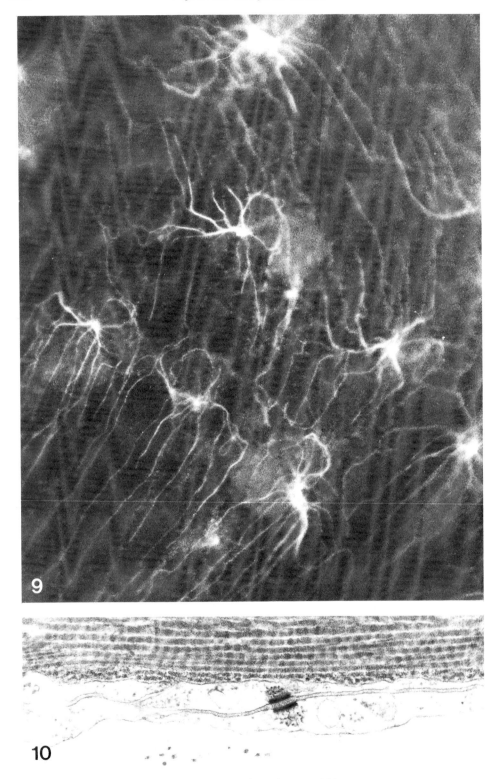

9

10

Figs 9, 10. For legends see p. 284

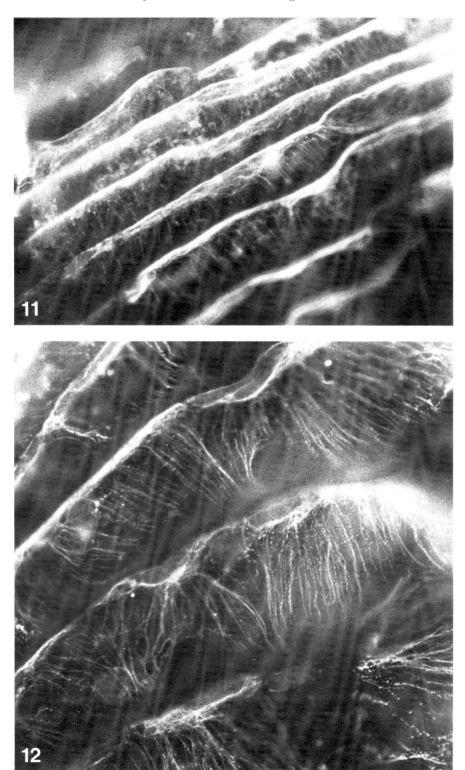

Figs 11, 12. For legends see p. 284

situated juxtanuclear centrosomes. Many osteoblasts in the central portions of scales where radii occur detach from scales during preparation for immunofluorescence microscopy. In those that remain, the radial arrangement of microtubules is usually more pronounced and orderly than it is in radius-associated osteoblasts of *Brachydanio* (compare Figs 8, 13, 14). In addition, groupings of microtubules extend around the margins of the flattened *Hyphessobrycon* osteoblasts. These groupings appear to be composed of the distal portions of the radially arranged microtubules that take up different orientations at cell margins where adjacent osteoblasts contact each other (Fig. 14).

Microtubule arrangement in fibroblasts is very similar to that described above for such cells in *Brachydanio*.

Microtubule arrangement and the scales of Salmo

The surface topographies of the osseous layers of the scales of *Salmo* (Order Isospondyli) are distinctly different from those of the cypriniform species considered above (compare Figs 2, 16). Circular concentrically arranged circuli are present in all regions of *Salmo* scales but there are no radii. The immunofluorescence procedure did not clearly reveal microtubule distribution in the fibroblast layers of *Salmo* scales and microtubules were not as readily detectable in the osteoblast layers as they were in those of the cypriniform species. Furthermore, microtubules do not exhibit

---

Fig. 9. Immunofluorescence micrograph of part of the fibroblast layer in *Brachydanio* showing that most of the microtubules in these cells radiate from a central site in each cell but possess distal portions that are aligned with each other and similar portions in neighbouring cells. ×1250.

Fig. 10. Section perpendicular to the plane of a decalcified *Brachydanio* scale showing thin peripheral portions of two adjacent fibroblasts where their edges overlap each other. The thickness of the fibroblast layer is not much greater than the spot desmosome and associated filament bundles. Part of the fibrillary plate and its collagen fibres is shown at the top of the micrograph. ×50 000.

Fig. 11. Immunofluorescence micrograph of part of the osteoblast layer near the anterior edge of a *Hyphessobrycon* scale showing microtubule arrangement. Circuli are oriented across the micrograph (from top right to bottom left). The more anterior portions of the scale are towards the top of the micrograph. ×1000.

Fig. 12. Immunofluorescence micrograph of part of a *Hyphessobrycon* osteoblast layer oriented as in Fig. 11 showing microtubule arrangement in a region where circuli are more widely spaced than they are in Fig. 11. ×1000.

Fig. 13. Immunofluorescence micrograph of an osteoblast in the central region of a *Hyphessobrycon* scale where circuli do not occur. Microtubules radiate from the centre of the cell and contribute to a marginal band of microtubules at the cell periphery. ×1100.

Fig. 14. Immunofluorescence micrograph of part of the osteoblast layer in the central region of a *Hyphessobrycon* scale. Microtubules radiate from the centres of cells and in some cases apparently curve (arrow) into alignment with the margins of cells. ×1250.

Fig. 15. Immunofluorescence micrograph of part of a *Hyphessobrycon* osteoblast showing curved portions of microtubules (arrow) that run between the portions that are aligned alongside a circulus (towards the top of the micrograph) and those that are aligned more or less at right angles to the circulus. ×3300.

well-defined patterns of alignment with respect to adjacent circuli even in regions where these are as closely juxtaposed and well aligned as circuli in *Brachydanio* and *Hyphessobrycon* (compare Figs 5, 11, 17).

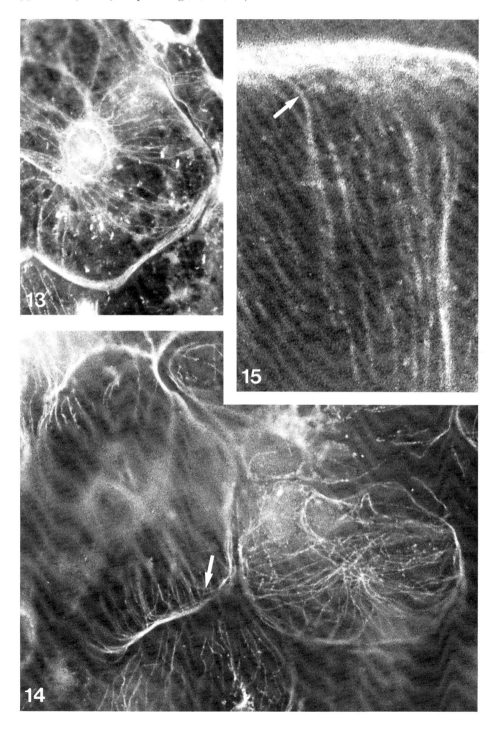

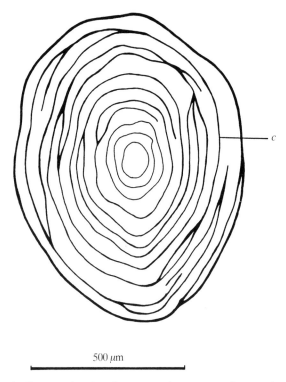

500 μm

Fig. 16. Schematic diagram showing the more or less concentric pattern of circuli (*c*) on the outer surface of a *Salmo* scale.

Influence of preparative procedures for immunofluorescence and electron microscopy

The fluorescent images of decorated microtubules in fibroblasts and osteoblasts that have been described above were probably obtained from portions of scales where only the osteoblast and/or fibroblast layers remained attached to scales. Evidence for this was obtained from light-microscopical examination of Methylene-Blue-stained 1 μm thick resin sections of non-decalcified *Brachydanio* scales and associated cells that had been removed from fishes in the same way as scales prepared for immunofluorescence studies (see Materials and Methods). In many regions of most scales the epidermal and dermal cells had sloughed away and only some regions of the fibroblast and osteoblasts cell layers shown in Fig. 1 remained attached to scales. However, layers of epithelial cells remained attached to the osteoblast layer of each scale for distances of up to 0·5 mm from the posterior edge of a scale. This was apparent in immunofluorescence preparations. The epithelial layers exhibited a fairly pronounced and diffuse fluorescence, which was probably due to uneluted non-specifically bound antibody. It was sufficiently substantial to mask fluorescent images of decorated microtubules that might otherwise have been discriminated in cells associated with the most posterior portions of scales.

Thin sectioning of non-decalcified scales and associated cells was attempted. Deformation and tearing of the sectioned resin was so extensive that most details of

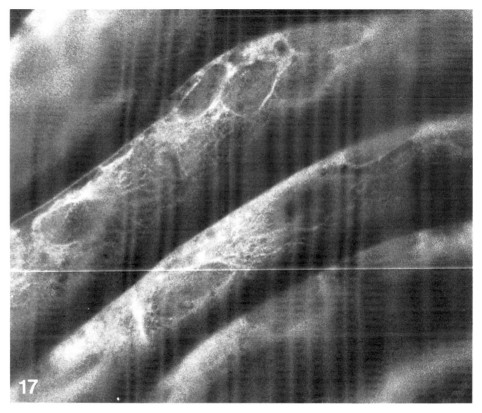

Fig. 17. Immunofluorescence micrograph of part of the osteoblast layer of a *Salmo* scale. Microtubules do not exhibit well-defined alignments with respect to circuli that are oriented across the micrograph (from top right to bottom left). The more peripheral portions of the scale are towards the top of the micrograph. ×1200.

cytoplasmic organization were obscured. These difficulties were not encountered after decalcification (see Materials and Methods) but there is evidence that substantial breakdown of microtubules occurred in some parts of the cells of decalcified material (see above).

DISCUSSION

Centrosomal microtubule-organizing centres and control of microtubule alignment

Investigation of several animal tissue cell types has shown that many of their microtubules grow out from their centrosomes (see Tucker, 1979; McIntosh, 1983; Bornens & Karsenti, 1984). Presumably this is also the case for microtubules that project from the vicinities of centrosomes in the cells examined in this study. These cells seem to provide examples of three types of situations where the distal portions of microtubules curve into orientations that are markedly different from those of their proximal portions (Fig. 18). For example, microtubules that are more or less radially oriented with respect to cell centres curve into alignment with each other and follow paths around the margins of flattened *Hyphessobrycon* osteoblasts that are positioned

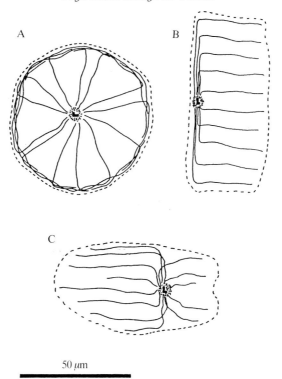

Fig. 18. Schematic diagrams showing the arrangement of microtubules with respect to the margins of cells (broken lines) and the apparent locations of the proximal ends of microtubules with respect to centrosomes. Centrosomes are represented by a pair of black rectangles (centrioles) surrounded by stippling (pericentriolar material). A. An osteoblast near the central portion of a *Hyphessobrycon* scale. B. An osteoblast near the anterior edge of a *Hyphessobrycon* or *Brachydanio* scale where circuli are most closely spaced. C. A fibroblast of a *Hyphessobrycon* or *Brachydanio* scale.

near the middles of scales (Fig. 18A). Such curving may be a response to interactions that are induced by encounters between microtubules and cell margins. The tendency for microtubules radiating from the centres of flattened cells to extend around the margins of such cells has been observed by others (e.g. see Brinkley *et al.* 1980; Byers *et al.* 1980). Conversely, microtubules bend *away* from their alignment alongside anterior cell margins into another alignment in osteoblasts that are located between closely spaced circuli (Fig. 18B). Individual microtubules, or small groups of microtubules, curve away from the main anterior bundle at a series of fairly numerous and regularly spaced loci. Evidently, conditions that promote re-alignment of certain microtubules at these loci do not modify the orientation of the remainder. In fibroblasts, on the other sides of scales, some radially oriented microtubules curve into alignment with each other in localities that are not associated with cell margins (Fig. 18C).

The changes in microtubule orientation and alignment considered above are situated at considerable distances (up to 40 μm) from centrosomes (Fig. 18). It is far from clear how such reorientations are accomplished. Presumably, the reorientations initially occur at the locations where the microtubule curves have been found. Such venues are too remote from the centrosomes for these microtubule-organizing centres to make direct contributions to the events that reorganize microtubule alignment. These observations for situations (in the fibroblasts at least) where the proximal ends of microtubules retain a close association with centrosomes, complement those for certain other cell types where microtubules may be detaching from centrosomes and migrating away from them as microtubule positioning proceeds (Warren, 1974; Vorobjev & Chentsov, 1983; Tucker, 1984; Murphy *et al.* 1986). In all these cases considerable 'decentralized' organization of microtubules apparently occurs in addition to initial specifications (such as those for control of microtubule number, polarity and composition), which may be provided by the centrosomal microtubule-organizing centres (Tucker, 1984).

Microtubule alignment and supracellular patterns in the extracellular matrix

What is the functional significance of microtubule alignments in the cell layers associated with the secretion of scales?

Microtubule alignment in goldfish scale fibroblasts is very similar to that described for fibroblasts above. It is strikingly correlated with the alignment of fibres in the collagen layer of the fibrillary plate that is closest to the secretory surfaces of the cells (Byers *et al.* 1980). This may also be the case for *Brachydanio* and *Hyphessobrycon* where there is a close similarity between supracellular patterns of microtubule alignment in fibroblasts and fibre alignment in collagen layers of fibrillary plates. Direct demonstration of microtubule/collagen fibre co-alignment in the goldfish was achieved by comparing phase-contrast images of fibres in collagen layers next to the secretory surfaces of fibroblasts with immunofluorescent images of micro-tubules in the same fibroblasts. This was not accomplished for *Brachydanio* and *Hyphessobrycon* because it was not possible to detect the orientation of the collagen fibres closest to the fibroblast layer using phase-contrast or differential interference contrast microscopy in examinations of scales and associated cells prepared for immunofluorescence microscopy. Transmission electron microscopy did not clarify this issue because most of the aligned portions of fibroblast microtubules were not preserved.

Microtubule alignments in osteoblasts are strikingly correlated with the arrange-ment of osseous circuli on *Brachydanio* and *Hyphessobrycon* scales. There is the intriguing possibility that the groupings of microtubules that run closely alongside circuli form part of a mechanism that specifies and maintains the orientation of circuli and determines where these ridge-shaped thickenings will be secreted onto the outer surface of an osseous layer. Microtubule portions that run at right angles to circuli often span the inter-circulus spaces. Are these microtubules used as intracellular rulers to measure out inter-circulus spacings? Admittedly, well-defined patterns of microtubule alignment were not detected in *Salmo* osteoblasts. However, the possibility that microtubule alignment does also occur in these osteoblasts, but is a transient phenomenon that is only associated with the initial establishment of circuli, cannot be discounted.

The possibilities outlined above are especially pertinent to the question of whether osteoblasts and their microtubules are involved in the formation and positioning of

growth annuli on the scales of certain teleosts. Growth annuli are zones that are
interpolated in the pattern of circuli where the spacing and/or arrangement of circuli
differs distinctly from that of circuli in the intervening regions (Tesch, 1968). The
number and spacing of a scale's growth annuli are sometimes used, rather like tree-
rings, to estimate the ages and growth rates of their owners (Van Oosten, 1957;
Tesch, 1968).

The orderly shaping and positioning of osteoblasts in the vicinities of circuli, and
the supracellular patterns of microtubule alignment in osteoblasts and fibroblasts,
may on the other hand, be features that occur as a response to, rather than being the
cause of, the orderly spatial patterns in the extracellular matrix material that they
secrete. For example, oriented locomotion and elongation of cells with respect to
aligned collagen fibres in the substratum is well established (see Dunn, 1982).
Indeed, one of the earliest demonstrations of this phenomenon used the oriented
collagen layers of fish-scale fibrillary plates as a substratum (Weiss & Taylor, 1956).

Hence, a major challenge now is to ascertain how the spatially correlated
supracellular patterns of *extracellular* matrix alignments and *intracellular* microtubule alignments are determined and whether they are causally related. Are the
alignments set up in response to the transmission of diffusible chemical signals
through the extracellular matrix of a scale and/or its associated cell layers? Intercellularly coordinated cytoskeletal/transmembrane interactions (Tucker, 1981) may
also be involved where the highly flattened cells come into close contact at their
margins.

Support from the Medical Research Council (UK) to P.J.D. in the form of a Research
Studentship is gratefully acknowledged.

REFERENCES

BAIRD, I. L., WINBOURNE, W. B. & BOCKMAN, D. E. (1967). A technique of decalcification suited
    to electron microscopy of tissues closely associated with bone. *Anat. Rec.* **159**, 281–290.
BORNENS, M. & KARSENTI, E. (1984). The centrosome. In *Membrane Structure and Function*,
    vol. 6 (ed. E. E. Bittar), pp. 99–171. New York: John Wiley.
BRINKLEY, B. R., FISTEL, S. H., MARCUM, J. M. & PARDUE, R. L. (1980). Microtubules in
    cultured cells; indirect immunofluorescent staining with tubulin antibody. *Int. Rev. Cytol.* **63**,
    59–95.
BYERS, H. R. & FUJIWARA, K. (1982). Stress fibres in cells *in situ*: immunofluorescence
    visualization with antiactin, anti-myosin and anti-alpha-actinin. *J. Cell Biol.* **93**, 804–811.
BYERS, H. R., FUJIWARA, K. & PORTER, K. R. (1980). Visualization of microtubules of cells *in situ*
    by indirect immunofluorescence. *Proc. natn. Acad. Sci. U.S.A.* **77**, 6657–6661.
DANE, P. J. & TUCKER, J. B. (1985). Modulation of epidermal cell shaping and extracellular matrix
    during caudal fin morphogenesis in the zebra fish *Brachydanio rerio. J. Embryol. exp. Morph.* **87**,
    145–161.
DUNN, G. A. (1982). Contact guidance of cultured tissue cells: a survey of potentially relevant
    properties of the substratum. In *Cell Behaviour* (ed. R. Bellairs, A. Curtis & G. Dunn),
    pp. 247–280. Cambridge University Press.
GORBSKY, G. & BORISY, G. G. (1985). Microtubule distribution in cultured cells and intact
    tissues: improved immunolabelling resolution through the use of reversible embedment cyto-
    chemistry. *Proc. natn. Acad. Sci. U.S.A.* **82**, 6889–6893.
GRIMSTONE, A. V. & SKAER, R. J. (1972). *A Guidebook to Microscopical Methods*. Cambridge
    University Press.

McINTOSH, J. R. (1983). The centrosome as an organizer of the cytoskeleton. In *Spatial Organization of Eukaryotic Cells. Modern Cell Biology*, vol. 2 (ed. J. R. McIntosh), pp. 115–142. New York: A. R. Liss.

MURPHY, D. B., GRASSER, W. A. & WALLIS, K. T. (1986). Immunofluorescence examination of beta tubulin expression and marginal band formation in developing chicken erythroblasts. *J. Cell Biol.* **102**, 628–635.

ONOZATO, H. & WATABE, N. (1979). Studies on fish scale formation and resorption. III. Fine structure and calcification of the fibrillary plates of the scales in *Carassius auratus* (Cypriniformes: Cyprinidae). *Cell Tiss. Res.* **201**, 409–422.

TESCH, F. W. (1968). Age and growth. In *Methods for Assessment of Fish Reproduction* (ed. W. E. Ricker), pp. 93–123. Oxford: Blackwell.

TUCKER, J. B. (1979). Spatial organization of microtubules. In *Microtubules* (ed. K. Roberts & J. S. Hyams) pp. 315–357. London: Academic Press.

TUCKER, J. B. (1981). Cytoskeletal coordination and intercellular signalling during metazoan embryogenesis. *J. Embryol. exp. Morph.* **65**, 1–25.

TUCKER, J. B. (1984). Spatial organization of microtubule-organizing centers and microtubules. *J. Cell Biol.* **99**, 55s–62s.

VAN OOSTEN, J. (1957). The skin and scales. In *The Physiology of Fishes* (ed. M. E. Brown), pp. 207–244. New York: Academic Press.

VOROBJEV, I. A. & CHENTSOV, Y. S. (1983). The dynamics of reconstitution of microtubules around the cell center after cooling. *Eur. J. Cell Biol.* **30**, 149–153.

WARREN, R. H. (1974). Microtubular organization in elongating myogenic cells. *J. Cell Biol.* **63**, 550–566.

WATERMAN, R. E. (1970). Fine structure of scale development in the teleost, *Brachydanio rerio*. *Anat. Rec.* **168**, 361–380.

WEBER, K. & OSBORN, M. (1979). Intracellular display of microtubular structures revealed by indirect immunofluorescence microscopy. In *Microtubules* (ed. K. Roberts & J. S. Hyams), pp. 279–313. London: Academic Press.

WEISS, P. & TAYLOR, A. C. (1956). Fish scales as substratum for uniform orientation of cells *in vitro*. *Anat. Rec.* **124**, 381.

J. Cell Sci. Suppl. 5, 293–310 (1986)
Printed in Great Britain © The Company of Biologists Limited 1986

MORPHOGENESIS AND THE CONTROL OF MICROTUBULE DYNAMICS IN CELLS

MARC KIRSCHNER AND ERIC SCHULZE

Department of Biochemistry and Biophysics, University of California at San Francisco, San Francisco, CA 94143-0448, USA

SUMMARY

Microtubules show unusual dynamic properties at steady state *in vitro*. While overall the polymer mass remains stable, individual polymers in the population are either growing or shrinking. This phenomenon called dynamic instability is best explained by the known coupling of polymerization to GTP hydrolysis, and the hypothesis that the stability or instability of the whole polymer is determined by whether GTP or GDP is bound to the terminal subunit. Similar unusual dynamics have now also been found *in vivo*. By visualizing new subunit assembly after injection of tubulin modified with biotin into living fibroblast cells, we can visualize new growth on individual microtubules with antibody to biotin. Microtubules grow *in vivo* at about $4\,\mu\text{m}\,\text{min}^{-1}$ and after rapid and precessive depolymerization old microtubules are replaced by new growth from the centrosome. Some microtubules turn over much more slowly and these stable microtubules have a different spatial distribution from the majority of dynamic ones. The existence of both stable and dynamic microtubules in the same cell suggests a model for morphogenesis of the microtubule cytoskeleton. The rapid turnover of microtubules in the cell provides a complex population upon which selective factors can act. Stability can be generated at the end of the polymer and affects the entire microtubule. This model of selective stabilization at the microtubule ends is discussed in terms of recent experiments on the establishment of kinetochore-pole microtubules during mitosis.

THE PROBLEM OF CELL MORPHOGENESIS

The allure of cell biology, to those willing to endure complex and often inelegant experimentation, has been the chance to understand the spatial organization of living things. In the past biologists have emphasized the chemical and molecular biological genesis of structure as the key to understanding this organization. But for all we have learned about metabolism and the molecular structure of proteins and nucleic acids, we are still unable to answer the basic question of how a cell organizes itself. The cytoskeleton is one aspect of cellular organization that has recently become amenable to investigation at the molecular level. In particular the microtubule cytoskeleton poses real morphogenetic questions and has been valuable as a model for the study of the self-assembly of large-scale intracellular structures.

The arrangement of microtubules in the cloned SKNSH retinoblastoma cells (Bluestein, 1978) serves as an example of how genetically identical cells express different cellular morphology and microtubule distributions (see Fig. 1). These same cells, however, will all produce functional mitotic spindles, and even respond in a similar manner to retinoic acid (a morphogenetic signal), by extending similar neurite processes (see Fig. 2). How can we explain the variability of structure in genetically identical cells in a nearly identical environment? How can we then explain

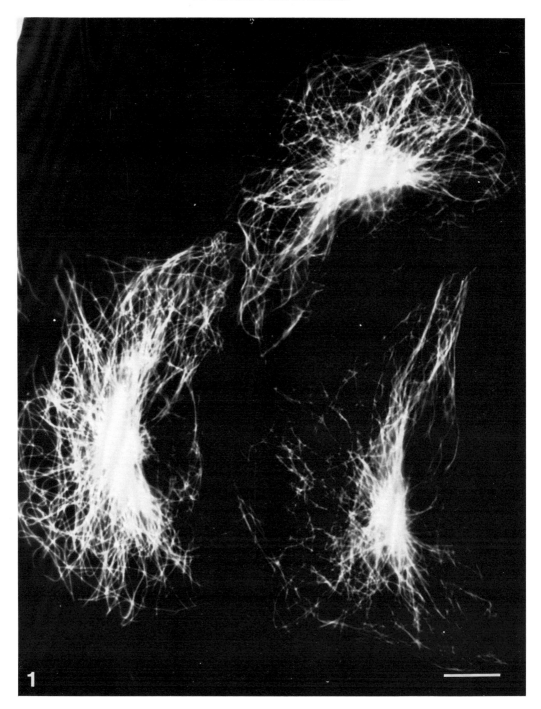

Fig. 1. Undifferentiated retinoblastoma cells stained with antibody to tubulin. Note the heterogeneity of both morphology and the distribution of microtubules between cells. Bar, 10 μm. Prepared according to the methods of Schulze & Kirschner (1986).

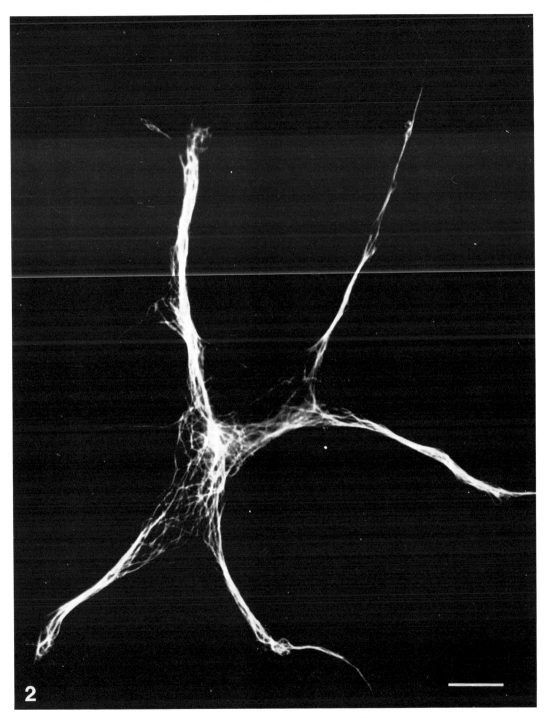

Fig. 2. Retinoblastoma cells exposed for 2 days to 30 μg ml^{-1} retinoic acid and stained with antibody to tubulin as stated in legend to Fig. 1. Bar, 10 μm.

the similar responses these cells make to extracellular signals such as retinoic acid or to internal cell cycle signals that will produce in each cell a functionally equivalent response? Although we will be concerned in this review mainly with the assembly and maintenance of microtubules in the cell, we must remember that this is only one aspect of cell organization and, as we shall see, poses many general questions about cellular morphogenesis.

In order to study the organization of the microtubule network, it is first necessary to understand the mechanism of assembly of the microtubule polymer. It was difficult initially to study the molecular mechanism of microtubule assembly *in vivo*, except in the special case of mitosis, and much investigation, therefore, has been done on microtubule assembly and dynamics *in vitro*. These studies have addressed the question of whether the microtubule polymer is in an equilibrium state, a steady state, a meta-stable state, or is simply a series of rapidly changing kinetic intermediates.

Any simple equilibrium process such as the addition of a subunit to the end of a linear polymer is governed by equation (1):

$$K_{diss} = \frac{k_{off}}{k_{on}}.$$ (1)

This equation, though simple in form ties the fraction of monomer in polymer to the off-and-on rate of subunit assembly. The dissociation constant K_{diss} represents the free monomer concentration in equilibrium with the polymer (Oosawa & Asakura, 1975). If tubulin subunits in the cell are used efficiently to make polymer, then K_{diss} will be low. The on rate, k_{on}, is ultimately limited by the diffusion of subunits to the end of the polymer. Measurements of subunit assembly *in vitro* suggest that the measured value is close to the theoretical limit of diffusion. The off rate k_{off} is in fact what is measured, when microtubules depolymerize if the free monomer pool is lowered either by dilution or by complexing the monomer with drugs such as colchicine or nocodazole. Given the physical limit on k_{on} it is clear from equation (1) that the extent of polymerization and k_{off} are inversely related and that polymers at true equilibrium within the cell can choose either efficient use of tubulin subunits (low K_{diss}) or rapid dynamics (high k_{off}) but not both. As we shall see, the unusual physical chemical properties of tubulin allow the cell to circumvent the physical limitations posed by equation (1).

Evidence that rates of exchange *in vivo* of the monomer of tubulin with the polymer were very rapid was previously found only for mitotic cells (Inoue, 1981; Saxton *et al.* 1984), but recently it has been demonstrated for interphase cells. Tubulin modified with fluorescein has been injected into cells and the rates of turnover have been measured by allowing the tubulin to exchange with the total monomer and polymer pool and then measuring the re-equilibration after photobleaching (Salmon *et al.* 1984; Saxton *et al.* 1984). These experiments confirmed the rapid microtubule turnover inferred previously in mitotic cells from polarization microscopy studies and extended these results to interphase cells where the dynamics were found to be slower but the microtubules are much longer. The question raised by the fluorescent photobleaching studies was: how could microtubules turnover so quickly and yet maintain appreciable polymer mass under the constraints imposed by equation (1)?

UNUSUAL PROPERTIES OF MICROTUBULES *IN VITRO*

An explanation for the puzzling *in vivo* properties of microtubules has come from recent *in vitro* experiments (Mitchison & Kirschner, 1984a,b). The microtubule is an unusual polymer in that it hydrolyses GTP during assembly. Assembly will proceed with non-hydrolysable analogues of GTP but the kinetics are somewhat different. For many years it was unclear what function was served by the input of energy and it was even questioned whether the hydrolysis activity was real or important. Since microtubules superficially resembled self-assembly systems that come to true equilibrium, there was no obvious function for GTP hydrolysis in assembly.

In the last few years, however, it has been increasingly clear that microtubules have unusual non-equilibrium properties (Hill & Carlier, 1983). Under assembly conditions where the amount of polymer does not change with time, the system is still far from equilibrium. For example, microtubules assembled to a plateau in polymer mass undergo dramatic changes in length and number (Mitchison & Kirschner, 1984b): there is a steady decrease in polymer number with a corresponding increase in polymer length. Further analysis showed that a majority of microtubules are growing, with a minority shrinking at a rapid rate, so that subunits freed by depolymerization are used for microtubule growth. Such dynamics have been termed dynamic instability.

Previous studies by Carlier *et al.* (1984) and by Farrell *et al.* (1983) showed that the rate of polymerization varied non-linearly with tubulin concentration, with the result that the measured rate of depolymerization was much faster than the rate expected from extrapolation to zero tubulin concentration of the net growth rate above the critical concentration. These results suggested that the mechanism of depolymerization was not the reverse process of the mechanism of polymerization. All of these results pointed to non-equilibrium behaviour requiring input of energy from GTP hydrolysis.

A model incorporating these new dynamic features is shown in Fig. 3 (Kirschner & Mitchison, 1986). It is based on the work of Hill, Carlier, Mitchison and Kirschner. In this model microtubules assemble from GTP-containing tubulin and hydrolyse their GTP to GDP during the course of assembly. As shown in Fig. 3, this hydrolysis can lag slightly behind polymerization to produce a chimaeric polymer with GTP bound to tubulin subunits at the ends of the polymer and GDP in the core subunits. The size of this 'GTP cap' depends on the relative rates of assembly and hydrolysis, but while the latter is fixed by the chemistry of tubulin, the former varies with the rate of polymerization, which at high concentrations of tubulin is directly proportional to the concentration of tubulin. In any case the addition of GTP-containing subunits to GTP ends is thought to be a favourable process with a low

K_{diss}. Again, according to the model, the size of the GTP cap should fluctuate statistically and if it falls below a minimum size and exposes the GDP-containing subunits the microtubules would enter a rapid depolymerization phase with a high K_{diss}. Several studies have documented the instability of GDP tubulin. Once in the depolymerizing phase, microtubules composed of pure GDP tubulin tend to depolymerize to completion (Kristofferson *et al.* 1986).

The model, although not proven directly, explains many features of microtubule growth and provides an interesting use of the energy of GTP hydrolysis. Persistent microtubule growth at high tubulin concentration is explained by the presence of a large GTP cap that has a small probability of disappearance. The sudden rapid depolymerization of microtubules is explained by the loss of the GTP cap. Polymerization of microtubules from centrosomes below the critical concentration of tubulin is explained by transient stability of the GTP cap, even though the microtubules are ultimately unstable. The picture of microtubule assembly from centrosomes at low concentration of tubulin that emerges from the *in vitro* studies is as follows. Centrosomes nucleate microtubules that are individually unstable. They

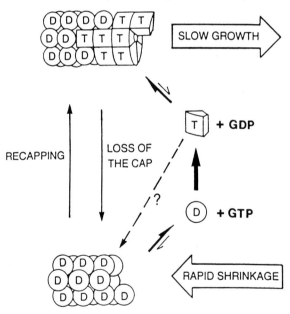

Fig. 3. Model for dynamic instability. Microtubules with a cap of GTP-containing subunits (denoted by T) are shown growing slowly by the addition of T-containing subunits. The free T subunits are shown to be in equilibrium with the T-containing end, with a very low dissociation constant. At some probability GTP hydrolysis catches up with assembly, the T cap disappears and the polymer transits to the 'rapid shrinkage' phase (all D) shown below. This polymer rapidly loses subunits from its end (high dissociation constant). The GDP-containing subunits that are released (denoted by D) exchange with free GTP in solution and form T subunits. It is not known whether T subunits can add to a depolymerizing end to recap the shrinking polymer.

each grow out and at some probability lose their GTP cap and quickly depolymerize. Since the centrosome is a permanent nucleation site it can continually renucleate microtubules. Thus although the individual microtubules are unstable, a stable array of polymers persists.

DYNAMIC INSTABILITY *IN VIVO*

We would like to know whether the unusual microtubule dynamics observed *in vitro* in fact apply *in vivo*. To study this we have microinjected cells with tubulin labelled with *N*-hydroxy succinimidyl biotin (Mitchison & Kirschner, 1985). These cells are allowed to incubate with the injected tubulin before permeabilization and fixation for immunofluorescence. The incorporated biotin–tubulin can be visualized with an antibody to biotin and the total microtubule distribution with antibody to tubulin. With this simple methodology we endeavoured to measure the assembly rate of individual microtubules in the cell, the sites of subunit addition, the extent and pattern of microtubule turnover and, by implication, the pattern of microtubule disassembly.

Fig. 4A shows the pattern of subunit addition 1 min after injection of biotin tubulin. Fig. 4B shows the total microtubule network in the same cell. Microtubule subunits are seen to assemble at the ends of existing microtubules and at the centrosomes. Fig. 5 shows the pattern of subunit incorporation 5 min after injection. Some microtubules extend to the periphery of the cell while other microtubules are seen as short segments. As shown by comparison with the total microtubule distribution (Fig. 5B) many microtubules remain unlabelled. Electron microscopy confirms the coexistence of labelled and unlabelled segments. The rate of subunit incorporation is $3 \cdot 7 \, \mu\text{m min}^{-1}$. For a fuller discussion of these results see Schulze & Kirschner (1986).

The picture that emerges for the microtubule arrays inside cells is not unlike that for microtubules *in vitro*. The so-called steady state *in vitro* is far from steady; the constancy of polymer mass obscures rapid changes in microtubule length and number. *In vitro* centrosomes can nucleate an array of microtubules, which grow transiently, depolymerize and then are replaced by new microtubule growth. The situation *in vivo* seems very much the same. The superficially steady state and apparently constant polymer mass *in vivo* in reality hide rapid turnover and dynamics. Microtubules are constantly growing and shrinking, and are constantly replaced by new nucleation from the centrosome.

STABLE MICROTUBULES IN THE CELL

In the biotin–tubulin injection experiments, we noticed that some microtubules do not appear to turnover with the rapid kinetics observed for the majority of microtubules in the cell. For example, if a fibroblast cell has typically 200 microtubules and the majority turnover with a half-time of 10 min, we expect that only one

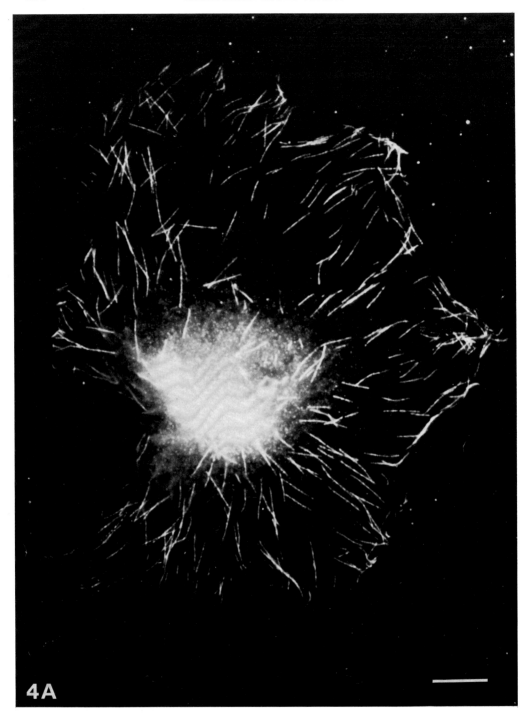

4A

Fig. 4. Pattern of subunit incorporation after injection of biotin–tubulin into a fibroblast cell 1 min before fixation. A. Stained with antibody to biotin. B. Stained with antibody to tubulin to show the total microtubule array. Bar, 10 μm.

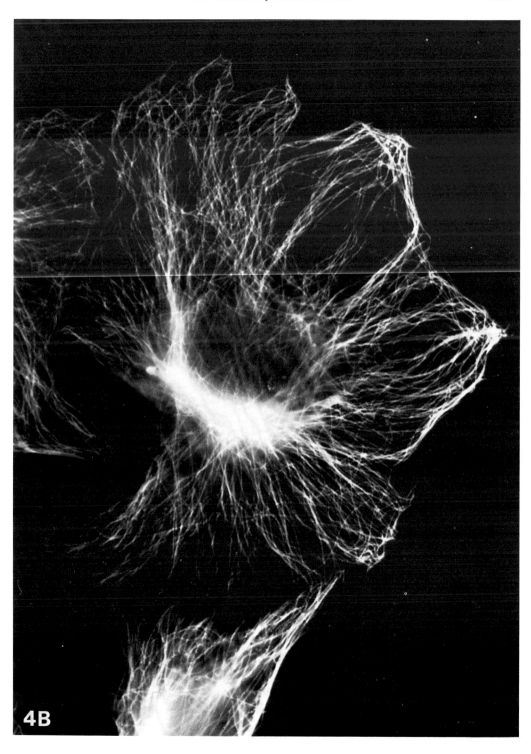

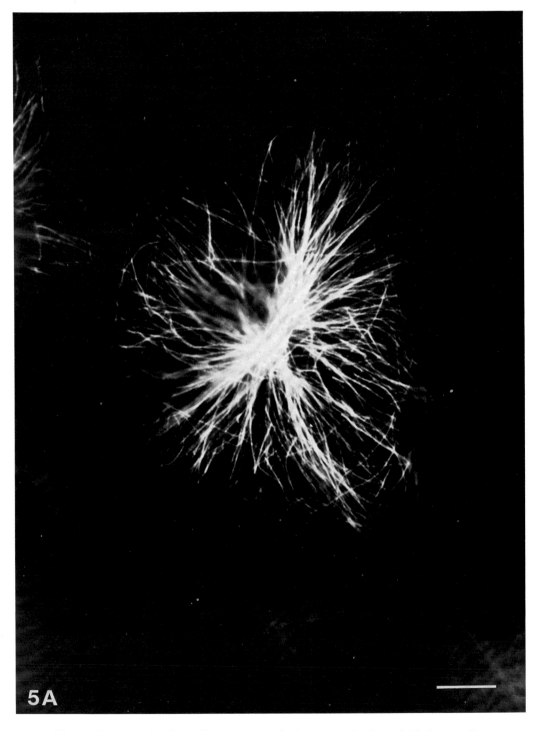

5A

Fig. 5. Pattern of subunit incorporation 5 min after injection of biotin tubulin. A. Stained with antibody to biotin to indicate new microtubule growth. B. Stained with antibody to tubulin to show entire microtubule array. Bar, 10 μm.

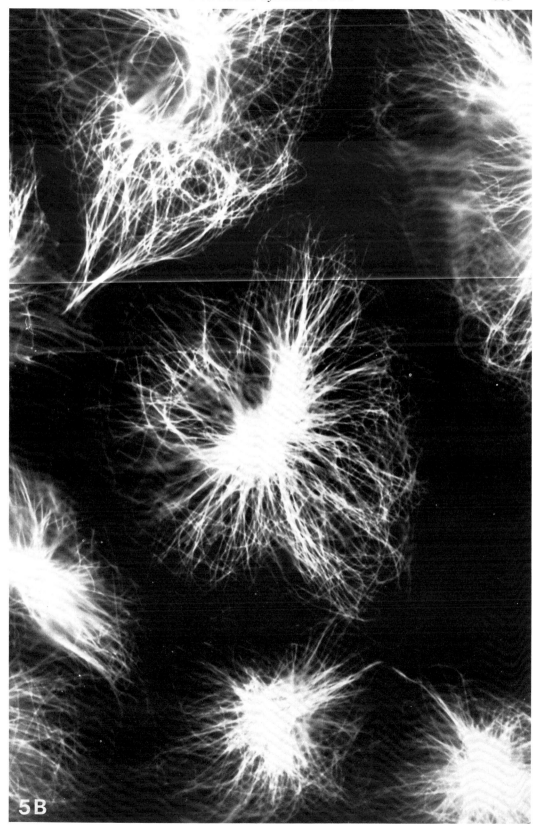

5B

or two microtubules would not have exchanged in 1 h. Yet we find 10–50 microtubules that have not exchanged and several that have not exchanged in 2 h. By 12 h all microtubules have exchanged their subunits.

Although it is possible to identify stable microtubule regions by comparing the total microtubule distribution with the biotin–tubulin distribution, it is not possible to trace their overall organization in the cell. To do this it would be desirable to label the stable microtubules directly, in a manner as direct as that used to label the dynamic microtubule with antibody to biotin. We have developed a new method for visualizing stable microtubules. Microtubules that have exchanged with biotin subunits are first labelled with anti-biotin and then with a fluorescent secondary antibody. Several more layers of antibody are then applied. The labelling reaction coats the biotin-containing microtubules with sufficient protein to block a subsequent reaction with anti-tubulin antibody. When the cell is subsequently stained with anti-tubulin and a secondary antibody labelled with a different fluorochrome only the stable microtubules are visualized (i.e. those that have not incorporated biotin–tubulin).

Fig. 6 shows a pair of micrographs illustrating stable (Fig. 6A) and dynamic (Fig. 6B) microtubules in a fibroblast cell. As can be seen these microtubules have a different distribution from the biotin-containing microtubules. They are curly, located near the centrosome, and generally do not extend out to the cell periphery.

IMPORTANCE OF STABLE MICROTUBULES FOR CELL MORPHOGENESIS

A fundamental problem in cell morphogenesis is the generation of cell asymmetries in response, usually, to extracellular signals. In many cases the extracellular signal is unknown but in some it is likely to be the extracellular matrix, growth factors or chemotactic agents. The response of cells to these signals has been well described and often includes asymmetric process formation (as is the case in neuronal cells), specialization of membrane domains, asymmetric positioning of the nucleus (as in columnar epithelial cells), movement of the centrosome and Golgi apparatus (in migrating cells), displacement of secretory vesicles or intracellular organelles (in secretory cells), etc. In many of these processes microtubules play an essential role in the generation of cell asymmetry. To some degree we can simplify the problem of cell morphogenesis to one of cytoskeletal morphogenesis and, although this is certainly an oversimplification, we can simplify it further to a problem of the regulation of the spatial arrangements of microtubules in cells.

There are two general classes of models for how the spatial organization of microtubules may be regulated. In the first, an extracellular signal would somehow induce repolymerization or reorganization of microtubules into a new configuration. In analogy with models of the immune system, one could call this an instructive model. In the second class, microtubules would polymerize at random and turn over rapidly. Virtually any configuration would appear at some point spontaneously, but would only be transiently stable. If the cell had some way of stabilizing the desired configuration, it would become the dominant configuration. Again in analogy with the immune system, this would be a selective model.

Dynamic instability suggests a mechanism by which a selective model would function for morphogenesis. As shown in Fig. 7, an extracellular signal can generate microtubule distribution by stabilizing the microtubules at the plasma membrane where the signal is presented. From an initially dynamic and random array would emerge the specific array of choice. Since stabilization near the end of a microtubule will stabilize the entire microtubule, information is in fact transferred from the end of the microtubule near the cell membrane to deep into the cell interior. This model predicts that microtubules of varying stability should be generated in cells and that these arrays should have some specific spatial organization.

As shown in Fig. 6, this is fulfilled for fibroblast cells although at present we do not know the function of stable microtubules or what signal induces their formation. Since these microtubules are often oriented to one side of the cell they may be related to the direction of cell movement. In more-polarized cells, such as epithelia or neurones, we hope to learn whether the disposition of stable microtubules is related to the polarization of the cell.

MICROTUBULE STABILITY AND POST-TRANSLATIONAL MODIFICATION

In the last several years two very interesting reports showed that microtubule populations in the same cell could be chemically differentiated. Gunderson *et al.* (1984) made antibody against the C-terminal peptide of α-tubulin and another against the C-terminal peptide lacking the last amino acid, tyrosine. When cells were stained with these two antibodies a non-overlapping set of microtubules were stained. Previously it had been shown that there is a cycle of tyrosine addition and removal at the C-terminal end that is specific for α-tubulin, but which has an unknown function. A similar result was obtained with a monoclonal antibody against the acetylated form of α-tubulin (Thompson *et al.* 1984), which also stained a subset of microtubules in the same cell.

An understanding of how microtubules can be modified along their entire length and yet occupy the same region of the cell as unmodified microtubules comes readily from our present knowledge of microtubule dynamics. As shown in Fig. 5 microtubules exchange one at a time by depolymerization back to the centrosome, followed by regrowth. Therefore the steady-state array of microtubules consists of populations of microtubules that differ in age. The age differences must be more extreme between tubulin in different microtubules than it is between the proximal and distal end of a given microtubule. These differences in age can easily be exploited to generate chemical differences between the microtubules. Microtubules that are older will, for example, be exposed longer to the specific carboxypeptidase responsible for removal of the C-terminal tyrosine or be exposed longer to other post-translational reactions such as phosphorylation or acetylation, or even to the binding of some associated protein.

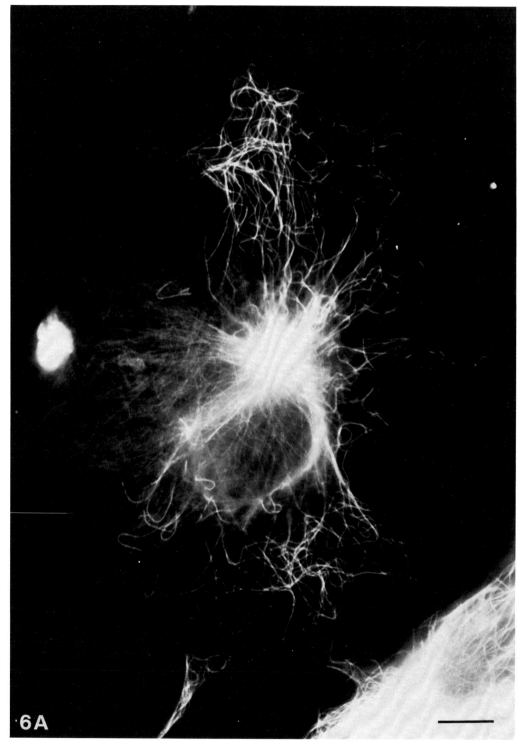

Fig. 6. Stable and unstable microtubules in the cell. Fibroblast cell injected with biotin–tubulin 1 h before fixation and immunofluorescence processing. A. Antibody to tubulin revealing microtubules that are stable to exchange over 1 h. Owing to multiple layers of antibody on the biotin–tubulin, the antibody to tubulin does not react appreciably with the microtubules containing biotin–tubulin. Bar, 10 μm.

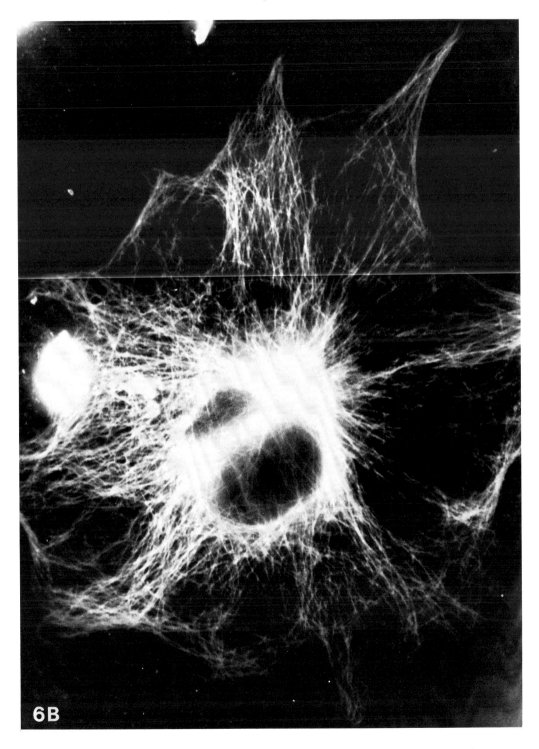

Fig. 6B. Biotin–tubulin detected with antibody to biotin and fluorescent secondary antibody showing all the microtubules that have exchanged in 1 h.

The overall distribution of detyrosinated tubulin seemed generally similar to the distribution of stable microtubules as shown in Fig. 6. The microtubules tended to be curly, shorter, and not extend into the cell periphery. To test this more directly we have recently begun to compare these microtubule distributions by double-label experiments. We have identified first the stable and unstable class by biotin–tubulin microinjection and in the same cell evaluated the presence of tyrosinated and de-tyrosinated tubulin. Preliminary results show that the stable microtubule class is enriched in detyrosinated tubulin, while the unstable class is enriched in tyrosinated tubulin. The segregation is not perfect since the definition of stable microtubules is to some degree arbitrarily fixed as those that have not exchanged subunits for a given amount of time. However, 1 h of stability seems to correlate well with post-translational modification in African Green monkey kidney fibroblast cells.

MICROTUBULE SPECIFICATION OF CELL MORPHOGENESIS

Spatial specialization or specification of microtubules is clearly an important part of cell morphogenesis. It is hard to evaluate how important it is, since after many

Morphogenesis by selective stabilization

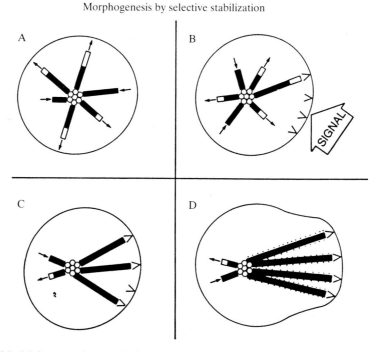

Fig. 7. Model for morphogenesis by selective stabilization of microtubules. In A we depict an unpolarized cell with microtubules growing out randomly with no preferred direction and spontaneously shortening by dynamic instability. In B a local extracellular signal activates some capping structures near the cell periphery. In C the selective stabilization of these capping structures leads gradually to a reorientation of the micro-tubule arrays. In D the polarization is complete with capped microtubules much less dynamic than the unpolarized ones. Here we also show chemical modification of the less-dynamic microtubules, as indicated by the dots.

years of study we are still uncertain about the function of microtubules. Microtubules may serve a morphogenetic function directly. However, with the emerging picture of the role of microtubules in intracellular transport (Vale *et al.* 1985), it is clear that they could regulate vesicular traffic in the cell. Microtubules also influence other cytoskeletal elements, such as intermediate filaments, and during mitosis they influence the distribution of actin filaments in the cleavage furrow.

Whatever their function in morphogenesis the distribution of microtubules serves as a paradigm for the problem of the generation of spatial organization. The genome determines the sequence of a polypeptide, which presumably can fold spontaneously to give a globular protein, which presumably can assemble spontaneously to give a cylindrical polymer made up of subunits held together by non-covalent interactions. Yet, complicated as the sequence of assembly events is, it still must follow directly from the linear genetic sequence. It is the problem of arranging these polymers in the cell and of choosing a distribution that serves some functional purpose that is not clearly connected with the linear genetic information. A similar failure to express in a determinative manner a perfectly defined structure from the blueprint in the genome occurs in the immune system and in evolution itself. In these cases, for example, a specific antibody directed against a novel antigen or a new organism evolved to fit a novel niche, the genome has merely provided a complex and even random mixture of possibilities upon which outside selective forces can act. It seems likely that this is the general strategy used to generate specific microtubule arrays in cells. For selection to work, a mechanism is needed to generate diversity. Dynamic instability with its rapid random growth and depolymerization is well suited to generating variable spatial arrangements of microtubules. We know nothing about the role of specific microtubule arrangements in cultured fibroblast cells or how selection takes place. In mitotic cells, however, recent evidence suggests that the kinetochore of metaphase chromosomes has as one of its functions the stabilization of the ends of microtubules that grow rapidly from the centrosome (Mitchison *et al.* 1986; Nicklas & Kubai, 1985; Mitchison & Kirschner, 1985). Once stabilization is achieved it may be rather transient and mechanisms should exist for converting a transient stabilization into a more permanent one. Post-translational modification, which can easily distinguish microtubules on the basis of their stability (age), could convert an initial stabilization into a more permanent one. Some modifications could also be used to specify the function of such stabilized microtubules; for example, by facilitating intracellular transport. Since microtubule stabilization can occur by a local interaction at the microtubule end, such stabilization could serve to communicate information from the cell periphery to the cell interior.

Although the microtubule polymer is not a very complicated structure, the dynamics of its assembly are very sophisticated. The energy of GTP hydrolysis is used to create different subunit conformations in the polymer that differ in stability. Most assembly systems such as viruses or oligomeric proteins, though structurally more complicated than microtubules, do not require an input of energy. It now appears that this energy input for microtubules is used to create an intrinsically dynamic population. For an equilibrium system rapid dynamics would require a high

k_{off} and, given a fixed limit on k_{on}, would mean a high K_{diss} or inefficient utilization of subunits. The use of GTP hydrolysis permits both a high k_{off} and efficient subunit utilization. Rapid dynamics leading to complex microtubule populations, followed by selective stabilization, are the mechanisms that can be used to achieve specific microtubule configurations in cells. Further stabilization or discrimination may then be achieved by post-translational modification.

We thank David Kristofferson and Tim Mitchison for experimental contributions to the work presented here, and Louise Evans and Cynthia Cunningham-Hernandez for preparation of the figures and the text. This work was supported by grants from the National Institute of General Medical Sciences (US) and the American Cancer Society.

REFERENCES

BLUESTEIN, H. G. (1978). Neurocytotoxic antibodies in serum of patients with systemic lupus erythematosus. *Proc. natn. Acad. Sci. U.S.A.* **75**, 3965–3969.

CARLIER, M.-F., HILL, T. L. & CHEN, Y. D. (1984). Interference of GTP hydrolysis in the mechanism of microtubule assembly: an experimental study. *Proc. natn. Acad. Sci. U.S.A.* **81**, 771–775.

FARRELL, K. W., HIMES, R. H., JORDAN, M. A. & WILSON, L. (1983). On the nonlinear relationship between the initial rates of dilution-induced microtubule disassembly and the initial free subunit concentration. *J. biol. Chem.* **258**, 14 148–14 156.

GUNDERSON, G. G., KALNOSKI, M. H. & BULINSKI, J. C. (1984). Distinct populations of microtubules: tyrosinated and nontyrosinated α-tubulin are distributed differently *in vivo. Cell* **38**, 779–789.

HILL, T. L. & CARLIER, M.-F. (1983). Steady-state theory of the interference of GTP hydrolysis in the mechanism of microtubule assembly. *Proc. natn. Acad. Sci. U.S.A.* **80**, 7234–7238.

INOUE, S. (1981). Cell division and the mitotic spindle. *J. Cell Biol.* **91**, 131s–147s.

KIRSCHNER, M. & MITCHISON, T. (1986). Beyond self-assembly: from microtubules to morphogenesis. *Cell* **45** (in press).

KRISTOFFERSON, D., MITCHISON, T. & KIRSCHNER, M. (1986). Direct observation of steady-state microtubule dynamics. *J. Cell Biol.* **102**, 1007–1019.

MITCHISON, T. J. & KIRSCHNER, M. W. (1985). Properties of the kinetochore *in vitro.* II. Microtubule capture and ATP-dependent translocation. *J. Cell Biol.* **101**, 766–777.

MITCHISON, T. & KIRSCHNER, M. (1984a). Microtubule assembly nucleated by isolated centrosomes. *Nature, Lond.* **312**, 232–237.

MITCHISON, T. & KIRSCHNER, M. (1984b). Dynamic instability of microtubule growth. *Nature, Lond.* **312**, 237–242.

NICKLAS, R. B. & KUBAI, D. F. (1985). Microtubules, chromosome movement and reorientation after chromosomes are detached from the spindle by micromanipulation. *Chromosoma* **92**, 313–324.

OOSAWA, R. & ASAKURA, S. (1975). *Thermodynamics of the Polymerization of Protein.* New York: Academic Press.

SALMON, E. D., LESLIE, R. J., SAXTON, W. M., KAROW, M. L. & McINTOSH, J. R. (1984). Spindle microtubule dynamics in sea urchin embryos: analysis using a fluorescein-labeled tubulin and measurement of fluorescence redistribution after laser photobleaching. *J. Cell Biol.* **99**, 2165–2174.

SAXTON, W. M., STEMPLE, D. L., LESLIE, R. J., SALMON, E. D., ZAVORTINK, M. & McINTOSH, J. R. (1984). Tubulin dynamics in cultured mammalian cells. *J. Cell Biol.* **99**, 2175–2186.

SCHULZE, E. & KIRSCHNER, M. (1986). Microtubule dynamics in interphase cells. *J. Cell Biol.* **102**, 1026–1031.

THOMPSON, W. C., ASAI, D. J. & CARNEY, D. H. (1984). Heterogeneity among microtubules of the cytoplasmic microtubule complex detected by a monoclonal antibody to alpha tubulin. *J. Cell Biol.* **98**, 1017–1025.

VALE, R. D., REESE, T. S. & SHEETZ, M. P. (1985). Identification of a novel force-generating protein, kinesin, involved in microtubule-based motility. *Cell* **42**, 39–50.

J. Cell Sci. Suppl. 5, 311–328 (1986)
Printed in Great Britain © The Company of Biologists Limited 1986

THE CYTOSKELETON OF THE EARLY *DROSOPHILA* EMBRYO

R. M. WARN

School of Biological Sciences, University of East Anglia, Norwich NR4 7TJ, Norfolk, UK

SUMMARY

The organization and roles of the cytoskeleton are described for a complex developing system (the early *Drosophila* embryo) at a time when the basic embryonic plan is mapped out. This type of embryo shows a separation of mitosis from cytokinesis during the early stages of development. Most cells are only formed when a syncytium of ≈6000 nuclei are present. The functions of the cytoskeleton are considered for the process of nuclear migration (pre-blastoderm), which distributes the nuclei throughout the embryo and brings most of them close to the surface. They are also described for the subsequent mitoses of the syncytial blastoderm where the cortex and its well-developed cytoskeleton is reorganized into cell-like surface protrusions known as 'caps' or 'buds'. A comparison is made of the very different cytoskeletal organization present during the cleavages that form the two cell types of early development (pole cell and blastoderm cell), together with information from mutations that affect various aspects of these cleavages *via* factors laid down during oogenesis.

INTRODUCTION

The cytoskeleton of early stage embryos is one of some complexity and of much interest from a developmental viewpoint. For the sub-division of the egg into cells creates the basic embryonic organization that will be subsequently elaborated into an organism. How the egg is divided into cells is a matter of much significance for further development. Therefore the genetic and cytoplasmic control of this process is likely to be elaborate, and must constitute a significant component of the programming of embryogenesis.

The early stage *Drosophila* embryo is a convenient material for studies of the cytoskeletal organization of embryos. Eggs are readily available and the embryos are fairly easily handled. Micro-injection can be done without difficulty and this enables *in vivo* studies to be carried out. Most importantly of all, the wealth of mutant forms available permits a genetic dissection of cytoskeletal action and its regulation.

To follow the workings of the cytoskeleton in the *Drosophila* embryo it is first necessary to describe briefly the pattern of cleavages and the process of cellularization (cf. Sonnenblick, 1950; Fullilove & Jacobson, 1978, for further details). The first nine cleavages are internal and occur without cytokinesis. Thus the embryo forms as a syncytium. During nuclear cycle 9 the first nuclei migrate into the cortical layer at the posterior pole. Cells are not formed but the nuclei are incorporated into specialized cytoplasmic domains known as caps. During the interphase of the next cycle the majority of the nuclei migrate out into the cortical layer and caps also form around them. After this has occurred the embryo is recognized as being in the syncytial blastoderm stage. During the mitosis of cycle 10 the caps at the posterior pole are cleaved to give rise to the pole cells, the precursors of the germ-cell line. The remainder of the embryo remains as a syncytium for three further divisions and then cell membranes extend simultaneously over the whole surface to form a monolayer of cells, the cellular blastoderm.

THE PRE-BLASTODERM EMBRYO

After fertilization the cytoskeleton is a major constituent of two types of domain within the embryo. The first of these is a well-defined cortex beneath the plasma-lemma, which forms a zone several micrometres deep. It is characterized by an absence of yolk granules and other large particles. At the poles the cortical layer is somewhat broader than elsewhere (Warn *et al.* 1979). This layer is characterized by the presence of a well-developed cytoskeletal organization with microfilaments, microtubules and intermediate filaments all present. Immunofluorescence studies using rhodamine–phalloidin (Warn *et al.* 1984) and anti-actin antibodies (Karr & Alberts, 1986) have shown that an actin-rich layer is present in the cortex of pre-blastoderm stages. Fig. 1A shows the F-actin organization found in the cortical layer. The surface is thrown up into many small folds, which stain strongly for actin. In the scanning electron microscope the surface plasmalemma is seen thrown into many micro-projections (Turner & Mahowald, 1976) and much of the surface-associated actin staining corresponds to these structures. These projections are also stained with the lectin concanavalin A (ConA) (Warn *et al.* 1984).

At a slightly lower level of focus many small dense aggregates of actin can be seen. These aggregates have an irregular form and vary in size up to several micrometres in diameter. They also occur during the subsequent syncytial and cellular blastoderm stages. The function of these intriguing aggregates is unknown. Actin aggregates are found in the cortex of amphibian oocytes (Franke *et al.* 1976) and early stage mouse embryos (Lehtonen & Badley, 1980). It seems possible that such aggregates may represent an inactive 'holding' form of actin in the polymerized state. Similar but rather larger aggregates have been found in the nurse cells of the *Drosophila* egg chamber during a stage of breakdown of the cytoplasmic contents and their transport into the oocyte (Warn *et al.* 1985*a*).

Using a taxol stabilization procedure Karr & Alberts (1986) have described an extensive microtubule network present within the cortex of pre-blastoderm stages. The microtubules in this region appear to be short and extend from many foci, which seem to connect up into a network over the surface. These foci may represent microtubule-organizing centres. The striking arrangement of these microtubules is quite different from that of other cell types, such as mammalian cultured cells, which normally radiate from centrosomes adjacent to the nucleus (see, e.g., Weber & Osborn, 1979). Centrosome-associated microtubules usually occur in the more central cytoplasm, and although they may turn fairly close to the plasmalemma and follow it over some distance they do not form part of the cortex itself. Thus microtubules might not be expected to be constituents of a cortical layer. There is, however, a precedent for such an arrangement. Oocytes of the starfish *Pisaster* possess an extensive microtubule network within their cortices (Otto & Schroeder, 1984; Schroeder & Otto, 1984). The *Pisaster* cortical microtubule network is rather different from that of *Drosophila* in that many long microtubules are present with few obvious foci. Immunofluorescence studies have also demonstrated the existence of

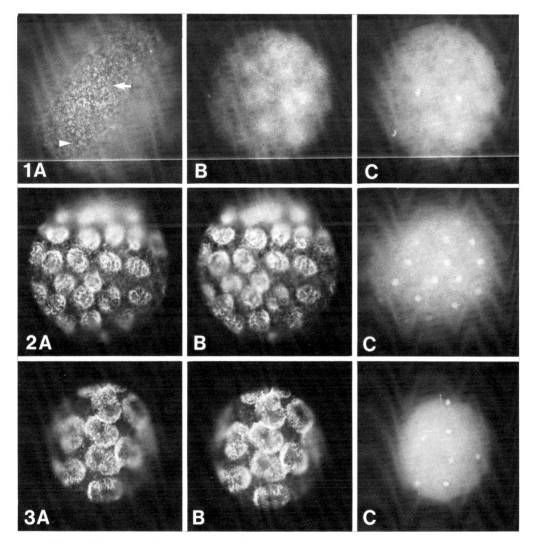

Figs 1–10 show embryos stained with rhodamine–phalloidin for F-actin and DAPI (4'-6,-diamidino-2-phenylindole) for nuclei according to Warn *et al.* (1985*b*).

Fig. 1. A. Cycle 9 embryo cortical layer. The field of focus progresses into the embryo from top right to bottom left. Arrow, staining at bases of microprojections; arrowhead, small aggregates. ×400 (same magnification, Figs 1–6, 9). B,C. Another embryo showing nuclear islands close to cortex. Nuclei in metaphase.

Fig. 2. A–C. A,B. Upper and lower levels of focus of newly formed cycle 10 somatic caps. C. Interphase nuclei of another embryo of same age.

Fig. 3. A–C. Cycle 10 somatic caps fully expanded. Metaphase.

intermediate filaments of the vimentin type present in the cortex, forming an irregular network throughout the structure (Walter & Alberts, 1984). What relationships may exist between the intermediate filaments and the other networks is unknown.

Thus an elaborate cytoskeleton is present in the cortex of the *Drosophila* preblastoderm embryo. What might its functions be? At present it is hard to give any precise answers in the case of the *Drosophila* embryo, but only reasonable speculations, until functional studies have been undertaken. Bearing this in mind there are a number of probable functions. First, the cortex would be anticipated to provide mechanical stiffening for the large egg cell. Such a role is also compatible with a second function. The early stage *Drosophila* embryo shows a phase of shortening that starts soon after fertilization and leads to fluid-filled pockets forming at both the anterior and posterior poles (Imaizumi, 1954). This process ceases shortly before the syncytial blastoderm stage is initiated and the embryo lengthens again, to return to its previous volume. Using indirect immunofluorescence myosin has been seen to be present in the cortical layer (Warn *et al.* 1979). The hypothesis is therefore proposed that the cortical actin network is under tension, causing the cortex to contract and hence the embryo to shorten. The network then gradually relaxes and the embryo lengthens. Another possible function is that cytoskeletal components laid down in the cortex are used during the subsequent blastoderm stages when the cytoskeleton is very active. A further likely function is that a variety of organelles, such as polar granules, and macromolecules including RNA, are localized by binding to the cytoskeleton in specific areas.

The cytoskeleton is also well-developed around the nuclei in the interior of the embryo during the pre-blastoderm stage. Each nucleus has a well-developed array of microtubules that form into spindles during successive mitoses (Karr & Alberts, 1986; Warn, unpublished results). Connections between the microtubules of the internal nuclei, which are organized from centrosomes, and those of the cortex have not been reported for *Drosophila*. However, temporary associations between the aster microtubules of the internal nuclei and the preiplasm have been noted in the dipteran *Wachtliella* (Wolf, 1978). Each nucleus is surrounded by a clear area known as a nuclear island, which is devoid of yolk granules, like the cortex. All the islands are interconnected by strands of cytoplasm. We have found that the nuclear islands stain strongly with rhodamine–phalloidin, evidence for a high local concentration of F-actin. This is shown for a stage 9 embryo in Fig. 1B.

The manner in which the nuclei migrate towards the surface is a matter of some interest, and suggests that factors providing directionality are associated with these internal cleavages. The first cleavage can apparently occur at any angle with respect to the egg axis (Parks, 1936). Zalokar & Erk (1976) noted that the second cleavage occurs roughly at right angles to the first. Subsequent cleavages do not show a very precisely defined pattern, but result in the nuclei moving outwards whilst occupying a roughly spherical area. After the fourth cleavage the organization of the nuclei changes towards an ellipsoid following the shape of the egg.

This movement of the nuclei toward the surface is dependent upon cytoskeletal action. Application of colchicine has been found to block movement, leaving the nuclei in metaphase. With time they then become scattered within the embryo (Zalokar & Erk, 1976). Cytochalasin B has no effect on lateral nuclear migration but movement towards the poles is stopped. As a result partial blastoderms form, with only the central region of periplasm occupied by nuclei (Zalokar & Erk, 1976).

In *Wachtliella* the nuclei are moved as a result of forces generated by microtubules extending from the nuclear islands to the embryo cortex (Wolf, 1978). In addition nuclei are also shifted passively by cytoplasmic flow. Such cytoplasmic flows also occur in *Drosophila* embryos (Kinsey, 1967; Foe & Alberts, 1983).

THE SYNCYTIAL BLASTODERM

By cycle 9 most of the nuclei are within 10 μm of the embryo surface. During this cycle the first nuclei migrate into the cortex at the posterior pole (cf. below, under POLE CELL FORMATION). After the next cleavage the majority of the nuclei migrate into the cortical layer. As this occurs there is a striking rearrangement of the cortex, which bulges out to form a protuberance above each nucleus (Ede & Counce, 1956; Bownes, 1975; Turner & Mahowald, 1976; Warn & Magrath, 1982; Foe & Alberts, 1983). We have termed this structure a 'cap' to emphasize the distrubution of the cytoskeleton above and around the nuclei. The caps at the posterior pole are referred to as polar caps whilst those found elsewhere on the blastoderm surface are known as somatic caps. Others have called these structures 'buds'. Cap formation is marked by a dramatic reorganization of the cytoskeleton in this region. The plasmalemma of the forming caps is thrown into many folds and the cortex underlying these micro-projections becomes more brightly stained by rhodamine–phalloidin (Fig. 2A; and Warn *et al.* 1984) or by anti-actin antibody staining (Karr & Alberts, 1986). The cytoplasm within the caps also stains quite brightly for F-actin (Fig. 2B). It may well be that this is because the actin-rich cytoplasm that surrounds the preblastoderm nuclei is incorporated into the forming caps. Around the edges of the caps and in regions between them small F-actin aggregates occur.

Studies on living embryos have demonstrated that a bilobed organization appears not long after, and sometimes with, the appearance of the caps during interphase of cycle 10 (Warn & Magrath, 1982). The plane of separation of the two halves indicates the subsequent plane of cap cleavage. Newly formed caps with a bilobed appearance are also found in fixed material (see Fig. 7). This early appearance of the site of future cleavage suggests a possible adaptation for the very rapid cleavage rates that occur during syncytial blastoderm. It may be that the caps create a pre-pattern that enables the subsequent rapid division to occur.

The pattern of cleavage of the caps shows some unusual features (Warn *et al.* 1984). After the caps have formed they then enlarge further and flatten, taking in increasing amounts of surface plasmalemma and associated cortical cytoplasm. By the time the cap nuclei are in metaphase a central region depleted in F-actin is obvious within the interior of the caps. These regions underlie parts of the central cortex that are rather less folded (Fig. 3A–C). During this stage the caps are quite flattened and bilobed in appearance. The caps cleave in two during the later stages of mitosis (Figs 4A–C, 5A–C, 8). Progressively later phases demonstrate that actin disappears between daughter caps whilst they separate and round up again. Fig. 8 shows a low-power photograph with caps in various stages of cleavage. Early in this process brightly fluorescent folds mark the boundaries in the central region (arrow in Fig. 8). At later stages there is a wider region marked by reduced F-actin staining between the forming daughter caps (arrowheads in Fig. 8; Fig. 4A–C). The caps then round up as they begin to protrude again (Fig. 5A–C). Fig. 5A,B also illustrate

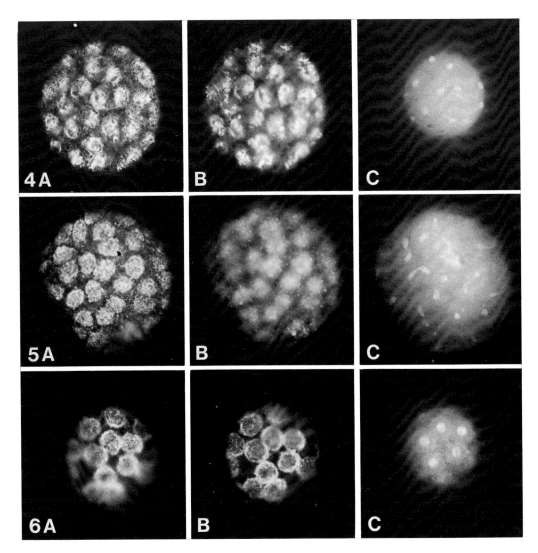

Fig. 4. A–C. Cycle 10 somatic caps in division. Telophase.

Fig. 5. A–C. Cycle 10 somatic caps reforming late in division. Telophase.

Fig. 6. A–C. Fully formed cycle 11 somatic caps. Interphase.

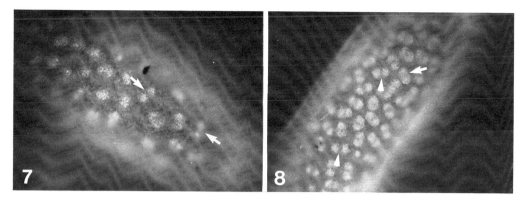

Fig. 7. Newly formed cycle 10 somatic caps. Arrows indicate groove in some caps. ×187.

Fig. 8. Cycle 10 somatic caps in division. Arrow, area of separation in cap beginning to cleave; arrowheads point to cleaving caps. ×120.

the small dense aggregates and actin threads that are present around the cap edges during the final phases of cap separation. At the end of the cycle fully reformed caps bulge out again (Fig. 6A–C). They have an irregularly folded sub-plasmalemma layer of staining with an interior cap cytoplasm that is also quite positively stained.

The caps cleave across the long axis of the area taken in during the expansion phase. This cleavage is not a furrowing into the embryo but rather a swelling out of the daughter caps from the ends of the parent caps coupled with a rupture of the original cap organization (Warn & Magrath, 1982; Foe & Alberts, 1983; Warn *et al.* 1984). The cycle of surface changes during the last cycle of syncytial blastoderm has also been clearly documented, using the scanning electron microscope, in the related dipteran *Calliphora* and shows a very similar pattern of changes (Lundquist & Lowkvist, 1984). The mechanism of cleavage is not well understood at present but the current evidence suggests that a contractile half-ring of F-actin filaments cutting the caps in two is unlikely to be the major agent of cleavage. F-actin is lost from the region of splitting at the time when the cap interiors show conspicuously bright fluorescence. Thus there may well be a migration of actin into the re-forming caps, perhaps as a result of contraction. This contraction coupled with insertion of membrane in regions between the new caps could comprise the major forces of the splitting process.

Stafstrom & Staehelin (1984) have described 'pseudo-cleavage furrows' between the caps during mitosis. These are in fact areas where caps abut as a result of their expansion. Where this occurs an apparent furrow is visible. With fluorescence optics lines of brighter staining occur wherever the sides of two caps come close enough together for the images to be summated. Regions of optical overlap can be found in cycle 10 embryos and become increasingly common in later syncytial stages where more caps occur closer together. Caps are therefore found with one edge brighter than the other, as can be seen in Fig. 9 (and see also Karr & Alberts, 1986). Furthermore, we have found no evidence of a contractile ring network like that of the cellular blastoderm during metaphase or anaphase, which would act to pull the membranes down. During telophase, prior to daughter cap formation, the caps are at their flattest and thus little membrane folding or overlap occurs giving the effect that the furrows disappear. Using the method of micro-injection of TMRITC–bovine serum albumin (BSA) into the perivitelline space (Warn & Magrath, 1982), we have failed to find any evidence of pseudo-cleavage furrows, nor has Foe, using Normarski optics (Foe & Alberts, 1983, and personal communication). If floor deepening does occur between caps in the later syncytial cycles during mitosis, the effect must be small.

Microtubule distribution has also been examined in detail during syncytial blastoderm by both indirect immunofluorescence and electron microscopy. Antibody staining methods have been based on modifications of the procedure of Mitchison & Sedat (1983). Warn & Warn (1986) used methanol as the primary fixative. This resulted in good fixation of spindle fibres but interphase microtubules were in general

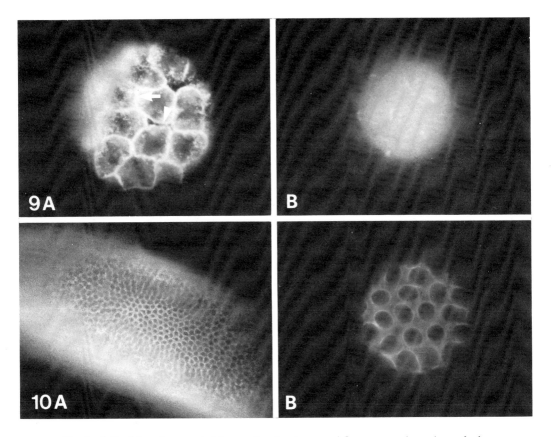

Fig. 9. A,B. Metaphase cycle 11 caps showing increased fluorescence in regions of edge overlap (arrow) compared with edges separated by a gap (arrowhead).

Fig. 10. A,B. A. Lower power (×160); and B, high power (×1000) view of cellular blastoderm stage at the level of the contractile ring network. Fixed with 8% paraformaldehyde in PHEM buffer.

not so well preserved. Large interphase centrosomes were seen with this procedure. Karr & Alberts (1986) used formaldehyde as the primary fixative and used a low concentration of taxol to stabilize the microtubules prior to fixation. With this fixation protocol interphase caps appear as richly endowed with microtubules. They surround the nuclei and penetrate some way into the underlying cytoplasm. However, centrosomes were not at all evident, due to the profusion of microtubules.

The changes in microtubule organization during the cap cycle, as perceived by combining the two fixation protocols, is given for cycle 10 embryos in Fig. 11. At interphase the centrosomes are already divided; a most unusual observation, for in most cells separation of the centrosomes occurs at prophase (Weber & Osborn, 1979). The early separation of the centrosomes was previously described for pre-blastoderm stages by Huettner (1933) using fixed material. This finding has recently been confirmed in living early syncytial blastoderm embryos (Warn *et al.* un-published results). A rich array of microtubules extends to the cap boundaries and underlies the sub-plasmalemma F-actin layer. This co-distribution of microfilaments and microtubules marks out the caps as special cytoplasmic domains each with an

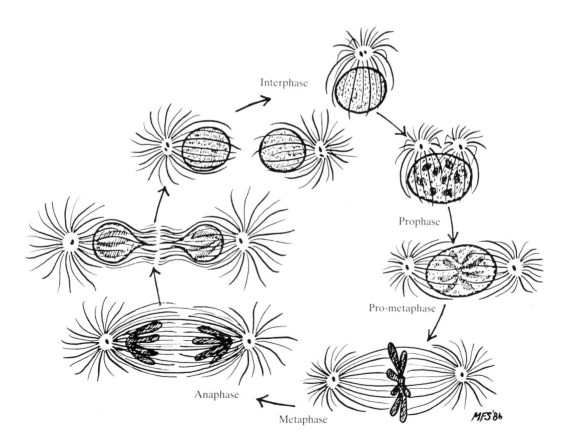

Fig. 11. Diagram illustrating microtubule distribution during cap cycle 10.

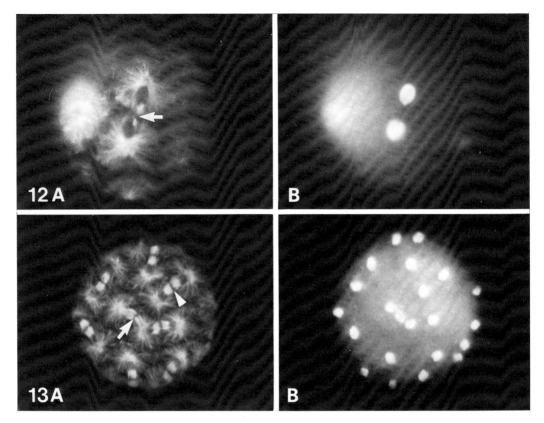

Fig. 12. A,B. Cycle 9 cap at late telophase. A. Microtubule arrays prepared by the method of Karr & Alberts (1986). Arrow, midbody. B. DAPI. ×1000.

Fig. 13. Cycle 11 caps showing midbody formation. A. Microtubules stained as in 12A. Arrow, anaphase spindle; arrowhead, forming midbody at telophase. B. DAPI. ×400.

integrated cytoskeletal organization and pattern of activity. Intermediate filaments are also present within the caps (Walter & Alberts, 1984).

During prophase the centrosomes migrate to the poles and initiate spindle formation. Whilst these processes are occurring the interphase microtubule array is lost, leaving much shorter astral fibres. Stafstrom & Staehelin (1984) have shown, using electron microscopy, that the spindle is of the closed type with microtubules growing in through the fenestrated ends of the nuclear envelope. Anaphase is marked by an elongation of the spindle and a gradual lengthening of the aster microtubules. During telophase a prominent stembody or midbody appears between the re-forming nuclei. As it forms, the microtubule connections to the spindle poles appear to be rapidly reduced, whilst the area between the nuclei remains strongly stained by antibodies. The midbody is very obvious in methanol-fixed embryos where it may represent a more stable microtubule population. It can be observed in taxol–formaldehyde-fixed embryos (Figs 12, 13) and also in living embryos micro-injected with a rhodamine-labelled anti-tubulin antibody (Warn *et al.* unpublished results). The midbody microtubules appear to terminate against the re-forming nuclei. Some microtubules run around the sides of the re-forming nuclei and attach to the centrosomes (arrowhead, Fig. 13A). The centre of the midbody appears lacking in microtubules, as judged by anti-tubulin staining. This is likely to be a masking artefact because electron microscopy reveals dense amorphous material coating the microtubules in this region, as occurs in the midbodies of cultured cells (Saxton *et al.* 1984). It is curious that the caps have such prominent midbodies, but a reasonable role for them is that they are somehow involved in the process of cap splitting. They appear during splitting and have disappeared by its completion. Whilst the caps go into the interphase of the next cycle the interphase array of microtubules is formed from the continued growth of the astral fibres and the caps are again filled with microtubules.

How is the process of mitosis triggered over the surface of the blastoderm? Foe & Alberts (1983) have produced evidence for a mitotic wave moving across the blastoderm surface, usually simultaneously from the anterior and posterior poles. The waves move rapidly with a velocity of $50-250 \, \mu m \, min^{-1}$. On occasions one end may lag up to 2 min behind the other. In these cases the wave that starts first does not pass further than the centre of the embryo. The mitotic waves are associated with movements of the inner yolk mass and the cortical cytoplasm, with the periplasm seeming to change its consistency as the wave front moves across. In the dipteran *Wachtliella* broadly similar changes accompanying mitosis have been reported, with spindles not entering anaphase until a wave of saltation passes around the nuclei (Wolf, 1985). The nature of the signal is unknown, although it has been suggested that they are triggered by a transient rise in the free Ca^{2+} level, which is subsequently sequestered again. Colchicine inhibits both nuclear division and the saltation wave in *Wachtliella*. Thus the target of the waves would seem to be microtubules.

The caps undergo four cleavages during the syncytial blastoderm stage. Each successive cycle is somewhat slower than its predecessor, ranging from 8 min for cycle 10 caps to $17\frac{1}{2}$ min for cycle 13 caps (Warn & Magrath, 1982). After each cleavage more of the surface is incorporated into the caps, which become progressively smaller. Successive cleavages have a tendency to divide roughly at right angles to the previous one and this corresponds to the pattern of centrosome migration. Sometimes the divisions are strikingly regular, as can be seen with the group of caps marked 8 in Fig. 14. However, caps can cleave at any angle with respect to the previous cleavage, as can also be seen in Fig. 14, e.g. cap 13. The caps follow Hertwig's Law and divide across the long axis of the area taken in after their expansion. Often it does not precisely correspond to the predicted angle of cleavage at right angles to the previous one. This finding implies that centrosome position may be altered, perhaps by forces involved in cap expansion or by the cytoplasmic streaming movements that accompany mitosis (Kinsey, 1967; Foe & Alberts, 1983). Rarely, caps divide into three portions instead of two halves and these may divide again, e.g. the lower cap 5 in cycle 11 of Fig. 14. In fixed material groups of very small caps lacking nuclei are sometimes found and these may correspond to such aberrant cleavages.

POLE CELL FORMATION

The caps of the posterior pole have a different history from those of the rest of the embryo (Huettner, 1923; Rabinowitz, 1941; Foe & Alberts, 1983; Warn *et al.* 1985*b*). During cycle 9, five to ten nuclei migrate into the posterior-pole plasm. Some regional mechanism presumably operates so that nuclei only migrate into the cortex in this region. The polar caps protrude somewhat more than the somatic caps, which bulge out during nuclear cycle 10. Prior to polar cap protrusion large club-shaped microvilli are present at the surface in this region only. As the polar caps form, these microvilli disappear except between the caps (Warn, 1979; Swanson & Poodry, 1980). Quite possibly the membrane present in these large microprojections is incorporated into the polar caps.

The process of polar cap formation and their first cleavage during cycle 9 is quite similar to that already described for the somatic caps (Warn *et al.* 1985*b*). The pattern of changes that occur during cycles 9, 10 and 11 is shown diagrammatically in Fig. 15. During cycle 10 the process of the polar caps bulging out and the surfaces then flattening down is as before. However, the caps do not flatten as much as before. At the end of mitosis a hoop of bright F-actin staining encircles the central region of each cap when plasmalemma begins to be drawn down between the daughter nuclei. The microfilament arrangement is strikingly different to that during the previous cleavage. As the pole cells form, the plasmalemma and associated actin layer move down towards the cell bases. The actin associated with the advancing plasmalemma is proposed to act as a contractile half-ring, which shortens as it contracts. The cortical F-actin at the bases of the forming pole cells is quite bright during this first cleavage process. When the plasmalemma reaches the cell bases, pairs of dark circles representing interior cytoplasm are visible, surrounded by bright fluorescence due to

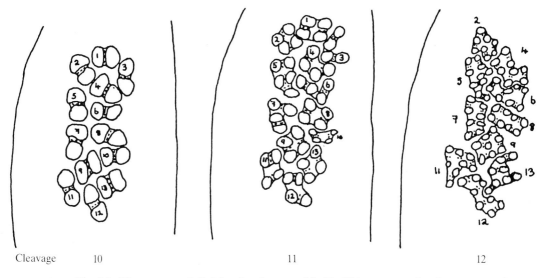

Cleavage   10   11   12

Fig. 14. The pattern of division for cleavages 10, 11, 12 in an area of embryo prepared and drawn out according to Warn & Magrath (1982).

surrounding cortical actin. The dark circles rapidly become smaller and disappear as the cells are pinched off from the underlying embryo cortex. This is postulated to occur by the operation of contractile rings located at the junctions between the pole cell bases and the embryo cortex; 20–30 pole cells are cleaved off as a result. This final phase of cleavage is the only one reported so far where microfilaments have been identified during pole cell formation by transmission electron microscopy (TEM) (Swanson & Poodry, 1980). However, *Drosophila* embryos are known to be difficult material for such electron-microscope (EM) studies (Rickoll, 1976).

The changing pattern of microtubule distribution during the two mitoses of the polar caps and subsequent pole cell formation has also been described. It appears very similar to that found for the somatic caps (Warn, 1986).

BLASTODERM CELL FORMATION

During cycle 14 all the somatic caps are simultaneously converted into cells at the cellular blastoderm stage. Cellularization is marked by a very active involvement of microfilaments (Fullilove & Jacobson, 1971; Rickoll, 1976; Warn & Magrath, 1983). At the beginning of this process each cap becomes surrounded by a roughly hexagonal ring of F-actin microfilaments. These microfilaments are associated with the tips of the inward moving cell membranes, the furrow canals. The microfilaments are interlinked over the surface to form a network. A low-power view of the network is given in Fig. 10A and a high-power view in Fig. 10B. At high power the network shows a rather uniform F-actin distribution. This embryo was prepared after fixation with PHEM buffer and 8% paraformaldehyde (Schliwa & van Blerkom, 1981). Using PHEM buffer there is less clumping of filaments and rupture of the networks compared with fixation using PBS as the buffer (Warn & Magrath, 1983) and thus better cellular blastoderm preparations can be obtained.

The process of cellularization occurs in two phases. The surfaces of the caps are thrown into many microprojections during phase I and are stained brightly for F-actin (Warn & Magrath, 1983). Because the microprojections increase in number during this phase it seems likely that they do not contribute significantly to the membrane extended during this time, and the actin presumably has a role in maintaining the structure of the microprojections. Once the canal furrows have reached to the bases of the nuclei, the rate of membrane growth doubles and the last $10\,\mu m$ of the cell sides are formed. At the same time the micro-projections rapidly disappear, suggesting that they are pulled down to form the new membrane. Simultaneously the actin associated with the micro-projections disappears.

What is the evidence that the ring network is a causal agent in membrane extension? First, as the membranes elongate into the embryo the gaps in the network gradually narrow (Warn & Magrath, 1983). This implies that the network shortens as it moves. Cytochalasin B suppresses plasmalemma extension, which strongly suggests that the network provides the force for extension (Zalokar & Erk, 1976; Foe & Alberts, 1983). Furthermore, myosin has been identified by immunofluorescence microscopy to be present in the rings (Warn *et al.* 1980), demonstrating a similar

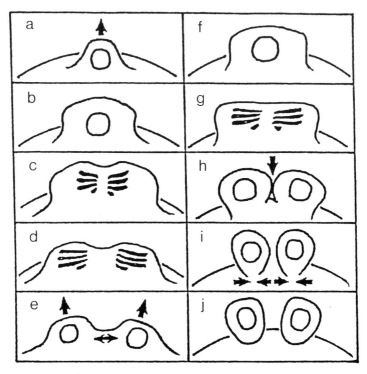

Fig. 15. Diagram to illustrate the shape changes of the polar caps: a–e, cycle 9; f–h, cycle 10; i,j, start of cycle 11. Arrows indicate movements of the cap surfaces. (From Warn *et al.* (1985).)

molecular organization as occurs in the cleavage furrows of cultured cells (Fujiwara & Pollard, 1976). The cell membranes move inwards to a depth of approximately $40\,\mu$m. Movement stops abruptly and the contractile network is replaced by small individual rings of F-actin microfilaments present in the remaining connections between the blastoderm cells and the yolk sac.

During blastoderm cellularization there is a change in the major axis of growth of both the nuclei and the microtubules (Fullilove & Jacobson, 1971; Warn & Warn, 1986). The nuclei elongate at right angles to the embryo surface, becoming oval. At approximately the same time microtubules grow down from pairs of centrosomes located immediately above the apical surfaces of the nuclei. They extend beside the nuclei, forming basket-like structures around them. These microtubules do not seem to run much beyond the distal ends of the nuclei. The microtubule 'baskets' appear to have several functions. If embryos are treated with colchicine early in cycle 14 the nuclei fail to elongate. They also lose their position at the surface and form irregular layers several nuclei deep (Zalokar & Erk, 1976). In addition, the vigorous saltation that accompanies cellularization is lost (Foe & Alberts, 1983). Microtubules therefore seem to act to hold the nuclei in place whilst cells form and also to influence nuclear elongation. The saltation effect also suggests that the microtubules translocate stores of materials required during cellularization.

MATERNAL EFFECTS AND THE CYTOSKELETON

Much information that influences subsequent development is stored in the egg cytoplasm. Some of these maternal 'determinants' act on the cytoskeleton, influencing patterns of cleavage in various types of embryos hours or days after their deposition within the egg. Pole cell formation has provided a particularly clear example where microfilament organization and action are influenced by a particular region of egg cytoplasm. There is a great deal of evidence that pole cells only form from pole plasm, as demonstrated by its micro-injection into other regions of the embryo, which causes ectopic pole cells to cleave (Illmensee & Mahowald, 1974; Niki, 1984). The determinants affect both the time of microfilament action and the kind of structures formed. What structural or regulatory differences may exist between different regions of the egg is a major question.

A variety of maternal-effect *grandchildless* mutants are known that affect pole cell formation. Most of these are pleiotropic in effect and only one found to date specifically affects pole cell formation (Niki & Okada, 1981). It appears that pole cells will only form during a certain time interval. If nuclear migration is held back experimentally and then nuclei allowed to move into the posterior pole, no pole cells form (Okada, 1982). If the posterior tips of pre-blastoderm cells are irradiated with ultraviolet (u.v.) light, no pole cells form unless unirradiated pole plasm is injected into this region (Okada *et al.* 1974; Warn, 1975; Ueda & Okada, 1982). After u.v. irradiation blastoderm cells form in this region and the pole plasm is incorporated into them. Thus some kind of regulatory switch with respect to the kind of cell cleaved off can be induced in the activity of the cytoskeleton in this region.

The egg cytoplasm also contains information for the regulation of blastoderm cell formation. Rice & Garen (1975) have isolated several maternal-effect mutants that affect this process. *mat(3)1* forms pole cells but not blastoderm cells. Two other mutants, *mat(3)3* and *mat(3)6*, form cells only in specific regions of the embryo, suggesting that some kind of positional information may regulate the contractile ring network, either directly or indirectly.

CYTOPLASMIC DOMAINS

The nuclear islands and the caps are good examples of cytoplasmic domains within the syncytial embryo, each with its own cycle of activity and yet also interacting with other domains. Each domain is organized around a nucleus and the cytoskeleton associated with it. In other egg types cytoplasmic domains occur but they are usually not directly associated with a nucleus, e.g. the yellow crescent in the Ascidian egg (Jeffery & Meier, 1983).

The inter-relationships of the different components of the cytoskeleton within the domains is a matter of some interest. The arrival of the nuclear islands at the periphery induces cap formation with striking rearrangements of the F-actin microfilaments, microtubules and intermediate filaments close to the surface. Karr & Alberts (1986) suggest that the microtubules of the islands may have a major role in inducing cap formation. The bilobed cap organization, which is often detectable during cap formation, is certainly consistent with a role for the pair of centrosomes and their associated microtubules in cap generation. During division the spindle poles mark regions where bright staining of F-actin occurs and also of rhodamine–ConA (Warn *et al.* 1984; Karr & Alberts, 1986). In contrast, the central regions stain comparatively weakly for actin and correspond to the spindle interzones. Also the distribution of the interphase microtubule arrays after mitosis corresponds well with the cortical F-actin layers of the new caps. However, such similar distribution of the two networks throughout the cap cycles is only indirect evidence that one cytoskeletal component (the microtubules) may influence or drive the changing distribution of the other (the microfilaments).

For a variety of cell types there is good evidence that the formation of the cleavage furrow is dependent upon the spindle (see Rappaport, 1973; Schroeder, 1975). The mechanism of how this occurs is not understood but the astral microtubules are the most likely candidates for initiating formation of a contractile ring of microfilaments within the cleavage furrow (White, 1985). A similar situation may well hold in the *Drosophila* embryo for the appearance of the contractile ring network. At the beginning of cellular blastoderm formation each cap becomes surrounded around its edges by the F-actin network. In these regions microtubules from adjacent caps abut and it may well be that the stimulation for contractile microfilaments to form emanates from these microtubules in analogous fashion to that occurring in mammals. Evidence in favour of such a hypothesis has been found by Foe & Alberts (1983). Micro-injection of colchicine into embryos just before the start of cellularization prevents it occurring. However, colchicine does not have this affect once plasmalemma extension has begun.

I thank Alba Warn and Ruth Magrath for their help over a number of years in all aspects of this work, M. Symmons for drawing Figs 10 and 15, J. P. Marshall for Figs 12 and 13, and Jill Gorton for putting the paper on disc. We are grateful to the Cancer Research Campaign for financial support.

REFERENCES

BOWNES, M. (1975). A photographic study of development in the living embryo of *Drosophila melanogaster*. *J. Embryol. exp. Morph.* **33**, 789–801.

EDE, D. A. & COUNCE, S. J. (1956). A cinematographic study of the embryology of *Drosophila melanogaster*. *Wilhelm Roux Arch. EntwMech. Org.* **148**, 402–415.

FOE, V. E. & ALBERTS, B. (1983). Studies of nuclear and cytoplasmic behaviour during the five mitotic cycles that precede gastrulation in *Drosophila* embryogenesis. *J. Cell Sci.* **61**, 31–70.

FRANKE, W. W., RATHKE, P. C., SEIB, E., TRENDELENBERG, M. F., OSBORN, M. & WEBER, K. (1976). Distribution and mode of arrangement of microfilamentous structures and actin in the cortex of the amphibian oocyte. *Cytobiologie* **14**, 111–130.

FUJIWARA, K. & POLLARD, T. D. (1976). Fluorescent antibody localization of myosin in the cytoplasm, cleavage furrow, and mitotic spindle of human cells. *J. Cell Biol.* **71**, 848–875.

FULLILOVE, S. L. & JACOBSON, A. G. (1971). Nuclear elongation and cytokinesis in *Drosophila montana*. *Devl Biol.* **26**, 560–577.

FULLILOVE, S. L. & JACOBSON, A. G. (1978). Embryonic development: descriptive. In *The Genetics and Biology of* Drosophila, vol. 2C (ed. M. Ashburner & T. R. F. Wright), pp. 105–227. New York: Academic Press.

HUETTNER, A. F. (1923). The origin of the germ cells in *Drosophila melanogaster*. *J. Morph.* **37**, 385–423.

HUETTNER, A. F. (1933). Continuity of the centrioles in *Drosophila melanogaster*. *Z. Zellforsch. mikrosk. Anat.* **19**, 119–134.

ILLMENSEE, K. & MAHOWALD, A. P. (1974). Transplantation of posterior pole plasm in *Drosophila*. Induction of germ cells at the anterior pole of the egg. *Proc. natn. Acad. Sci. U.S.A.* **71**, 1016–1020.

IMAIZUMI, T. (1954). Recherches sur l'expression des facteurs létaux héréditaires chez l'embryon de la *Drosophile*. *Protoplasma* **44**, 1–10.

JEFFERY, W. R. & MEIER, S. (1983). A yellow crescent cytoskeletal domain in Ascidian eggs and its role in early development. *Devl Biol.* **96**, 125–143.

KARR, T. L. & ALBERTS, B. M. (1986). Organization of the cytoskeleton in early *Drosophila* embryos. *J. Cell Biol.* **102**, 1494–1509.

KINSEY, J. D. (1967). Studies on an embryonic lethal hybrid in *Drosophila*. *J. Embryol. exp. Morph.* **17**, 405–423.

LEHTONEN, E. & BADLEY, R. A. (1980). Localization of cytoskeletal proteins in preimplantation mouse embryos. *J. Embryol. exp. Morph.* **55**, 211–225.

LUNDQUIST, A. & LOWKVIST, B. (1984). Cell surface changes during cytokinesis in a dipteran egg. *Differentiation* **28**, 101–108.

MITCHISON, T. & SEDAT, J. (1983). Localization of antigenic determinants in whole *Drosophila* embryos. *Devl Biol.* **99**, 261–264.

NIKI, Y. (1984). Developmental analysis of the grandchildless (gs(1)N26) mutation in *Drosophila melanogaster*: Abnormal cleavage patterns and defects in pole cell formation. *Devl Biol.* **103**, 182–189.

NIKI, Y. & OKADA, M. (1981). Isolation and characterization of *grandchildless*-like mutants of *Drosophila melanogaster*. *Wilhelm Roux Arch. Devl Biol.* **190**, 1–10.

OKADA, M. (1982). Loss of the ability to form pole cells in *Drosophila* embryos with artificially delayed nuclear arrival at the posterior pole. In *Embryonic Development*, part A, *Genetic Aspects*, pp. 363–372. New York: Alan R. Liss.

OKADA, M., KLEINMAN, I. A. & SCHNEIDERMAN, H. A. (1974). Restoration of fertility in sterilized *Drosophila* eggs by transplantation of polar cytoplasm. *Devl Biol.* **37**, 43–54.

OTTO, J. J. & SCHROEDER, T. S. (1984). Microtubule arrays in the cortex and near the germinal vesicle of immature starfish oocytes. *Devl Biol.* **101**, 274–281.

PARKS, H. B. (1936). Cleavage patterns in *Drosophila* and mosaic formation. *Ann. ent. Soc. Am.* **29**, 350–392.

RABINOWITZ, M. (1941). Studies on the cytology and early embryology of the egg of *Drosophila melanogaster*. *J. Morph.* **69**, 1–49.

RAPPAPORT, R. (1973). Cleavage furrows establishment – a preliminary to cylindrical shape change. *Am. Zool.* **13**, 941–948.

RICE, T. B. & GAREN, A. (1975). Localized defects of blastoderm formation in maternal effect mutants of *Drosophila*. *Devl Biol.* **43**, 277–286.

RICKOLL, W. L. (1976). Cytoplasmic continuity between embryonic cells and primitive yolk sac during early gastrulation in *Drosophila melanogaster*. *Devl Biol.* **49**, 304–310.

SAXTON, W. M., STEMPLE, D. L., LESLIE, R. J., SALMON, E. D., ZAVORTINK, M. & MCINTOSH, J. R. (1984). Tubulin dynamics in cultured mammalian cells. *J. Cell Biol.* **99**, 2175–2186.

SCHLIWA, M. & VAN BLERKOM, J. (1981). Structural interactions of cytoskeletal components. *J. Cell Biol.* **90**, 222–235.

SCHROEDER, T. E. (1975). Dynamics of the contractile ring. In *Molecules and Cell Movements* (ed. S. Inoue & R. E. Stephens), pp. 305–334. New York: Rouen Press.

SCHROEDER, T. E. & OTTO, J. J. (1984). Cyclic assembly–disassembly of cortical microtubules during maturation and early development of starfish oocytes. *Devl Biol.* **103**, 493–503.

SONNENBLICK, B. P. (1950). The early embryology of *Drosophila melanogaster*. In *Biology of Drosophila* (ed. M. Demerec), pp. 62–167. New York: John Wiley and Sons.

STAFSTROM, J. P. & STAEHELIN, L. A. (1984). Dynamics of the nuclear envelope and of nuclear pore complexes during mitosis in *Drosophila* embryo. *Eur. J. Cell Biol.* **34**, 179–189.

SWANSON, M. M. & POODRY, C. A. (1980). Pole cell formation in *Drosophila melanogaster*. *Devl Biol.* **75**, 419–430.

TURNER, F. R. & MAHOWALD, A. P. (1976). Scanning electron microscopy of *Drosophila* embryogenesis. I. The structure of the egg envelopes and the formation of the cellular blastoderm. *Devl Biol.* **50**, 95–108.

UEDA, R. & OKADA, M. (1982). Induction of pole cells in sterilized *Drosophila* embryos by injection of subcellular fraction from eggs. *Proc. natn. Acad. Sci. U.S.A.* **79**, 6946–6950.

WALTER, M. F. & ALBERTS, B. M. (1984). Intermediate filaments in tissue culture cells and early embryos of *Drosophila melanogaster.* In *Molecular Biology of Development, UCLA Symp. Mol. Cell. Biol. New Series* (ed. E. H. Davidson & R. A. Firtel), pp. 263–272. New York: Alan R. Liss.

WARN, R. M. (1975). Restoration of the capacity to form pole cells in U.V. irradiated *Drosophila* embryos. *J. Embryol. exp. Morph.* **33**, 1003–1011.

WARN, R. M. (1979). The pole plasm of *Drosophila.* In *Maternal Effects in Development* (ed. D. R. Newth & M. Balls), pp. 199–219. Cambridge University Press.

WARN, R. M. (1986). Microtubule organization during polar cap mitosis and pole cell formation in the *Drosophila* embryo. In *Progress in Developmental Biology*, part B (ed. H. Slavkin), pp. 361–364. Alan R. Liss.

WARN, R. M., BULLARD, B. & MAGRATH, R. (1980). Changes in the distribution of cortical myosin during the cellularization of the *Drosophila* embryo. *J. Embryol. exp. Morph.* **57**, 167–176.

WARN, R. M., BULLARD, B. & MALEKI, S. (1979). Myosin as a constituent of the *Drosophila* egg cortex. *Nature, Lond.* **278**, 651–653.

WARN, R. M., GUTZEIT, H. O., SMITH, L. & WARN, A. (1985*a*). F-actin rings are associated with the ring canals of the *Drosophila* egg chamber. *Expl Cell Res.* **157**, 355–363.

WARN, R. M. & MAGRATH, R. (1982). Observations by a novel method of surface changes during the syncytial blastoderm stage of the *Drosophila* embryo. *Devl Biol.* **89**, 540–548.

WARN, R. M. & MAGRATH, R. (1983). F-actin distribution during the cellularization of the *Drosophila* embryo visualized with FL-phalloidin. *Expl Cell Res.* **143**, 103–114.

WARN, R. M., MAGRATH, R. & WEBB, S. (1984). Distribution of F-actin during cleavage of the *Drosophila* syncytial blastoderm. *J. Cell Biol.* **98**, 156–162.

WARN, R. M., SMITH, L. & WARN, A. (1985*b*). Three distinct distributions of F-actin occur during the divisions of polar surface caps to produce pole cells in *Drosophila* embryos. *J. Cell Biol.* **100**, 1010–1015.

WARN, R. M. & WARN, A. (1986). Microtubule arrays present during the syncytial and cellular blastoderm stages of the early *Drosophila* embryo. *Expl Cell Res.* **163**, 201–210.

WEBER, K. & OSBORN, M. (1979). Intracellular display of microtubule structures revealed by indirect immunofluorescence microscopy. In *Microtubules* (ed. K. Roberts & J. S. Hyams), pp. 279–313. London: Academic Press.

WHITE, J. G. (1985). The astral relaxation theory of cytokinesis revisited. *Bioessays* **2**, 267–292.

WOLF, R. (1978). The cytaster, a colchicine sensitive migration organelle of cleavage nuclei in an insect egg. *Devl Biol.* **62**, 464–472.

WOLF, R. (1985). Migration and division of cleavage nuclei in the gall midge *Wachtliella persicariae*. III. Pattern of anaphase – triggering waves altered by temperature gradients and local gas exchange. *Wilhelm Roux Arch. Devl Biol.* **194**, 257–270.

ZALOKAR, M. & ERK, I. (1976). Division and migration of nuclei during early embryogenesis of *Drosophila melanogaster. J. Microsc. Biol. Cell* **25**, 97–106.

J. Cell Sci. Suppl. 5, 329–341 (1986)
Printed in Great Britain © The Company of Biologists Limited 1986

CYTOSKELETAL CHANGES DURING OOGENESIS AND EARLY DEVELOPMENT OF *XENOPUS LAEVIS*

C. C. WYLIE[1], JANET HEASMAN[1], JUDY M. PARKE[2], BRIAN ANDERTON[2] AND PETER TANG[1,2]

Departments of Anatomy[1] and Immunology[2], St George's Hospital Medical School, Cranmer Terrace, London SW17 0RE, UK

SUMMARY

The frog oocyte is well known for studies on the control of gene expression, but has been used much less in studies on the cytoskeleton. However, frog oocytes are very large single cells, whose cytoplasmic movements and asymmetries are fundamental to the correct development of the subsequent embryo. One particular example of asymmetrically distributed cytoplasm is germ plasm, thought to be important in the formation of the germ line. Data are presented that show that germ plasm is a highly concentrated mass of cytoskeletal elements, which include tubulin, and an intermediate filament protein of molecular weight 55×10^3. The distribution of these molecules has been studied during oogenesis and during early post-fertilization development. The implications of these findings are discussed.

WHY USE *XENOPUS* OOCYTES OR EGGS IN STUDIES ON THE CYTOSKELETON?

The frog oocyte is well known for its usefulness in studies of transcription and translation. When oocytes are removed from the frog ovary and put into suitable media, they can be regarded for short periods (up to several days) as free-living single cells whose ease of manipulation and microinjection has led to their widespread use in studies on the control of gene expression by the injection of macromolecules (see Gurdon & Melton, 1981; Lane, 1983, for reviews).

The fertilized egg is also a short-lived free-living single cell, which will develop, by process of division, growth and differentiation, into a swimming larva. In order to discover the factors that govern developmental regulation of genes that are only expressed in certain lineages, the eggs of many species have become favourite targets for introduction of new genetic material (Hammer *et al.* 1986; Orr-Weaver *et al.* 1986).

Oocytes and eggs have been used much less in studies on the cytoskeleton. Indeed, their usefulness is less immediately obvious, and the components of their cytoskeleton poorly characterized. However, recent experiments with eggs and early embryos of *Xenopus* have made it increasingly obvious that large-scale cytoplasmic movements take place during oocyte differentiation, oocyte maturation, and the first cell cycle after fertilization of the egg. Asymmetries produced by these cytoplasmic movements are causal factors in the earliest and most fundamental developmental decisions.

It is worth digressing to review some of these rearrangements, because they indicate areas where it is possible to study the functional role of individual cyto-skeletal components.

The formation of the dorsal axis

During the first cell cycle following fertilization, a period of about 75 min in *Xenopus*, a complex series of cytoplasmic movements takes place. These have been the subjects of several studies (Ancel & Vintemberger, 1948; Elinson, 1983; Ubbels *et al.* 1983), and have recently been analysed in some detail (Vincent *et al.* 1986). Following these movements, the egg becomes bilaterally symmetrical, with recognizable prospective dorsal and ventral hemispheres. When the vegetal pole of the egg is damaged by ultraviolet light this causes a progressive loss of dorsal structures (such as nervous system and somites) in the ensuing embryo (Malacinski *et al.* 1977). This effect can be mimicked by cold or compression treatment of the egg (Scharf & Gerhart, 1980), both of which are known to disrupt microtubules (see also Elinson, 1985, for the possible role of microtubules in this process). These effects can be rescued simply by rotating the egg to 90° from its normal axis (Scharf & Gerhart, 1980). This rotation causes gravity-driven movement of the heavier yolky cytoplasm in the vegetal hemisphere of the egg in a way that mimics the normal cytoplasmic movements in the untreated egg (see Gimlich, 1985, for review). These observations led to the hypothesis that axis-reducing treatments such as ultraviolet (u.v.) irradiation do not damage localized 'dorsal determinants', but interfere with the cytoplasmic movements essential for dorsal axis formation later in development. The truth of this was elegantly shown by grafting experiments in early blastulae (Gimlich & Gerhart, 1984) in which the u.v. effect could be rescued by grafting into treated embryos blastomeres from normal embryos. Vegetal cells from the prospective dorsal side of the embryo would rescue the dorsal reduction effect, but those from the prospective ventral side would not. The dorsal structures themselves are not formed from these cells, but from animal hemisphere cells on the same side of the embryo. Thus the dorsal vegetal cells are able to instruct neighbouring cells to form the dorsal axis, a property they acquired during the cytoplasmic movements of the first cell cycle. The identities of the molecules that are moved by this process, and the way they act in later cell interactions, are not known. However, several genes involved in dorsal axis formation have been identified in *Drosophila* (Anderson *et al.* 1985*a,b*). No doubt if there are sequences homologous to these in vertebrates they will soon be identified. If so, then the *Xenopus* egg will prove an extremely useful system in which to identify the nature of their action.

Germ plasm

Another well-known asymmetry of the fertilized egg is the germ plasm, which refers to a collection of small basophilic masses just below the surface of the vegetal hemisphere. These aggregate during the first few cleavages to form a small number, usually around four, of larger masses each of which is inherited by one of the vegetal blastomeres of the dividing embryo. These blastomeres give rise later in development to the progenitors of the germ line, the primordial germ cells. When germ plasm is examined by transmission electron microscopy (TEM) it is found to consist of mitochondria and electron-dense granulofibrillar masses known as germinal granules (see Heasman *et al.* 1984, for review). Other species have similar cytoplasmic organelles in the egg, which become incorporated into the germ line, e.g. the polar granules of *Drosophila* (see Mahowald & Boswell, 1983, for review) and the P granules of *Caenorhabditis* (Strome & Wood, 1983). The exact role of these organelles is unknown; however, there is good evidence to suggest they are important for germ cell formation. If they are damaged by localized ultraviolet irradiation (Bounoure, 1939) or physical ablation (Buehr & Blackler, 1970) there is a reduction in the number of germ cells that reach the gonad. This effect can be rescued by microinjection of unirradiated vegetal but not animal pole egg cytoplasm (Smith, 1966). There is also evidence that germ cell number can be enhanced in untreated eggs by microinjection of extra vegetal cytoplasm (Wakahara, 1978). All this suggests that germ plasm is important in the establishment of the germ line in *Xenopus*. However, its exact role is unknown.

Asymmetries of macromolecules in the egg

There are now several reports of asymmetries in both RNA and protein species in the egg, the functional significance of which is unknown. Using differential screening, maternal RNA species concentrated in either the animal hemisphere or the vegetal hemisphere have been identified, and their cDNAs cloned (Rebagliati *et al.* 1985). The heterogeneous distribution of proteins along the animal–vegetal axis has been identified by dividing large numbers of eggs into transverse slices and analysing the soluble proteins in these slices by sodium dodecyl sulphate–polyacrylamide gel electrophoresis (SDS–PAGE) (Moen & Namenwirth, 1977). In view of the experiments on dorsal axis formation described above, it is surprising that the prospective dorsal and ventral regions of the egg have not been compared by these methods.

Monoclonal antibody analysis has also revealed heterogeneous distribution of antigens in the oocyte and egg. Two monoclonal antibodies, termed VC1 and MC3, raised against vegetal cortices of eggs and mitochondrial clouds of oocytes, respectively, show interesting distributions (a preliminary report of these results has been presented by Wylie *et al.* 1985). Both antibodies are found throughout oogenesis in only the most superficial cytoplasm of the oocyte. After fertilization most of the embryonic cells become labelled, since as the egg cleaves the new superficial cytoplasm of each blastomere becomes positive for the antibodies. However, during the organogenesis period staining becomes restricted to the germ line cells and a small number of other lineages. VC1 stains the germ cells and the endodermally derived gut, whereas MC3 stains germ cells and only scattered other cells in the foregut.

The developmental significance of these asymmetrically distributed macromolecules is unknown. However, they will provide useful tools with which to analyse the importance of such molecules. This is being done by microinjection of anti-sense strands and monoclonal antibodies. Although something of a needle-in-a-haystack approach, this method is potentially extremely important since it should produce phenocopies of mutations affecting these gene products.

All these asymmetries in the egg must be initiated during the period of oocyte differentiation. It therefore becomes interesting to study the cytoskeleton of the oocyte and egg not as an exercise in embryology but in applied cell biology, since this is where the two fields meet. There are two possible ways to perturb the developmental systems described above: either by blocking the action of developmentally important molecules whose identity we do not know, or by interfering with their correct localization in the oocyte or egg by the cytoskeleton. This latter can be done by cytoskeleton-disrupting drugs or by microinjection of specific antibodies. In this way the functions of individual cytoskeletal elements and their associated molecules can be studied. The oocyte/egg system offers advantages for such analysis that are greater than for any other cell type, since the assay system for such experimental intervention is of course abnormal embryonic development.

In most somatic cell types the cytoskeleton-generated asymmetries play roles in cell function that are quite difficult to assay, particularly *in vitro* where both normal function and normal polarity are lost. The *Xenopus* egg, however, is a single large free-living cell whose cytoplasmic asymmetries serve eventually to produce a normal embryo.

THE ORIGINS OF EGG ASYMMETRY DURING OOGENESIS AND THEIR
RELATION TO THE CYTOSKELETON

The account that follows concentrates to a large extent on the nature, origin and localization of germ plasm, and its relation to the cytoskeleton. Germ plasm seemed particularly attractive since it is so easy to identify, and because it is apparently associated so clearly with only one cell lineage.

Germ plasm can be traced back to the pre-vitellogenic stages of oogenesis. Fig. 1A shows a fragment of ovary under the dissecting microscope, showing oocytes at most developmental stages (for staging system, see Dumont, 1972, or a brief review by Wylie *et al.* 1985). A characteristic feature of the pre-vitellogenic oocyte is a dense cytoplasmic mass known as the mitochondrial cloud. The main function of this organelle was thought to be the source of oocyte mitochondria. Under Nomarski optics the cloud is seen to be a phase-dense mass connected to the developing filament system of the oocyte (Fig. 1B). At the beginning of vitellogenesis the cloud breaks down and most of its fragments spread to the sub-cortical cytoplasm at one pole of the oocyte (Fig. 1C). Careful electron-microscopic observations of the cloud itself and its breakdown products reveal that they contain the germinal granules characteristic of the germ plasm of the egg (Heasman *et al.* 1984; Wylie *et al.* 1985). The pole to which the mitochondrial cloud fragments spread becomes the vegetal pole later on during vitellogenesis. Clearly then, animal–vegetal polarity is already established at pre-vitellogenic stages, and at least one role of the mitochondrial cloud

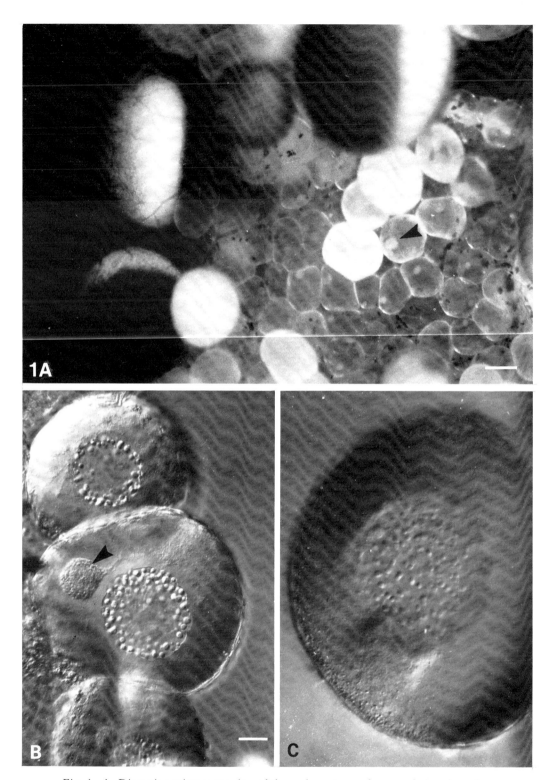

Fig. 1. A. Dissecting microscope view of the various stages of oogenesis seen in a piece of adult ovary. The mitochondrial clouds of the stage I oocytes are shown (arrowhead). Bar, 200 μm. B. Differential interference contrast (Nomarski) micrograph of a single living pre-vitellogenic oocyte, showing the mitochondrial cloud (arrowhead). Bar, 25 μm. C. Nomarski image of an early vitellogenic living oocyte (stage II) to show the mito-chondrial cloud breaking down and moving peripherally. Bar, 25 μm. B,C. From Heasman *et al.* (1984); A, unpublished observation.

is to sequester the germinal granules and localize them to the correct region of the differentiating oocyte (Heasman et al. 1984).

Staining of the pre-vitellogenic oocyte with antibodies against components of the cytoskeleton showed that the mitochondrial cloud and its breakdown products react strongly with anti-tubulin and anti-mammalian vimentin antibodies (Godsave et al. 1984a; Wylie et al. 1985). Furthermore, the cloud was found to be surrounded by a shell of anti-cytokeratin staining material, which partially divides it into segments, thus presaging the breakdown of the cloud (Godsave et al. 1984b).

The anti-vimentin antibodies enable the appearance and changing distribution of germ plasm to be followed throughout oogenesis and early development. This cycle of events is shown in Fig. 2.

One problem with the observations documented above is the identity of the material stained by the anti-mammalian vimentins. Three different antibodies gave essentially the same staining patterns in Xenopus oocytes (Godsave et al. 1984a). However, these were not always monospecific on Western blots though they all reacted with a band of approximately $55 \times 10^3 M_r$, the published molecular weight of Xenopus vimentin (Nelson & Traub, 1982).

We therefore screened a large number of monoclonal antibodies for ones that would be monospecific by immunoblotting and would give the vimentin-type staining pattern in Xenopus oocytes. Preliminary data on these will be presented here and will be published more fully elsewhere.

Two antibodies were found that fulfilled the above criteria, designated C26 and C41. Fig. 3 shows their staining pattern in vitellogenic oocytes, which is identical to that shown for anti-mammalian vimentin by Godsave et al. (1984a). In the animal hemisphere of the oocyte dense strands of stained material pass radially outward from the nucleus towards the oocyte surface. In the vegetal hemisphere staining is extremely sparse except for the sub-cortical islands of germ plasm.

Immunoblotting data are shown in two parts. In Fig. 3D, oocyte Triton-insoluble extracts are blotted with an antibody (known as α-IFA) that cross-reacts with all intermediate filament proteins (Pruss et al. 1981). One track is blotted with a monoclonal antibody against β-tubulin, which has a molecular weight of 55×10^3 in Xenopus. This antibody was raised against Physarum tubulin (Birkett et al. 1985) and was kindly provided by Dr C. R. Birkett. Anti-IFA blots bands of approximately 70, 60, 55, 50 and 44 $(\times 10^3) M_r$ in Xenopus oocytes, and these therefore represent their spectrum of intermediate filament proteins. Fig. 3E shows Triton-insoluble

---

Fig. 2. Immunofluorescence images using anti-intermediate filament antibodies of various stages in the life-cycle of germ plasm in Xenopus. A. Mitochondrial cloud in pre-vitellogenic (stage I) oocyte. B. Mitochondrial cloud fragmenting and moving to future vegetal pole. C. Mitochondrial cloud fragments remain in cortical cytoplasm of vegetal hemisphere of full-grown oocyte. D. Diagram to show orientation of sections shown in E–G. These are grazing sections of the vegetal pole of fertilized egg (E), four-cell stage (F) and 32-cell stage (G) to show stages in the aggregation of germ plasm. The germ plasm surrounds the nucleus of the cells that inherit it at the gastrula stage (H). Bars, 50 μm for all micrographs. A. From Wylie et al. (1985); C, from Godsave et al. (1984a); the rest, unpublished observations.

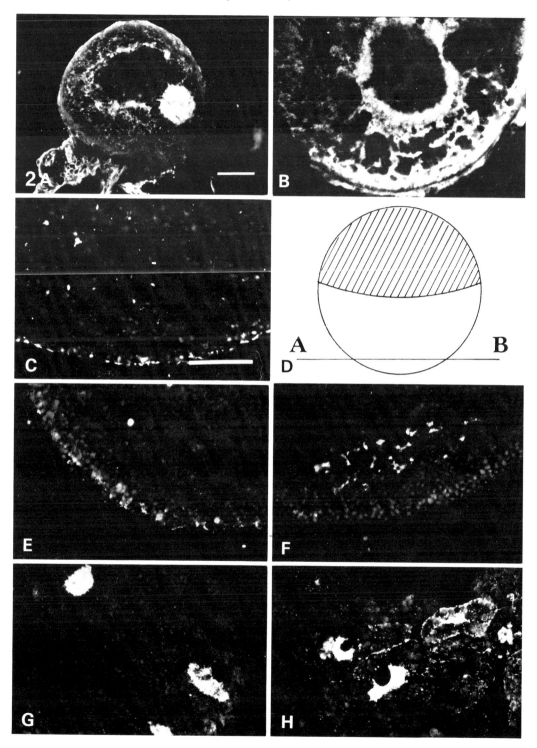

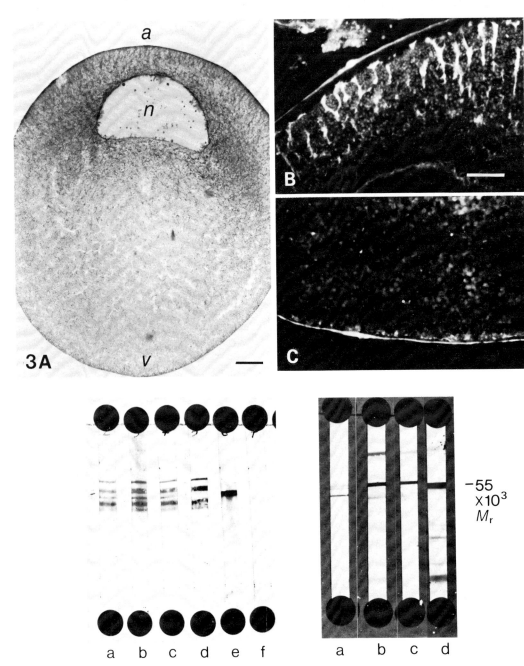

Fig. 3. C26 and C41 monoclonal antibodies give the same pattern of immunofluorescent staining in oocytes, and react with the same major band on immuno-blots. A. Low-power image of whole section of full-grown oocyte. a, animal pole; v, vegetal pole; n, oocyte nucleus. B,C. C41 stains radial strands of cytoplasm in animal pole (B), and islands of germ plasm in cortex of vegetal pole (C). The solid outermost line of staining in B and C is due to the surrounding follicle cells. Bars, $100\,\mu$m (A); $50\,\mu$m (B,C). D. Immunoblot of Triton extracts of oocytes separated by SDS–PAGE. Primary antibodies were anti-IFA (tracks a–d), anti-β-tubulin (M_r 53×10^3, track e), non-immune monoclonal supernatant (track f). Secondary antibody in each case was gold-conjugated goat anti-mouse immunoglobulin G (IgG) (Janssen), followed by silver enhancement. E. Immunoblot of Triton-extracted oocyte separated by SDS–PAGE and reacted with LE65 (track a), C41 (track b), C26 (track c) and anti-β-tubulin (track d). C26 and C41 react with the same major band of slightly heavier molecular weight than β-tubulin (approx. 55×10^3). LE65 reacts with a major band at approx. $44\times10^3\,M_r$ and two minor bands. Methodology as for D (C. C. Wylie & Peter Tang, unpublished observations).

extracts of *Xenopus* oocytes that have been blotted with anti-β-tubulin, C41, C26 and LE65 (a monoclonal anti-cytokeratin that stains *Xenopus* oocytes, see Godsave *et al.* 1984*b*). Both C41 and C26 blot the $55\times10^3 M_r$ intermediate filament protein extremely strongly, with little cross-reaction with other bands. LE65 blots predominantly the $44\times10^3 M_r$ intermediate filament protein, with lesser cross-reactions around 50 and 55 $(\times10^3) M_r$.

C41 and C26 were then shown to cross-react with *Xenopus* intermediate filaments by immunocytochemistry at both light and electron-microscope levels. Fig. 4B shows a *Xenopus* XL177 cell in culture stained with C41, compared with anti-actin (Fig. 4A). Fig. 4C shows an intermediate filament bundle in a Triton-extracted early oocyte stained by the immuno–gold method with C41.

It is clear, therefore, that these antibodies, which give the same staining and blotting patterns, do cross-react with *Xenopus* intermediate filaments, and do cross-react with only one intermediate filament protein, of molecular weight approximately 55×10^3, in the oocyte. This does not unequivically identify this molecule as vimentin, however. A cytokeratin of $56\times10^3 M_r$ has been reported in *Xenopus* oocytes by Franz *et al.* (1983). This is presumably the molecule that is also blotted by LE65 in Fig. 3E. Also, these two antibodies, C41 and C26, must react with other intermediate filament proteins in tissues other than oocytes, since they stain a variety of tissues including neurones, glial cells, epithelia, muscle and connective tissue in pre-metamorphic *Xenopus* tadpoles and adults (data not shown). Of course we know little of the amphibian intermediate filament protein family, which is virtually uncharacterized. We are currently using C41 and C26 to screen an oocyte DG11 expression library in order to identify and characterize their coding sequences.

The distribution of both the $55\times10^3 M_r$ intermediate filament protein and tubulin has also been studied in eggs and early cleavage stages of *Xenopus* (Fig. 5). Both stain germ plasm strongly, indicating that this organelle contains a large store of both cytoskeletal elements (Fig. 5A,B). The $55\times10^3 M_r$ protein is also distributed in a filamentous network in all blastomeres, being most easily seen in animal pole blastomeres, which have less yolk to confuse the picture. This filamentous framework extends radially outwards from the area of the nucleus in each blastomere (Fig. 5C,D). Tubulin is also found in a radial array, but focussed more obviously on microtubule-organizing centres (Fig. 5E,F).

Whatever the intermediate filament class to which it belongs, therefore, it is clear that the $55\times10^3 M_r$ protein plays a major role in the cytoskeletal framework of the oocyte, egg and early embryo. It will be interesting to establish whether this intermediate filament protein is one of the adult types and becomes confined to only certain cell types later in development. We do not know whether the dense arrays of $55\times10^3 M_r$ protein in the animal pole of the oocyte are a maternal stockpile for early development, or whether it is synthesized on maternally inherited message after fertilization. If it is stored, it will be interesting to know whether it is polymerized into filaments, and if so, how these become re-arranged during cytoplasmic movements of the oocyte and egg, and during cleavage. Using these monospecific antibodies, it will be worth studying the effects of localized disruption of this skeletal

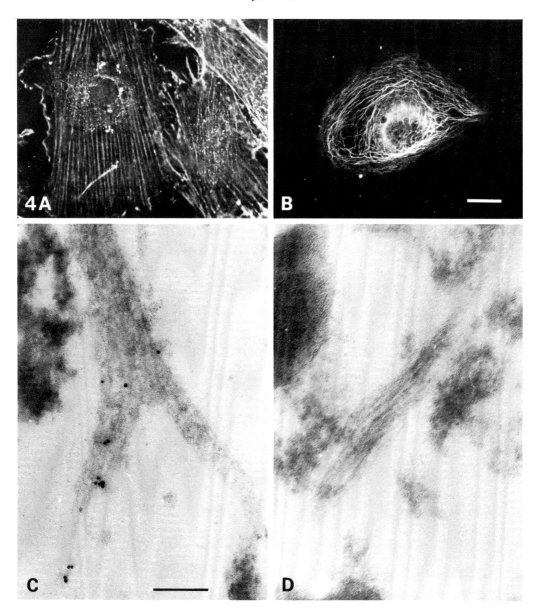

Fig. 4. C26 and C41 have the same staining reaction in *Xenopus* cells in culture. C41 also stains intermediate filament bundles in stage II oocytes. Cells of a *Xenopus* cell line (XL177) were stained with anti-actin (A) and C26 (B). C26 stains the intermediate filament pattern, as does C41 (not shown). Triton extracts of stage II oocytes are shown in C and D. Whole extracted oocytes were stained unfixed in C41 neat supernatant (C), or non-immune monoclonal supernatant from X-63 cells (D). They were then reacted with 4 nm gold-conjugated goat anti-mouse IgG (Janssen) before fixation and processing for electron microscopy. Sections are shown without further heavy-metal staining. C41 reacts with intermediate filament bundles in the Triton extracts. Bars, 20 μm (A,B); 100 nm (C,D). (C. C. Wylie, unpublished data.)

framework on the maintenance of polarity in the oocyte during its differentiation, and on early development.

The role of such a large concentration of an intermediate filament protein in germ plasm is very puzzling. It is well known, of course, that *Xenopus* eggs contain large maternal stores of cytoskeletal elements such as actin and tubulin. These are required for cell division during the period of rapid cleavage that takes place without

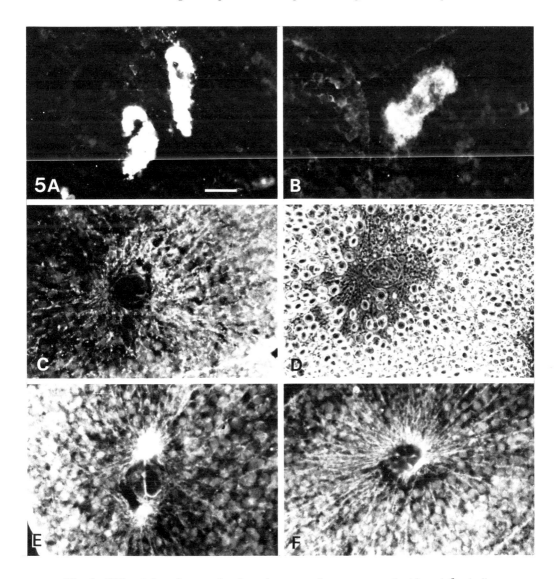

Fig. 5. C26 staining of egg and early embryo cytoplasm, compared with anti-β-tubulin. Germ plasm is stained at the 32-cell stage by both C26 (A) and anti-β-tubulin (B). C26 stains a radially arranged irregular pattern of phase-dense filaments extending outwards from the nuclear area of each blastomere (C,D). Anti-β-tubulin stains straighter radially arranged microtubules centred on either asters or possibly microtubule-organizing centres (E,F). Bar, 25 μm.

concomitant levels of transcription and translation. It is possible that germ plasm represents a large store of cytoskeletal elements that are required by early germ line cells for their migration to the gonad, or for establishing their cytoarchitecture. It is possible that the initiation of polarity in the primordial germ cells depends on cytoskeletal elements present in the germ plasm. This polarity will in turn dictate the polarity and cytoarchitecture of the differentiating gametes, and thus be important in the early developmental asymmetries of the next generation. It will be extremely interesting to establish the role of these and other asymmetrically localized cytoskeletal elements in *Xenopus* development.

I am grateful to the Cancer Research Campaign and the Science and Engineering Research Council for their financial support of this work.

The expert technical assistance of Claire Varley is also gratefully acknowledged.

REFERENCES

ANCEL, P. & VINTEMBERGER, P. (1948). Recherches sur le determinanisme de la symetrie bilaterale dans l'oeuf des amphibiens. *Bull. biol. Fr. Belg. Suppl.* **31**, 1–182.

ANDERSON, K. V., BOKLA, L. & NUSSLEIN-VOLHARD, C. (1985a). Establishment of dorsal–ventral polarity in the *Drosophila* embryo: the induction of polarity by the *Toll* gene product. *Cell* **42**, 791–798.

ANDERSON, K. V., JURGENS, G. & NUSSLEIN-VOLHARD, C. (1985b). Establishment of dorsal–ventral polarity in the *Drosophila* embryo: genetic studies on the role of the *Toll* gene product. *Cell* **42**, 779–789.

BIRKETT, C. P., FOSTER, K. E., JOHNSON, L. & GULL, K. (1985). Use of monoclonal antibodies to analyse the expression of a multi-tubulin family. *FEBS Lett.* **187**, 211–218.

BOUNOURE, L. (1939). *L'Origine des Cellules Reproductive et le Problem de la Lignee Germinale.* Paris: Gauthier-Villrs.

BUEHR, M. & BLACKLER, A. W. (1970). Sterility and partial sterility in the South African clawed toad following pricking of the egg. *J. Embryol. exp. Morph.* **23**, 375–384.

DUMONT, J. N. (1972). Oogenesis in *Xenopus laevis* (Daudin). I. Stages of oocyte development in laboratory maintained animals. *J. Morph.* **136**, 153–180.

ELINSON, R. P. (1983). Cytoplasmic phases in the first cell cycle of the activated frog egg. *Devl Biol.* **100**, 440–451.

ELINSON, R. P. (1985). Changes in levels of polymeric tubulin associated with activation and dorso ventral polarization of the frog egg. *Devl Biol.* **109**, 224–233.

FRANZ, J. K., GALL, L., WILLIAMS, M. A., PICHERAL, B. & FRANKE, W. W. (1983). Intermediate-sized filaments in a germ cell: expression of cytokeratins in oocytes and eggs of the frog *Xenopus*. *Proc. natn. Acad. Sci. U.S.A.* **80**, 6254–6258.

GIMLICH, R. L. (1985). Cytoplasmic localization and chordamesoderm induction in the frog embryo. *J. Embryol. exp. Morph.* **89 Suppl.**, 89–111.

GIMLICH, R. L. & GERHART, J. C. (1984). Early cellular interactions promote embryonic axis formation in *Xenopus laevis*. *Devl Biol.* **104**, 117–130.

GODSAVE, S. F., ANDERTON, B. H., HEASMAN, J. & WYLIE, C. C. (1984a). Oocytes and early embryos of *Xenopus laevis* contain intermediate filaments which react with anti-mammalian vimentin antibodies. *J. Embryol. exp. Morph.* **83**, 169–187.

GODSAVE, S. F., WYLIE, C. C., LANE, E. B. & ANDERTON, B. H. (1984b). Intermediate filaments in the *Xenopus* oocyte: the appearance and distribution of cytokeratin-containing filaments. *J. Embryol. exp. Morph.* **83**, 157–167.

GURDON, J. B. & MELTON, D. A. (1981). Gene transfer in amphibian eggs and oocytes. *A. Rev. Genet.* **15**, 189–218.

HAMMER, P. E., PALMITER, P. D. & BRINSTER, R. L. (1986). Expression of bovine and human growth hormone fusion genes in transgenic mice. *Cold Spring Harbor Symp. quant. Biol.* **50** (in press).

HEASMAN, J., QUARMBY, J. & WYLIE, C. C. (1984). The mitochondrial cloud of *Xenopus* oocytes: the source of germinal granule material. *Devl Biol.* **105**, 458–489.

LANE, C. D. (1983). The fate of genes, messengers and proteins introduced into *Xenopus* oocytes. *Curr. Top. devl Biol.* **18**, 89–117.

MAHOWALD, A. P. & BOSWELL, R. E. (1983). Germ plasm and germ cell development in invertebrates. In *Current Problems in Germ Cell Differentiation* (ed. A. McLaren & C. C. Wylie). Cambridge University Press.

MALACINSKI, G. M., BROTHERS, A. J. & CHUNG, H.-M. (1977). Destruction of components of the neural induction system of the amphibian egg with ultraviolet irradiation. *Devl Biol.* **56**, 24–39.

MOEN, T. L. & NAMENWIRTH, M. (1977). The distribution of soluble proteins along the animal–vegetal axis of frog eggs. *Devl Biol.* **58**, 1–10.

NELSON, W. J. & TRAUB, P. (1982). Intermediate (10 nm) filament proteins and the Ca^{2+}-activated proteinase specific for vimentin and desmin in the cells from fish to man: an example of evolutionary conservation. *J. Cell Sci.* **57**, 25–49.

ORR-WEAVER, T., DECICCIO, D., KALFAYEN, L., KELLEY, R., LEVINE, J., PARKS, S., WAKIMOTO, B. & SPRADLING, A. (1986). Amplification and expression of *Drosophila* chorion genes. *Cold Spring Harbor Symp. quant. Biol.* **50** (in press).

PRUSS, R. M., MIRSKY, R., RAFF, M. C., THORPE, R., DOWDING, A. J. & ANDERTON, B. H. (1981). All classes of intermediate filaments share a common antigenic determinant defined by a monoclonal antibody. *Cell* **27**, 419–428.

REBAGLIATI, M. R., WEEKS, D. L., HARVEY, R. P. & MELTON, D. A. (1985). Identification and cloning of localized maternal RNAs from *Xenopus* eggs. *Cell* **42**, 769–777.

SCHARF, S. R. & GERHART, J. C. (1980). Determination of the dorso–ventral axis in eggs of *Xenopus laevis*: Complete rescue of UV impaired eggs by oblique orientation before first cleavage. *Devl Biol.* **79**, 181–198.

SMITH, L. D. (1966). The role of a germinal plasm in the formation of primordial germ cells in *Rana pipiens*. *Devl Biol.* **14**, 330–347.

STROME, S. & WOOD, W. B. (1983). Generation of asymmetry and segregation of germ line granules in early *C. elegans* embryos. *Cell* **35**, 15–25.

UBBELS, G. A., HARA, K., KOSTER, C. H. & KIRSCHNER, M. (1983). Evidence for a functional role of the cytoskeleton in determination of the dorso–ventral axis in *Xenopus laevis* eggs. *J. Embryol. exp. Morph.* **77**, 15–37.

VINCENT, J. P., OSTER, G. F. & GERHART, J. C. (1986). Kinematics of gray crescent formation in *Xenopus* eggs: the displacement of subcortical cytoplasm relative to the egg surface. *Devl Biol.* **113**, 484–500.

WAKAHARA, M. (1978). Induction of supernumerary primordial germ cells by injecting vegetal pole cytoplasm into *Xenopus* eggs. *J. exp. Zool.* **203**, 159–164.

WYLIE, C. C., BROWN, D., GODSAVE, S. F., QUARMBY, J. & HEASMAN, J. (1985). The cytoskeleton of *Xenopus* oocytes and its role in development. *J. Embryol. exp. Morph.* **89 Suppl.**, 1–15.

J. Cell Sci. Suppl. 5, 343–359 (1986)
Printed in Great Britain © The Company of Biologists Limited 1986

CYTOSKELETAL DYNAMICS IN THE MOUSE EGG

BERNARD MARO

Département de Différenciation Cellulaire, Centre de Génétique Moléculaire du CNRS, 91190 Gif sur Yvette, France

SARAH K. HOWLETT

AFRC Institute of Animal Physiology, 307 Huntingdon Road, Cambridge CB3 0JQ, UK

AND EVELYN HOULISTON

Department of Anatomy, University of Cambridge, Downing Street, Cambridge CB2 3DY, UK

SUMMARY

The distribution and roles of the microtubule and microfilament networks in the mouse egg following fertilization are described. The role of the chromosomes in the control of the egg cytoskeleton organization is discussed and a model for polar body formation proposed. Finally we describe the changes occurring in the pattern of proteins synthesized during this period, these being discussed in relation to cell cycle events and to changes in cytoskeleton organization.

INTRODUCTION

At the time of ovulation the mouse egg has reached and become arrested at metaphase of the second meiotic division (metaphase II). Fertilization triggers the completion of meiosis and thus the entry into the first mitotic cell cycle. Here we shall concentrate on the first 24 h of development and consider the mechanisms within the egg that act in concert to produce a biparental, diploid two-cell embryo. Cytoskeletal elements are probably involved in these events, since we are mainly dealing with changes in the spatial organization within the cell. Both microtubules and microfilaments are present in the egg (Wassarman & Fujiwara, 1978; Abreu & Brinster, 1978), the presence of intermediate filaments being more controversial. We will discuss the reorganization of the cytoskeleton (microfilaments and microtubules) following fertilization and the way in which this is controlled. We will also describe the changes in the pattern of proteins being synthesized in the egg. There is virtually no detectable RNA synthesis during this initial period (as the first synthesis of embryonic RNA takes place in the early two-cell embryo; Young *et al.* 1978; Piko & Clegg, 1982; Flach *et al.* 1982) and therefore, if the reorganization within the embryo is orchestrated by changes in proteins, these should result from differential mRNA usage or post-translational modification.

TIMING OF MORPHOLOGICAL EVENTS WITH RELATION TO THE CELL CYCLE PHASES

Fertilization triggers the completion of meiosis and a sequence of events leading to cell division and differentiation. Meiosis resumes within 30 min after the fusion of the two gametes (Sato & Blandau, 1979), resulting in the formation of the second polar body and the establishment of a haploid set of female chromosomes 2 h after fertilization, the time at which the first mitotic cycle starts (Fig. 1). The sperm nucleus enters the egg, loses its nuclear membrane and the chromosomes decondense. The subsequent sequence of first cell-cycle events has been examined in detail for (C57Bl.10 × CBA)F1 mice (Howlett & Bolton, 1985; Maro *et al.* 1984). In this strain of mice the male and then the female pronucleus forms at the egg periphery 2–3 h into G_1. Later, the male pronucleus migrates to the centre of the egg to be met by the female pronucleus (5–7 h into G_1). S phase lasts about 5 h while G_2 phase is very short and only lasts 1 h. The two pronuclei enter mitosis I together and the two sets of condensed chromosomes become aligned on a common metaphase plate at 16–17 h post-fertilization. Thus the first interphase period (interphase I) lasts 14–15 h whilst first mitosis (mitosis I) lasts 2 h and gives rise to a two-cell embryo 18–19 h post-fertilization.

CYTOSKELETAL ORGANIZATION DURING THE FIRST CELL CYCLE

Microfilaments

In the metaphase II egg, microfilaments are found mainly in the cortex but with a greater concentration in the area overlying the meiotic spindle that is located near, and parallel to, the cell surface (Fig. 2; Maro *et al.* 1984; Longo & Chen, 1985). This area of the cell surface is also devoid of microvilli (Fig. 3; Eager *et al.* 1976; Maro *et al.* 1984; Longo & Chen, 1985) and has relatively few binding sites for concanavalin A, a lectin that binds to some surface molecules (Johnson *et al.* 1975; Maro *et al.* 1984). Usually, spermatozoa do not fertilize the egg in this area (Johnson *et al.* 1975; Nicosia *et al.* 1977). After fertilization the meiotic cleavage-furrow forms in this actin-rich domain of the cortex at the equator of the spindle (Fig. 4). Two actin-rich shoulders are thereby created on each side of the furrow, and one of these subsequently shrinks while the other expands causing a rotation of the spindle and leading to the formation of the second polar body (Sato & Blandau, 1979; Maro *et al.* 1984). In addition, following fertilization, an area free of microvilli and rich in microfilaments develops near the decondensing sperm nucleus forming the incorporation cone (Fig. 4; Stefanini *et al.* 1969; Shalgi *et al.* 1978; Maro *et al.* 1984).

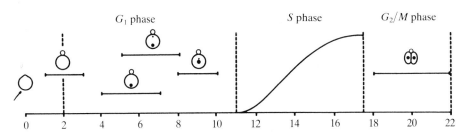

Fig. 1. Schematic representation of the morphological events in relation to cell cycle phases taking place during the first 24 h of mouse development.

These two actin-rich, microvillous-free domains disappear when the pronuclei form and migrate towards the egg centre. By which time, numerous microfilaments can be observed around the pronuclei (Maro *et al.* 1984).

Microtubules

In most animal cells the microtubule-organizing centre (MTOC) is composed of a pair of centrioles surrounded by electron-dense material, the peri-centriolar material (PCM), and it is within this material that the MTOC activity is located (Gould & Borisy, 1977). The mouse egg does not have centrioles and the poles of the meiotic spindle are composed of bands of PCM (Szollosi *et al.* 1972; Calarco-Gillam *et al.* 1983; Maro *et al.* 1985). In addition to the polar bands of PCM, numerous cytoplasmic PCM foci can be observed in the egg cortex (Fig. 3; Maro *et al.* 1985). However, whereas the PCM foci are dispersed, microtubules themselves are seen exclusively within the spindle (Fig. 3; Wassarman & Fujiwara, 1978; Maro *et al.* 1985; Schatten *et al.* 1985). Although the cytoplasmic PCM foci in the egg are evidently inactive as MTOCs (Maro *et al.* 1985; Schatten *et al.* 1985), they can be

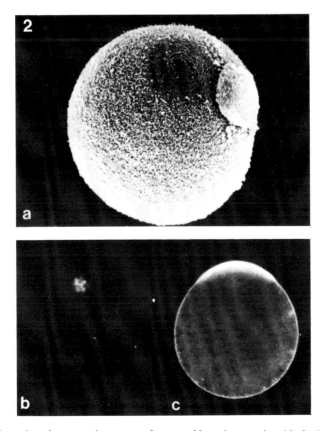

Fig. 2. a. Scanning electron microscopy of an egg. Note the area devoid of microvilli near the first polar body. b,c. Egg double stained for chromatin (b) and actin (c). (From Maro *et al.* (1986*b*).)

shown to have a nucleating capacity by the addition of taxol (a drug that decreases the critical concentration for tubulin polymerization; Schiff *et al.* 1979), which induces multiple asters to form around each cytoplasmic PCM focus (Maro *et al.* 1985; see also Fig. 6). It seems that usually the critical concentration for tubulin polymerization in the egg is high, such that microtubules can only polymerize in the region of the chromosomes. In contrast, following fertilization and passage of the egg from

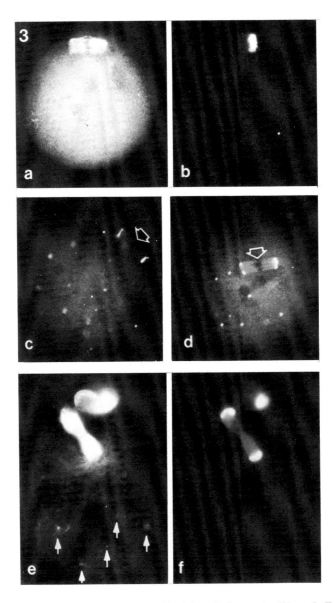

Fig. 3. a,b. Egg double stained for tubulin (a) and chromatin (b). c,d. Eggs stained for pericentriolar material. Arrowheads indicate the position of the metaphase plate. e,f. Parthenogenetically activated telophase egg double stained for tubulin (e) and chromatin (f). Arrows indicate microtubule asters. (a–d from Maro *et al.* (1985).)

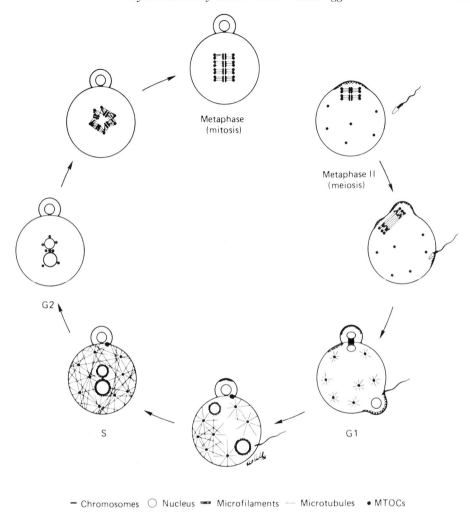

— Chromosomes ○ Nucleus ▰▰ Microfilaments — Microtubules • MTOCs

Fig. 4. Schematic representation of the distribution of cytoskeletal elements during the first cell cycle of mouse development in relation to the cell cycle phases. (From Maro (1985).)

meiosis II to interphase I, a drop in the critical concentration for tubulin polymerization seems to occur and multiple cortical asters form spontaneously around the PCM foci (Fig. 4; Maro *et al.* 1985; Schatten *et al.* 1985). During completion of meiosis, G_1 phase and early S phase, the cytoplasmic MTOCs remain in a peripheral position near the cell cortex. Numerous asters of microtubules form at the end of mitosis (Fig. 3E,F) and then enlarge to form a dense cytoplasmic network that remains until the end of interphase before being disassembled (Fig. 4; Schatten *et al.* 1985; B. Maro, unpublished observations). Then towards the end of S phase they migrate centrally towards the pronuclei (Maro *et al.* 1985). When the two pronuclear membranes break down, at prometaphase of mitosis I, numerous MTOCs are found around the two sets of chromosomes, and many half-spindles

Table 1. *Cytoskeletal dependence of the sequence of events occurring during the 24 h following fertilization*

Event	Microfilament dependence	Microtubule dependence
Activation	−	−
Sperm entry	−	−
Metaphase–anaphase transition	−	+
Spindle rotation	+	−
Second meiotic cleavage (polar body)	+	−
Disappearance of microvilli over the sperm head	−	−
Formation of pronuclei	−	−
Restoration of microvilli over the sites of pronuclear formation	+	+
Pronuclear migration	+	+
Entry into mitosis I	−	−
Mixing of chromosomes	−	+
Metaphase–anaphase transition	−	+
First mitotic cleavage	+	−
Re-formation of nuclear membranes	−	−

Data from Maro *et al.* (1984, 1985, 1986*a*) and Howlett (1986*b*).

originate from these MTOCs invading the pronuclei (Zamboni *et al.* 1972; B. Maro & S. K. Howlett, unpublished observations). All these MTOCs then align to form the poles of the barrel-shaped mitotic spindle (Calarco-Gillam *et al.* 1983; Maro *et al.* 1985).

Role of the cytoskeletal elements during the first cell cycle

Some indication of the role of the cytoskeletal elements can be assessed by the use of specific disruptive drugs such as cytochalasin D (CD) for microfilaments and nocodazole for microtubules. The results obtained are summarized in Table 1.

If the spindle of a metaphase II egg is destroyed by nocodazole, both the chromosomes and the polar aggregates of PCM disperse independently into small clusters around the cell cortex (Maro, 1985; Maro *et al.* 1985, 1986*a*; Longo & Chen, 1985). This process of dispersal is sensitive to CD and thus seems to be microfilament-dependent (Maro *et al.* 1986*a*). Eggs can nonetheless be activated either by fertilization or by parthenogenetic stimuli, in the presence of nocodazole but they remain in a metaphase state with condensed chromosomes until the drug is removed (Maro *et al.* 1986*a*; S. K. Howlett and B. Maro, unpublished observations). Microfilaments and microtubules are not required for sperm entry at fertilization (Maro *et al.* 1984, 1986*a*). Microfilaments are necessary for spindle rotation and polar body formation (Maro *et al.* 1984). Both microtubules and microfilaments are involved in the migration of the pronuclei and the restoration of a normal cortex over the sites of sperm entry and polar body extrusion after formation of the pronuclear membranes (Maro *et al.* 1984, 1986*a*). Microtubules are needed for the mixing of the two sets of condensed chromosomes during metaphase of mitosis I.

CONTROL OF CYTOSKELETON ORGANIZATION IN THE EGG

Microfilaments

A close association exists between the egg cortex and both the meiotic female and, after fertilization, the newly introduced male chromosomes (Fig. 5A–D). In both cases it seems that the chromosomes induce the formation of a cortical focus of stable polymerized actin.

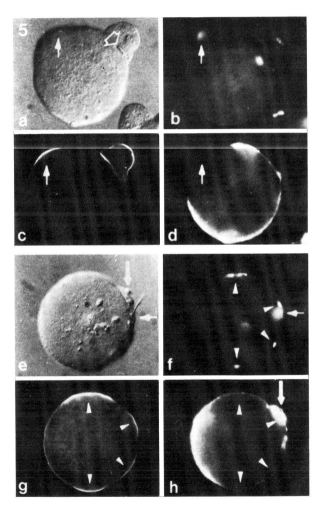

Fig. 5. a–d. Egg 2 h post-fertilization triple stained for chromatin (b), actin (c) and concanavalin A (ConA) (d). Note sperm entry point (arrow) and spindle (arrowhead) in the differential interference contrast (DIC) picture (a), which are associated with cortical actin (c) and loss in ConA binding (d). e–h. Egg treated with 10 μM-nocodazole for 1 h prior to fertilization and then triple stained for chromatin (f), actin (g) and ConA (h) at 6 h post-fertilization. Note in the DIC picture (e) sperm entry point (small arrow) and degenerating first polar body (large arrow), which binds ConA strongly (h). Egg chromosome clusters are dispersed (arrowheads) round the cortex and associated with cortical actin (g) and loss of ConA binding (h) as is the sperm-derived chromatin (small arrow, slightly off the plane of focus). (Adapted from Maro *et al.* (1986*a*).)

The influence of metaphase II chromosomes on their immediate environment was investigated following their dispersal after nocodazole-induced dissolution of the spindle (Maro *et al.* 1986a). Each maternal chromosome cluster, as well as the non-dispersed sperm-derived chromosomes, induces a focal accumulation of cortical microfilaments and a loss of surface microvilli in the overlying membrane (Fig. 5E–H). If, however, nocodazole is removed later, multiple polar bodies form in many of the microfilament-rich, microvilli-free cortical domains associated with the chromosomes, suggesting that the meiotic cleavage-furrow is limited to these areas, thereby yielding unequal cleavage (Maro *et al.* 1986a).

The hypothesis that the actin-rich cortical area that overlies the meiotic spindle forms a domain to which the meiotic cleavage-furrow is restricted is strengthened by experiments in which the cytoskeletal organization of the egg was studied during ageing (Webb *et al.* 1986). The earliest change observed is the disappearance of the microfilament-rich area overlying the meiotic spindle and this is followed by the migration of the spindle towards the centre of the egg. This suggests that the microfilament-rich domain is responsible for the maintenance of the spindle in a peripheral position. Finally, the spindle breaks down and the chromosomes become dispersed. This spindle disruption may result from changes in the microtubule-nucleating material of the spindle poles and/or from a global increase in the critical concentration for tubulin polymerization. It is possible to correlate the changes in the cytoskeletal organization of the egg occurring during ageing with the different types of parthenogenetic embryos obtained after activation with ethanol (Fig. 6). The normal formation of a polar body is related to, and therefore may be dependent upon, the existence of a microfilament-rich domain overlying the spindle. With the actin distributed uniformly around the egg, a successful but symmetrical cleavage may occur if the spindle is centrally located within the egg, leading to a polar body and an embryo of similar size. Embryos with two haploid pronuclei may be derived from eggs in which the spindle remains peripheral but in which the cortical actin had become uniform so that a polar body cannot form. Finally, embryos with one single pronucleus may be derived from eggs in which the central spindle has been destroyed.

The effect of chromatin on the cell cortex also explains the existence of the incorporation cone that develops at the sperm entry site. The sperm nuclear envelope breaks down because of the meiotic environment in the egg during the first 30 min after fertilization (Sato & Blandau, 1979). The presence of the non-enveloped male chromatin then alters the cortical domain.

Microtubules

Various observations also point to an effect of chromosomes on tubulin polymerization. First, chromosome clusters observed in nocodazole-treated eggs promote the formation of large microtubule bundles after taxol treatment despite the fact that most of them are not associated with MTOCs (Fig. 7; Maro *et al.* 1986a). Second, if nocodazole-treated eggs are removed from the presence of the drug, each dispersed chromosome cluster promotes local tubulin polymerization and also recruits MTOCs that organize the microtubules into a spindle that rotates to yield a polar body (Maro *et al.* 1986*a*). Third, inactive PCM foci exist in the cytoplasm of the metaphase II egg, but they do not nucleate microtubules, whereas microtubules are clearly present in the vicinity of the chromosomes (Maro *et al.* 1985). Calmodulin is known to be located at the poles of the mitotic spindles (Welsh *et al.* 1978; Zavortink *et al.* 1983). It is also present at the meiotic spindle poles but not associated with inactive cytoplasmic MTOCs (E. Houliston & B. Maro, unpublished observations). However, after taxol treatment, calmodulin is seen in the centre of the asters nucleated by

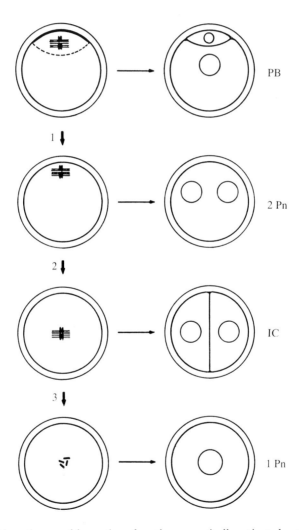

Fig. 6. Possible pathways of formation of parthenogenetically activated eggs. Changes in cytoskeletal organization during ageing (left panel) and types of parthenogenetic embryos obtained after activation with ethanol (right panel). (Adapted from Webb *et al.* (1986).) Changes in cytoskeletal organization during ageing: 1, disappearance of the actin-rich cortical domain; 2, central migration of the spindle; 3, spindle disruption. Types of parthenogenetic embryos: PB, 1 haploid pronucleus with second polar body; 2 Pn, 2 haploid pronuclei; IC, immediate cleavage; 1 Pn, 1 diploid pronucleus.

cytoplasmic MTOCs. This suggests that calmodulin is associated with microtubules during *M* phase, possibly modulating their assembly (Welsh *et al.* 1979; Vantard *et al.* 1985), rather than being involved in the regulation of the nucleating capacity of the MTOCs. A decrease in the apparent critical concentration for tubulin polymerization around the chromosomes has also been observed in *Xenopus* eggs (Karsenti *et al.* 1984). In this case, centrosomes injected into the cytoplasm of the metaphase II arrested egg were not able to nucleate microtubules unless located close to the chromosomes. However, following fertilization (or activation) of both *Xenopus* and mouse eggs, all of the MTOCs are able to nucleate, suggesting that there is a drop in the cytoplasmic critical concentration for tubulin polymerization during interphase (Karsenti *et al.* 1984; Maro *et al.* 1985; Schatten *et al.* 1985).

Polar body formation

It appears that chromosomes control the spatial organization of the cytoskeleton in the egg. Although the precise mechanism by which they are able to induce a reorganization of both microfilaments and microtubules is unclear, it is nevertheless possible to propose a sequence for the various events leading to polar body formation. First, it seems that at the end of meiotic maturation (just before germinal vesicle breakdown), the chromosomes gain the capacity to modify the organization of actin

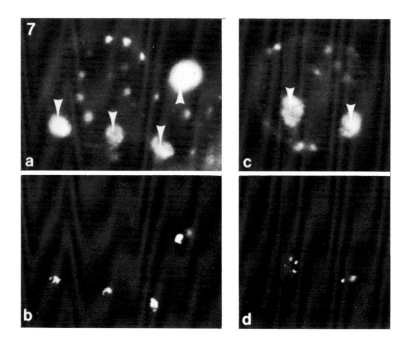

Fig. 7. a–d. Eggs treated with 10 µm-nocodazole for 6 h, washed and immediately incubated in 6 µM-taxol for 5 min at 37 °C, fixed and double stained for tubulin (a,c) and chromatin (b,d). Note large microtubule bundles associated with chromosome clusters (arrowheads) and the small asters nucleated by cytoplasmic MTOCs. (From Maro *et al.* (1986*a*).)

in their vicinity (Van Blerkom & Bell, 1986). Second, when the oocyte enters metaphase I (after germinal vesicle breakdown), the PCM, which was associated previously with the nuclear envelope, becomes dispersed in several foci within the cytoplasm (Calarco *et al.* 1972; Maro *et al.* 1985). A spindle is formed because of the effect of the chromosomes on tubulin polymerization during metaphase (Karsenti *et al.* 1984; Maro *et al.* 1985, 1986*a*) in conjunction with the recruitment of nearby MTOCs. Third, the spindle movement towards the cell periphery is dependent upon microfilaments (Longo & Chen, 1985), probably because of the effect of chromatin on microfilaments (Van Blerkom & Bell, 1986). Finally, when peripheral, the chromosomes induce the formation of an actin-rich, microvillous-free domain in the cortex (Maro *et al.* 1984; Longo & Chen, 1985; Van Blerkom & Bell, 1986). After fertilization (or activation), meiosis resumes and the cleavage-furrow forms only in this microfilament-rich domain (Maro *et al.* 1984). The rotation of the spindle follows (probably as a consequence of the limited area available for the development of the furrow), cleavage is completed, and the polar body forms (Maro *et al.* 1984, 1986*a*).

PROTEIN SYNTHETIC REQUIREMENTS

In the absence of novel gene expression this period of development must be controlled exclusively at a translational/post-translational level involving (mostly) the maternal components inherited by the egg. We have used various inhibitors of protein synthesis (PSI) in order to determine where translational controls are involved and which processes have no requirement for continuous protein synthesis and therefore are presumably under post-translational control (see Table 2).

Eggs fertilized in the presence of protein synthesis inhibitors complete meiosis and form pronuclei on schedule with control fertilized eggs. However, in the presence of PSI such eggs are unable to enter mitosis I and so remain blocked as single cells with intact pronuclear membranes (interphase I; Howlett, 1986*a*). Unfertilized eggs cultured *in vitro* remain arrested in metaphase II for at least 48 h, although the meiotic spindle undergoes some disruption after about 30 h (see Microfilaments, above; Webb *et al.* 1986). However, unfertilized eggs cultured in the presence of PSI are activated (parthenogenetically) to enter interphase I over a period of 1–6 h (Siracusa *et al.* 1975; Clarke & Masui, 1983; S. K. Howlett & B. Maro, unpublished observations). Pronuclear membranes form around: (1) a single haploid maternal complement if the second meiotic division is completed; (2) a single diploid maternal complement if the meiotic spindle is destroyed prior to the metaphase–anaphase II transition; (3) two haploid maternal complements if the spindle is destroyed after the metaphase–anaphase II transition but the cleavage division does not occur. Such activated eggs remain in interphase I and are unable to divide.

We have shown that eggs fertilized in the presence of nocodazole remain blocked in metaphase II until washed free of the drug (Maro *et al.* 1986*a*). However, some eggs fertilized in the presence of both nocodazole and PSI are able to enter interphase I by 4–6 h. Similarly, unfertilized eggs cultured in the presence of nocodazole and PSI overcome the metaphase II block and enter interphase after 5–9 h, forming mini-nuclei around each of the dispersed groups of chromosomes. Therefore, the natural and nocodazole-induced metaphase II block in the egg is overcome if protein synthesis is inhibited, suggesting a role for unstable proteins in the maintenance of the metaphase (*M* phase) state (Howlett, 1986*a*).

Fertilized eggs placed into PSI at any point during G_1 or S phases remain blocked in interphase I, with intact pronuclei, and are unable to cleave. However, beyond a point near the S/G_2 phase border entry into and successful completion of mitosis I can occur in the absence of further protein synthesis; these cells divide and enter the second cell cycle (interphase II; Howlett, 1986*b*). Similarly, cells that have been artificially arrested in mitosis I by the use of nocodazole will return to interphase (without cell division because of the absence of a spindle) if PSI are added. Therefore, entry into mitosis I requires protein synthesis until within about 2 h, but once initiated the completion of mitosis and entry into interphase II requires no further protein synthesis just as with the transition from meiosis II into interphase I (Howlett, 1986*b*).

THE PATTERN OF PROTEIN SYNTHESIS

Having established that some of the steps during cell cycle progression require continuous protein synthesis whilst others do not, can we identify potential functional candidates amongst the proteins being synthesized?

The pattern of [^{35}S]methionine-labelled proteins remains broadly similar from the metaphase II egg through the first and into the second cell cycle (Pratt *et al.* 1983;

Table 2. *Effect of nocodazole and protein synthesis inhibitors on cell cycle progression*

Initial state	Treatment	Final state
Metaphase II	None	Metaphase II
Metaphase II	Fertilization	Interphase I ...
Metaphase II	NZ*,†	Metaphase II
Metaphase II	PSI*,‡	Interphase I
Metaphase II	NZ + PSI*	Interphase I
Interphase I	None	Mitosis I ...
Interphase I	NZ	Mitosis I
Interphase I	PSI	Interphase I§
Mitosis I	None	Interphase II ...
Mitosis I	NZ	Mitosis I
Mitosis I	PSI	Interphase II
Mitosis I	NZ + PSI	Interphase II¶

* With or without fertilization.
† NZ, nocodazole.
‡ PSI, protein synthesis inhibitors (puromycin, anisomycin).
§ Note that protein synthesis is required for entry into mitosis I up to about the S/G_2 border (1–2 h prior to pronuclear membrane breakdown).
¶ Note that cells return to interphase without cell division.

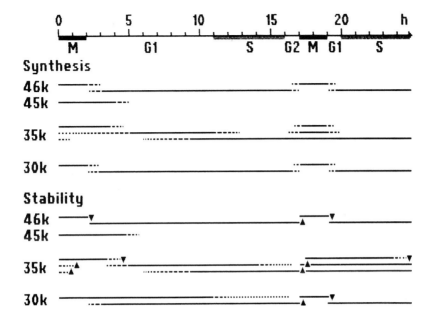

Fig. 8. Schematic view of the synthetic profile (upper panel) and stability (lower panel) of the polypeptides of the three complexes discussed in the text in relation to the cell cycle phases. Arrowheads in lower panel indicate interconversion (possibly by phosphorylation/dephosphorylation). k denotes $10^3 M_r$. (Upper panel adapted from Howlett (1986*b*).)

Howlett & Bolton, 1985). The pattern then changes dramatically as a result of translation from the new embryonic transcripts (Flach *et al.* 1982; Bolton *et al.* 1984). There are, however, a few proteins or groups of proteins that do exhibit changes prior to the embryonic genome activation (Fig. 8; and Howlett & Bolton, 1985; Howlett, 1986*b*).

The 35 000 M$_r$ complex

This prominent group is composed of several polypeptides (about 15) that are separable into three bands in one-dimensional gels (called upper, middle and lower bands). In the metaphase II egg essentially only the largest, upper band polypeptides are produced. During passage through interphase I there is a gradual progression from the production of upper, to upper and middle, to middle and lower and to only lower band polypeptides by late *S* phase. Coincident with the entry into mitosis I, synthesis of middle and upper band polypeptides resumes and continues during mitosis I but ceases abruptly upon entry into interphase II.

It appears that most, if not all, of these polypeptides are formed by multiple post-translational modifications to primary translation products that represent lower band polypeptides (Van Blerkom, 1981; Howlett & Bolton, 1985). Thus, both newly and previously synthesized lower band polypeptides are rapidly modified (probably by phosphorylation) during mitosis I, so explaining the reappearance of upper and middle band polypeptides. Once formed, upper and middle band polypeptides are relatively stable with only a slow dephosphorylation during interphase II. Similarly, during meiosis (metaphase I and II) all of the lower band polypeptides produced are converted into upper band polypeptides that are only slowly dephosphorylated during interphase I (Howlett, 1986*b*).

The 30 000 M$_r$ complex

This group is composed of two distinct polypeptides separable into two bands in one-dimensional gels (bands y and z). Synthesis of band y is restricted to the metaphase II egg and the period of mitosis I, whilst the slightly lower molecular weight band z is produced during interphase I and II. It appears that these two bands are interconvertible, probably again by phosphorylation/dephosphorylation. Thus, we propose that band z is the primary translation product that remains unmodified during interphase. However, during *M* phase of meiosis II or mitosis I it is rapidly phosphorylated to produce band y. Dephosphorylation of band y, although rapid following mitosis I, is apparently very slow following meiosis II (Howlett, 1986*b*).

The 46 000 M$_r$ complex

This group of polypeptides is complicated by the synthesis of several polypeptides of similar molecular weight; however, it appears that there are probably two polypeptides that are involved, the larger one of which is called band c. Thus, production of band c is marked in the metaphase II egg, ceases abruptly upon entry into interphase I, and resumes during mitosis I only to cease again upon entry into interphase II. It appears that the phosphorylation producing band c is completely and rapidly reversible on exit from *M* phase (Howlett, 1986*b*).

The 45 000 M$_r$ complex

A single polypeptide (band a) is synthesized during meiosis and continues in the metaphase II egg. Within about 4 h of fertilization (although rather variably), or within about 8–10 h if the ovulated egg remains unfertilized, synthesis of band a ceases. This polypeptide is apparently a remarkably unstable protein with a half-life of only 1–2 h, unlike the majority of proteins, which are very stable (Howlett & Bolton, 1985).

Changes in proteins and the cell cycle

Although it was quite encouraging to have demonstrated that many, if not all, of the detectable changes in the proteins reflect the cell cycle state, it still remains to be determined whether any of the proteins described are in fact functionally involved in cell cycle progression. However, since phosphorylations occur coincident with mitosis I and since there is a 2 h period prior to mitosis I that does not require protein synthesis it seems unlikely that the phosphorylated forms of the proteins described are responsible for triggering entry into mitosis I. It seems more likely that these proteins are substrates for protein kinases that are activated during *M* phase.

Whereas the phosphorylation within each complex seems to occur simultaneously upon entry into and continues during M phase, the dephosphorylation is variable with only some occurring on exit from M phase.

CONCLUSION

It appears that in the mouse most of the changes observed during the first 24 h of development are related to the phases of the cell cycle (either interphase or M phase). Thus, the chromosomes are able to induce local polymerization of both actin and tubulin during M phase. Whilst the effect of the chromosomes on the cortex is restricted to meiotic M phase, the effect on tubulin polymerization is probably more general, occurring during meiosis and mitosis. What is observed as a local effect induced by the chromosomes is probably due to global alterations within the egg; the complete cell cortex is able to respond by removing microvilli from the cell surface and by forming a subcortical network of microfilaments, whilst it becomes more difficult to polymerize microtubules within the M phase cytoplasm. These effects could perhaps be linked to post-translational changes of cytoskeleton-associated proteins and/or to changes in the intracellular concentrations of ions such as Ca^{2+}. In addition, protein kinases are active during M phase and act upon several newly synthesized proteins, and probably also upon existing proteins (such as lamins; Gerace & Blobel, 1980), within the egg.

Maturation or M phase promoting factor (MPF) has been identified as a trigger for the transition from interphase to M phase during meiotic (Masui & Markert, 1971) and mitotic (Wasserman & Smith, 1978) cell cycles. There is indirect evidence to suggest that MPF is a kinase (Maller *et al.* 1977; Gerhart *et al.* 1984). Thus, it is possible that MPF initiates a phosphorylation cascade so that directly or indirectly the 46, 35 and 30 ($\times 10^3$) M_r proteins (together with others such as the lamins; Miake-Lye & Kirschner, 1985) become phosphorylated as the cell enters M phase. MPF is an unstable activity, and provides only a transient signal for each M phase. Also, we know that entry into M phase is dependent upon protein synthesis but exit from it is not. In order to explain the apparent paradox of the transient nature of M phase and yet the indefinite arrest of vertebrate eggs in meiotic M phase, the stabilizing influence of a factor termed cytostatic factor (CSF) has been invoked (Masui *et al.* 1980). We might expect CSF, if a protein, to behave in a manner similar to that observed for the unstable $45\,000\,M_r$ protein, whose absence may be permissive for the exit from meiotic M phase II. This protein may alternatively be linked to the capacity of the cell cortex to respond to the chromosomes. Interestingly, in the unfertilized egg of *Xenopus*, a $45\,000\,M_r$ protein has been observed that also disappears immediately after activation (M. Kirschner & E. Karsenti, personal communication). However, the nature of MPF and CSF is elusive. Further analysis of the changing distribution and modification of cytoskeletal proteins in relation to fertilization and early cell cycle events in the mouse, and in other organisms, may throw more light on their nature.

We thank G. Flach and S. J. Pickering for their technical assistance, and M. H. Johnson for his continuous support during the course of these studies. We are indebted to M. H. Johnson, M. Webb and V. N. Bolton for permission to cite some of the data presented in this study. This work was funded by an MRC grant to M. H. Johnson and by an INSERM grant to B. Maro.

REFERENCES

ABREU, S. L. & BRINSTER, R. L. (1978). Synthesis of tubulin and actin during the preimplantation development of the mouse. *Expl Cell Res.* **114**, 134–141.

BOLTON, V. N., OADES, P. J. & JOHNSON, M. H. (1984). The relationships between cleavage, DNA replication, and gene expression in the mouse 2-cell embryo. *J. Embryol. exp. Morph.* **79**, 139–163.

CALARCO, P. G., DONAHUE, R. P. & SZOLLOSI, D. (1972). Germinal vesicle breakdown in the mouse oocyte. *J. Cell Sci.* **10**, 369–385.

CALARCO-GILLAM, P. D., SIEBERT, M. C., HUBBLE, R., MITCHISON, T. & KIRSCHNER, M. (1983). Centrosome development in early mouse embryos as defined by an autoantibody against pericentriolar material. *Cell* **35**, 621–629.

CLARKE, H. S. & MASUI, Y. (1983). The induction of reversible and irreversible chromosome decondensation by protein synthesis inhibitors during meiotic maturation in mouse oocytes. *Devl Biol.* **97**, 291–301.

EAGER, D., JOHNSON, M. H. & THURLEY, K. W. (1976). Ultrastructural studies on the surface membrane of the mouse egg. *J. Cell Sci.* **22**, 345–353.

FLACH, G., JOHNSON, M. H., BRAUDE, P. R., TAYLOR, R. A. S. & BOLTON, V. N. (1982). The transition from maternal to embryonic control in the 2-cell mouse embryo. *EMBO J.* **1**, 681–686.

GERACE, L. & BLOBEL, G. (1980). The nuclear envelope lamina is reversibly depolymerized during mitosis. *Cell* **19**, 277–287.

GERHART, J., WU, M. & KIRSCHNER, M. (1984). Cell-cycle dynamics of an *M*-phase-specific cytoplasmic factor in *Xenopus laevis* oocytes. *J. Cell Biol.* **98**, 1247–1255.

GOULD, R. R. & BORISY, G. G. (1977). The pericentriolar material in Chinese Ovary Cells nucleates microtubule formation. *J. Cell Biol.* **73**, 601–615.

HOWLETT, S. K. (1986*a*). A set of proteins showing cell cycle-dependent modification in the mouse embryo. *Cell* **45**, 387–396.

HOWLETT, S. K. (1986*b*). Control of cell cycle events during meiotic maturation and early cleavage in the mouse. PhD thesis, University of Cambridge.

HOWLETT, S. K. & BOLTON, V. N. (1985). Sequence and regulation of morphological and molecular events during the first cell cycle of mouse embryogenesis. *J. Embryol. exp. Morph.* **87**, 175–206.

JOHNSON, M. H., EAGER, D., MUGGLETON-HARRIS, A. L. & GRAVES, H. M. (1975). Mosaicism in the organisation of concanavalin A receptors on surface membrane of mouse eggs. *Nature, Lond.* **257**, 321–322.

KARSENTI, E., NEWPORT, J., HUBBLE, R. & KIRSCHNER, M. (1984). Interconversion of metaphase and interphase microtubule arrays as studied by the injection of centrosomes and nuclei into *Xenopus* eggs. *J. Cell Biol.* **98**, 1730–1745.

LONGO, F. J. & CHEN, D. Y. (1985). Development of cortical polarity in mouse eggs: Involvement of the meiotic apparatus. *Devl Biol.* **107**, 382–394.

MALLER, J., WU, M. & GERHART, J. (1977). Changes in protein phosphorylation accompanying maturation of *Xenopus laevis* oocytes. *Devl Biol.* **58**, 298–312.

MARO, B. (1985). Fertilisation and the cytoskeleton in the mouse. *BioEssays* **3**, 18–21.

MARO, B., HOWLETT, S. K. & JOHNSON, M. H. (1986*b*). A cellular and molecular interpretation of mouse early development: the first cell cycle. In *Gametogenesis and the Early Embryo* (ed. J. G. Gall), pp. 389–407. New York: A. Liss Inc.

MARO, B., HOWLETT, S. K. & WEBB, M. (1985). Non-spindle MTOCs in metaphase II-arrested mouse oocytes. *J. Cell Biol.* **101**, 1665–1672.

MARO, B., JOHNSON, M. H., PICKERING, S. J. & FLACH, G. (1984). Changes in the actin distribution during fertilisation of the mouse egg. *J. Embryol. exp. Morph.* **81**, 211–237.

MARO, B., JOHNSON, M. H., WEBB, M. & FLACH, G. (1986a). Mechanism of polar body formation in the mouse oocyte: an interaction between the chromosomes, the cytoskeleton and the plasma membrane. *J. Embryol. exp. Morph.* **92**, 11–32.

MASUI, Y. & MARKERT, C. L. (1971). Cytoplasmic control of nuclear behavior during meiotic maturation of frog oocytes. *J. exp. Zool.* **117**, 129–146.

MASUI, Y., MEYERHOF, P. G. & MILLER, M. A. (1980). Cytostatic factor and chromosome behaviour in early development. In *The Cell Surface*, pp. 235–256. New York, London: Academic Press.

MIAKE-LYE, R. & KIRSCHNER, M. W. (1985). Induction of early miotic events in a cell-free system. *Cell* **41**, 165–175.

NICOSIA, S. V., WOLF, D. P. & INOUE, M. (1977). Cortical granule distribution and cell surface characteristics in mouse eggs. *Devl Biol.* **57**, 56–74.

PIKO, L. & CLEGG, K. B. (1982). Quantitative changes in total RNA, total poly A and ribosomes in early mouse embryos. *Devl Biol.* **89**, 362–378.

PRATT, H. P. M., BOLTON, V. N. & GUDGEON, K. A. (1983). The legacy from the oocyte and its role in controlling early development of the mouse embryo. *CIBA Fdn Symp.* 98 *Molecular Biology of Egg Maturation*, pp. 197–227. London: Pitman Books.

SATO, K. & BLANDAU, R. J. (1979). Second meiotic division and polar body formation in mouse eggs fertilised *in vitro*. *Gamete Res.* **2**, 283–293.

SCHATTEN, G., SIMERLY, C. & SCHATTEN, H. (1985). Microtubule configuration during fertilization, mitosis and early development in the mouse. *Proc. natn. Acad. Sci. U.S.A.* **82**, 4152–4156.

SCHIFF, P. B., FANT, J. & HORWITZ, S. B. (1979). Promotion of microtubule assembly *in vitro* by taxol. *Nature, Lond.* **277**, 665–667.

SHALGI, R., PHILLIPS, D. M. & KRAICER, P. F. (1978). Observations on the incorporation cone in the rat. *Gamete Res.* **1**, 27–37.

SIRACUSA, G., WHITTINGHAM, D. G., MOLINARO, M. & VIVARELLI, E. (1978). Parthenogenetic activation of mouse oocytes induced by inhibitors of protein synthesis. *J. Embryol. exp. Morph.* **43**, 157–166.

STEFANINI, M., OURA, C. & ZAMBONI, L. (1969). Ultrastructure of fertilization in the mouse: penetration of sperm into the ovum. *J. submicrosc. Cytol.* **1**, 1–23.

SZOLLOSI, D., CALARCO, P. & DONAHUE, R. P. (1972). Absence of centrioles in the first and second meiotic spindles of mouse oocytes. *J. Cell Sci.* **11**, 521–541.

VAN BLERKOM, J. (1981). Structural relationship and post-translational modification of stage-specific proteins synthesised during early preimplantation development in the mouse. *Proc. natn. Acad. Sci. U.S.A.* **78**, 7629–7633.

VAN BLERKOM, J. & BELL, H. (1986). Regulation of development in the fully grown mouse oocyte: chromosome-mediated temporal and spatial differentiation of cytoplasm and plasma membrane. *J. Embryol. exp. Morph.* (in press).

VANTARD, M., LAMBERT, A. M., DE MEY, J., PICQUOT, P. & VAN ELDIK, L. J. (1985). Characterization and immunocytochemical distribution of calmodulin in higher plant endosperm cells: localization in the mitotic apparatus. *J. Cell Biol.* **101**, 488–499.

WASSARMAN, P. M. & FUJIWARA, K. (1978). Immunofluorescent anti-tubulin staining of spindles during meiotic maturation of mouse oocytes *in vitro*. *J. Cell Sci.* **29**, 171–188.

WASSERMAN, W. J. & SMITH, L. D. (1978). The cyclic behavior of a cytoplasmic factor controlling nuclear membrane breakdown. *J. Cell Biol.* **78**, R15–R22.

WEBB, M., HOWLETT, S. K. & MARO, B. (1986). Parthenogenesis and cytoskeleton organisation in aging mouse oocytes. *J. Embryol. exp. Morph.* **95**, 131–145.

WELSH, M. J., DEDMAN, J. R., BRINKLEY, B. R. & MEANS, A. R. (1978). Calcium-dependent regulator protein: localization in the mitotic apparatus of eukaryotic cells. *Proc. natn. Acad. Sci. U.S.A.* **75**, 1867–1871.

YOUNG, R. J., STULL, G. B. & BRINSTER, R. L. (1973). RNA in mouse ovulated oocytes. *J. Cell Biol.* **59**, 372a.

ZAMBONI, L., CHAKRABORTY, J. & MOORE-SMITH, D. (1972). First cleavage division of the mouse zygote: an ultrastructural study. *Biol. Reprod.* **7**, 170–193.

ZAVORTINK, M., WELSH, M. J. & MCINTOSH, J. R. (1983). The distribution of calmodulin in living mitotic cells. *Expl Cell Res.* **149**, 375–385.

The Company of Biologists Limited, founded in 1925, is a 'Company Limited by Guarantee' having tax-exempt charitable status. There is a Board of Directors consisting of about 20 professional biologists, two of them appointed annually by the Society for Experimental Biology, who receive no salary or fees for their services. The Company's main function is to own and produce *The Journal of Experimental Biology*, the *Journal of Cell Science*, and the *Journal of Embryology and Experimental Morphology*, and to appoint the Editors of these journals. These are part-time appointments held by established professional biologists of some eminence, and once they have been appointed the Company exercises no control over editorial policy.

The Company is precluded by its charitable status from making a commercial profit on its operations, and its aim is to produce high-quality journals at the lowest possible price. Any surplus on publishing not required for the journals' reserves is transferred to an Educational Trust Fund, which makes substantial grants in aid of societies concerned with the fields of interest covered by the Company's journals. Grants are also made to conferences and summer schools in the fields of its journals.

The Company's independence of commercial publishers enables it to choose the most effective form of publishing to give papers accepted the widest possible circulation in journals of high quality and prestige. Planned changes in production and distribution of the journals should result in significant increases in the speed of publication, and it is hoped to reduce the time between the acceptance of a paper and its publication to no more than 13 weeks in the near future.

Other projects of benefit to biology are being developed.

The Company of Biologists Limited
Department of Zoology, Downing Street, Cambridge CB2 3EJ